The Petraeus Doctrine

The Field Manual on

COUNTERINSURGENCY OPERATIONS

Joint Chiefs of Staff Joint Publication 3-24

Cover design by Smerdloff Graphics.

ISBN: 9781449929916

Printed in USA.

13 12 11 10 09 5 4 3 2 1

TABLE OF CONTENTS

PAGE

APPENDIX

GLOSSARY

FIGURE

Intentionally Blank

EXECUTIVE SUMMARY
COMMANDER'S OVERVIEW

- **Provides the foundation for defining insurgency and counterinsurgency (COIN)**
- **Describes the relationships between COIN, irregular warfare, counterterrorism, and foreign internal defense**
- **Gives a doctrinal baseline to understanding insurgencies**
- **Describes strategic and operational approaches to COIN**
- **Introduces the principles of COIN**
- **Emphasizes the need for "unity of effort" in COIN operations and how to achieve it through "unified action"**
- **Explains the dynamic relationship between intelligence and COIN operations**
- **Provides principles of intelligence operations in COIN**
- **Describes supporting operations for COIN**
- **Addresses component contributions to COIN**
- **Describes the COIN operation environment and use of the joint intelligence preparation of the operational environment process in analyzing it**
- **Discusses COIN planning, execution, and assessment**

Foundation for Counterinsurgency

Insurgencies are complex, dynamic, and adaptive; they can rapidly shift, split, combine, or reorganize.

The twenty-first century is typified by a volatile international environment, persistent conflict, and increasing state fragility. Long-standing external and internal tensions tend to exacerbate or create core grievances within some states, resulting in political strife, instability, or even insurgency. Moreover, some transnational terrorists/extremists with radical political and religious ideologies may intrude in weak or poorly governed states to form a wider, more networked threat.

Insurgents seek to gain power to overthrow or force change of a governing authority.

Insurgency is an internal threat that uses subversion and violence to reach political ends. Conversely, counterinsurgents seek to defeat insurgents and address core grievances to prevent insurgency's expansion or regeneration. Typically the insurgents will solicit or be offered some type of support from state or non-state actors, which can include transnational terrorists who take advantage of the situation for their own benefit. Affected nations may request United States support in countering an insurgency, which is typically the circumstances under which US forces become involved in counterinsurgency (COIN) operations.

Counterinsurgency (COIN) is comprehensive civilian and military efforts taken to simultaneously defeat and contain insurgency and address its core grievances.

COIN is primarily political and incorporates a wide range of activities, of which security is only one. Unified action is required to successfully conduct COIN operations and should include all host nation (HN), US, and multinational agencies or actors. Civilian agencies should lead COIN efforts. When operational conditions do not permit a civilian agency to lead COIN within a specific area, the joint force commander (JFC) must be cognizant of the unified action required for effective COIN.

The fragile states framework, used in interagency fora, can help the joint force commander (JFC) develop a foundational understanding of the operational environment (OE).

The term "fragile states" describes a broad range of failing, failed, and recovering states. The framework has three categories of states: failed, failing, and recovering, although the distinction or exact transition between categories is rarely clear.

Failed State. A failed state is unable to effectively protect and govern the population.

Failing State. The failing state is still viable, but it has a reduced capability and capacity to protect and govern the population.

Recovering State. The recovering state is moving towards normalcy but may have an imperfect level of viability. This state is able to protect and govern its population to some degree.

There are several operations, programs, and activities that may be interdependent with COIN, including nation assistance, foreign internal defense (FID), security force assistance, security cooperation,

In traditional warfare the conflict focuses on defeating the opposing military through force-on-force engagements, and influencing the government by taking control of their territory, and influencing the people generally through intimidation, fear, and deception; whereas in irregular warfare (IW), the conflict focuses more on the control or influence over, and the support of, a relevant population and not on the control of an adversary's forces or territory. Some military operations, such as foreign internal defense (FID), *unconventional warfare, combating terrorism, peace operations, and psychological operations.*

COIN, combating terrorism, and unconventional warfare (UW) are primarily conducted during IW. COIN requires joint forces to both fight and build sequentially or simultaneously, depending on the security situation and a variety of other factors.

There are several operations, programs, and activities that may be interdependent with COIN, including nation assistance, FID, security force assistance, security cooperation, UW, combating terrorism, peace operations, and psychological operations (PSYOP).

Balance and Simultaneity of Offense, Defense, and Stability Operations.

COIN requires joint forces to both fight and build sequentially or simultaneously, depending on the security situation and a variety of other factors. The balance of these operations must be appropriate to accomplish the current phase's objectives. Offensive and defensive operations in COIN that are predominantly aimed at insurgent combatants are counterguerrilla operations. Stability operations are consequently fundamental to COIN—stability operations address the core grievances of insurgency as well as drivers of conflict and are therefore essential to long-term success.

Insurgency

Insurgency is the organized use of subversion and violence by a group or movement that seeks to overthrow or force change of a governing authority. Insurgency can also refer to the group itself.

Successful COIN operations require comprehensive knowledge of the operational environment (OE) including an understanding of the insurgents, the scope of the insurgency, any external supporting elements, and the other players (e.g., terrorists and criminals) that may benefit from a protracted conflict and especially the relevant population. An insurgency typically succeeds or fails based on the support of the population. This understanding acts as a foundation on which the joint force can plan, prepare, execute, and assess COIN operations.

Understanding an insurgency's motivations, breadth of activity and support, and core grievances is essential to successful COIN.

Ends, scope, and core grievances are three of the most important aspects of an insurgency.

Ends. Insurgencies generally share some combination of four common objectives: political change, overthrow of the government, resistance against an outside actor, or nullifying political control in an area.

Scope. There are four general categories for the scope of insurgencies; however, there is no clear-cut delineation between categories: local, local-external support, local-global support, and global.

Core Grievances. The core grievances are issues, real or perceived, in the view of some of the population. Additionally, insurgents can be adept at manipulating or creating core grievances to serve their purpose.

The dynamics of insurgency are a framework to assess an insurgency's strengths and weaknesses.

The dynamics of insurgency are a framework to assess an insurgency's strengths and weaknesses. The dynamics can be examined separately, but studying their interaction is an indispensable part of COIN mission analysis. The dynamics include leadership, objectives, ideology, OE, external support, internal support, phasing and timing, and organizational and operational approaches, though they should be examined with the underlying understanding that insurgents are a product of their culture, society, and history.

There are three prerequisites for an insurgency to be successful in an area—a vulnerable population, leadership available for direction, and lack of government control.

When all three prerequisites exist in an area, insurgency can operate with some freedom of movement, gain the support of the people, and become entrenched over time. A population is vulnerable if the people have real or perceived grievances that insurgents can exploit. If insurgents can recruit, co-opt, or coerce local leaders or the local leaders are part of the insurgency, these leaders can direct the frustrations of the populace. Real or perceived lack of governmental control can allow insurgents to operate with little or no interference from security forces or other agencies.

There are shared general organizational characteristics that provide a general framework for analysis of insurgencies.

Components. Insurgent structure may be generally broken down into two wings [components]: political and military. The political wing is primarily concerned with undermining the legitimacy of the HN government and its allies while building up support for the insurgency. The military wing of the insurgency conducts combat operations.

Elements. The elements are the basic organizational "building blocks" of insurgencies. Leaders provide overall direction in more organized insurgencies. The underground is that element of the insurgent organization that conducts operations in areas normally denied to the auxiliary and the guerrilla force. Guerrillas conduct the actual fighting and provide security. Cadre element forms the political or ideological core of the insurgency. The auxiliary is the support element of the insurgent organization.

Some key approaches or strategies used by insurgencies include: conspiratorial, military-focused, terrorism, identity-focused, subversive, and composite and coalitions.

A **conspiratorial approach** involves a few leaders and a militant cadre or activist party seizing control of government structures or exploiting a revolutionary situation.

Users of **military-focused approaches** aim to create revolutionary possibilities or seize power primarily by applying military force.

A terrorism-focused approach is waged by small, independent cells that require little or no popular support. This approach uses terrorist tactics to accomplish the following: sow disorder, incite sectarian violence, weaken the government, intimidate the population, kill government and opposition leaders, fix and intimidate police and military forces, attempt to create government repression, and, in cases where foreign forces may occupy the country, force their withdrawal.

The **identity-focused approach** mobilizes support based on the common identity of religious affiliation, clan, tribe, or ethnic group.

A **subversive approach** either attempts to transform an illegal political entity into a legitimate political party or to use an existing legitimate political party. This party will attempt to subvert the government from within.

A **composite approach** includes tactics drawn from any or all of the other approaches. Also, different insurgent forces using different approaches may form loose **coalitions** when it serves their interests.

Counterinsurgents should seek to create or exploit potential vulnerabilities.

Insurgencies have aspects that can be strengths or vulnerabilities. Some insurgency vulnerabilities are: secrecy, recruitment and message, base of operations, external support, finances, internal divisions, maintaining momentum, defectors and informants, attrition of human resources, and leadership.

Devolution and Decline

Many insurgencies can devolve into organizations merely focused on terrorism or criminality. Devolution may occur due to one or a combination of counterinsurgent pressure, lack of popular support, loss of leadership, organizational fragmentation, or atrophy during long periods of stalemate. The counterinsurgents must ameliorate the core grievances of the insurgency to bring the insurgents to their breaking point. If core grievances remain, the insurgency will remain at least latent and incipient.

Counterinsurgency

The support of the people is the most vital factor in the long-term success of any COIN effort.

Mindset. Conducting successful COIN operations requires an adaptive and flexible mindset. Counterinsurgents must make every effort to reinforce the legitimacy of the HN government in the eyes of the people. Counterinsurgents must understand that **the military instrument is only one part of a comprehensive approach for successful COIN** Counterinsurgents must also understand the core grievances, drivers of conflict, and friction points between different groups. Cultural awareness facilitates accurate anticipation of the population's perception of COIN operations. These perceptions can determine the success or failure of COIN operations.

Strategic Direction.

The military contribution to countering insurgency, while vital, is not as important as political efforts for long-term success. Military efforts are especially important initially to gain security. The national strategy, military strategy, and theater strategy play key roles in determining COIN strategic context. There are three possible general strategic settings for US involvement in COIN: assisting a functioning government as part of FID, as an adjunct to US major combat operations, or US operations in an ungoverned area.

Strategic Approach.

The potential global and regional scope of contemporary insurgency has added to the complexity and therefore the challenge of conducting COIN. This challenge requires a global or regional COIN strategic approach for success. A strategy of disaggregation includes the following activities: containment, isolation, disruption, and resolution of core grievances, and neutralization in detail.

Operational Approaches.

There are a range of possible operational approaches to COIN. COIN should strive to move from direct to balanced and balanced to indirect. The **direct approach** focuses on protecting US and HN interests while attacking the insurgents. The **indirect approach** focuses on the actions to establish conditions (a stable and more secure environment) for others to achieve success with the help of the US.

Principles of COIN.

The **principles of COIN** are derived from the historical record and recent experience. These principles do not replace the principles of joint operations, but rather provide focus on how to successfully conduct COIN.

Counterinsurgents Must Understand the OE.

This understanding includes the political, military, economic, social, information, infrastructure, and other aspects of the OE. Counterinsurgents must pay special attention to society, culture, and insurgent advantages within the OE.

Legitimacy Is the Main Objective.

The primary objective of any COIN operation is to foster development of effective governance by a legitimate government. Counterinsurgents achieve this objective by undertaking appropriate actions and striving for a balanced application of both military and nonmilitary means as dictated by the situation.

Unity of Effort is Essential.

Unity of effort must be present at every echelon of a COIN operation. Otherwise, well-intentioned but uncoordinated actions can cancel each other or provide vulnerabilities for insurgents to exploit.

Political Factors are Primary.

At the beginning of a COIN operation, military actions may appear predominant as security forces conduct operations to secure the populace and kill or capture insurgents. However, **political objectives must guide the military's approach.** Commanders must consider how operations contribute to strengthening the HN government's legitimacy and achieving US goals—the latter is especially important if there is no HN.

Intelligence Drives Operations.

Effective COIN is shaped by timely, specific, and reliable intelligence, gathered and analyzed at all levels and disseminated throughout the force. Reporting by units, members of the country team, and information derived from interactions with civilian agencies is often of equal or greater importance than reporting by specialized intelligence assets.

Insurgents Must be Isolated from Their Cause and Support.

While it may be required to kill or capture insurgents, **it is more effective in the long run to separate an insurgency from the population and its resources**, thus letting it die. Confrontational military action, in exclusion is counterproductive in most cases; it risks generating popular resentment, creating martyrs that motivate new recruits, and producing cycles of revenge.

Security Under the Rule of Law is Essential.

To establish legitimacy, commanders transition security activities from military operations to law enforcement as quickly as feasible. **When insurgents are seen as criminals, they often lose public support.**

Counterinsurgents Should Prepare for a Long-Term Commitment.

Insurgencies are protracted by nature, and history demonstrates that they often last for years or even decades. Thus, COIN normally demands considerable expenditures of time and resources, especially if they must be conducted simultaneously with conventional operations in a protracted war combining traditional and IW.

Manage Information and Expectations.

To limit discontent and build support, the HN government and any counterinsurgents assisting it **create and maintain a realistic set of expectations** among the populace, friendly military forces, and the international community. Information operations (IO), particularly PSYOP and the related activities of public affairs (PA) and civil-military operations (CMO), are key tools to accomplish this.

Use the Appropriate Level of Force.

Even precise and tailored **force must be executed legitimately and with consideration for consequent effects.** An operation that kills five insurgents is counterproductive if collateral damage leads to the recruitment of fifty more insurgents.

Learn and Adapt.

An effective counterinsurgent force is a learning organization. Insurgents constantly shift between military and political phases and tactics. **Every unit needs to be able to make observations, draw and apply lessons, and assess results.**

Empower the Lowest Levels.

Successful COIN is normally conducted with decentralized execution based upon centralized vision and orders that include clear and concise rules for the use of force and rules of engagement.

Support the Host Nation (HN).

US forces committed to supporting COIN are there to assist a HN government. **The long-term goal is to leave a government able to stand by itself,** which is also normally the goal even if the US begins COIN in an area that does not have a HN government. US forces and agencies can help, but HN elements must accept responsibilities to achieve real victory.

Unity of Effort in Counterinsurgency

Unified action refers to the synchronization, coordination, and/or integration of military operations with the activities of governmental and nongovernmental entities to achieve unity of effort.

Unified action includes a "whole-of-government" or "comprehensive approach" that employs all instruments of national power. Achieving unity of effort is challenging in COIN due to the normally complex OE and its many potential actors—friendly, neutral, and adversarial. The military contribution to COIN must be coordinated with the activities of US Government (USG) interagency partners, intergovernmental organizations (IGOs), nongovernmental organizations (NGOs), regional organizations, the operations of multinational forces, and activities of various HN agencies to be successful. The joint military contribution is essential to provide security that enables other COIN efforts. Joint forces contribute to unified action through unity of command and a solid command and control architecture that integrates strategic, operational, and tactical COIN.

The internal defense and development strategy is the overarching strategy in a FID mission.

When a HN is dealing with an insurgency and the US supports the HN, COIN is one aspect of a larger FID mission. **Internal defense and development (IDAD) is the HN's plan that US FID supports; the HN does not support the US FID plan.** The purpose of the IDAD strategy is to promote HN growth and its ability to protect itself from subversion, lawlessness, and insurgency.

There are several United States (US) civil-military integration mechanisms that facilitate unified action for COIN.

Civil-military integration mechanisms fall into two general areas: those that are located outside of the theater and those that are located in theater.

Civil-military mechanisms in the US include the National Security Council and policy operations groups.

Civil-military integration mechanisms in theater may include: joint interagency coordination group, US country team, advance civilian team, executive steering group, regional authority, civil-military coordination board, joint civil-military operations task force, national-level governmental assistance teams, provincial reconstruction teams, civil-military operations centers, and joint interagency task force.

Military unity of command is achieved by establishing

Unity of command should extend to all military forces engaged in COIN—US, HN, and other multinational

and maintaining formal command or support relationships.

forces. No single command structure meets the needs of every multinational command but one absolute remains constant; political considerations will heavily influence the ultimate shape of the command structure. Regardless of the command structure, coalitions and alliances require a significant liaison structure, and liaisons are even more important in COIN in order to coordinate many disparate and highly politically sensitive efforts.

Intelligence Support to Counterinsurgency

Purposes of Joint Intelligence in a Counterinsurgency

The purpose of joint intelligence in counterinsurgency is to inform the commander; identify, define, and nominate objectives; support the planning and execution of operations; counter adversary deception and surprise; support friendly deception efforts; and assess the effectiveness of operations. As in any joint operation, intelligence and operations have a cyclical relationship. **This dynamic relationship is particularly important in COIN—intelligence drives operations and successful operations generate additional intelligence.** COIN efforts conducted without accurate intelligence may alienate the population, which results in their offering less information

Principles of Intelligence Operations in COIN.

Bottom-Up Intelligence Flow. The fact that all units collect and report information, combined with the mosaic nature of insurgencies, means that the intelligence flow in COIN is more bottom up than top down.

Feedback. Feedback from analysts and intelligence consumers to collectors is important to synchronizing the intelligence, surveillance, and reconnaissance (ISR) effort in COIN.

Intelligence Collection Considerations. Because all counterinsurgents are potential collectors, the collection plan addresses all day-to-day tactical operations.

Nontraditional ISR Assets. Commanders should consider use of assets not traditionally used for ISR to fill gaps in ISR coverage. Commanders should ensure intelligence from nontraditional assets is fused with other analytical efforts in order to maintain the appropriate situational awareness.

Intelligence disciplines are core competencies of the intelligence community involved in intelligence planning, collection, processing, exploitation, analysis, production, and dissemination using a specific category of technical or human resources.

Some Intelligence disciplines specifics for COIN are:

Geospatial intelligence, the combination of imagery, the intelligence derived from imagery, and geospatial information, provide the ability to visualize the OE and establish a shared situational awareness picture.

Human intelligence is a category of intelligence derived from information collected and provided by human sources; and, **during COIN operations, actionable intelligence is often based on information gathered from people.**

Signal intelligence collection is a good source for determining adversary locations, intentions, capabilities, and morale.

Measurement and signature intelligence sensors can provide remote monitoring of avenues of approach or border regions for smugglers or insurgents. They can also be used to locate insurgent safe havens and cache sites and determining insurgent activities and capabilities.

Civil information is information developed from data about civil areas, structures, capabilities, organizations, people, and events (ASCOPE) that can be fused or processed to increase interagency, IGO, and NGO situational awareness.

Technical intellegence on insurgent equipment can help understand insurgent capabilities. These may include how insurgents are using improvised explosive devices, homemade mortars, and other pieces of customized military equipment.

All-Source Intelligence.

The multidisciplinary fusion of information by intelligence organizations at all echelons results in the production of all-source intelligence products. Analysis for COIN operations is very challenging, due in part to the need to understand perceptions and culture, the need to track hundreds or thousands of personalities, the local nature of insurgencies, and the tendency of insurgencies to change over time.

Factors effecting intelligence collaboration include: complexity, intelligence cells and working groups,

Effective intelligence collaboration organizes the collection and analysis actions of counterinsurgent organizations into a coherent, mutually supportive intelligence effort. The intelligence portion of understanding the OE and other supporting intelligence for *intelligence sharing, host-nation integration, and infiltration of HN intelligence.*

COIN operations is complex. It is important not to oversimplify an insurgency.

Supporting Operations for Counterinsurgency

Information operations employ capabilities that will significantly contribute to the achievement of the end state.

A strong IO plan when integrated effectively in military operations will assist the HN government in acquiring control of legitimate social, political, economic and security institution; marginalize or separate, both physically and psychologically, insurgency and its leaders from the population; and help demobilize and reintegrate armed insurgents forces into the political, economic and social structures of the population.

Public affairs activities are critical for informing and influencing the populace's understanding and perceptions of events.

Public opinion, perceptions, media, public information, and rumors influence how the populace perceives the HN legitimacy. PA shapes the information environment through public information activities and facilitates media access to preempt, neutralize, or counter adversary disinformation efforts.

Through professional relationships, military leaders should strive to ensure that the media's audiences understand the counterinsurgents' efforts from the counterinsurgents' perspective.

Embedded media representatives experience the joint force perspective of operations in the COIN environment. Commanders may hold periodic press conferences to explain operations and provide transparency to the people most affected by COIN efforts. However, **counterinsurgents must strive to avoid the perception of attempting to manipulate the population or media. Even the slightest appearance of impropriety can undermine the credibility of the COIN force and HN legitimacy.**

Counterinsurgents must carefully consider who will be detained, and the manner and methods that will be used to detain them.

While detainees can be vital sources of information, how counterinsurgents treat captured insurgents has immense potential impact on insurgent morale, retention, and recruitment. Humane and just treatment may afford counterinsurgents many short-term opportunities as well as potentially damaging insurgent recruitment. Abuse may foster resentment and hatred; offering the enemy an opportunity for propaganda and assist potential insurgent recruitment and support.

Security sector reform is the set of policies, plans, programs, and activities

National defense and internal security are the traditional cornerstones of state sovereignty. Security is essential to legitimate governance and participation, effective rule of *that a government undertakes to improve the way it provides safety, security, and justice.*

law, and sustained economic development. Security sector reform (SSR) aims to provide an effective and legitimate public service that is transparent, accountable to civilian authority, and responsive to the needs of the public. **SSR must be part of any COIN plan, including the IDAD strategy, from the outset.**

Disarmament, demobilization, and reintegration attempts to stabilize the OE by disarming and demobilizing insurgents and by helping return former insurgents to civilian life.

The objective of the disarmament, demobilization, and reintegration process is to contribute to security and stability in post-conflict environments so that recovery and development can begin. **Disarmament** is the collection, documentation, control, and disposal of small arms, ammunition, explosives, and light and heavy weapons of former insurgents and the population. **Demobilization** is the process of transitioning a conflict or wartime military establishment and defense-based civilian economy to a peacetime configuration while maintaining national security and economic vitality. **Demobilization for COIN normally involves the controlled discharge of active combatants from paramilitary groups, militias, and insurgent forces that have stopped fighting. Reintegration** is the process through which former combatants, belligerents, and dislocated civilians receive amnesty, reenter civil society, gain sustainable employment, and become contributing members of the local population.

Component Contributions to Counterinsurgency

All components of the joint force are essential for the overall military contribution to COIN.

Joint warfare is a team effort and air, land, maritime, and special operations components of the joint force make vital contributions in support of all instruments of national power in achieving national security objectives.

HN Land Contribution to COIN.

Much of securing or protecting the population is done by deploying land forces within the population and with an enduring presence. Normally, US land forces will operate in designated contiguous operational areas that coincide with HN national political boundaries.

Air Contribution to COIN.

Air forces and capabilities play a vital role in the military contribution to COIN. These forces and capabilities are especially critical for successful counterguerrilla, intelligence, combating weapons of mass destruction, humanitarian, and informational efforts. Air contributions include close air support, precision strikes, armed overwatch, personnel recovery, air interdiction, ISR, communications, electronic warfare, combat support, and air mobility.

Maritime Contribution to COIN.

For COIN, the maritime component plays a critical role in controlling the seas, which may be vital to isolating an insurgency physically and psychologically. **The expeditionary character and versatility of maritime forces provide an advantage in areas where access is denied or limited.** Maritime forces may provide direct support to the joint task force that does not include combat operations, to include CMO, logistic support, intelligence/communication sharing, humanitarian relief, maritime civil affairs, and expeditionary medical aid and training.

Special Operations Forces Contribution to COIN.

Special operation forces are vitally important to successful COIN operations. **Their capacity to conduct a wide array of missions, working by, with, and through HN security forces or integrated with US conventional forces make them particularly suitable for COIN campaigns.** They are particularly important when the joint force is using an indirect approach to COIN. In a more balanced or direct approach to COIN, however, they should be used to complement rather than replace conventional forces in traditional warfare roles.

Operational Environment

Understanding of the COIN environment begins with understanding the population, then the insurgents, and finally the counterinsurgents.

The OE for all joint operations is the sum of the conditions, circumstances, and influences that affect how the commander uses the available capabilities and makes decisions. The OE encompasses physical domains, nonspatial environments and other factors. The OE includes the information environment, sociocultural considerations, and civil considerations. A holistic understanding of the OE includes all of these aspects and helps the commander to understand how the OE constrains or shapes options, how the OE affects capabilities, and how friendly, adversary, and neutral actors' actions affect or shape the OE.

Initial Joint Intelligence Preparation of the Operational Environment (JIPOE) must focus on having enough detail to

Joint intelligence preparation of the operational environment (JIPOE) in COIN follows the process described in Joint Publication 2-01.3, *Joint Intelligence Preparation of the Operational Environment,* **with an emphasis of sociocultural and civil factors.** The joint *complete mission analysis of the joint operation planning process.*

force should include HN representatives if possible in the JIPOE process.

Step one of the JIPOE process is to "Define the OE".

The first step of the JIPOE process is defining the OE by identifying those aspects and significant characteristics that may be relevant to the joint force's mission. Defining the OE must include the many military and nonmilitary organizations involved in the COIN effort. When working to determine the significant characteristics of the OE, for COIN this step should pay special attention to the sociocultural factors, civil factors, root causes of the insurgency, insurgent desired end state, and insurgent narratives

Step two of the JIPOE process is to "Describe the Impact of the OE".

This JIPOE step continues to develop a holistic view of the OE by analyzing the nonphysical and physical aspects of the OE, developing a systems perspective of relevant political, military, economic, social, information, and infrastructure links and nodes. COIN operations require a detailed understanding of sociocultural factors and civil factors from three perspectives: the population, the insurgent, and the counterinsurgent. To understand the population the following five sociocultural factors should be analyzed: society, social structure, culture, power and authority, and interests. Civil factors include areas, structures, capabilities, organizations, people, and events (ASCOPE). ASCOPE analysis will help determine COIN impact on neutral, adversarial, and friendly systems.

JIPOE must determine the sources of frustration or anger within the population, from their perspective. JIPOE also must determine if the three prerequisites for insurgency are present: a vulnerable population, leadership available for direction, and lack of government control. When all three exist in an area, insurgency can operate with some freedom of movement, gain the support of the people, and become entrenched over time.

Step three of the JIPOE process is to "Evaluate the Adversary".

JIPOE uses the eight dynamics as a framework to analyze insurgencies. While each dynamic is important, analyzing their overarching interaction is essential to understand the insurgency holistically. Not only are insurgent activities indicators of what approach or approaches an insurgency is using, they will help determine what counters can be used. A thorough and detailed center of gravity analysis helps commanders and staffs to understand the systemic nature of the OE and the actions necessary to shape the conditions that define the desired end state.

Step four of the JIPOE process is to "Determine Adversary Courses of Action"

The fourth step of the JIPOE process builds upon this holistic view to develop a detailed understanding of the adversary's plan and probable courses of action. The insurgency's overall approach, or combination of approaches, the insurgent senior leaders have selected to achieve their goals and their recent tactics are key indicators of their plan. From these indicators a model of the insurgent plan can be constructed.

Planning in Counterinsurgency

Planning involves thinking about ways to influence the future rather than responding to events.

Because COIN operations require comprehensive solutions, planning horizons in COIN are normally longer than other operations, despite increased uncertainties associated with these longer planning horizons. The unified action required to achieve the comprehensive solutions that will bring success during COIN operations, in turn requires interorganizational planning efforts among all interagency, intergovernmental, and nongovernmental partners involved.

Through early and continuous assessment during COIN execution, the staff and JFC monitor the OE and progress toward accomplishing tasks and achieving objectives.

Joint operation planning blends two complementary processes. The first is the **joint operational planning process**. The second process is **operational design**, the use of various design elements in the conception and construction of the framework that underpins a joint operation plan and its subsequent execution. The initial observable symptoms of an insurgency often do not reflect the true nature and core grievances of the insurgency, so the JFC and staff must devote sufficient time and effort early in planning to correctly frame the problem and design a broad approach to a solution. Because there is only one IDAD strategy or campaign, there should only be one operational design.

Logical lines of operations (LOOs) describe the linkage of various actions on nodes and decisive points with an operational or strategic objective and the conditions of the end state. **COIN requires the synchronization of activities along multiple and complementary logical LOOs in order to work through a series of tactical and operational objectives to attain the military end state.**

Execution in Counterinsurgency

COIN is fundamentally a counterstrategy for insurgency. While a counter effort, COIN does not concede the initiative.

There are many ways to achieving success in COIN. The components of each form of execution are not mutually exclusive. These forms are not the only choices available and are neither discrete nor exclusive. They may be combined, depending on the environment and available resources, and they have proven effective. **The approaches must be adapted to the demands of the local environment.** Three examples are: Clear-hold-build, combined action, and limited support.

A clear-hold-build operation is executed in a specific, high-priority area experiencing overt insurgent operations.

A clear-hold-build operation has the following objectives: create a secure physical and psychological environment, establish firm government control of the populace and area, and gain the populace's support.

Clear operation's purpose is to disrupt insurgent forces and force a reaction by major insurgent elements in the area.

For COIN, **clear is a task that requires the commander to remove all guerrilla forces and eliminate organized resistance in an assigned area.** The force does this by destroying, capturing, or forcing the withdrawal of guerrilla combatants.

Ideally HN forces or combined HN and coalition forces execute the hold portion of clear-hold-build approach

Hold operations are designed to continuously secure the people and separate them from the insurgents; establish a firm government presence and control over the area and populace; recruit, organize, equip, and train local security forces; and establish a government political apparatus to replace the insurgent apparatus. The success or failure of the effort depends, first, on effectively and continuously securing the populace and, second, on effectively reestablishing a HN government presence at the local level.

Progress in building support for the HN government requires protecting the local populace.

The most important activities during the build stage are conducted by nonmilitary agencies. HN government representatives reestablish political offices and normal administrative procedures. National and international development agencies rebuild infrastructure and key facilities. Local leaders are developed and given authority.

Combined action is a technique that involves joining US and HN ground troops in a single

Commanders use the combined action approach to hold and build while providing a persistent counterinsurgent presence among the populace. This approach attempts to first achieve security and stability in a local area, followed by offensive *organization, usually a platoon or company, to conduct COIN operations.*

operations against insurgent forces now denied access or support.

The limited support approach focuses on building HN capability and capacity.

In many cases US support is limited or focused on missions like advising security forces and providing fire support or sustainment. Under this approach, HN security forces are expected to conduct combat operations, including any clearing and holding missions.

Targeting is conducted for all COIN efforts, not just attacks against the insurgent military wing (counterguerrilla operations).

Targeting is the process of selecting and prioritizing targets and matching the appropriate response to them, considering operational requirements and capabilities. The targeting process facilitates achieving effects that support the logical LOOs in a COIN campaign plan. The targeting process can support IO, CMO, and even meetings between commanders and HN leaders.

Assessment is a process that measures progress of the counterinsurgent team toward mission accomplishment.

Effective assessment in COIN operations is necessary for counterinsurgents to recognize changing conditions and determine their meaning. Assessment requires determining why and when progress is being achieved along each logical LOO. It is important for the commander to understand the larger context of the assessment as it relates to the OE and the principles guiding the USG response. A USG framework for assessment whose principles have been approved is the Interagency Conflict Assessment Framework (ICAF). The purpose of the ICAF is to develop a commonly held understanding across relevant USG departments and agencies of the dynamics driving and mitigating violent conflict within a country that informs US policy and planning decisions.

CONCLUSION

This publication provides joint doctrine for the planning, execution, and assessment of COIN operations across the range of military operations. This will include the description of relationships between COIN, IW, counterterrorism, and FID.

CHAPTER I
FOUNDATION FOR COUNTERINSURGENCY

"In counterinsurgency, military forces are a delivery system for civilian activity: their role is to afford sufficient protection and stability to allow the government to work safely with its population and for economic revival and political reconciliation to occur."

Counterinsurgency: A Guide for Policy-Makers
United States Government, Interagency Counterinsurgency Initiative
May 2008

1. Introduction

a. The twenty-first century is typified by a volatile international environment, persistent conflict, and increasing state fragility. Long-standing external and internal tensions tend to exacerbate or create core grievances within some states, resulting in political strife, instability, or even insurgency. Moreover, some transnational terrorists/extremists with radical political and religious ideologies may intrude in weak or poorly governed states to form a wider, more networked threat.

b. Insurgency is an internal threat that uses subversion and violence to reach political ends. Typically the insurgents will solicit or be offered some type of support from state or non-state actors, which can include transnational terrorists who take advantage of the situation for their own benefit. Affected nations may request US support in countering an insurgency, which is typically the circumstances under which US forces become involved in counterinsurgency (COIN) operations. Whatever the mix of actors and level of conflict, and despite the broadly applied label of insurgency, the motivation and objectives of the various belligerents must be understood to be effectively countered.

c. **Insurgency.** Insurgency is the organized use of subversion and violence by a group or movement that seeks to overthrow or force change of a governing authority. Insurgency can also refer to the group itself. An insurgent is a member of that group. When compared to their adversaries, insurgents generally have strong will but limited means. Although some insurgents have no interest in working within any political system, it is this relative disparity of means that normally drives groups to use insurgency to alleviate core grievances. Additionally, this relative disparity of means also drives the insurgents to use subversion, guerrilla warfare, and terrorism, in the face of capable counterinsurgent forces. Insurgency requires few resources to initiate, yet it ties up significant resources to counter as the insurgents seek to exhaust the government in an effort to be effective in the long term. Insurgency allows a group time to potentially gain public support, expand, and secure external moral and material support; it seeks to erode the opposition's will, influence, and power. In its early phases, insurgency may only be loosely organized with competing interests amongst its subgroups. For example, subgroups may differ on their views of foreign support to the host nation (HN). Additionally, some subgroups may focus more on fighting other groups in the region than they focus on the overall insurgent efforts. Typical insurgencies only become a military concern when normal political process and law enforcement methods are insufficient. Insurgencies are complex, dynamic, and adaptive; they can rapidly shift, split, combine, or reorganize.

For more detail on insurgency, see Chapter II, "Insurgency."

d. **Counterinsurgency.** COIN is comprehensive civilian and military efforts taken to defeat an insurgency and to address any core grievances. COIN is primarily political and incorporates a wide range of activities, of which security is only one. Unified action is required to successfully conduct COIN operations and should include all HN, US, and multinational agencies or actors. Civilian agencies should lead US efforts. When operational conditions do not permit a civilian agency to lead COIN within a specific area, the joint force commander (JFC) must be cognizant of the unified action required for effective COIN. Ideally, all COIN efforts protect the population, defeat the insurgents, reinforce the HN's legitimacy, and build HN capabilities. COIN efforts include, but are not limited to, political, diplomatic, economic, health, financial, intelligence, law enforcement, legal, informational, military, paramilitary, psychological, and civic actions. As capable insurgents evolve and adapt, counterinsurgents must evolve and adapt.

e. **Insurgency and Counterinsurgency.** Insurgency and COIN are two sides of one conflict. Insurgents seek to gain power to overthrow or force change of a governing authority. Conversely, counterinsurgents seek to defeat insurgents and address core grievances to prevent insurgency's expansion or regeneration. Local and global popular perception and support are vital considerations for both insurgents and counterinsurgents. Insurgency and COIN tend to be nested in larger, complex, and irregular conflicts; therefore, understanding and appreciating the strategic context and operational environment (OE) of an insurgency are essential to success of the COIN operations.

2. Fragile States Framework and Governance

a. **Fragile States Framework.** The fragile states framework, used in interagency fora, can help the JFC develop a foundational understanding of the OE. A fragile state is a country that suffers from institutional weaknesses serious enough to threaten the stability of its central government. This is normally a function of the government's legitimacy and effectiveness. The term "fragile states" describes a broad range of failing, failed, and recovering states (see Figure I-1). However, the distinction among them is not always clear in practice, as fragile states rarely travel a predictable path of failure and recovery, and the labels may mask other important factors (e.g., insurgencies, factions). It is more important to understand in which direction a state is moving along the framework and how quickly than it is to categorize a state as failed or not. Therefore, the JFC must distinguish between fragile states that are vulnerable to failure and those that are already in crisis.

b. **Insurgency in a Fragile State.** Insurgency can be a significant contributor to a state's weakness, though other factors usually contribute as well. When joint forces

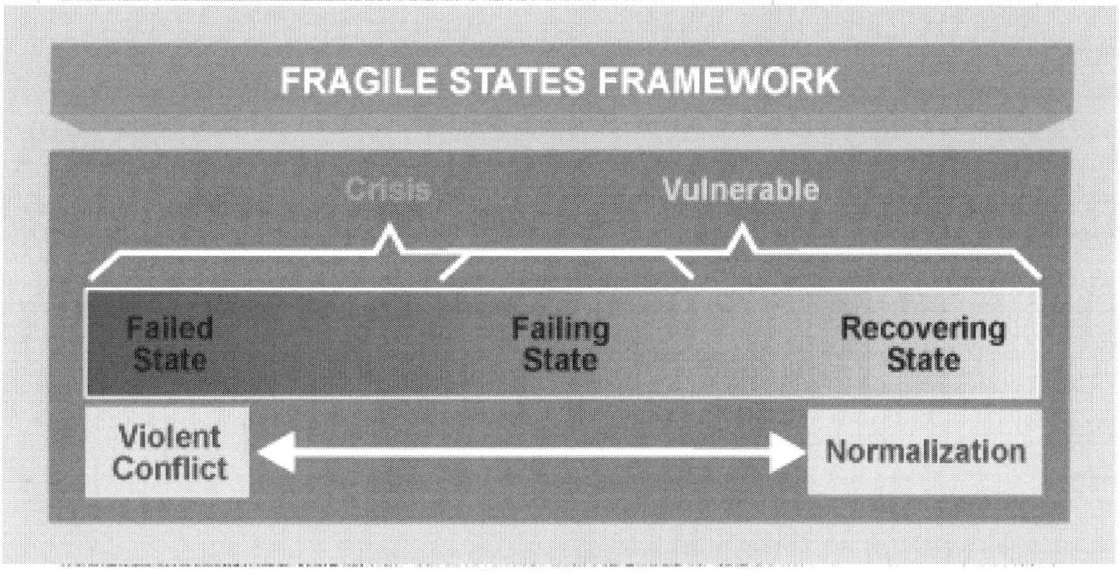

Figure I-1. Fragile States Framework

become involved in COIN, the state may be at any point along the fragile states framework; thus, the starting conditions may range from a failed state to a recovering state. From that point, the joint and coalition forces will attempt to move towards normalization, while insurgents will attempt to move toward increased violent conflict. Movement along the framework does not have to be linear; the conditions can decline and improve in separate iterations. Conditions on the left end of the framework require more military effort to eliminate threats and reduce violence. As conditions improve, military forces and civilian agencies focus on building capacity and encouraging sustained development. COIN can be conducted at any point within the framework.

c. **Failed, Failing, and Recovering States.** The framework has three categories of states: failed, failing, and recovering, although the distinction or exact transition between categories is rarely clear.

(1) **Failed State.** A failed state may only have remnants of a government due to collapse or regime change or it may have a government that exerts weak governance in all or large portions of its territory. A failed state is unable to effectively protect and govern the population. A failed state may not have a national government with which to work and, consequently, conducting COIN is difficult, especially with respect to legitimacy at the national level. Under these extreme circumstances, the intervening authority has a legal and moral responsibility to install a transitional military authority.

(2) **Failing State.** The failing state is still viable, but it has a reduced capability and capacity to protect and govern the population. When a state is fighting an insurgency and its ability to protect and govern the population starts to decline, the pace of that state's decline tends to accelerate towards collapse. Outside support for a failing state's COIN efforts may halt and reverse this trend; however, assistance becomes more difficult based on the level of decline at the time of intervention.

(3) **Recovering State.** The recovering state is moving towards normalcy but may have an imperfect level of viability. This state is able to protect and govern its population to some degree. A key consideration is whether the population considers the level of protection and governance acceptable and normal. A recovering state may still suffer from insurgency, although any insurgency in a recovering state will be relatively weak. When dealing with a recovering state, US efforts focus on building HN capability and capacity and preventing a latent insurgency from emerging.

d. When considering the OE, the JFC considers whether the HN is vulnerable to failure or already in crisis. This may be different in different parts of the country.

(1) **Vulnerable States.** Vulnerable states are those states unable or unwilling to adequately assure the provision of security and basic services to significant portions of their populations and where the legitimacy of the government is in question. This includes states that are failing or recovering from crisis.

(2) **Crisis States.** Crisis states are those states where the central government does not exert effective control over its own territory or is unable or unwilling to assure the provision of vital services to significant parts of its territory, where legitimacy of the government is weak or nonexistent, and where violent conflict is a reality or a great risk.

For further details on the fragile states framework, refer to United States Agency for International Development's (USAID's) Fragile States Strategy *(2005).*

e. **Governance.** Governance is the state's ability to serve the citizens through the rules, processes, and behavior by which interests are articulated, resources are managed, and power is exercised in a society. A state's ability to provide effective governance rests on its capability and capacity to establish rules and procedures for political decision making, strengthen public sector management and administrative institutions and practices, provide public services in an effective and transparent manner, and provide civil administration that supports lawful private activity and enterprise. An ungoverned area (UGA) is a place where the state or the central government is unable or unwilling to extend control, effectively govern, or influence the local population, and where a provincial, local, tribal, or autonomous government does not fully or effectively govern, due to inadequate governance capacity, insufficient political will, gaps in legitimacy, the presence or recent presence of conflict, or restrictive norms of behavior. UGA is a broad term that encompasses under-governed, misgoverned, contested, and exploitable areas as well as UGAs.

f. **Source of Governance.** A fundamental issue is who provides governance to the population during a COIN operation. Figure I-2 depicts three potential sources of governance: the HN government, transitional civilian authority, and transitional military authority. For an UGA, the establishment of a transitional civilian authority or transitional military authority may be required until the HN indigenous populations and institutions (IPI) can resume their functions and responsibilities. For a failed state, a

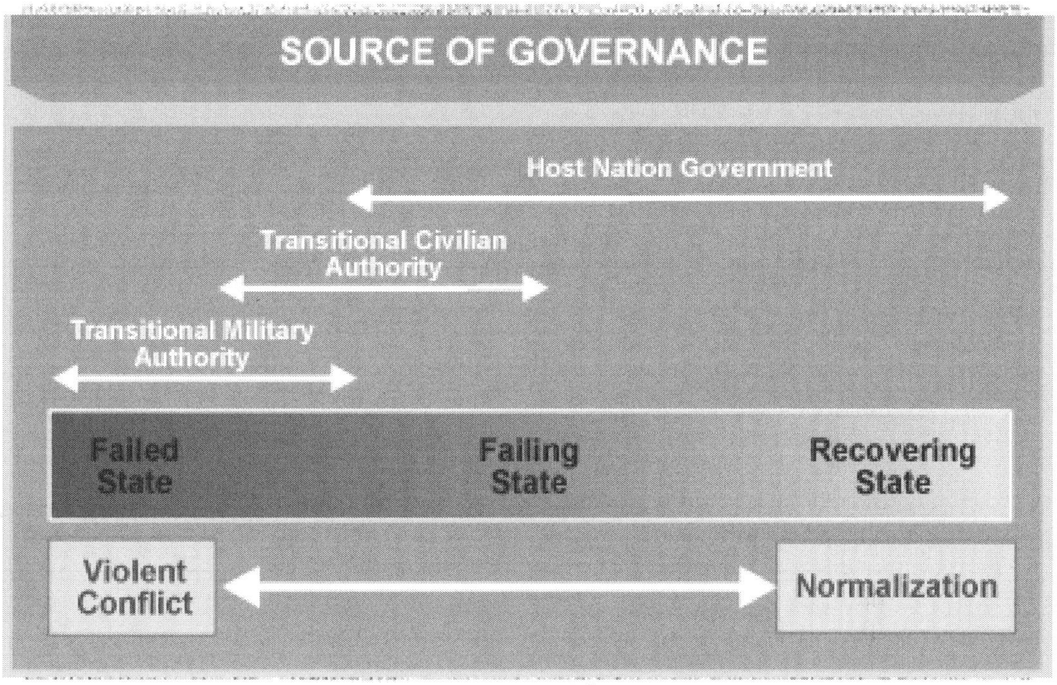

Figure I-2. Source of Governance

transition to a new HN government or former government-in-exile should begin as soon as feasible.

g. **Vulnerabilities of Governance and Authority.** A state's authority is dependent upon the successful amalgamation and interplay of four factors: mandate, manner, support and consent, and expectations. When the relationship between the governing and the governed breaks down, challenges to authority are likely. If the population, or a significant section of it, cannot achieve a remedy through established political discourse, they are likely to resort to insurgency.

(1) **Mandate.** The perceived legitimacy of the mandate that establishes a state authority, whether through the principles of universal suffrage, a recognised or accepted caste/tribal model, or an authoritarian rule.

(2) **Manner.** The perceived legitimacy of the way in which those exercising that mandate conduct themselves, both individually and collectively.

(3) **Support and Consent.** The extent to which factions, local populations and others consent to, comply with, or resist the authority of those exercising the mandate. Consent may range from active resistance, through unwilling compliance, to freely given support.

(4) **Expectations.** The extent to which the expectations and aspirations of factions, local populations, and others are managed or are met by those exercising the mandate.

h. **Transitional Military Authority.** Joint or multinational military forces may initially have to govern an area through a transitional military authority, which provides civil administration. This may occur because forces have occupied foreign territory or because the security situation may not permit civilian agencies to function effectively. Use of a transitional military authority should be of as short duration as practicable and should continue only until a civil authority can assume or resume its functions and responsibilities.

i. **Transitional Civilian Authority.** If deemed necessary by US and multinational leaders, a transitional civilian authority may be formed. A transitional civilian authority may be formed to immediately provide governance in some cases. Alternatively, as the level of security improves, transitional civilian authority may replace a transitional military authority. The exact nature and tempo of the transition period will be determined by US and multinational decision makers based on the security conditions in the OE. Like a transitional military authority, transitional civilian authority should be of as short duration as practicable and should continue only until the HN can assume or resume its functions and responsibilities.

j. **Support to Civil Administration (SCA).** SCA helps continue or stabilize management by an existing governing body of a HN's civil structure. The joint force may provide SCA when a HN requests support for their COIN efforts or as a continuation of a transitional military authority and/or transitional civilian authority. Civil administration in friendly territory may include advising friendly authorities and performing specific functions within the limits of authority and liability established by international treaties and agreements.

For more information on SCA, refer to Joint Publication (JP) 3-57, Civil-Military Operations.

3. Warfare and Counterinsurgency

War is a violent contest of wills between sociopolitical groups. Carl von Clausewitz proposed that the nature of war is unchanging in that there are three key forces—passion and enmity, chance and creativity, and policy and reason. These forces often are expressed as the population, the military, and the government, respectively. While the nature of war is unchanging, there are differences in the way wars are waged, and we refer to the way war is waged as "warfare." While the way any war is fought is unique, JP 1, *Doctrine for the Armed Forces of the United States*, discusses traditional warfare and irregular warfare (IW). The important distinction between these is focus. In traditional warfare the conflict focuses on defeating the opposing military through force-on-force engagements, and influencing the government by taking control of their territory, and influencing the people generally through intimidation, fear, and deception;

whereas in IW, the conflict focuses more on the control or influence over, and the support of, a relevant population and not on the control of an adversary's forces or territory. Even while understanding the differing contexts for military operations, it is important to understand that and all wars involve the full range of capabilities available to an actor's strategy. Nations have historically used subversion, unconventional warfare, guerrilla warfare and other means focused on influence over relevant populations during traditional war; likewise, states and other actors use missiles, aircraft, troop formations and other conventional means to strike at enemy military forces during IW.

a. **Irregular Warfare.** IW is a violent struggle among state and nonstate actors for legitimacy and influence over the relevant populations. IW favors indirect and asymmetric approaches, though it may employ the full range of military and other capacities, in order to erode an adversary's power, influence, and will. Enemies of the United States may be loosely organized networks or entities with no discernible hierarchical structure. Nevertheless, they have critical vulnerabilities to be exploited within their interconnected political, military, economic, social, information, and infrastructure systems. These actors often wage protracted conflicts in an attempt to break the will of the state. Military operations alone rarely resolve such conflicts. This publication will address all the instruments of national power. States have sovereign rights and a social contract with their inhabitants; therefore, they have sovereign responsibilities to combat these irregular threats. What makes IW "irregular" is the focus of its operations—the population—and its strategic purpose—to gain or maintain control or influence over, and the support of that population through various efforts.

(1) **Credibility and Legitimacy.** An adversary waging IW often attempts to protract the conflict to break the will of its opponent and control the relevant population. The belligerents, whether states or other armed groups, seek to undermine their adversaries' legitimacy and credibility and to isolate their adversaries from the relevant population, physically as well as psychologically. At the same time, they also seek to bolster their own legitimacy and credibility to exercise authority over that same population.

(2) **Means.** IW, as practiced by our adversaries, typically manifests itself as one or a combination of several possible means, including guerrilla warfare, terrorism, subversion, information operations (IO), strikes, and raids. The specific form or combination will vary according to the adversary's capabilities and objectives.

(3) **Selection.** The context of warfare in which forces operate, whether insurgent or counterinsurgent is driven by many different factors including the protagonist's culture, capabilities, and means; adversary capabilities, vulnerabilities, and actions; and the strategic objectives and end state. Failure of one side or the other to recognize the context in which they and their adversary operate will normally result in strategic failure, even in the wake of tactical success. The relative disparity of means between insurgents and governments often drives insurgents to nontraditional devices, particularly during the early and middle stages of an insurgency. If a parity of means

becomes more attainable and domination of influence with the relevant population is achieved, the insurgents may turn to more traditional means of conducting warfare.

(4) **Range of Military Operations.** The joint force operates across the range of military operations to counter the enemy during IW with military operations and other capabilities. Some military operations, such as foreign internal defense (FID), COIN, combating terrorism, and unconventional warfare (UW) are primarily conducted during IW.

For additional information on IW, see JP 1, Doctrine for the Armed Force of the United States, *JP 3-0,* Joint Operations, *JP 3-05,* Joint Special Operations, *JP 3-22,* Foreign Internal Defense, *and JP 3-26,* Counterterrorism.

b. **Traditional Warfare.** Traditional warfare is characterized as a confrontation between states or coalitions/alliances of states. This confrontation is predominately between belligerents pitting one side's government and military against the opposition's government and military. The objective is to defeat an adversary's armed forces, destroy an adversary's war-making capacity, or seize or retain territory in order to force a change in an adversary's government or policies. Military operations in traditional warfare normally focus on an adversary's armed forces and critical infrastructure to ultimately influence the adversary's government.

For additional information on traditional warfare, see JP 1, Doctrine for the Armed Force of the United States, *and JP 3-0,* Joint Operations.

4. Related Operations and Activities

There are several operations, programs, and activities that may be interdependent with COIN, including nation assistance, FID, security force assistance (SFA), security cooperation, UW, combating terrorism, peace operations (PO), and psychological operations (PSYOP).

a. **Nation Assistance.** Nation assistance is civil or military assistance (other than foreign humanitarian assistance) rendered to a nation by US forces within that nation's territory during peacetime, crises or emergencies, or war, based on agreements mutually concluded between the United States and that nation. Nation assistance operations support the HN by promoting sustainable development and growth of responsive institutions. The goal is to promote long-term regional stability. Nation assistance programs include, but are not limited to, security assistance, FID, and humanitarian and civic assistance.

b. **Foreign Internal Defense.** FID refers to the participation by civilian and military agencies of a government in any of the action programs taken by another government or other designated organization to free and protect its society from subversion, lawlessness, insurgency, terrorism, and other threats to their security. The focus of all US FID efforts is to support the HN's program of internal defense and development (IDAD). **FID can only occur when there is a HN that has asked for assistance.** The US will generally employ a mix of diplomatic, economic, informational, and military instruments of national power in support of these objectives. Military assistance is often necessary in order to provide the secure environment for the above efforts to become effective. For example, a FID program may help a HN to improve the capability or capacity of one of its programs such as counterdrug activities or quell the nascent stages of an insurgency.

(1) **Relation to COIN.** FID may or may not include countering an insurgency. **When FID includes countering an insurgency, COIN is part of FID. COIN only refers to actions aimed at countering an insurgency whereas FID can aim at dealing with any one or a combination of subversion, lawlessness, and insurgency.** In most cases, the joint force conducts COIN as part of a larger FID program supporting the HN government. **COIN that is not part of FID is an uncommon situation, and it should be a transitory situation where the US and any multinational partners should work to establish or reestablish HN sovereignty.** Figure I-3 depicts where COIN is distinct, where COIN supports FID, and where FID is distinct. There are three Department of Defense (DOD) categories of FID programs.

(2) **Indirect Support.** DOD FID indirect support consists of security assistance, exchange programs, and joint/multinational exercises. These programs can have either a small or no US footprint in the HN, and they can support issues not related to insurgency, issues related to a latent insurgency, or programs related to an entrenched insurgency.

(3) **Direct Support Not Involving Combat Operations.** DOD FID military direct support that does not involve combat operations includes civil-military operations (CMO), PSYOP, SFA, military training support, logistics support, mobility support, and intelligence and communications sharing. These programs have varying US footprints in the HN. They can be in support of a HN of any kind, but large efforts in this area tend to assist a HN with an extant insurgency.

(4) **US Combat Operations.** The introduction of US combat forces into FID operations requires a Presidential decision and serves only as a temporary solution until HN forces can stabilize the situation and provide security for their populace. If this involves COIN, US efforts can vary from providing advisors that fight alongside HN forces to the US conducting COIN in support of the larger HN IDAD. Consequently, the US footprint could vary from a few advisors to a large joint force. Control must transition to the HN as soon as practical to ensure the population perceives its government as legitimate.

For further details on FID, see JP 3-05, Joint Special Operations, *and JP 3-22,* Foreign Internal Defense.

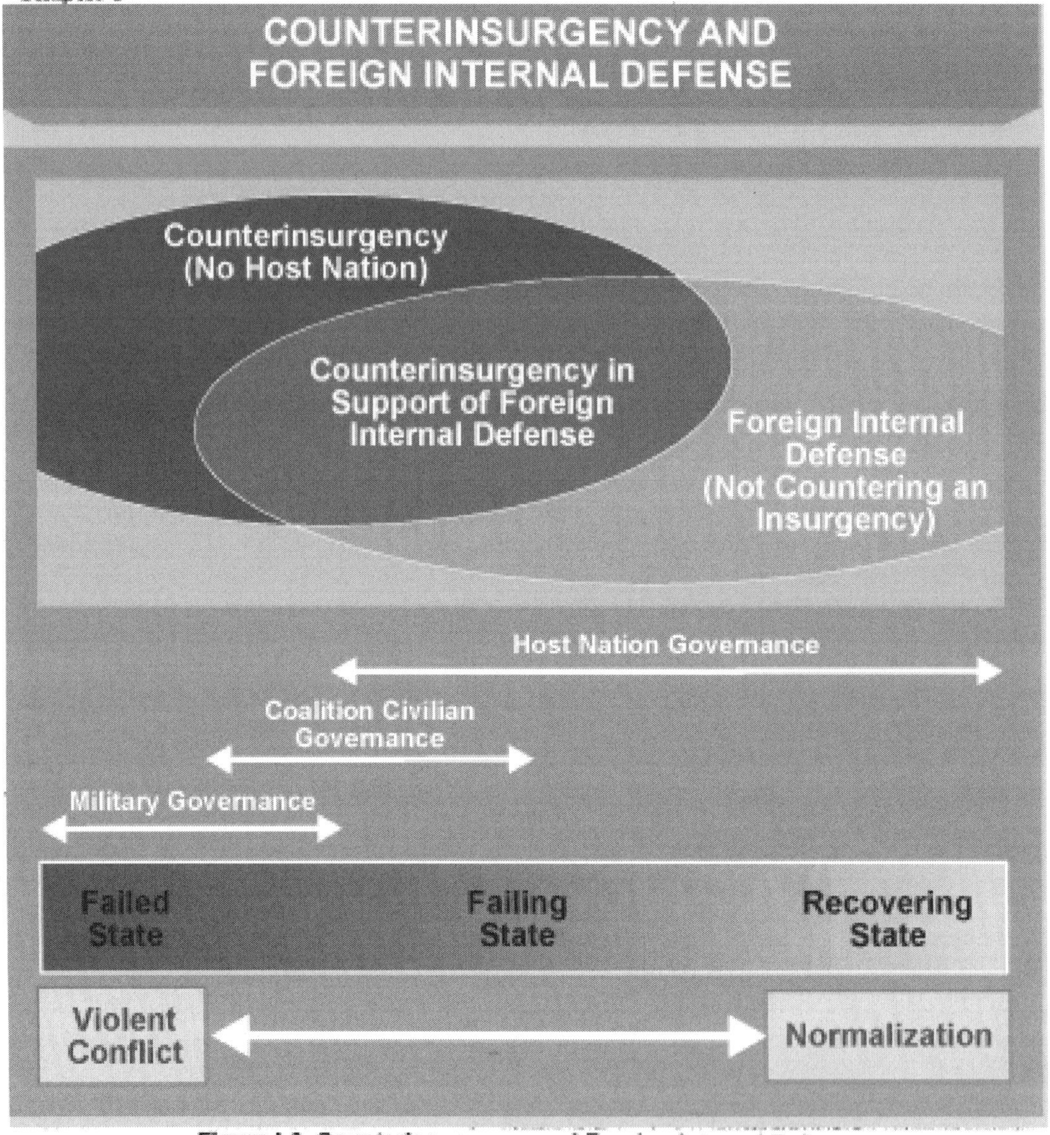

Figure I-3. Counterinsurgency and Foreign Internal Defense

c. **Security Force Assistance.** Security forces comprise both civilian and military participants, to include law enforcement, border security, intelligence, special operations forces (SOF), and conventional military forces. Security forces can be at the regional level, such as United Nations (UN) forces, and all levels of the HN from local to national. Many actors can participate in SFA, including joint, intergovernmental, interagency, multinational, nongovernmental, and others. These efforts focus on the HN's efforts to increase its security forces' capability and capacity.

For further information, see JP 3-22, Foreign Internal Defense.

(1) **Relationship to COIN.** SFA and security forces are integral to successful FID, COIN, and stability operations. SFA includes organizing, training, equipping, rebuilding, and advising various components of security forces in support of a legitimate authority; however, actors performing SFA have to initially assess the security forces they will assist and then establish a shared, continual way of assessing the security forces.

(2) **Organizing.** SFA includes organizing institutions and units, which can range from standing up a ministry to improving the organization of the smallest maneuver unit. Building capability and capacity in this area includes personnel, logistics, and intelligence and their support infrastructure. Developing HN tactical capabilities alone is inadequate; strategic and operational capabilities must be developed as well. HN organizations and units should reflect their own unique requirements, interests, and capabilities—they should not simply mirror existing external institutions.

d. **Security Cooperation.** Security cooperation interactions build defense relationships that promote specific US security interests, develop allied and friendly military capabilities for self-defense and multinational operations, and provide US forces with peacetime and contingency access to a HN. These activities help the US and HN gain credibility and help the HN build legitimacy. These efforts can help minimize the effects of or prevent insurgencies and thwart their regeneration.

e. **Unconventional Warfare.** UW is a special operations mission. UW is a broad spectrum of military and paramilitary operations normally of long duration and conducted by, with, and through indigenous or surrogate forces. These surrogate forces are organized, trained, equipped, supported, and directed in varying degrees by an external source. UW activities include, but are not limited to, insurgency, guerrilla warfare, subversion, sabotage, intelligence, PSYOP, and unconventional assisted recovery. UW most frequently refers to the military and paramilitary aspects of an insurgency designed to resist, overthrow, or gain political autonomy from an established government or used to resist or expel a foreign occupying power. However, UW can also refer to military and paramilitary support to an armed group seeking increased power and influence relative to its political rivals without overthrowing the central government and in the absence of a foreign occupying power.

For further details on UW, see JP 3-05, Joint Special Operations.

f. **Counterterrorism (CT).** Terrorism is the calculated use of unlawful violence or threat of unlawful violence to inculcate fear; which is intended to coerce or to intimidate governments or societies in the pursuit of goals that are generally political, religious, or ideological. Terrorism can be a standalone activity when the terrorists have no intent to control territory but instead focus on political impact to further their agenda. Terrorism is often used in conjunction with insurgency. CT can be applied directly against terrorist networks and indirectly to influence and render global environments inhospitable to terrorist networks.

For further details on CT, see JP 3-05, Joint Special Operations, *and JP 3-26,* Counterterrorism.

g. **Peace Operations.** For the Armed Forces of the United States, PO are **crisis response and limited contingency operations** involving all instruments of national power and also include international efforts and military missions to contain conflict, restore the peace, and shape the environment to support reconciliation and rebuilding and to facilitate the transition to legitimate governance. PO include peacekeeping operations (PKO), peace enforcement operations (PEO), peace building (PB) post-conflict actions, peacemaking (PM) processes, and conflict prevention. PO may be conducted under the sponsorship of the UN, another intergovernmental organization (IGO), within a coalition of agreeing nations, or unilaterally.

(1) **Peacekeeping Operations.** PKO consist of **military operations undertaken with the consent of all major parties to a dispute.** PKO may be part of a larger COIN framework when some parties come to a diplomatic agreement. When all parties have agreed to a diplomatic agreement, PKO can replace COIN over time.

(2) **Peace Enforcement Operations.** PEO are generally coercive in nature and rely on the threat of or use of force; however, PEO also rely on the development of working relationships with the local population. **The impartiality with which the PO force treats all parties and the nature of its objectives separate PEO from COIN and major combat operations.**

(3) **Peacemaking.** PM is a **diplomatic process** that may include mediation, negotiation, or conciliation. PM efforts may take advantage of seams in insurgent organizations by establishing separate agreements with individual organizations or groups that make up an insurgency movement. Commanders should constantly seek opportunities for PM throughout COIN.

(4) **Peace Building.** PB is an important aspect of a larger COIN effort. PB covers several post conflict actions including diplomatic, economic, and security related activities aimed at strengthening political settlements and legitimate governance, and rebuilding governmental infrastructure and institutions, in order to establish sustainable peace and security, foster a sense of confidence and well-being, and support the conditions for economic reconstruction.

(5) **Conflict Prevention.** Conflict prevention consists of diplomatic initiatives and other actions taken in advance of a crisis to prevent or limit violence, deter parties, and reach an agreement short of conflict. Conflict prevention also occurs in the post-conflict phase in order to prevent a return to conflict. Military deployments designed to deter and coerce parties will need to be credible, and this may require a combat posture and an enforcement mandate under the principles of Chapter VII of the UN Charter. Conflict prevention activities range from diplomatic initiatives to deployments designed to resolve disputes. Early efforts to prevent insurgency are covered in Chapter III, "Counterinsurgency."

For further details on PO, see JP 3-07.3, Peace Operations.

h. **Psychological Operations.** By lowering insurgent morale and reducing their operational or combat effectiveness, PSYOP can discourage aggressive actions and create dissension and disaffection within insurgent ranks. When properly employed, PSYOP can save lives of friendly, noncombatant, and insurgent forces by reducing insurgent will to fight.

(1) **Purpose.** The purpose of PSYOP in COIN is to induce or reinforce attitudes and behavior that support HN legitimacy and are favorable to the end state, including addressing perceived core grievances, drivers of conflict, and the illegitimacy of the insurgents. PSYOP efforts in COIN are most effective when personnel with a thorough understanding of the language and culture of the target audience (TA) are included in the review of PSYOP materials and messages. The dissemination of PSYOP includes print, broadcast, Internet, facsimile messaging, text messaging, and other emerging media. However, face-to-face communications are the most effective and preferred method of communicating with local audiences, especially in COIN.

(2) **Employment.** PSYOP employed at the strategic, operational, and tactical levels, are used to establish and reinforce foreign perceptions of counterinsurgent credibility and HN legitimacy. PSYOP conducted at the strategic level are international information activities conducted by United States Government (USG) agencies to influence foreign attitudes, perceptions, and behavior in favor of US goals and objectives during peacetime and in times of conflict. These programs are conducted predominantly outside the military arena but typically utilize DOD assets. PSYOP conducted at the operational level are in a defined operational area to promote the effectiveness of COIN, and PSYOP conducted at the tactical level are employed in the area assigned a maneuver commander to COIN tactical efforts. PSYOP forces are vital at the tactical level in COIN. They build rapport for US/coalition forces, enhance legitimacy and populace support for the HN, and support on-going CMO, as well as reduce combat effectiveness of the insurgents.

(3) **The PSYOP program.** The PSYOP program forms the legal authority to integrate PSYOP in Secretary of Defense (SecDef) approved missions in a theater of operation. The program establishes the parameters for the execution of PSYOP. The components of a PSYOP program provide the necessary guidelines from which to develop and approve PSYOP series to target foreign audiences. The program is staffed and coordinated through the Joint Staff and interagency process and approved by the SecDef to ensure PSYOP products reflect national and theater policy, strategy and also receive the broadest range of policy considerations.

(4) **PSYOP Product Approval.** Under US policy and the PSYOP Supplement to the Joint Strategic Capabilities Plan, PSYOP product approval authority may be sub-delegated by the Under Secretary of Defense for Policy to the geographic combatant commander (GCC) and further to the commander, joint task force through official

message traffic. When required or requested, the SecDef can authorize PSYOP product approval authority to be delegated down to the brigade combat team in order to facilitate responsive PSYOP support. Current policy facilitates decentralized PSYOP execution and allows for commanders with product approval authority to develop a streamlined time sensitive product approval process. **A JFC must have an approved PSYOP program, execution authority, and delegation of product approval authority before PSYOP execution can begin.**

For more discussion on PSYOP see JP 3-13.2, Psychological Operations.

i. **Counterguerrilla Operations.** Counterguerrilla operations are operations and activities conducted by armed forces, paramilitary forces, or nonmilitary agencies against guerrillas. Counterguerrilla operations essential supporting efforts, or a subset, of COIN operations focused on the insurgents' military forces.

j. **Example of Related Operations.** The complex nature of COIN often requires many types of operations to effectively shape the OE and set the conditions to reach the desired end state. For example, all or part of unsuccessful PEO can transition to COIN as the situation devolves and becomes more unstable. COIN and PEO can also occur simultaneously if some parties have agreed to peace while one or more use insurgency to reach their goals. More importantly, successful COIN can become long-term PEO as part of a larger FID framework. Figure I-4 depicts an example nexus of COIN, CT, and PEO.

5. Balance and Simultaneity of Offense, Defense, and Stability Operations

Simultaneity and Balance. COIN requires joint forces to both fight and build sequentially or simultaneously, depending on the security situation and a variety of other factors. Although offense, defense, or stability levels of effort will change over time, there will be some offensive, defensive, and stability operations occurring simultaneously. The balance of these operations must be appropriate to accomplish the current phase's objectives.

a. **Offensive and Defensive Operations. Offensive and defensive operations in COIN that are predominantly aimed at insurgent combatants are counterguerrilla operations.** Counterguerrilla operations are focused on countering the military aspect of insurgencies. The joint force, however, must never lose sight of the broader COIN effort and not merely focus on lethal efforts. Although the political dimension of COIN is paramount for the long-term, counterguerrilla operations are essential to protect the population. A balance of counterguerrilla, CT, collection, counterintelligence (CI), information, and other operations are necessary to secure the population.

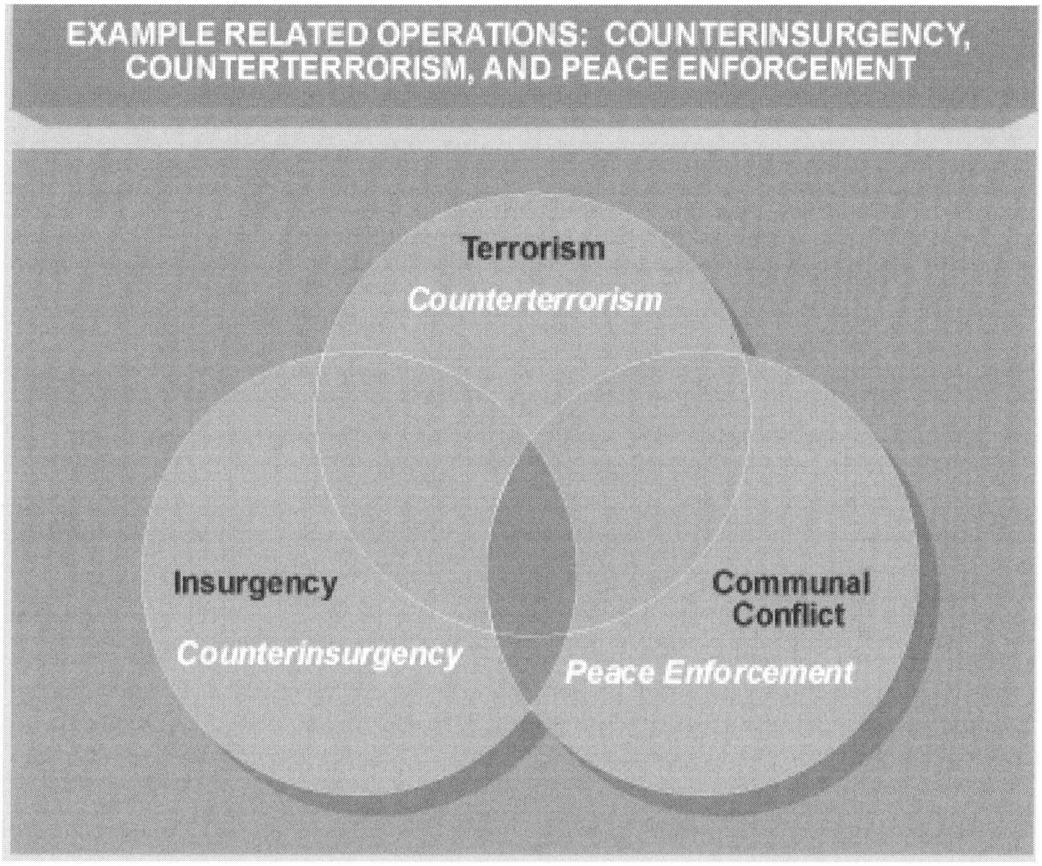

Figure I-4. Example Related Operations: Counterinsurgency, Counterterrorism, and Peace Enforcement

b. **Stability Operations.** Stability operations refer to various military missions, tasks, and activities conducted outside the US in coordination with other instruments of national power to maintain or reestablish a safe and secure environment and provide essential governmental services, emergency infrastructure reconstruction, and humanitarian relief. **Stability operations are consequently fundamental to COIN—stability operations address the core grievances of insurgency as well as drivers of conflict and are therefore essential to long-term success.** US military forces should be prepared to lead the activities necessary to accomplish these tasks when indigenous civil, USG, multinational, or international capacity does not exist or is not yet capable of assuming responsibility. Once a legitimate civil authority is prepared to conduct such tasks, US military forces may support such activities as required. Integrated civilian and military efforts are essential to success and military forces need to work competently in this environment while properly supporting the agency in charge. Effectively planning and executing stability operations require a variety of perspectives and expertise. The Department of State (DOS) is charged with responsibility for a whole-of-government approach to stability operations that includes USG departments and agencies (including DOD), the HN, alliance or coalition partners, nongovernmental organizations (NGOs),

IGOs, and other actors. Military forces should be prepared to work in informal or formal integrated civilian-military teams that could include, and in some cases be led by, representatives from other US departments and agencies, foreign governments and security forces, IGOs, NGOs, and members of the private sector with relevant skills and expertise.

For further details on stability operations, refer to JP 3-0, Joint Operations, *JP 3-07.3,* Peace Operations, *and Department of Defense Directive (DODD) 3000.05,* Military Support for Stability, Security, Transition, and Reconstruction (SSTR) Operations.

CHAPTER II
INSURGENCY

> *"The beginning of wisdom is to grasp and hold on tightly to the idea that insurgency is a profoundly political problem."*
>
> **Anthony James Joes**
> ***Resisting Rebellion: The History and Politics of Counterinsurgency***

1. Introduction

Successful COIN operations require comprehensive knowledge of the OE including an understanding of the insurgents, the scope of the insurgency, any external supporting elements, and the other players (e.g., terrorists and criminals) that may benefit from a protracted conflict and especially the relevant population. An insurgency typically succeeds or fails based on the support of the population. This understanding acts as a foundation on which the joint force can plan, prepare, execute, and assess COIN operations. This chapter provides COIN practitioners a doctrinal baseline to understand their adversaries.

a. **Nature.** Insurgencies are primarily internal conflicts that focus on the population. An insurgency aims to gain power and influence, win a contest of competing ideologies, or both. The insurgent goal of gaining power, influence, and freedom of action may not extend to overthrowing the HN government, but only to gaining power and influence at a greater rate or extent than other means would peacefully or legally allow. Some insurgent leaders may use ideology to gain power but not actually subscribe to the ideology—the ideology can be a means to another end. To survive, insurgencies must adapt to environmental and operational changes and new threats. This need to adapt also applies to any significant subgroups in an insurgency. Insurgents strive to adapt to change more quickly and effectively than the counterinsurgents. The use of subversion and violence is what makes insurgency distinct from the culturally accepted political process or culturally accepted nonviolent means of political protest.

b. **An Approach.** The use of insurgency is normally necessary because of the inherent weakness of insurgent forces relative to the state or external forces. This relative weakness forces insurgents to avoid an initial direct confrontation and instead look for ways to attack asymmetrically. While combatants generally prefer a quick, cheap, overwhelming victory over a protracted struggle, insurgents often must prolong their effort to gain in relative strength and erode the will of opponents over time.

c. **Focus.** Insurgencies may focus at the local, state, or regional level. The focus depends on the insurgents' endstate and phase. They may focus current operations on a small area and later expand their efforts geographically.

d. **Subversion and Violence**

(1) Subversion. Subversion describes actions designed to undermine the military, economic, psychological, or political strength or morale of a governing

authority. Insurgents may stage violent acts for their subversive impact, such as fomenting violent civil unrest, such as violent riots or strikes. Insurgents may also use nonviolent subversive efforts, such as political fronts, infiltration of government agencies, or nonviolent civil unrest (nonviolent strikes or peaceful public demonstrations). Subversion is most effective when consistently conducted over a long period of time. Insurgent use of propaganda, sabotage, and other means to influence audiences often seeks to undermine the legitimacy of the HN government and other counterinsurgent forces and increase support for the insurgency. These efforts are often focused on the HN population, but they may be focused on counterinsurgent forces or foreign audiences. Despite the lack of formal doctrine for these efforts, insurgents will often have honed propaganda skills and will quickly master skills in the manipulation of international media. Successful insurgents will plan activities and supporting influence efforts; they will have propaganda and media messages ready for immediate implementation. Furthermore, the eagerness of international media to obtain inside, exclusive stories may allow insurgents to control messages and present images and stories that support their narrative, their core grievances, and representation of themselves as victims.

(2) Violence. Insurgents use violence, which may include guerrilla warfare, terrorism, and even conventional operations to erode the strength and numbers of counterinsurgent forces, weaken the HN government, undermine the HN government's legitimacy, and promote their influence. The insurgents may only seek the population's acquiescence through violence. To gain popular support, the insurgents may use violence to make the government look incompetent or provoke an inappropriate HN government response. An inappropriate response could be HN government repression of the population that does no actual harm to the insurgents.

e. **Organization.** There may be many insurgent groups or other destabilizing actors involved in one area. Insurgency may be conducted by a highly organized single movement or by a loose coalition of poorly organized groups. Individual insurgencies may have several factions or subgroups that have varying degrees of unity, ideological or otherwise. Insurgent organization may also change. This can take varying forms, from splitting into smaller groups to separate insurgencies forming a loose coalition or permanent larger insurgency. Loose coalitions may cooperate only to achieve a certain goal, so the groups that make up the loose coalition may be unable to cooperate on fundamental ideological issues or be unwilling to share power if the insurgency succeeds. Some insurgencies have members that work towards a common goal with little or no central direction. The potential involvement or support of international terrorists, criminals, and other actors may further impact insurgent organization.

f. **Characteristics.** While each insurgency is unique and often adaptive, there are basic similarities among insurgencies. In all cases, insurgent military action is secondary and subordinate to a larger end, which differentiates insurgency from lawlessness. However, counterinsurgent commanders may face a confusing and shifting coalition of many kinds of opponents, some of whom may be at odds with one another. Additionally, some of these adversaries are insurgents and some are not. Characteristics of insurgencies can be found in Figure II-1.

CHARACTERISTICS OF INSURGENCIES

1. Ends, Scope, Core Grievances, and Prerequisites
2. Dynamics
3. Organization
4. Approaches
5. Recruitment, Causes, Resources, and Information
6. Vulnerabilities
7. Devolution and Decline

Figure II-1. Characteristics of Insurgencies

g. **Inherent Advantages.** The counterinsurgents normally have initial advantage over insurgents in means and resources; however, that edge is counterbalanced by the counterinsurgents' requirement to maintain a degree of order throughout the operational area. On the other hand, insurgents only need to sow chaos and disorder. A small number of highly motivated insurgents with simple weapons, good operations security (OPSEC), and limited mobility can undermine security over a large area. A coordinated COIN effort requires political and military leaders to recognize that an insurgency exists and determine its makeup and characteristics. While the government prepares to respond, the insurgents gain strength and foster increasing disruption throughout the state or region. Some insurgents are successful at disguising their intentions, so potential counterinsurgents are at a disadvantage; however, the exposure of disingenuous insurgent goals often proves advantageous to the HN's COIN efforts.

h. **Protraction and Success.** It is not necessary for the insurgency to "win" in a traditional Western sense—an insurgency wins by not losing. As long as the insurgency survives to regenerate and fight another day, it continues to erode the counterinsurgents' capabilities and will. If the counterinsurgents are not effective in dealing with the insurgency, they are usually losing relative strength, credibility, and legitimacy. Counterinsurgents must first contain and then defeat an insurgency as well as address the insurgency's core grievances. If core grievances are not addressed sufficiently, the insurgency will regenerate and prolong the conflict.

i. **Will, Time, and Space.** Insurgent strategies seek to achieve their political aims by using time, space, and will. They normally accept temporary setbacks with respect to time and space to reach their long-term goals.

(1) **Will.** The ideological nature and core grievances of insurgency often result in insurgencies having a strong collective will. This sense of collective will is often relatively much greater than that of fragile states' governments. The insurgent thus seeks to make the struggle a protracted "contest of wills."

(2) **Time.** Due to their relative strong will, insurgents can afford to be patient. When their relative weakness requires, insurgents can erode their opponents' will through various means, such as guerrilla warfare, subversion, terrorism, and propaganda. Thus, capable insurgents use time as a resource that effective insurgents manage at all levels, especially the strategic.

(3) **Space.** Like their use of time, insurgents can use space to wear down their opponents' will. Like conventional operations, they may seek to attack relatively weak areas. However, capable insurgents will be fluid. They will fight on ground of their choosing, wear down their opponent, yet avoid becoming decisively engaged or destroyed. In this fashion, they will seek to wear down their opponents' actual strength and force their opponent to react to insurgent efforts. Sanctuaries and porous border regions also offer insurgent's transnational lines of communication, escape routes, and havens to recuperate, train, and plan future operations.

2. Ends, Scope, Core Grievances, and Prerequisites

Ends, scope, and core grievances are three of the most important aspects of an insurgency. Understanding an insurgency's motivations, breadth of activity and support, and core grievances is essential to successful COIN.

a. **Ends.** Insurgencies generally share some combination of four common objectives: political change, overthrow of the government, resistance against an outside actor, or nullifying political control in an area. Insurgencies may have more than one end, and the ends can change with circumstances; however, ends tend to be ideologically driven. In some cases, insurgents may only seek to goad the international community to intervene, which may force political change, or the presence of foreigners may help fuel support for the insurgency.

(1) **Change.** Many insurgencies center on forcing the HN into significant political or economic change. This change can have multiple forms. Moreover, the level of violence and subversion may be beyond the HN's capability to address with nonmilitary means. Change can include issues such as political processes, religious practices, or secession of a region.

(2) **Overthrow.** Insurgents may seek to overthrow governments. The actual efforts to overthrow a regime can range from an unplanned, spontaneous explosion of popular will to a coup d'état with little support from the population. Most insurgencies fall between these two extremes and are characterized more by a strategy of protracted attrition than broad-based populist revolutions or coup d'état. They normally seek to achieve at least one of two goals: to overthrow the existing social order and reallocate power.

(3) **Resistance.** In some cases indigenous elements seek to expel or overthrow perceived "occupiers" or "outsiders," particularly when local groups initially resist the joint force during or in the aftermath of major operations. These resistance groups may initially have little or no central direction, or they may have been part of a preplaned resistance effort. Either way, the actions of these small groups can have a cumulative impact. Counterinsurgents must address these nascent insurgencies as quickly as possible, before resistance efforts gain momentum and organization. Resistance is usually more easily addressed if action is taken early. Some resistance groups could come under the control of a government in exile or by factions competing for that role. It is important to note that the joint force may be unwelcome or seen as "occupiers" or "outsiders" in an UGA just as they might in a state. As in many situations, the objective of general resistance is often to protract the war until the "outsiders" tire of the struggle and withdraw.

(4) **Nullification.** Some non-state actors seek to create or maintain a region where there is no governmental control or governmental control that they can co-opt. For example, powerful criminal organizations desire a space where they can conduct their activities unrestrained by a government. If these criminal organizations can challenge a HN's control beyond the local level of government, they have become an insurgency. Additionally, some insurgencies may have the goal of nullifying one state's control of a region with the intent to form a sanctuary in support of action elsewhere. Such a sanctuary may be safely over an international border from the real (or current) focus of the insurgency or may be far from the seat of the insurgency, serving as a safe haven for training and other preparation.

b. **Scope.** There are four general categories for the scope of insurgencies; however, there is no clear-cut delineation between categories. The first two categories are more common forms of insurgency. The latter two categories refer to more broadly-based insurgencies made more potent and prevalent by globalization.

(1) **Local.** These insurgencies are local-national in scope and end state; however, these insurgencies do not enjoy any substantive external support.

(2) **Local-External Support.** Like the previous category, these insurgencies are local-national in scope and end state. What makes these insurgencies different from the previous category is that they enjoy external support from other actors. External support may come from diverse sources and may be either overt or covert. Support may

come from states in any combination of diplomatic, informational, military, or economic efforts, although an important form of support is another nation's allowing the insurgents to use its territory as a safe haven. Support from non-state actors is generally smaller in size and scope than a state's support.

(3) **Local-Global Support.** These insurgencies focus on a particular area, but supporters and elements can be found globally. For example, some insurgencies use subversion and violence in a localized area while using IO for a more regional or global impact; these IO often originate from a site geographically separate from the area where the insurgency is physically operating. Thus, the support network of these insurgencies may be global in scope, especially when there is a sympathetic diaspora or émigré population. By definition the operations of insurgencies of this kind can be found in multiple states, which adds to the difficultly of effectively dealing with them in a coherent fashion. A good example of this type of insurgency is the Liberation Tamil Tigers Elam—their efforts are focused on one island while their support has taken on a global scale.

(4) **Global.** These insurgencies are committed to a radical end state—they wish to force major change in the world. The theater for these insurgencies is politically, logistically, and operationally global. Global insurgencies often seek to first transform regions and then eventually the world. Global insurgencies often are willing to use any means to achieve their end state, including forming coalitions with or amalgamating other smaller-scoped insurgencies. Portions of these insurgencies can be found globally, although they may concentrate in ungoverned spaces or within sympathetic states. Global insurgencies can exploit local grievances and may transform these grievances from mundane to more religious or philosophical ones. They are often willing to support causes they view as compatible with their own goals through the provision of funds, volunteers, and propaganda. Some of these insurgents also attempt to leverage religious or ideological identity to create and support a transnational array of insurgencies. The world-wide communist efforts during the Cold War and Al Qaeda are examples of such groups. As the scope of these groups increases, the scope and therefore the complexity of COIN also increases. Traditional COIN methods still apply—isolation and disaggregation of the insurgencies to deal with them in detail coupled with addressing the core grievances. Defeating such enemies requires a global, strategic response; such a response addresses the array of linked resources and conflicts that sustain these movements while tactically addressing the local grievances that feed them. While globalization makes these insurgencies very difficult to destroy, their extreme beliefs and dispersion make it difficult for them to hold any territory for any duration.

c. **Core Grievances.** The core grievances are issues, real or perceived, in the view of some of the population. Some or all may fuel insurgency to varying degrees. The importance of the core grievances, or even their existence, can change over time. Additionally, insurgents can be adept at manipulating or creating core grievances to serve their purpose. The following represent common core grievances:

(1) **Identity.** There are many factors that shape a person's sense of identity, but identity is sociocultural in character. Strong feelings based on identity can be in conflict with the HN government, potentially leading to insurgencies with secession, border changes, or political overthrow as goals. External actors with similar identity as the insurgents may assist.

(2) **Religion.** Religious fundamentalism or extremism can become a core grievance of insurgency in and of itself. External groups with similar extremist religious views as the insurgents often provide support.

(3) **Economy.** Pervasive and desperate poverty often fosters and fuels widespread public dissatisfaction. Young people without jobs or hope are ripe for insurgent recruitment. Additionally, a perceived disparity of means can be an economic core grievance, for example a gap between a large poor majority and a small wealthy minority.

(4) **Corruption.** Corruption of national politics, HN government, or key institutions or organizations can be a core grievance. Institutional corruption is systemic and ongoing, unfair or illegal actions or policies. Political corruption is the dysfunction of a political system. For example, corruption in government development programs can cause resentment by the aggrieved group. Corruption leads to loss of HN legitimacy and is often a key core grievance.

(5) **Repression.** Repression can take many forms, such as discriminatory policies, rights violations, police brutality, or imprisonment. Like corruption, repression can lead to popular dissatisfaction with the current government and leads to the reduction of HN legitimacy.

(6) **Foreign Exploitation or Presence.** The perception that outsiders exploit the HN or the HN government excessively panders to foreigners can be a core grievance. For example, if foreign businesses dominate critical portions of the local economy, some of the population may feel that they or their country are being exploited by outsiders. A foreign military presence or military treaty may offend national sentiment as well. Finally, the mere presence or specific actions of foreigners may offend local religious or cultural sensibilities.

(7) **Occupation.** Foreign military forces' occupation of another state is often a core grievance. If groups within the population have the will to fight on after a regime change or occupation, they may form a resistance movement.

(8) **Essential Services.** Essential services provide those things needed to sustain life. Examples of these essential needs are availability of food, law enforcement, emergency services, water, electricity, shelter, health care, schools, transportation, and sanitation (trash and sewage). Stabilizing a population requires meeting these basic needs. People pursue essential needs until they feel they are met, at any cost and from any source. People support the source that meets their needs.

d. **Prerequisites.** There are three prerequisites for an insurgency to be successful in an area—a vulnerable population, leadership available for direction, and lack of government control. When all three exist in an area, insurgency can operate with some freedom of movement, gain the support of the people, and become entrenched over time.

(1) **Vulnerable Population.** A population is vulnerable if the people have real or perceived grievances that insurgents can exploit. The insurgents can exploit the population by offering hope for change as well as exploiting political, economic, or social dissatisfaction with the current government. A gap between population's expectations and the capability to meet these expectations may cause unrest within the population, including turning to insurgency. The larger the gap, the greater the population's perceived or relative, deprivation between what they have and what they perceive they should have. Similarly, the larger the gap, the more susceptible the population is to insurgent influence through promises to close the gap.

(2) **Leadership Available for Direction.** A vulnerable population alone will not support an insurgency. There must be a leadership element that can direct the frustrations of a vulnerable population. If insurgents can recruit, co-opt, or coerce local leaders or the local leaders are part of the insurgency, these leaders can direct the frustrations of the populace. If the HN government alienates the intelligentsia, religious leaders, middle class, or other influential people in their society, these influential people may start or become part of an insurgency. This may be very important as these people often bring special skills and leadership to an insurgency.

(3) **Lack of Government Control.** Real or perceived lack of governmental control can allow insurgents to operate with little or no interference from security forces or other agencies. Greater government control decreases the likelihood of insurgent success. The opposite is also true. If the people feel the government is inadequate in meeting their needs, insurgents may provide an alternative, or "shadow," government, or they may merely nullify governance to allow freedom of action and movement. HN failure to see or admit that there is an issue, or outright refusal to change, can further strengthen this prerequisite.

3. Dynamics of Insurgency

The dynamics of insurgency are a framework to assess an insurgency's strengths and weaknesses. The dynamics can be examined separately, but studying their interaction is an indispensable part of COIN mission analysis. The interplay of these dynamics influences an insurgency's approach. A change in location or the amount of external support might lead insurgents to adjust their approach and organization. Effective counterinsurgents identify the organizational pattern these dynamics form and closely monitor its evolution. The dynamics include leadership, objectives, ideology, OE, external support, internal support, phasing and timing, and organizational and operational approaches, though they should be examined with the underlying understanding that insurgents are a product of their culture, society, and history (see Figure II-2).

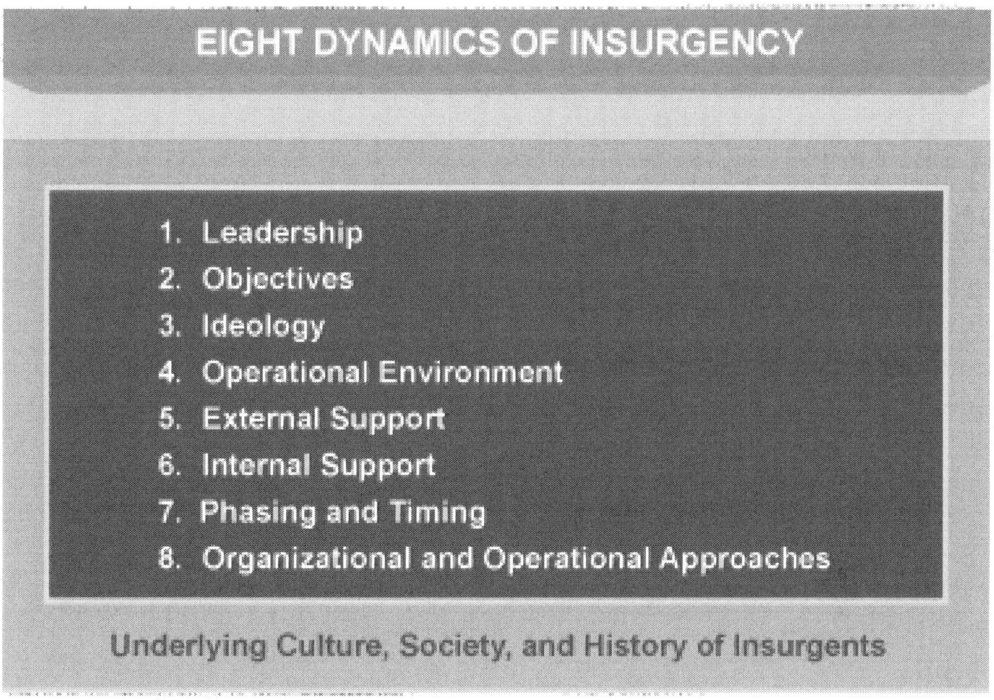

EIGHT DYNAMICS OF INSURGENCY
1. Leadership
2. Objectives
3. Ideology
4. Operational Environment
5. External Support
6. Internal Support
7. Phasing and Timing
8. Organizational and Operational Approaches
Underlying Culture, Society, and History of Insurgents

Figure II-2. Eight Dynamics of Insurgency

a. **Leadership.** Like any organization, leadership is critical to any insurgency. Leaders must provide vision, direction, guidance, coordination, and organizational coherence. This may come at the strategic level in an organized insurgency, or direction may initially come locally in a disparate resistance movement. Successful insurgent leaders' key tasks are to break the ties between the people and the government, build physical and psychological ties between the insurgency and the people, and to establish credibility for insurgent efforts. Leader education, background, family and social connections, and experiences contribute to their ability to organize and inspire the people who form the insurgency. Insurgent leaders ultimately advance alternatives to existing conditions.

(1) **Distributed Leadership.** In some cases, insurgencies have multiple important leaders. They are often from the elite, middle class, or intellectual segments of society. These leaders may separately recruit, indoctrinate, and use other members of the insurgency to carry out tasks. Consequently, these kinds of insurgent leadership structures are difficult to penetrate and can continue to operate efficiently despite the loss of any single leader, and sometimes even multiple leaders.

(2) **Collective Leadership.** Some insurgencies operate from a collective power base that does not depend on specific leaders or personalities. This kind of collective leadership arrangement may require physical meetings, which often require a sanctuary

for security. Insurgencies with this style of leadership are easier to penetrate but recover rapidly when they lose key personnel.

(3) **Charismatic Leadership.** Some insurgencies depend on a charismatic personality to provide cohesion, motivation, and a focal point for the movement. Some charismatic leaders are traditional authority figures such as tribal leaders, local warlords, or religious leaders. These traditional authority figures often wield enough power to single-handedly drive an insurgency. Identity-focused insurgencies can be defeated in some cases by co-opting the responsible traditional authority figure; in others, the authority figures have to be discredited or eliminated. Organizations led in this way make decisions and initiate new actions rapidly, but they are vulnerable to disruption or collapse if the charismatic leader is removed.

b. **Objectives. Effective analysis of an insurgency requires identifying its strategic, operational, and tactical objectives. This analysis must be from the insurgent perspective, rather than that of the counterinsurgent.** Insurgents do not normally plan specifically in terms of strategic, operational, or tactical objectives. Insurgents use physical or psychological effects to connect strategic and operational objectives to tactical actions. Insurgent objectives may be achieved through lethal or nonlethal actions. For instance, to achieve a strategic objective of discouraging support for the government, insurgents may conduct operations to assassinate government officials or may delegitimize the HN in the eyes of the population by damaging or seizing a key facility. Identifying direct and indirect effects of insurgent actions within the OE and understanding the insurgent's strategic, operational, and tactical objectives are key to countering insurgent operations.

(1) **Strategic.** The insurgents' strategic end state is related to the ends and scope of the insurgency. The end state is a set of conditions that describe victory. During insurgency, these conditions usually describe a government that is either unable or unwilling to control regions of the state, or the conditions may include the fall of the existing government. Strategic objectives are developed by insurgents that will bring about the end state conditions. A common strategic objective among insurgencies is a population that perceives the government as illegitimate and ineffective. Other strategic objectives may include popular support for the insurgency and negation of COIN forces.

(2) **Operational.** Insurgents pursue operational objectives that support their strategic objectives. Operational objectives will substantially increase insurgent control and influence and erode government legitimacy and counterinsurgent credibility. Operational objectives exploit the three prerequisites of an insurgency. Continued successful achievement of operational objectives will progressively establish the insurgents' desired end state. For example, successful derailment of a national election may be an operational objective that will produce reduced confidence in government legitimacy - an effect that will lead to the achievement of a strategic objective.

(3) **Tactical.** Insurgents conduct missions, tasks, and actions to produce effects that achieve tactical objectives. The insurgent operational objectives often require

cumulative tactical efforts over a protracted period. Tactical objectives vary substantially in size and scope. For example, a large tactical objective could be successfully derailing a national election in one province and a small tactical objective may be successfully terrorizing a single family to not vote.

c. **Ideology.** Insurgents promise reforms or improvements and can present membership as an alternative to what otherwise may be a dull, impoverished existence. Thus, some join an insurgency due to poverty or lack of other opportunities. In other cases, insurgencies can recruit and gain popular support by appealing to the cause and the narrative. Finally, recruits may join an insurgency simply because they are seeking to belong to a community or because insurgents exploit recruits' religious beliefs or ideological views.

(1) **Narrative.** The narrative is the central mechanism through which ideologies are expressed and absorbed. A narrative is an organizational scheme expressed in story form, and a good narrative is rooted in the local culture. Narratives are central to representing identity, particularly the collective identity of religious sects, ethnic groupings, and tribal elements. Stories about a community's history provide models of how actions and consequences are linked. Stories are often the basis for strategies and actions, as well as for interpreting others' intentions.

(2) **Ideological Dogma.** Many insurgents hold all-encompassing worldviews; they are ideologically rigid and uncompromising, seeking to control their members' private thought, expression, and behavior. Seeking power and believing themselves to be ideologically pure, these insurgents often brand those they consider insufficiently orthodox as enemies. Extremist beliefs can also fortify the will of insurgents. For instance, their dogmas often confirm the idea, common among hard-core transnational terrorists, that unlimited means are appropriate to achieve their often unlimited goals—the means are justified by the ends and mitigated by the vilification and dehumanization of the target. Some insurgent groups employ religious concepts to portray their efforts favorably and mobilize followers in pursuit of their political goals. However, these insurgents often pursue their ends in highly pragmatic ways based on realistic assumptions. Even the most rigid insurgents may seek cease fires and participate in elections when such actions support their short-term interests.

d. **Operational Environment.** The OE—including sociocultural factors and civil factors—affects all participants in a conflict, including insurgents. The effects of these factors are immediately visible at the tactical level, where they are perhaps the predominant influence on decisions. For example, insurgencies in urban environments present different planning considerations from insurgencies in rural environments. Similarly, border areas contiguous to states that may actively or passively provide external support and sanctuary to insurgents create a distinct vulnerability for counterinsurgents.

e. **External Support.** External support to insurgency can provide political, psychological, and material resources that might otherwise be limited or unavailable.

External support for an insurgency can be provided by a state, organization, or non-state actor. Assistance can come from outside state governments or political entities that may provide support by recognizing an insurgency or political party sympathetic to the insurgency. Political support is the most dangerous form of support and can result in the insurgency's gaining legitimacy, which may force limitations on the counterinsurgent operations. Psychological support to insurgency is sympathy for, or acknowledgement of, the insurgent cause. Support in the form of resources may include fighters, money, weapons, equipment, food, intelligence, advisors, and training. Insurgencies may turn to transnational criminal elements for funding or use the Internet to create a support network. Ethnic or religious communities in other states may also provide external support.

(1) **Sanctuaries.** Sanctuaries provide insurgents with safe havens from which to prepare or conduct further operations. This may include physical sanctuaries where insurgents may plan, train, or otherwise prepare for ongoing operations. These sanctuaries may be located areas external to a HN from which operations are launched and to which insurgents may retire. Physical safe havens may be in areas with sympathetic governments or, more often, UGAs. In either case, sanctuaries challenge or prevent COIN efforts to enter these areas that protects insurgents. Similarly, insurgents may be able to use safe havens created by cultural sanctuaries, such religious or other culturally significant areas (e.g., churches, mosques, museums), or in locations among historically protected populations, such as women and children. Insurgents also draw on virtual sanctuaries such as websites, chatrooms, and blogs. These virtual sanctuaries are used to transmit propaganda, recruit, issue directives or orders, and conduct various other activities. For these virtual sanctuaries, the complexity of cyberspace can impede counterinsurgent efforts.

(2) **Urban Sanctuaries.** Modern target acquisition and intelligence collection technology make insurgents in isolation, even in neighboring states, more vulnerable than those hidden among the population. Thus, contemporary insurgencies often develop in urban environments, using formal and informal networks. Human intelligence (HUMINT) and other forms of intelligence, surveillance, and reconnaissance (ISR) are vital to understanding and defeating these underground networks.

(3) **Non-state Actors.** Non-state actors often team with insurgents and profit from the conflict. Non-state actors, such as transnational terrorist organizations, often represent a security threat beyond the areas they inhabit.

f. **Internal Support.** Internal support is vital for insurgencies, especially when insurgencies are latent or incipient. Insurgents must recruit or mobilize elements of the population to provide practical internal support and maintain momentum if an insurgency is to survive. In many cases neutrals are neither recognized nor tolerated by insurgents; they need to be persuaded or coerced. Therefore, the insurgents may have to eliminate some to persuade the remainder.

(1) **Level of Internal Support.** The reality is that neither side will ever enjoy the support of the entire population. The support of the population will fluctuate due to many factors. Assessing why groups within the population favor the HN or an insurgent group(s) is difficult. Measuring the population's support is important and asking the population directly or using surveys can produce valuable insight into popular support and attitudes. Figure II-3 depicts an insurgency's range of popular support.

(2) **Types of Internal Support.** Popular support can be either active or passive. It may come from only a small segment of the population or from a broad base of the population. Support for an insurgency may also be open or hidden, depending on the overall situation. Local insurgents normally exploit local core grievances when conducting recruiting. Normally insurgents link their messages with tangible solutions and actions.

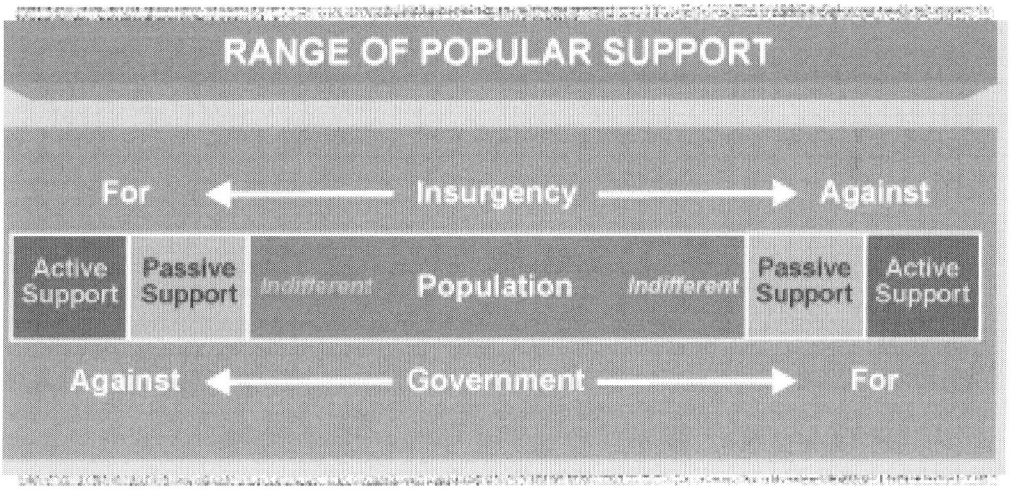

Figure II-3. Range of Popular Support

g. **Phasing and Timing.** Most insurgencies pass through three common phases of development. Within those phases, insurgencies may evolve through radicalization, popular unrest, civil disobedience, subversion, localized guerrilla activity, widespread guerrilla warfare, and conventional warfare. Alternatively, they may wither away to dormancy if effectively countered or if they fail to capture sufficient popular support. Not all insurgencies experience a phased or neatly evolving development, and linear progression is not required for insurgent success. Moreover, a single insurgency may be in different phases in different parts of a country simultaneously, and they often continue activities they began in earlier phases with new activities. Insurgencies under pressure can also revert to an earlier phase, as needed. They then resume development when favorable conditions return. This flexibility is the key strength of a phased approach, which provides fallback positions for insurgents when threatened. Movement from one phase to another does not end the operational and tactical activities typical of earlier phases; it incorporates them. The phases of the protracted model below may not provide a complete template for understanding contemporary insurgencies; however, they do explain the shifting mosaic of activities usually present in some form.

(1) **Phase I—Strategic Defensive (Latent and Incipient).** The first phase of an insurgency normally begins with the HN government's having stronger forces than the insurgents, when the insurgency is on the strategic defensive. In this situation insurgents must concentrate on survival and building support. There are two distinct, common stages within the first phase: latent and incipient.

(a) **Latent.** A latent insurgency is not yet ready to begin significant subversive or violent activities—it has not manifested or openly conducted operations. A latent insurgency usually begins with a group of like-minded individuals discussing core grievances. This exchange of ideas may occur through many mediums, including the Internet or recorded video. The involved individuals may discuss challenging authority or correcting perceived core grievances, which may lead to a conspiracy and plan for action. During this period the insurgency establishes an identity, cause, narrative, and a firm ideological or political base. This period tends to be a vulnerable and crucial time for the insurgents, and it can be a period of frequent fracturing or splintering due to ideological or other internal disputes. Insurgents often try to keep their activities hidden from the HN government and the majority of the population due to their potential vulnerability in this period. There are two key tasks insurgents perform during the latent stage: recruitment and infiltration (see Figure II-4). Counterinsurgents must take great care to differentiate between the activities of a latent insurgency and the activities of like-minded individuals of a political group lawfully exercising their rights to challenge the viewpoints of a sovereign government. Ignoring this, counterinsurgents may unwittingly drive these groups to support insurgency.

(b) **Incipient.** There is usually a period of time for any latent insurgency to transform to an incipient insurgency. When the insurgents have a sufficient foundation to begin more activities, they move into the incipient stage. During this stage an insurgency is becoming more active. In addition to expanding the tasks from the latent stage, insurgents will begin efforts to subvert and influence. They will also expand their efforts into using armed force. The insurgents often declare their existence through IO in the incipient stage (see Figure II-4).

(2) **Phase II—Strategic Stalemate (Guerrilla Warfare).** When the insurgents have reached rough strategic parity with counterinsurgent forces, they often begin to emphasize guerrilla warfare. Guerrilla warfare is military and paramilitary operations conducted in enemy-held or hostile territory by irregular, predominantly indigenous forces. This emphasis on guerrilla warfare characterizes the second phase. Guerrilla warfare is characterized by guerrillas' striking at the time and place of their choosing and disappearing back into the population. The size and intensity of such attacks will depend on the situation and objectives of the insurgency. Insurgents will normally continue other efforts used in the latent and incipient phase; however, these efforts often change to support guerrilla warfare (see Figure II-4).

Figure II-4. Insurgent Actions, Underground and Military

(3) **Phase III—Strategic Counteroffensive (War of Movement).** The third phase begins if insurgents feel they have superior strength and they choose to employ a

portion of their forces to fight in a conventional manner. These conventional insurgent forces often attempt to hold terrain and expand insurgent-controlled areas. To prepare for these conventional insurgent efforts, guerrilla forces normally combine and train to fight as conventional forces, which often takes place in cross-border sanctuaries. These forces may form multiple echelons. They often acquire sophisticated, modern weapons and the skill to employ them. Insurgents may also obtain support from external combat forces, such as advisors or even conventional forces from a friendly border nation.

h. **Organizational and Operational Approaches.** Insurgencies develop operational approaches from the interaction of various factors. Insurgencies will adapt their approaches and organizational structure to the current conditions of the OE. More specifically, insurgent organizational and operational approaches are directly related to the strength of the HN government. If the HN is strong, the insurgency will have to be more secretive and selective. Conversely, the insurgency can be bolder if the HN is weak.

4. Organization

While each insurgency will have its own unique organization that may change over time, there are shared general organizational characteristics that provide a general framework for analysis of insurgencies. There are two basic organizational structures that comprise most insurgent organizations: components and elements.

a. **Components.** Insurgent structure may be generally broken down into two wings: political and military. Insurgent sociocultural factors, approaches, and resources tend to drive its organization, and most insurgencies. Figure II-4 depicts the many activities that these two wings may perform, from exploiting root causes to overt guerrilla warfare. Progression up the diagram does not have to be linear; insurgencies can perform any of these activities at any time, in any order or combination.

(1) **Political Wing.** Insurgencies will have some form of political wing, although some ends or approaches may only require a nascent political wing. The political wing is primarily concerned with undermining the legitimacy of the HN government and its allies while building up support for the insurgency. This may be accomplished by participation of members of the political wing in legitimate elections and political processes in order to infiltrate the government and undermine it from within. The political wing of the insurgency builds credibility and legitimacy for the insurgency within the population and potentially with the international community. The political wing may downplay insurgent violence and subversion, some to the point of outright deception.

(a) **Shadow Government.** An insurgency and its political wing may become strong enough to not only challenge the HN government, but it may act as an alternative government. It may provide some or all of the functions or services of a government, for example food distribution, health care, and security. Normally the shadow government will attempt to satisfy grievances in local areas first. They may attempt to transfer blame for any residual issues to foreign presence or the HN government in order to facilitate popular support. This approach is used in Lebanon and has become widely known as the "Hezbollah model." This model is being explicitly replicated by other insurgents in the region, including in Iraq.

(b) **Supportive Parties.** While not part of the insurgency, an existing legal political party may come to support the insurgency or may form a legal political party that supports the insurgency. These legal political parties may become the insurgents' conduit for diplomacy and political reconciliation. In some cases, the political party may consist of former insurgent strategic leaders and cadre. Efforts should be made to open and maintain these avenues for reconciliation.

(2) **Military Wing.** The military wing of the insurgency conducts combat operations. Most insurgencies will initially have few combatants; however, military-focused insurgencies will focus on this wing. Most insurgencies build the military wing's capability and capacity over time. The military wing may have to execute its overt operations and go back into hiding to survive. As the insurgency grows in relative strength, however, its military wing may be able to continuously operate in an overt fashion. Insurgent military forces usually start with paramilitary forces, but advanced insurgencies may transition some paramilitary forces to more traditionally-organized military forces. Thus, if security is ineffective or the insurgency has grown powerful relative to the HN, the insurgent elements may exist openly. If the state maintains a continuous and effective security presence, some part of the insurgent organization will likely maintain a secret existence.

b. **Elements.** The elements are the basic organizational "building blocks" of insurgencies. The proportion or presence of each element relative to the larger organization depends on the strategic approach the insurgency uses. Figure II-5 depicts an example of the insurgency's elements.

(1) **Strategic Leaders.** Leaders provide overall direction in more organized insurgencies. These leaders are the "key idea people" or strategic planners. They usually exercise leadership through force of personality, the power of revolutionary ideas, and personal charisma. In some insurgencies, they may hold their position through religious, clan, or tribal authority. A loosely organized insurgency may not have strategic leaders, but they will have leaders of smaller groups that happen to act towards the same goals, such as expelling an "occupier."

(2) **Underground.** The underground is that element of the insurgent organization that conducts operations in areas normally denied to the auxiliary and the guerrilla force. The underground is a cellular organization within the insurgency that conducts covert or clandestine activities that are compartmentalized. This secrecy may be by necessity, by design, or both depending on the situation. Most underground operations are required to take place in and around population centers that are held by counterinsurgent forces. Underground members often fill leadership positions, overseeing specific functions that are carried out by the auxiliary. The underground and

auxiliary—although technically separate elements—are, in reality, loosely connected elements that provide coordinated capabilities for the insurgent movement. The key distinction between them is that the underground is the element of the insurgent organization that operates in areas denied to the guerrilla force. Members of the underground often control cells used to neutralize informants and collaborators from within the insurgency and the population.

(3) **Guerrillas.** Guerrillas conduct the actual fighting and provide security. They support the insurgency's broader agenda and maintain local control. Guerrillas protect and expand the counterstate, if the insurgency establishes such an institution. They also protect training camps and networks that facilitate the flow of money, instructions, and foreign and local fighters. Guerrillas include any individual member of the insurgency who commits or attempts an act of overt violence or terrorism in support of insurgent goals. Guerrilla leaders are considered part of the combatant element for analyzing insurgencies.

(4) **Cadre.** Although few contemporary insurgencies would use the term "cadre," this element forms the political or ideological core of the insurgency. If present, the cadre is part of the underground. Some cadre activities are violent deeds, but their fundamental role is enforcement of political and ideological discipline, subversion of opponents, and co-optation of social power to support the insurgent strategy. Cadre leaders maintain organizational discipline and may perform key "shadow government" or government-in-exile functions. Cadres wage the battle of ideas and lead other insurgents in this respect. Cadre activities may include: control of intelligence and CI networks; focus and integration of IO capabilities against the government, the population, and the international community; direction and coordination of acts of sabotage; and operation of the command structure or shadow government, if present. Parts of the cadre may act as a formal political party. Movements based on religious extremism usually include religious and spiritual advisors among their cadre.

(5) **Auxiliary.** The auxiliary is the support element of the insurgent organization. The auxiliary's organization and operations are secretive in nature, and members do not openly indicate their sympathy or involvement with the insurgent movement. This support enables the combatant force to survive and function. This support can take the form of logistics, labor, or intelligence. Auxiliary members are active sympathizers who provide important support services but do not generally participate in combat operations. Typical auxiliary activities include: running safe houses; storing weapons and supplies; acting as couriers; providing intelligence collection; giving early warning of counterinsurgent movements; providing funding from lawful and unlawful sources; and providing forged or stolen documents and access or introductions to potential supporters.

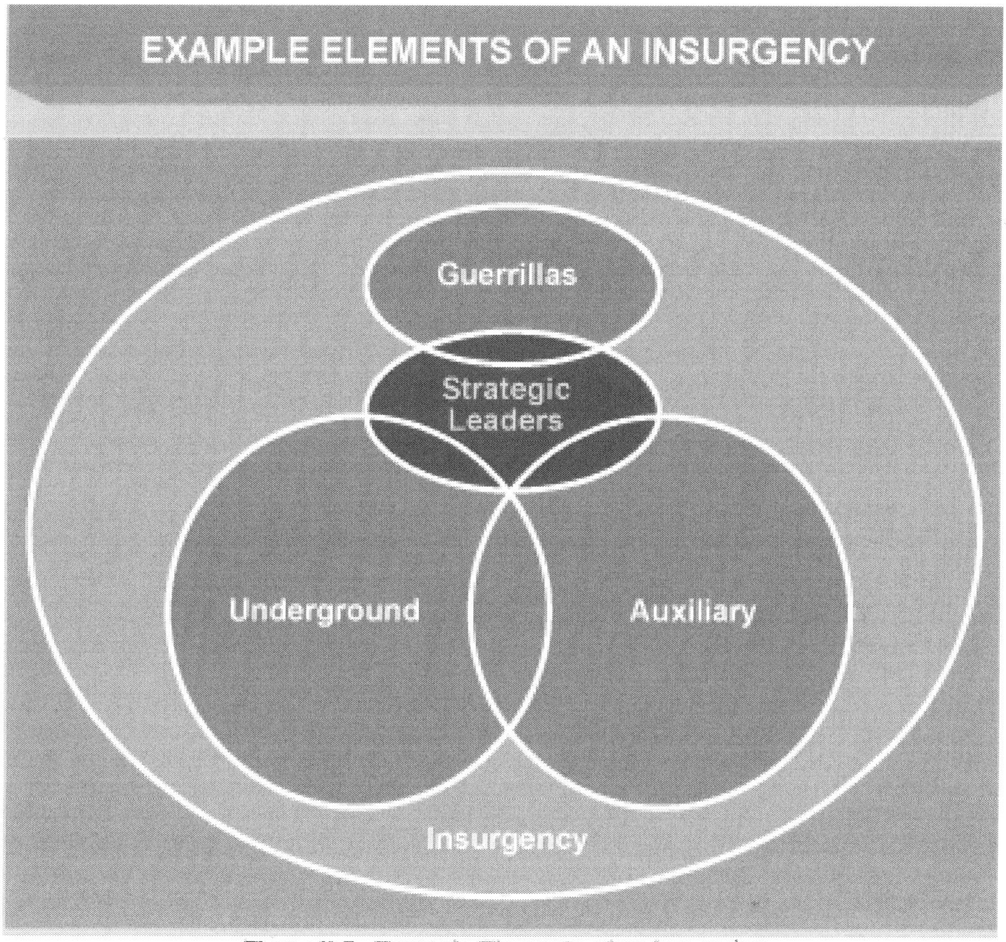

Figure II-5. Example Elements of an Insurgency

c. **Networks.** Insurgents are often organized as a network. A network is a series of direct and indirect ties from one actor to a collection of others. Networking extends the range and variety of both their military and political actions. Networked organizations are difficult to destroy; they tend to heal, adapt, and learn rapidly. However, such organizations have a limited ability to attain strategic success because they cannot easily muster and focus power. The best outcome they can expect is to create a security vacuum leading to a collapse of the targeted regime's will and then to gain in the competition for the spoils, thus moving to the strategic offensive without building combat superiority. Their enhanced capabilities to sow disorder, survive, and protract the struggle, however, present particularly difficult problems for counterinsurgents.

d. **Mass Base.** The mass base consists of the population indigenous to an area that insurgent forces are from and from whom support for an insurgent effort can be wittingly or unwittingly drawn. Organization of the larger indigenous population from which the insurgent forces are drawn is conducted primarily by the political cadre; often through, or with the assistance of, the underground and auxiliary. The primary value of the mass base to the insurgency is less a matter of formal organization than it is a marshalling of population groups to act in specific ways that support the insurgency. Elements of the mass base are divided into three distinct groups in relation to the insurgent cause or movement: pro-insurgent; anti-insurgent; and uncommitted, undecided, or ambivalent. The political cadres then conduct activities to influence or leverage these groups. These groups may or may not be knowledgeable of the insurgent nature of the operations or activities in which they are utilized.

5. Approaches

This section examines some of the key approaches or strategies used by insurgencies. The first four approaches often make winning the peace difficult for former insurgents. This may begin a cycle of collapsing or changing governments or, in the worst case, lead to poorly governed areas.

a. **Conspiratorial.** A conspiratorial approach involves a few leaders and a militant cadre or activist party seizing control of government structures or exploiting a revolutionary situation. Such insurgents remain secretive as long as possible. They emerge only when success can be achieved quickly. This approach usually involves creating a small, secretive, "vanguard" party or force. Insurgents who use this approach successfully may have to create or co-opt security forces and generate mass support to maintain power. Outside state complicity or support may be necessary to promulgate a successful *coup de main* at the onset of the conspiracy.

b. **Military-Focused.** Users of military-focused approaches aim to create revolutionary possibilities or seize power primarily by applying military force. Leaders of this form of insurgency assert that an insurrection itself can create the conditions needed to overthrow a government. They often believe that a small group of guerrillas operating in a rural environment can eventually gather enough support to achieve their aims. In contrast, some secessionist insurgencies have relied on major conventional forces to try to secure their independence. Military-focused insurgencies may have little or no political structure; they may spread their control through movement of combat forces rather than political subversion. Other military-focused insurgencies may attempt to politicize controlled areas. The insurgents will use varying levels of coercion, indoctrination, direct military control of civil institutions, and martial law to solidify their position. Political subversion in areas outside of those under insurgent military control remains infrequent.

c. **Terrorism-Focused.** Protracted terrorism is waged by small, independent cells that require little or no popular support. As societies have become more interconnected and insurgent networks more sophisticated, this approach has become more effective. When facing adequately run internal security forces, insurgencies typically assume a conspiratorial, underground cellular structure recruited along lines of close association—family, religious affiliation, political party, or social group. This approach uses terrorist tactics to accomplish the following: sow disorder, incite sectarian violence, weaken the government, intimidate the population, kill government and opposition leaders, fix and intimidate police and military forces, attempt to create government repression, and, in cases where foreign forces may occupy the country, force their withdrawal.

d. **Identity-Focused.** The identity-focused approach mobilizes support based on the common identity of religious affiliation, clan, tribe, or ethnic group. Some movements may be based on an appeal to a religious identity, either separately from or as part of other identities. This approach is common among contemporary insurgencies and is sometimes combined with the military-focused approach. The insurgent organization may not have the dual military/political hierarchy evident in a protracted popular war approach. Rather, communities often join the insurgent movement as a whole, bringing with them their existing social/military hierarchy. Additionally, insurgent leaders often try to mobilize the leadership of other clans and tribes to increase the movement's strength.

e. **Protracted Popular War.** Protracted conflicts favor insurgents, and no approach makes better use of strength and patience asymmetries than the protracted popular war. There are three strategic phases: defensive, stalemate, and counteroffensive. These phases are not necessarily linear and can overlap depending on the situation. The aim is to erode the strength and will of the HN. A key objective for a protracted insurgency is to preserve insurgent forces and attrite the enemy. Thus, an insurgency must constantly attack yet avoid being decisively engaged and potentially destroyed. That is why many insurgencies never progress past guerrilla warfare.

f. **Subversive.** Although subversive activities may take place in other strategies, particularly in the protracted popular war approach, a subversive approach either attempts to transform an illegal political entity into a legitimate political party or to use an existing legitimate political party. This party will attempt to subvert the government from within. The insurgency will use this political party in conjunction with violent and subversive activities to delegitimize the HN and its allies; however, there may be a reduction in overt violent actions. This approach is marked by sophisticated IO, aimed at specific TAs with appropriate messages. Overall, the insurgent purpose is not to integrate into the national government, but to undermine and even overthrow the government.

g. **Composite and Coalitions.** Contemporary insurgents may use different approaches at different times, applying approaches that take best advantage of circumstances. Insurgents may also apply a composite approach that includes tactics drawn from any or all of the other approaches. In addition, different insurgent forces using different approaches may form loose coalitions when it serves their interests. This is often the case with a local insurgency's aligning with an insurgency of regional or global scale. However, these same insurgents may fight among themselves, even while engaging counterinsurgents. Within a single operational area there may be multiple competing entities, each seeking to maximize its survivability and influence—and this situation may be duplicated several times across a joint operations area. This reality further complicates both the mosaic that counterinsurgents must understand and the operations necessary for victory.

6. Recruitment, Causes, Resources, and Information

Competent insurgents and counterinsurgents seek to establish control of the population and to rally cooperation and popular support for their cause. Counterinsurgents who do not gain the control and support of the population will normally fail. Counterinsurgents gain control and popular support through providing security and governance, and through overt and lawful mobilization. The insurgents, however, use recruitment and causes. When both insurgents and counterinsurgents vie for support of the population, both try to sustain their efforts while discouraging support for their adversaries.

a. **Recruitment.** A mixture of recruitment means may motivate an individual. There are normally six means to recruit: persuasion, coercion, reaction to abuses, foreign support, apolitical motivations, and deception.

(1) **Persuasion.** Political, social, security, religious, and economic benefits can often entice people to support one side or the other in times of turmoil. Ideology and religion are means of persuasion, especially for the elites and leadership. In this case, legitimacy derives from the consent of the governed, though leaders and followers can have very different motivations.

(2) **Coercion.** In the eyes of some, a government that cannot protect its people forfeits the right to rule. Legitimacy is accorded to the element that can provide security. Insurgents may use coercive force to provide security for people or to intimidate them and the legitimate security forces into active or passive support. Kidnapping or killing local leaders or their families is a common insurgent tactic to discourage working with the government, as is killing or intimidating local government officials such as schoolteachers or police. Insurgents sometimes use security, or the threat to remove it, to maintain control of cities and towns. Some members and supporters may simply be more afraid of the insurgents than they are of counterinsurgents.

(3) **Reaction to Abuses.** Though firmness by security forces is often necessary to establish a secure environment, a government that exceeds accepted local norms and abuses its people or is tyrannical generates resistance to its rule. People who have been maltreated or have had close friends or relatives killed by the government may strike back at their attackers. Security force abuses and the social upheaval caused by collateral damage from combat can be major escalating factors for insurgencies.

(4) **Foreign Support.** Foreign governments can provide the expertise, international legitimacy, and money needed to start or intensify a conflict. Also of note, NGOs, even those whose stated aims are impartial and humanitarian, may wittingly or unwittingly support insurgents. For example, funds raised overseas for professed charitable purposes can be redirected to insurgent groups, or funds and aid can permit both the HN and insurgents to concentrate scarce resources elsewhere.

(5) **Apolitical Motivations.** Deteriorating conditions may prompt otherwise law-abiding citizens to see an insurgency as the only viable means of support. In effect, the insurgency may enjoy a "poverty draft." Insurgencies often attract criminals and mercenaries seeking illicit rewards. Some individuals inspired by the romanticized image of the revolutionary or holy warrior and others who imagine themselves as fighters for a cause might also join. It is important to note that a political solution will probably not satisfy many of the people enough to end their participation.

(6) **Deception.** Deception is rarely a stand-alone means of recruitment, but rather a means of supporting other motivators. Persuasive and coercive approaches may contain deceptive elements. Insurgents may be deliberately deceptive of their goals, support levels, and strength. They may manufacture abuses by counterinsurgents and mask their own. Stated insurgent policies and platforms may be deceptive as well. Insurgents may target recruits who do not understand the larger implications of joining. In illiterate population's deception by insurgents is usually more successful.

(7) **Acquiescene.** In some cases, the local populace is unable or unwilling to resist those wielding de facto control of the local area.

b. **Causes.** A cause is a principle that the insurgents are willing to militantly defend or support.

(1) **Potential Causes.** Insurgents can capitalize on a number of potential causes. Any country ruled by a small group without broad, popular participation provides a political cause for insurgents. Exploited or repressed social groups—be they entire classes, ethnic or religious groups, or small elites—may support larger causes in reaction to their own narrower grievances. Economic inequities can nurture revolutionary unrest. So can real or perceived persecution. Insurgents may create artificial or deceptive grievances using propaganda and misinformation. Typically these will be extrapolations of previously held grievances and will play on stereotypes, xenophobia, racism, classism or other arguments conducive to shallow emotional appeal and jingoism.

(2) **Exploiting Causes.** Insurgents employ deep-seated, strategic causes as well as temporary, local ones, adding or deleting them as circumstances demand. Insurgents can gain more support by not limiting themselves to a single cause. By selecting an assortment of causes and tailoring them for various groups within the society, insurgents increase their base of sympathetic and complicit support. Insurgent leaders often use a bait-and-switch approach. They attract supporters by appealing to local grievances; then they lure followers into the broader movement. Without an attractive cause, an insurgency might not be able to sustain itself. But a carefully chosen cause is a formidable asset; it can provide a fledgling movement with a long-term, concrete base of support. The ideal cause attracts the most people while alienating the fewest and is one that is the most difficult for counterinsurgents to defeat or co-opt. It must be remembered that due to the austere nature of an insurgency, especially in its infancy, most of an insurgency's resources may be obtained through or from the local population.

c. **Resources.** Insurgents resort to such tactics as guerrilla warfare and terrorism for any number of reasons. These may include disadvantages in manpower or organization, relatively limited resources compared to the government, and, in some cases, a cultural predisposition to an indirect approach to conflict. To strengthen and sustain their effort once manpower is recruited, insurgents require weapons, supplies, and funding. Insurgents often use crime as a source of sustainment.

(1) **Weapons.** Acquiring weapons is a critical task to an insurgency movement. In some parts of the world, lack of access to weapons may forestall insurgencies. In some cases there is widespread availability of weapons in many areas, with especially large surpluses in the most violent regions of the world. Availability and sales of small arms can lend legitimacy to insurgent forces, especially if insurgents reach combat parity with HN security forces. Explosive hazards, such as mines and improvised explosive devices (IEDs), are likely to be common weapons in insurgencies. Insurgents can obtain weapons through legal or illegal purchases or from foreign sources. A common tactic is to capture them from government forces. Homemade weapons and parts may be used as well. As insurgents gain secure locations, this may progress to cottage industry.

(2) **Supplies.** Insurgencies require a wide variety of supplies to support their efforts. As with any major undertaking, supplies can come in many forms, from ammunition to foodstuffs. Circumstances will dictate how difficult it is for an insurgency to acquire supplies and which supplies are more challenging to acquire. For example, acquiring sufficient small arms ammunition may be more difficult than acquiring the weapons themselves. The current phase and level of operations also impacts insurgent supply needs and difficulties. For example, foodstuffs may also be difficult to acquire in sufficient quantities to support large-scale guerrilla warfare.

(3) **Funding.** Income is essential for insurgents to purchase weapons, pay recruits, provide patronage to subordinates and the population, and bribe corrupt officials. Money and supplies can be obtained through many sources. Foreign support has already been mentioned. Local supporters or international front organizations may provide donations. Sometimes legitimate businesses are established to furnish funding. In areas controlled by insurgents, confiscation or taxation may be utilized. Another common source of funding is criminal activity. Devoting exceptional amounts of time and effort to fund-raising can require an insurgent movement to shortchange ideological or armed action. Indeed, the method of raising funds is often at the heart of internal debates among insurgents. Funding greatly influences an insurgency's character and vulnerabilities; the insurgents' approach determines its requirements.

(4) **Insurgent Criminal Sustainment.** Insurgent funding requirements often drive insurgents into relationships with organized crime or into criminal activity themselves, usually due to the ease of reaping windfall profits compared to securing external support or taxing a mass base. Kidnapping, extortion, bank robbery, slavery, piracy, intellectual property piracy, smuggling, and drug trafficking are common lucrative criminal activities that insurgents use. However, the insurgents' descent into

crime risks alienating the population. On the other hand, some powerful criminal organizations take on aspects of or evolve into insurgencies.

For more details on insurgent criminal activity, see Appendix A, "Insurgency and Crime."

d. **Information Environment.** The information environment is a critical dimension for insurgents. Insurgents can have an advantage in shaping the information environment in that counterinsurgents must stick to the truth and make sure that words are backed up by deeds. On the other hand, insurgents can make exorbitant promises and point out government shortcomings, many caused or aggravated by the insurgency. As insurgents achieve more success and begin to control larger portions of the populace, many of these asymmetries diminish, which may provide new vulnerabilities that adaptive counterinsurgents can exploit. Counterinsurgents can overcome this insurgent advantage with a comprehensive IO plan.

(1) **Propaganda of the Deed.** These efforts, which include such acts as homicides, have little military value but are a key tool of insurgents as it creates fear and uncertainty within the IPI. These actions are executed to attract high-profile media coverage or local publicity and inflate perceptions of insurgent capabilities. Resulting stories often include insurgent fabrications designed to undermine the government's legitimacy. The actual danger to the population posed by insurgent operations, notably terrorist tactics, is often far lower than the perceived danger. The insurgents often only need to foster the perception in the general populace of counterinsurgent helplessness and the inevitability of insurgent victory.

(2) **Technology.** Globalization, interconnectedness, and information technology are key aspects for twenty-first century insurgencies. Insurgents virtually link with allied groups throughout the world. This is especially difficult to counter as insurgents do not recognize established international laws or the same moral restraints. Counterinsurgents must strive to build the capability to rapidly and credibly counter the insurgents' efforts and send their own message.

e. **Weapons of Mass Destruction (WMD).** If they become available, insurgents may attempt to integrate WMD into their arsenal for physical destruction and, more importantly, psychological and political impact. Insurgents will try to use WMD as part of terrorism and will attempt to integrate their use with their IO. The type of WMD and available means of delivery will constrain insurgent targets. Insurgents may attack conventional forces with WMD out of necessity or by choice. Insurgent concepts for employment of WMD may include conventional and clandestine delivery of chemical, biological, radiological, and nuclear (CBRN) weapons for the purposes of disruption, destabilization, coercion, or revenge. Broad objectives for acquisition and employment of CBRN weapons may include the capabilities to:

(1) Defeat, influence, intimidate, and deter an opponent.

(2) Disrupt HN, US, and multinational forces and operations.

(3) Forestall defeat or prolong the struggle.

(4) Punish opponents for countering insurgent efforts.

7. Vulnerabilities

Most insurgencies have aspects that can be strengths or vulnerabilities. Counterinsurgents should seek to create or exploit potential vulnerabilities.

a. **Secrecy.** An insurgency that starts from a position of weakness that intends to use violence to pursue its political aims must initially adopt a secret approach for its planning and activities. This practice can become counterproductive once an active insurgency begins. Excessive secrecy can limit insurgent freedom of action, reduce or distort information about insurgent goals and ideals, and restrict communication within the insurgency. Some insurgent groups try to avoid the effects of too much secrecy by using the political wing.

b. **Recruitment and Message.** In the early stages of an insurgency, a movement may be tempted to go to almost any extreme to attract followers. To mobilize their base of support, insurgent groups use a combination of propaganda and intimidation, and they may overreach in both. Effective counterinsurgents use IO to exploit inconsistencies in the insurgents' message as well as their excessive use of force or intimidation. The insurgent cause itself may also be an exploitable vulnerability.

c. **Base of Operations.** Insurgents can experience serious difficulties finding a viable base of operations. A base too far from the major centers of activity may be secure but risks being out of touch with the populace. It may also be vulnerable to isolation. A base too near centers of government activity risks opening the insurgency to observation and perhaps infiltration. Bases close to national borders can be attractive when they are beyond the reach of counterinsurgents yet safe enough to avoid suspicions of the neighboring authority or population. In the information environment, bases of operation may be easy for insurgents to establish, especially if these bases are physically distant from the actual conflict.

d. **External Support.** Insurgencies often rely heavily on freedom of movement across porous borders, and insurgencies often cannot sustain themselves without substantial external support. An important feature of many transnational terrorist groups is the international nature of their basing. Terrorists may train in one country and fight or conduct other types of operations in another country. The movements of fighters and their support are vulnerable to intervention or attack.

e. **Finances.** All insurgencies require funding to some extent. Criminal organizations are possible funding sources; however, these groups may be unreliable. Such cooperation may attract undue attention from HN authorities and create vulnerabilities to counterinsurgent intelligence operations. In addition, cooperating with criminals may not be ideologically consistent with the movement's core beliefs, although it often does not prevent such cooperation. Funding from outside donors may come with a political price that can affect the overall aim of an insurgency and weaken its popular appeal.

f. **Internal Divisions.** Counterinsurgents must remain alert for signs of divisions within an insurgent movement. A series of successes by counterinsurgents or errors by insurgent leaders can induce some insurgents to question their cause or challenge their leaders. In addition, relations within an insurgency do not remain harmonious when factions form to vie for power.

g. **Maintaining Momentum.** Controlling the pace and timing of operations is vital to the success of any insurgency. Insurgents seek to control when the conflict begins and have some measure of control over subsequent activity. However, many insurgencies fail to capitalize on their initial opportunities. Others allow counterinsurgents to dictate the pace of events and scope of activities. Initiative is paramount in terms of the psychological struggle for the population's support.

h. **Defectors and Informants.** Nothing is more demoralizing to insurgents than realizing that people inside their organization or trusted supporters among the public are deserting or providing information to government authorities. Counterinsurgents may attract deserters or informants by arousing fear of prosecution or by offering rewards. However, informers must be confident that the government can protect them and their families against retribution.

i. **Attrition of Human Resources.** Regardless of how an insurgency loses combatants, leaders, auxiliaries, and supporters, it cannot maintain its momentum if attrition outpaces recruiting. An insurgency that sustains heavy attrition of human resources will have to adjust its current activities or assume risk. Reduction of observable and verifiable insurgent effectiveness and actions will usually translate into loss of political support. However, attrition or reduction of insurgent activity does not eliminate the possibility of regeneration and reinvigoration if the core grievances of the insurgency are not addressed. Moreover, a strategy of attrition can provide additional motivation to insurgents when attrition is accompanied by substantial collateral casualties. Attrition is ultimately only valuable when exploited politically and informationally. An insurgency need not have many combatants to cause a tremendously disproportional amount of disruption in a nation.

j. **Leadership.** Leadership is essential to all organizations, including insurgencies. Disrupting leadership, however, is not always equal to direct attack on leaders. It is more important to first disrupt the leadership function than to kill or capture individual leaders. Actions that disrupt an organization's leadership—including attacking the will and capability of the leaders to communicate with their followers as well as exacerbating distrust between leaders and followers—may diminish an insurgency's effectiveness. An insurgency with centralized leadership is vulnerable to effective decapitation, be it physical or psychological. Even if the insurgency's leadership is distributed, commanders can find ways to disrupt communications and sow discord within the insurgent network. These actions are unlikely to produce decisive effects on their own, but when incorporated into a multifaceted plan designed to expose insurgents to broad, simultaneous pressure, they can produce critical effects such as denying sanctuary and inducing fog and friction.

8. Devolution and Decline

a. Many insurgencies can devolve into organizations merely focused on terrorism or criminality. Devolution may occur due to one or a combination of counterinsurgent pressure, lack of popular support, loss of leadership, organizational fragmentation, or atrophy during long periods of stalemate. Long periods of equilibrium or decline may cause an insurgency to reach a spoiling point where it fails, changes radically, or devolves. Insurgencies devolve with changes in the three prerequisites as vulnerable population grievances are mitigated, insurgent leadership is eliminated or discredited, or government control and legitimacy increases.

(1) **Terrorists.** Insurgencies that lose strength and momentum over time may regress to the point of only having terrorism as a means. When this occurs, the focus of the organization often becomes solely deed rather than the end; thus, the organization is essentially no longer an insurgency. Moreover, most insurgencies have a narrative that includes an alternative to the status quo, which terrorist groups may not have or be interested in.

(2) **Criminals.** Some insurgencies can compartmentalize criminal activity, keeping it ancillary to the main effort and preventing it from affecting the organization and its unity. However, some insurgencies can become focused on criminal activity that once only served as a funding mechanism. This can occur as the primary organization disintegrates and the remaining elements are cast adrift. Such disintegration is exploitable. Because the desire for a particular end state is the organizing force behind insurgency, when it devolves to crime, that desired end state no longer serves to organize insurgent efforts nor provides an avenue to political support. Hierarchical control may disappear and what remains may be incapable of or unwilling to conduct any coordinated action. Cellular leaders may become crime bosses and a security threat requiring military action may be transformed into a law-and-order concern. The HN can vilify the criminals by PSYOP. Successful counterinsurgents foment and address this devolution.

b. **Insurgent Decline.** Historically, when an insurgency starts to decline, the pace of its decline tends to decelerate over time (see Figure II-6). In many ways this deceleration is because a declining insurgency tends to grow smaller and can therefore better blend into the population. COIN efforts, lack of popular support, and failed insurgent efforts can contribute to the decline of the insurgency; however, these factors have diminishing impact on reducing the insurgency. The counterinsurgents must ameliorate the core grievances of the insurgency to bring the insurgents to their breaking point. If core grievances remain, the insurgency will remain at least latent and incipient.

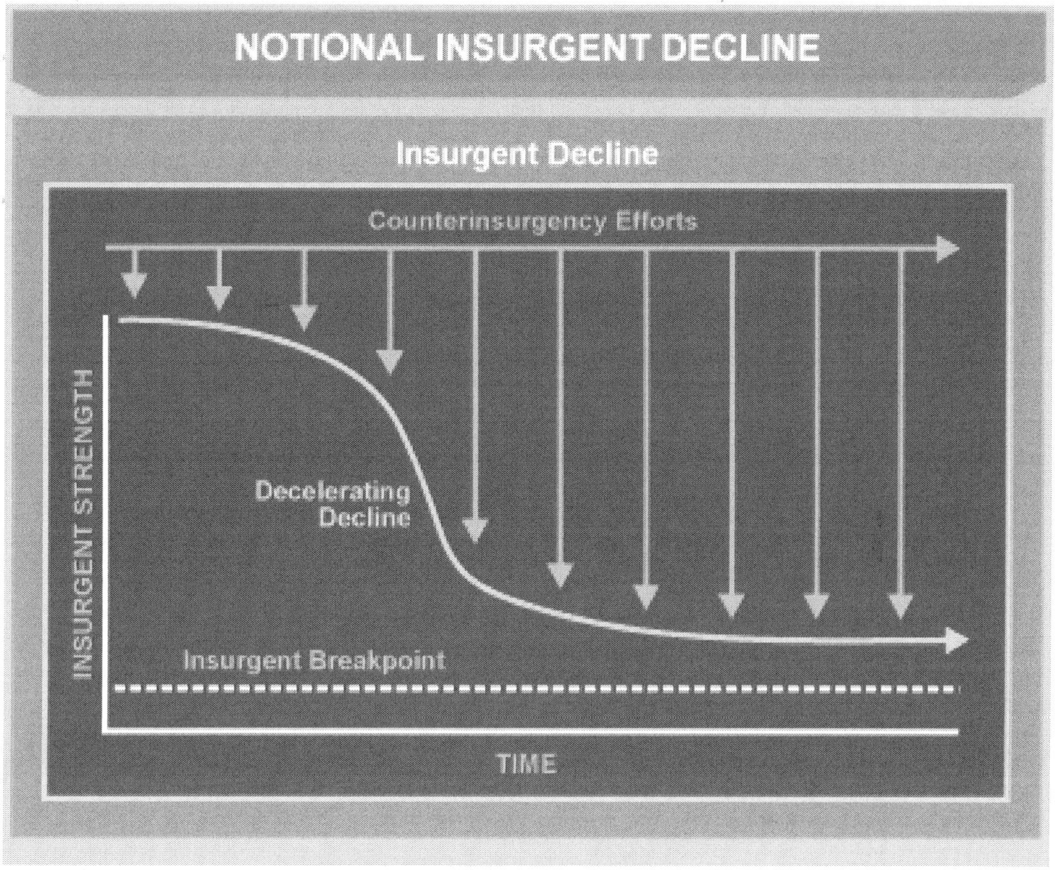

Figure II-6. Notional Insurgent Decline

Intentionally Blank

CHAPTER III
COUNTERINSURGENCY

"In small wars, caution must be exercised, and instead of striving to generate the maximum power with the forces available, the goal is to gain decisive results with the least application of force. In small wars, tolerance, sympathy, and kindness should be the keynote of our relationship with the mass of the population. Small wars involve a wide range of activities including diplomacy, contacts with the civil population and warfare of the most difficult kind."

Small Wars Manual
United States Marine Corps, 1940

1. Introduction

a. **Mindset.** Conducting successful COIN operations requires an adaptive and flexible mindset. First and foremost, **the population is the critical dimension of successful COIN.** Understanding the population is to successful COIN as understanding physical terrain is to successful conventional land operations. Understanding the population requires an intimate knowledge of the causes and ongoing grievances of the insurgency. A second aspect of the counterinsurgent mindset is being able to **think like an insurgent** to stay ahead of the actual insurgents' decisions and actions. Third, successful counterinsurgents must understand it is essential to **establish an enduring presence within the population** to provide continuous security and development efforts vital to assuring the population's sense of security and long-term outlook. Finally, counterinsurgents must understand that **the military instrument is only one part of a comprehensive approach for successful COIN,** although the security situation may require the joint force to execute tasks that other organizations are better suited to conduct.

b. **Popular Support.** The support of the people is the most vital factor in the long-term success of any COIN effort. Gaining and maintaining the population's support can be a formidable challenge. It is imperative that the population have trust and confidence in their government and its institutions. Counterinsurgents must make every effort to reinforce the legitimacy of the HN government in the eyes of the people (see Figure III-1).

c. **Cultural Understanding.** Forces or agencies supporting or conducting COIN must understand and be aware of the local and national culture. More specifically, counterinsurgents must understand the core grievances, drivers of conflict, and friction points between different groups. Only when counterinsurgents understand the relationships of these factors can their COIN efforts be effective. Cultural awareness facilitates accurate anticipation of the population's perception of COIN operations. These perceptions can determine the success or failure of COIN operations. By simultaneously addressing the core grievances and drivers of conflict and taking measures against the insurgencies themselves, COIN attacks the problem indirectly and directly, thus providing the best chance for success. Insurgency and COIN also tend to be

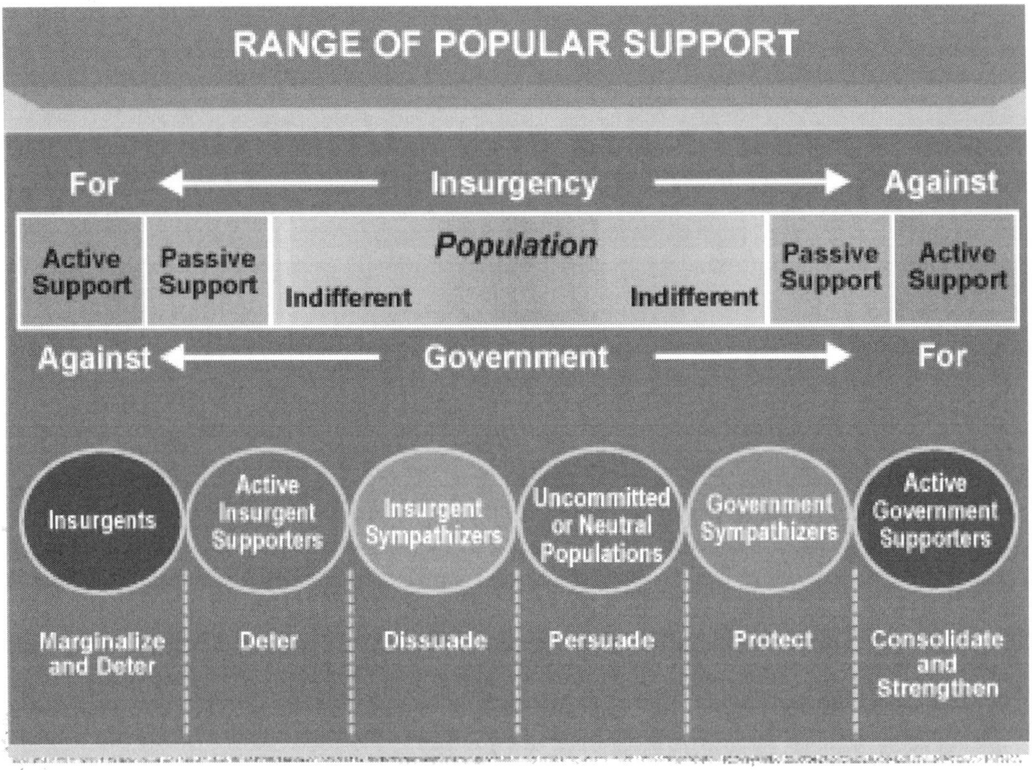

Figure III-1. Range of Popular Support

nested in larger, complex, and irregular conflicts; therefore, understanding and appreciating the strategic context and OE are essential to success.

d. **Military and Nonmilitary Contributions.** Although COIN may emphasize military actions in some phases, nonmilitary contributions are essential for COIN to be successful in the long term. COIN military efforts focused on destroying the military wing of insurgencies are counterguerrilla operations. In addition to its military contribution, the joint force may initially be responsible for and heavily involved in diplomatic, informational, and economic aspects until civil agencies construct, install, or build HN capability and capacity to provide governance. These military efforts will be coordinated and incorporated with other civil agencies at the first opportunity.

e. **Civilian agencies should lead COIN efforts.** Unified action that includes all HN, US, and multinational agencies is essential for COIN. This can be challenging due to the wide array of potential actors in COIN, regardless of who leads the overall effort. Whenever possible, civilian agencies should lead COIN efforts. Military participation in COIN is focused on establishing security, assistance in security sector reform, and supporting other stability operations as required. Although JFCs should be prepared to lead COIN efforts if required, the JFC must normally focus military operations as part of a comprehensive solution under civilian agency leadership.

For more information on core grievances, see Chapter II, "Insurgency." *For more information on IDAD and civil-military integration see Chapter IV,* "Unity of Effort in Counterinsurgency." *For more information on the population and drivers of conflict see Chapter VIII,* "Operational Environment."

2. Context of Counterinsurgency

The military contribution to countering insurgency, while vital, is not as important as political efforts for long-term success. Military efforts are especially important initially to gain security.

a. **Counterinsurgency Situations.** There are two fundamental ways in which joint forces may be involved with COIN: support to COIN or conduct of COIN.

(1) **Support to Counterinsurgency.** Joint forces normally conduct COIN to support a HN. Ideally, political and military COIN efforts gain credibility with the relevant population, reinforce the HN's legitimacy and capabilities, and reduce insurgent influence over the population. Joint forces' support to a HN's COIN is normally an aspect of FID and normally supports a HN's IDAD plan.

(2) **Counterinsurgency.** In some rare cases, joint forces may conduct COIN without a HN. The US can conduct COIN in a UGA should our national interest require. Second, joint forces may have to conduct COIN against general resistance when occupying foreign territory as part of a larger operation. This occurs when joint forces are required by US and international law to provide military governance to the local population when there is no HN governance.

For additional detail on the COIN environment, please see Chapter VIII, "Operational Environment," *and JP 2-01.3,* Joint Intelligence Preparation of the Operational Environment.

b. **Force Levels.** No force level guarantees victory for either side, insurgent or counterinsurgent. No predetermined, fixed ratio of friendly forces to enemy forces ensures success in COIN. The OE and insurgents' approaches vary too widely. Such calculations remain very dependent upon the assets available and the situation. A better force requirement gauge is counterinsurgent force density, which is the ratio of land security forces (including both indigenous and foreign contributions) and supporting elements (which must account for technological sophistication and applicability) to inhabitants. Force density will depend on the overall context, especially the size and density of the population, and can change over time. In some situations, the necessary force ratio may be unattainable. In these situations, the commander will have to determine if there are ways to leverage other advantages through innovative operational design and interdependent joint operations. If not, this may lead the commander to adopt limited objectives or plan for a prolonged, multiphased campaign as alternatives.

c. **Manpower and Support.** As in any operation, the size of the force needed to execute the concept of operations and attain the commander's vision depends on the situation and support. Although advanced technology can make counterinsurgents more effective, COIN is manpower- and resource-intensive because counterinsurgents (indigenous or foreign) must maintain widespread order and security—capable insurgents will occupy any vacuum. The ratio of US and coalition forces to HN forces will evolve. Moreover, counterinsurgents typically have to adopt different approaches to address each element of the insurgency. For example, some members of the organization or supporters among the population might be co-opted by economic or political reforms, while more fanatic insurgents will most likely have to be killed or captured.

d. **Preventing Insurgency.** When a potential insurgency is identified, HN leaders may request US or multinational assistance to prevent insurgency through the use of diplomatic, informational, military, and economic efforts. The chief of mission (COM) can request assistance, help mobilize international support through multilateral diplomacy, and engage NGOs to help address the causes of unrest before the crisis escalates and limits political alternatives to the use of force. The COM, along with the country team, must take an active role in helping the HN develop or revise an effective IDAD strategy to address core grievances which may result in an insurgency. It is vital for the US to recommend action and, if necessary, assist a HN as early as possible. The nature of the HN government and its potential willingness to make necessary reforms must be taken into account. Even the best support to COIN cannot overcome unresolved core grievances. Preventative strategy should develop mechanisms to integrate and co-opt talented and ambitious people from the disaffected segment of the population, as well as prevent those who cannot be integrated and co-opted from joining or supporting insurgency.

e. **Early Intervention.** An insurgency is generally more easily dealt with in its early stages, although it may be difficult to detect. Successfully identifying an insurgency requires accurate intelligence, recognition of an insurgency's potential or existence, a decision to act, and actual COIN efforts. The earlier that COIN begins the better. Normally efforts to deal with latent or incipient insurgencies are less extensive and less expensive in lives and materiel than dealing with an insurgency that is already using guerrilla warfare and has some popular support. This is true for COIN or for support to COIN. However, members of the counterinsurgent force must take great care to differentiate between the activities of a latent insurgency and the activities of a political group lawfully exercising their right to challenge the viewpoints of a sovereign HN government. If they ignore this, counterinsurgents may unwittingly drive these groups to support insurgents.

f. **Defining Success.** The meaning of success in COIN operations may be different from that in other operations. Long-term strategic success in COIN normally depends on the HN institutions effectively governing and the population's consenting to the government's rule. In generic terms, the strategic objective normally is isolation of the insurgents from the population, and this isolation is maintained by, with, and through the population—not forced upon the population. From the US perspective, policymakers determine the precise meaning of strategic success; however, the first military objective is to protect the population. Subsequent security and development efforts are interrelated and interdependent—a secure environment is necessary for successful development, and successful development is necessary to facilitate a secure environment.

(1) **Setting Conditions.** Achieving the conditions necessary for strategic success normally requires the HN government to eliminate the key grievances that are fueling the insurgency. However, reform often directly conflicts with long-seeded political and financial interest of families, tribes, clans, and even entire ethnic groups in the HN. Encouraging necessary reform requires careful diplomacy. As long as there are significant grievances, there may be a latent insurgency. COIN can include killing, capturing, or neutralizing extremists whose beliefs prevent them from ever reconciling with the government. Over time, counterinsurgents aim to enable a country or regime to provide the security and rule of law that allow establishment of social services and growth of economic activity. COIN involves the comprehensive and integrated application of the instruments of national power. Political and military leaders and planners should not underestimate its scale and complexity; moreover, they should recognize military operations alone cannot force success.

(2) **General Conditions of Success.** COIN is successful when three general conditions are met. First, the HN government effectively controls legitimate social, political, economic, and security institutions that meet the population's general expectations, including adequate mechanisms to address the grievances that may have fueled support of the insurgency. Second, the insurgency and its leaders are effectively co-opted, marginalized, or separated physically and psychologically from the population, with the voluntary assistance and consent of the population. Third, armed insurgent forces have been destroyed or demobilized and reintegrated into the political, economic, and social structures of the population.

3. Strategic and Operational Approaches

a. **Strategic Direction.** The national strategy, military strategy, and theater strategy play key roles in determining COIN strategic context.

(1) **National Strategy.** Interagency unity, or a whole-of-government approach, is required to create and support national strategy; moreover, this unity must extend from the national strategic to the tactical level for COIN to be effective.

(2) **Military Strategy.** Military strategy, derived from national strategy and policy and shaped by the appropriate ambassador's guidance and joint doctrine, provides a framework for conducting COIN operations.

(3) **Theater Strategy.** Ideally, campaign planning should be done in conjunction with the country team and those responsible for the production of the US ambassador's mission strategic plan so the campaign plan is coordinated and does not contradict the long-term USG plan for the country. The combatant commander's

(CCDR's) operation plan establishes the military strategic objectives, operational concepts, and resources that contribute to attainment of the national strategic end state. These plans must be flexible enough to take advantage of insurgents who lose momentum so counterinsurgents can regain the initiative. Theater strategy formulation normally involves key leaders and their staffs: Chairman of the Joint Chiefs of Staff (CJCS), GCCs, and, if established, joint task force (JTF) commanders. Every effort must be made to include all USG agencies and NGOs involved in COIN operations, as security requirements and organizational cultures allow. There are three possible general strategic settings for US involvement in COIN: assisting a functioning government as part of FID, as an adjunct to US major combat operations, or US operations in an UGA. These three settings could occur in any combination at the same time in the same theater.

b. **Strategic Approach.** The potential global and regional scope of contemporary insurgency has added to the complexity and therefore the challenge of conducting COIN. This challenge requires a global or regional COIN strategic approach for success. **While each situation will be unique, there are some general guidelines for strategies to deal with a global or regional insurgency.**

c. **Disaggregation.** Some insurgencies aspire to regional and even global ends; however, these groups are not one monolithic entity—they consist of smaller groups. These smaller groups can be subordinate parts of one insurgency or willing partners who share similar goals. The progress behind the association can range from a temporary coalition to achieve a shared objective to actually beginning the process of becoming one group of subordinate parts. The first step in disaggregation is cognitive: identify fissures in the supposed monolith. To do this counterinsurgents must have a deep understanding of the OE and, more specifically, an understanding of the adversaries. Subsequently, a strategy of disaggregation includes the following activities: containment, isolation, disruption, and resolution of core grievances, and neutralization in detail. Containment, isolation, and disruption should be implemented as soon as possible and simultaneously. While the previous three aspects require political consensus, the choice of what insurgency to neutralize in detail is a shared strategic policy decision amongst all nations involved.

(1) **Containment.** Diplomatic, informational, intelligence, economic, financial, law enforcement, and military efforts should focus on containing the spread of the insurgency. Diplomatic efforts should attempt to gain international support to politically contain the insurgency, and subsequently bring other instruments in line with political containment efforts. Public affairs (PA) and IO capabilities play a key role in combating the insurgent's narrative. Successful containment depends heavily on FID and CT efforts. These efforts should focus on denying the insurgency the ability to link with and amalgamate or exploit new local actors or local insurgencies.

(2) **Isolation.** Efforts to isolate the insurgency must be made concurrently with efforts to contain the insurgency. Superficially these two efforts may seem to be the same; however, efforts to *contain* an insurgency prevent its spread, where efforts to *isolate* focus on separating the insurgency physically and psychologically from other

parts of the insurgency and the population. In addition to physical and psychological isolation, efforts to isolate the insurgency economically are necessary, but must be narrowly focused on the activities of insurgents. These efforts seek to isolate the insurgency as much as possible, as complete isolation of the insurgency is not realistic. If implemented too broadly, efforts to isolate may have a negative effect on the population and strengthen the insurgency.

(a) **Physical Isolation.** One of the initial steps of isolation is to physically isolate insurgents. This means that all efforts strive to physically isolate the insurgency in all physical domains—air, land, maritime, and space—as well as the information environment (which includes cyberspace). Ultimately this means controlling the physical domains as well as controlling borders; however, completely controlling the physical domains or border at all times is not realistic. It also means impeding the insurgents' physical means of transmitting information.

(b) **Psychological Isolation.** Psychologically isolating insurgencies is arguably the most important part of isolating an insurgency; however, it is difficult, resource intensive, and time consuming. This isolation has two aspects: first to break the psychological links between the insurgent and the population and, second, to degrade the psychological links between the insurgent and the remainder of the insurgent organization or support base. Psychological isolation requires success in the overall information environment, which includes the physical dimension, informational dimension, and the cognitive dimension.

(c) **Economic Isolation.** Successfully isolating the insurgents from funding can severely undermine their operations. Economic isolation requires both physical and informational interruption of financial, business, and criminal enterprises. Attempting to economically isolate insurgents from the population must be narrowly focused on the insurgents and minimize the effect on the population, by offering viable replacement sources of employment and revenue. This needs to be communicated to the affected population. Applying economic isolation of insurgents must be planned and implemented in coordination with civilian agency specialists who are skilled in the aspects of the local economy and culture and individuals representing significant knowledge of the local business and financial sectors. Improperly implementing economic isolation will have the opposite of the intended effect and may further strengthen an insurgency.

(3) **Disruption.** Disruption focuses on degrading the overall coherence and operations of an insurgency. Disruption can come in many forms—diplomatic, informational, military, economic, financial, and legal. An insurgency that is left unhindered will continue to grow and strengthen, so disruption is essential to degrade an insurgency and to keep it off balance. Disruption efforts are secondary to the main effort of neutralizing in detail.

(4) **Addressing Core Grievances.** To defeat insurgency, counterinsurgents must address the core grievances fuelling the insurgency. The joint force should

contribute to the comprehensive approach to address the core grievances of the conflict, focusing on the causes which have generated the insurgency, and minimize its effects. Effectively addressing core grievances will facilitate isolating the insurgent from the population. It is vital to note that addressing core grievances is not the same as solving all of the core grievances.

(5) **Neutralizing in Detail.** Defeating a global or regional insurgency is an immense task. The previous aspects of a strategy of disaggregation all occur simultaneously to deal with these insurgencies. However, countering these insurgencies across a wide geographic area may preclude being able to bring enough assets to bear simultaneously. Thus, political and military decision makers must choose where to focus or, in other words, where to counter the insurgency. When more assets are available or the first area is secured, a subsequent area on which to focus can be identified. Thus, where to neutralize the insurgency in detail is fundamentally an issue of how to allocate scarce means and where to accept risk. The COIN efforts in an area chosen to defeat the insurgency in detail resemble "classic" COIN efforts of the past.

d. **Operational Approaches.** There are a range of possible operational approaches to COIN (see Figure III-2). Careful consideration and coordination determines what initial approach is appropriate given the starting conditions; however, the earlier efforts can begin, the more likely an indirect approach is appropriate. Commanders adjust their approach as circumstances change, especially the security situation. COIN should strive to move to the right on the scale—to move from direct to balanced and balanced to indirect. The direct approach focuses on protecting US and HN interests while attacking the insurgents. The indirect approach focuses on the actions to establish conditions (a stable and more secure environment) for others to achieve success with the help of the United States.

(1) **Direct.** A direct approach may be required where a HN government is losing ground in its struggle with an insurgency or there is no viable HN government. The first task in this situation is to establish security and control in as wide an area and extent as possible. Once security and control are established, the counterinsurgent approach should strive to become more balanced. If COIN efforts start without a viable HN governing body, the JFC will most likely have to use a direct approach until security and control allow transitioning authority to the HN or other specified organization. The direct approach may also be appropriate when facing an insurgency that is not concerned with the support of the population and the population supports the HN government. In this situation, the COM leads all US efforts in support of the IDAD.

(2) **Balanced.** This approach is a more even blend of US diplomatic, development and military efforts. The balanced approach is led by the COM and supported by the JFC, but all efforts support the HN's IDAD. While the overall level of effort is balanced, military efforts are secondary and subordinate to diplomacy and development activities when using this approach. Removing the fuel that keeps the insurgency going—the core grievances and narrative—is more effective in the long-term than attacking or destroying the military wing of the insurgency.

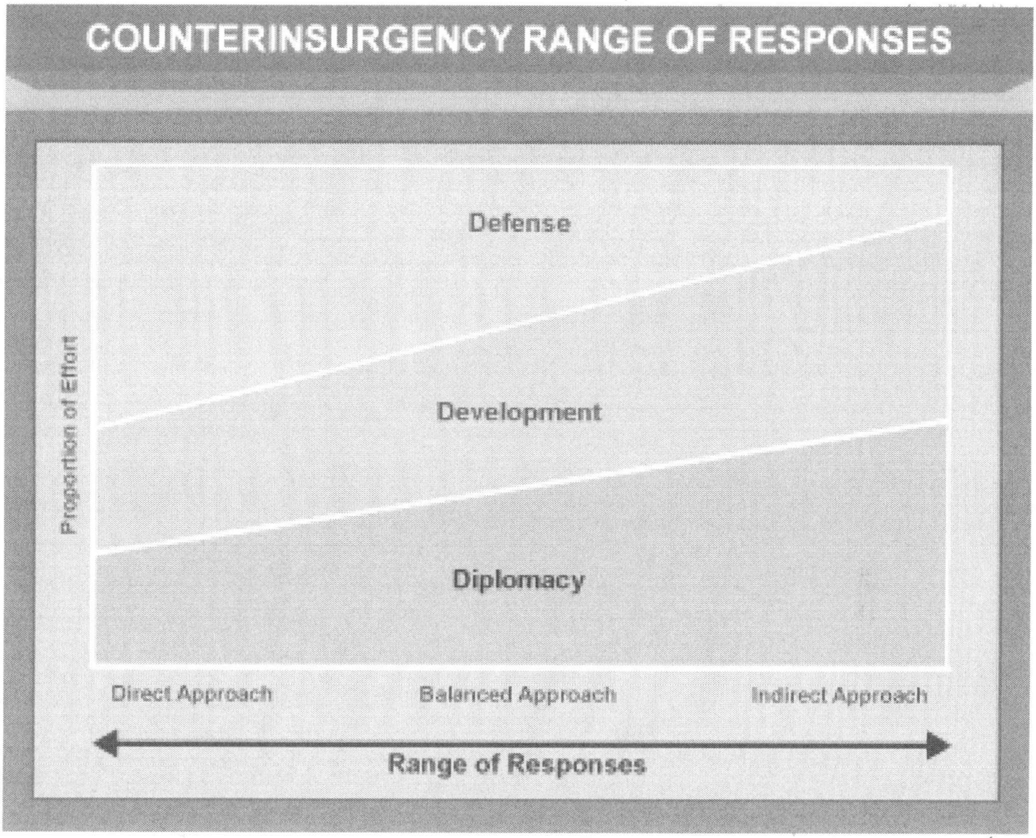

Figure III-2. Counterinsurgency Range of Responses

(3) **Indirect.** An indirect approach utilizes more development and political efforts than military efforts to address the insurgency. The ability to use the indirect approach is based on the security situation. If the insurgency is at least in military stalemate, counterinsurgents can avoid direct military confrontation and instead focus on addressing the core grievances and combating the insurgency's narrative. The indirect approach also requires that the HN be viable. If the HN is viable, US and other coalition partners can support the HN's COIN efforts. A US indirect approach will assist the HN as part of a larger FID effort. This FID mission is led by the COM, supported by the JFC, and planned to support the HN's IDAD plan. SFA and other advisory efforts are normally an essential part of the indirect approach. Finally, the indirect approach is best suited to early intervention and must be a holistic effort.

e. **Progression.** Figure III-3 is an example of how a COIN operation might move from a direct approach to a balanced approach and is currently using an indirect approach, yet the COIN operation has not reached its end state and is consequently

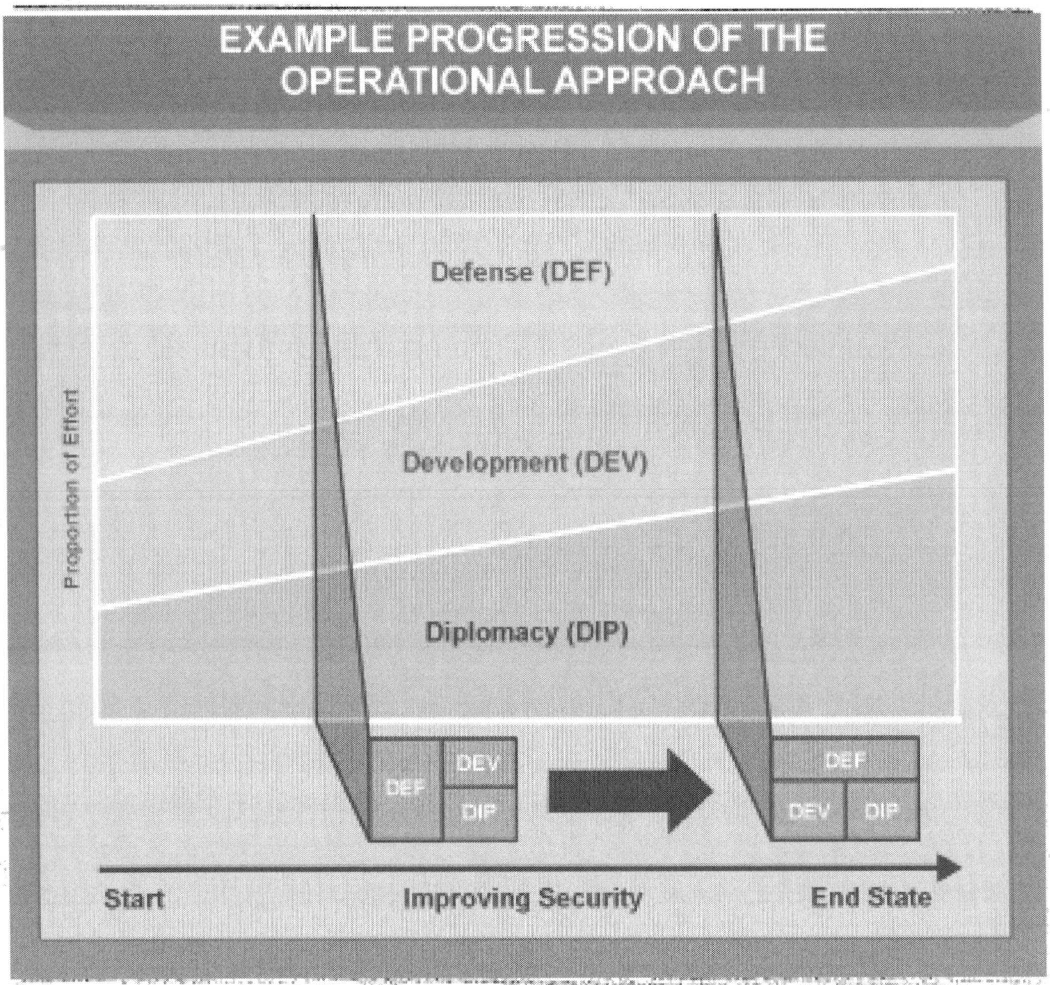

Figure III-3. Example Progression of the Operational Approach

ongoing. This reinforces that US long-term efforts should aim to be more developmental and political than military until the presence of US forces is no longer required.

4. Principles of Counterinsurgency

The principles of COIN are derived from the historical record and recent experience. They are detailed below to provide guideposts for the joint force in COIN. These principles do not replace the principles of joint operations, but rather provide focus on how to successfully conduct COIN.

a. **Counterinsurgents Must Understand the Operational Environment.** This understanding includes the political, military, economic, social, information, infrastructure, and other aspects of the OE. Counterinsurgents must pay special attention to society, culture, and insurgent advantages within the OE. Counterinsurgents also must understand the broader context within which they are operating. A mission to assist a functioning government offers different options from situations where no such viable entity exists or where a regime has been changed by conflict. The joint force may support a HN that has been heavy-handed or excessive in the past; thus, the HN's security apparatus may have inadvertently assisted the insurgency in its incipient stages. Counterinsurgents must also be prepared to identify their opponents and their opponents' approach to insurgency. Effective counterinsurgents understand the insurgents' approach and act accordingly.

(1) **Cultural Knowledge.** Cultural knowledge is essential to successful COIN. American ideas of what is "normal" or "rational" are not universal. To the contrary, members of other societies often have different notions of rationality, appropriate behavior, level of religious devotion, and norms concerning gender. Thus, what may appear abnormal or strange to an external observer may appear as self-evidently normal to a group member. For this reason, US counterinsurgents—especially commanders, planners, and small-unit leaders—should strive to avoid imposing their ideal of normalcy on a foreign cultural problem. Joint forces should receive appropriate cultural awareness training before joining specific COIN operations.

(2) **Leaders.** Accurately determining whether a leader can be dissuaded from insurgency and won over to counterinsurgency is crucial. However, counterinsurgent attempts to win over traditional leaders can backfire if those leaders choose to oppose the COIN. Leaders who refuse to accept counterinsurgent overtures can strengthen their standing as they gain power and influence among insurgents, especially if this refusal is well exploited through subsequent propaganda. Insurgent authority figures need to be neutralized; preferably through co-option or by bringing discredit to the leader or his position. While eliminating the insurgent leader may greatly harm or defeat the insurgency, it may have unwanted results such as creating a martyr for the insurgents or causing popular backlash.

(3) **Insurgent Advantages.** In most COIN operations in which joint forces participate, insurgents hold a distinct advantage in their level of local knowledge. They speak the language, move easily within the society, and are more likely to understand the population's interests. Thus, effective COIN operations require a greater emphasis on certain skills, such as language and cultural awareness, than do operations in traditional warfare. Successful COIN operations require joint forces at every echelon to possess a clear appreciation of the essential nature and nuances of the conflict, an understanding of the motivation, strengths, and weaknesses of the insurgents, and knowledge of the roles of other actors in the area.

b. **Legitimacy Is The Main Objective. The primary objective of any COIN operation is to foster development of effective governance by a legitimate government.** Counterinsurgents achieve this objective by undertaking appropriate actions and striving for a balanced application of both military and nonmilitary means as dictated by the situation. All governments rule through a combination of consent and coercion. Governments described as "legitimate" rule primarily with the consent of the governed; those described as "illegitimate" tend to rely mainly or entirely on coercion.

Citizens of the latter obey the state for fear of the consequences of doing otherwise, rather than because they voluntarily accept its rule. A government that derives its powers from the governed tends to be accepted by its citizens as legitimate. It still uses coercion—for example, against criminals—but most of its citizens voluntarily accept its governance.

(1) **Legitimacy and Governances.** Legitimacy makes it easier for a state to carry out its key functions. These functions include the authority to regulate social relationships, extract resources, and take actions in the public's name. Legitimate governments can develop these capabilities more easily, which usually allows them to competently manage, coordinate, and sustain collective security as well as political, economic, and social development. Illegitimate states (sometimes called "police states") typically regulate society by applying overwhelming coercion. Legitimate governance is inherently more stable. The societal support it engenders allows it to adequately manage the internal problems, change, and conflict.

(2) **Indicators of Legitimacy.** There are six possible indicators of legitimacy that can be used to analyze threats to stability. First, the ability to provide security for the populace, including protection from internal and external threats, is a key indicator of legitimacy. Second, the selection of leaders at a frequency and in a manner considered just and fair by a substantial majority of the populace strengthens the legitimacy of the HN. Other indicators of legitimacy include: a high level of popular participation in or support for political processes; a culturally acceptable level of corruption; a culturally acceptable level and rate of political, economic, and social development; the existence and acceptance of laws; and a high level of regime acceptance by major social institutions.

(3) **Cultural Lens.** Governments that have many of the indicators of legitimacy probably have the support of a sufficient portion of the population. Different cultures, however, may see acceptable levels of development, corruption, and participation differently. For some societies providing security and some basic services may be enough for citizens to see a government as legitimate. Additionally, the importance of security in situations where violence has escalated cannot be overemphasized. In such cases, establishing security can win the people's confidence, gain credibility, and enable the government to develop legitimacy in other areas.

(4) **Population Perception of Credibility and Legitimacy.** In working to understand the problem, joint forces must determine what the HN population defines as effective, credible, and legitimate governance. This understanding continues to evolve as information is developed. Joint forces must continually evaluate what legitimacy means to the HN population. The population's expectations will influence all ensuing operations. Additionally, planners may also consider perceptions of credibility and legitimacy held by outside supporters of both the HN government and the insurgents. Joint force efforts may have to strive to win the hearts and minds of the local population to change their views on legitimacy if the local population considers genocide or the exclusion of some ethnic groups as legitimate. The often-used phrase "winning hearts and minds" should not be taken to mean that the goal is for the population to like

counterinsurgent forces, but rather is a more subtle and indirect influence aimed at establishing the legitimacy and effectiveness of the government in the eyes of the people through the provision of basic services in a secure environment and having a voice and stake in the system. Ultimately people must be convinced that supporting the COIN effort is in their best interest. Calculated self-interest, not emotion, is what counts. Over time, successful trusted networks grow in the populace. They displace enemy networks, which forces enemies into the open, letting military forces seize the initiative and destroy the insurgents.

(5) **Rule of Law.** The presence of the rule of law is a major factor in assuring voluntary acceptance of a government's authority, and therefore its legitimacy. A government's respect for a preexisting and impersonal legal system as well as the population's perception of the rule of law, can provide the key to gaining widespread, enduring societal support. Such government respect for rules is the essence of the rule of law. As such, it is a powerful potential tool for counterinsurgents.

c. **Unity of Effort is Essential.** Unity of effort must be present at every echelon of a COIN operation. Otherwise, well-intentioned but uncoordinated actions can cancel each other or provide vulnerabilities for insurgents to exploit. Ideally, a single counterinsurgent leader has authority over all government agencies involved in COIN. Usually, JFCs work to achieve unified action through liaison with the leaders of a wide variety of government, nongovernmental, and international agencies, including the HN and the US. The ambassador, when present, is the central figure to be supported as the representative of the President. The ambassador and country team, along with senior HN representatives, are key players in higher level planning; similar connections are needed throughout the chain of command.

d. **Political Factors are Primary.** At the beginning of a COIN operation, military actions may appear predominant as security forces conduct operations to secure the populace and kill or capture insurgents. However, political objectives must guide the military's approach. Commanders must consider how operations contribute to strengthening the HN government's legitimacy and achieving US goals—the latter is especially important if there is no HN. This means that political and diplomatic leaders must actively participate throughout the conduct (planning, preparation, execution, and assessment) of COIN. The political and military aspects of insurgencies are so bound together as to be inseparable. Military actions executed without properly assessing their diplomatic and political effects at best result in reduced effectiveness and at worst are counterproductive. Resolving most insurgencies requires a political solution. It is imperative that counterinsurgent actions do not hinder achieving that solution. Moreover, most solutions involve some sort of political compromise and are rarely a "winner take all" situation.

e. **Intelligence Drives Operations.** Effective COIN is shaped by timely, specific, and reliable intelligence, gathered and analyzed at all levels and disseminated throughout the force. A cycle develops where operations produce intelligence that drives subsequent operations. Reporting by units, members of the country team, and information derived from interactions with civilian agencies is often of equal or greater importance than reporting by specialized intelligence assets. This reporting may be both solicited and unsolicited information from the relevant population or defectors. In all cases corroboration of the information retains significant importance to prevent acting upon false, misleading, or circular reporting. These factors, along with the need to generate a favorable operational tempo, drive the requirement to produce and disseminate intelligence at the lowest practical level.

f. **Insurgents Must be Isolated from Their Cause and Support.** While it may be required to kill or capture insurgents, it is more effective in the long run to separate an insurgency from the population and its resources, thus letting it die. Confrontational military action, in exclusion is counterproductive in most cases; it risks generating popular resentment, creating martyrs that motivate new recruits, and producing cycles of revenge.

(1) **Expropriating the Insurgent Cause.** Skillful counterinsurgents can deal a significant blow to an insurgency by expropriating its cause. Insurgents often exploit multiple causes, however, making counterinsurgents' challenges more difficult. In the end, any successful COIN operation must address the legitimate grievances insurgents exploit to generate popular support. These may be different in each local area, in which case a complex set of solutions will be needed. A mix of usurpation and direct refutation may also be used. Counterinsurgents may champion portions of the insurgents' cause while directly refuting others. This approach may be especially useful when stated insurgent goals are clearly disproportionally beneficial to one group. Counterinsurgents may be able to also "capture" an insurgency's cause and exploit it. For example, an insurgent ideology based on an extremist interpretation of a holy text can be countered by appealing to a moderate interpretation of the same text. When a credible religious or other respected leader passes this kind of message, the counteraction is even more effective.

(2) **Cutting Logistics.** Counterinsurgents must cut off the flow of arms and ammunition into the area and eliminate their sources. An effective weapon in denying logistics to an insurgency is populace and resource control. These two controls are distinct, yet linked, normally a responsibility of indigenous civil governments. They are defined and enforced during times of civil or military emergency.

(a) Populace control provides security for the populace, mobilizes human resources, denies personnel to the enemy, and detects and reduces the effectiveness of enemy agents. Populace control measures include curfews, movement restrictions, travel permits, registration cards, and relocation of the population.

(b) Resource control regulates the movement or consumption of materiel resources, mobilizes materiel resources, and denies materiel to the enemy. Resources control measures include licensing, regulations or guidelines, checkpoints (for example, roadblocks), ration controls, amnesty programs, and inspection of facilities.

(3) **Reducing Finances.** Counterinsurgents can exploit insurgent financial weaknesses. Controls and regulations that limit the movement and exchange of materiel and funds may compound insurgent financial vulnerabilities. These counters are especially effective when an insurgency receives funding from outside the state. Additionally, effective law enforcement can be detrimental to an insurgency that uses criminal means for funding. Department of the Treasury designations and other diplomatic tools outside the scope of DOD are key to countering threat finance. The JFC must work closely with the COM to identify and target threat finance sources, and may even consider the creation of interagency and threat finance cell to enhance the collection, analysis, and dissemination of intelligence to support and strengthen US, coalition, and HN efforts to disrupt and eliminate key insurgent financial network nodes.

(4) **Momentum. As the HN government increases its legitimacy, the populace begins to assist it more actively.** Eventually, the people marginalize and stigmatize insurgents to the point that the insurgency's claim to legitimacy is destroyed. However, victory is gained not when this isolation is achieved, but when legitimate government functions are maintained by and with the people's active support and when insurgent forces lose legitimacy.

g. **Security Under the Rule of Law is Essential.** To establish legitimacy, commanders transition security activities from military operations to law enforcement as quickly as feasible. When insurgents are seen as criminals, they often lose public support. Using a legal system established in line with local culture and practices to deal with such criminals enhances the HN government's legitimacy. Joint forces help establish HN institutions that sustain that legal regime, including police forces, court systems, and penal facilities. In support of this process, a reduced level of violence must be established to permit police forces to maintain order. It is a paradox of COIN that the increased use of force required to maintain order decreases the perceived legitimacy of counterinsurgent actions. The key to establishing legitimate and effective HN security institutions is to limit the use of force to the minimum necessary, while taking care to ensure that legitimacy is established when the use of force is required.

(1) **Illegitimate Actions.** Illegitimate actions are those involving the use of power without authority—whether committed by government officials, security forces, or counterinsurgents. Such actions include unjustified or excessive use of force, unlawful detention, torture, and punishment without trial. Illegitimate actions to build a legitimate government are self-defeating, even against insurgents who conceal themselves amid civilians and flout the law. Moreover, US forces participation in COIN operations must follow US laws, applicable HN and international laws, as well as certain international treaties or pacts. Any abuses or legal violations committed by US forces quickly become known throughout the local populace and eventually around the world. Illegitimate actions undermine both long- and short-term COIN efforts.

(2) **Evidence Gathering.** Every action by insurgents and counterinsurgents leaves a "forensic trace" that may be required sometime later in a court of law. Joint forces working with or in support of appropriate police agencies should support to the

maximum extent possible actions to preserve a chain of evidence. Accurate documentation can be an important means to counter insurgent propaganda. Although evidence gathering resembles intelligence efforts, appropriate evidentiary standards are more stringent.

h. **Counterinsurgents Should Prepare for a Long-Term Commitment.** Insurgencies are protracted by nature, and history demonstrates that they often last for years or even decades. Thus, COIN normally demands considerable expenditures of time and resources, especially if they must be conducted simultaneously with conventional operations in a protracted war combining traditional and IW. The relevant population may prefer the HN government to the insurgents; however, people do not actively support a government unless they are convinced that the counterinsurgents have the means, ability, stamina, and will to win—credibility. The insurgents' primary battle is against the HN government, not the US; however, US support can be crucial to building public faith in that government's viability. The population must have confidence in the staying power of both the counterinsurgents and the HN government. Insurgents and relevant population often believe that a few casualties or a few years will cause the US to abandon a COIN effort. Constant reaffirmations of commitment, backed by deeds, can overcome that perception and bolster US credibility. Even the strongest US commitment, however, will not succeed if the population does not perceive the HN government as having similar credibility. US forces must help create crucial HN capabilities and capacities to sustain the HN's credibility and legitimacy. It is also important to note that US support to a HN's COIN efforts can decrease or even cease while the HN's COIN efforts are still fighting an insurgency. This normally is because the HN can successfully deal with the insurgency.

(1) **Preparation.** Preparing for a protracted COIN effort requires establishing headquarters and support structures designed for long-term operations. Planning and commitments should be based on sustainable operating tempo and personnel tempo limits for the various components of the force. Even in situations where the US goal is reducing its military force levels as quickly as possible, some support for HN institutions usually remains for a long time. US preparatory actions for long-term support must come at the public request of the HN and be focused on supporting the IDAD strategy.

(2) **US Public Support.** At the national strategic level, gaining and maintaining US public support for a protracted deployment is critical. Demonstrating incremental success is essential to maintaining support.

i. **Manage Information and Expectations.** Information and expectations are related; capable counterinsurgents manage both. To limit discontent and build support, the HN government and any counterinsurgents assisting it create and maintain a realistic set of expectations among the populace, friendly military forces, and the international community. IO (particularly PSYOP and the related activities of PA and CMO) are key tools to accomplish this. Achieving steady progress toward a set of reasonable expectations can increase the populace's tolerance for the inevitable inconveniences entailed by ongoing COIN. Where a large US force is present to help establish a legitimate government, due care must be taken to avoid the negative repercussions that are often involved when a country is legally occupied by US or allied forces.

(1) **Expectations.** US agencies trying to build enthusiasm for their efforts should avoid making unrealistic promises. In some cultures, failure to deliver promised results is automatically interpreted as deliberate deception, rather than good intentions gone awry. Effective counterinsurgents understand local norms; they use locally tailored approaches to control expectations. Managing expectations also involves demonstrating economic and political progress to show the populace how life is improving. Expectation management is a process that enforces reasonable expectations, and is intended to prevent unrealistic expectations. Increasing the number of people who feel they have a stake in the success of the state and its government is a key to successful COIN. In the end, victory comes, in large measure, by convincing the populace that their life will be better under the HN government than under an insurgent regime. However, sometimes societies are most prone to unrest not when conditions are the worst, but when the situation begins to improve and people's expectations rise. For example, the indigenous population may have unrealistic expectations of the ability of the United States to improve their lives. The resulting discontent can fuel unrest and insurgency. At such times, the influences of globalization and the international media may create a sense of relative deprivation, contributing to increased discontent.

(2) **Actions.** Both counterinsurgents and the HN government must ensure that their deeds match their words. Any action also has a consequent information reaction. Counterinsurgents and the HN government must carefully consider that impact on the many audiences involved in the conflict and on the sidelines and work actively to shape responses that further their ends. In particular, messages to different audiences must be consistent and crafted with their views in mind. In the global information environment, people in the area can access the Internet and satellite television to determine the messages counterinsurgents are sending to the international community and the US public. Any perceived inconsistency reduces credibility and undermines COIN efforts.

j. **Use the Appropriate Level of Force.** Even precise and tailored force must be executed legitimately and with consideration for consequent effects. Overwhelming effort may prove necessary to destroy an opponent, especially extremist insurgent combatants. However, counterinsurgents should carefully calculate the type and amount of force and who applies it, regardless of the means of applying force. An operation that kills five insurgents is counterproductive if collateral damage leads to the recruitment of fifty more insurgents. Thus, careful targeting is required to weigh the potential effects and perceptions of the relevant population, the US population, the multinational partner populations, and international opinion.

(1) **Security.** Counterinsurgents undertake offensive and defensive operations to regain the initiative and create a secure environment. However, killing insurgents—while often necessary, especially with respect to extremists—by itself cannot defeat an insurgency. Gaining and retaining the initiative requires counterinsurgents to address the population's core grievances through stability operations as well as providing security

from insurgent activities. To achieve this goal, counterinsurgents must initially establish a trusted presence within the population. As security improves, joint resources contribute to supporting government reforms and reconstruction projects.

(2) **Restraint.** Normally, counterinsurgents can use rules of engagement (ROE) to minimize potential loss of life. ROE should address lesser means of force when such use is likely to create the desired effects and joint forces can do so without endangering themselves, others, or mission accomplishment. Escalation of force procedures do not limit the right to use deadly force when such force is necessary to defend against a hostile act or demonstrated hostile intent. Commanders ensure that their forces are properly trained in such procedures and, more importantly, in methods of shaping situations so that small unit leaders have to make fewer split-second, life-or-death decisions.

(3) **Law Enforcement Use of Force.** The perception of legitimacy with respect to the use of force is also important. If the HN police have a reasonable reputation for competence and impartiality, it is better for them to execute urban raids, as the population is likely to view that application of force as more legitimate than military action. This is true even if the police are not as well armed or as capable as military units. However, local circumstances affect this decision. If the police are seen as part of an ethnic or sectarian group oppressing the general population, their use may be counterproductive. Effective counterinsurgents thus understand the character of the local police and popular perceptions of both police and military units. This understanding helps ensure that the application of force is appropriate and reinforces the rule of law.

k. **Learn and Adapt.** An effective counterinsurgent force is a learning organization. Insurgents constantly shift between military and political phases and tactics. In addition, networked insurgents constantly exchange information about their enemy's vulnerabilities—even with insurgents in distant theaters. However, skillful counterinsurgents can adapt at least as fast as insurgents. Every unit needs to be able to make observations, draw and apply lessons, and assess results. Commanders must develop an effective system to circulate best practices throughout their command. Commanders might also need to seek policies that authorize or resource necessary changes. Insurgents shift where they operate to look for weak links, so widespread competence is required throughout the counterinsurgent force.

l. **Empower the Lowest Levels.** Successful COIN is normally conducted with decentralized execution based upon centralized vision and orders that include clear and concise rules for the use of force and ROE.

(1) **Initiative.** Successful decentralized execution results from exercise, by subordinate leaders at all echelons, of disciplined initiative within the commander's intent to accomplish missions. It requires an environment of trust and mutual understanding and is the preferred method for commanding and controlling COIN forces. Commanders must provide subordinates with a mission, commander's intent, a concept of operations, and resources adequate to accomplish the mission. Higher commanders empower subordinates to make decisions within the commander's intent. They leave details of

execution to their subordinates and expect them to use initiative and judgment to accomplish the mission.

(2) **Mosaic Nature.** The mosaic nature of COIN is ideally suited to decentralized execution. On-scene commanders often have the best grasp of their tactical situations. Counterinsurgents that win this kind of mosaic war are those able to respond to all forms of insurgent operations, often simultaneously; thus, commanders must allow them access or control of the resources needed to produce timely intelligence, conduct effective tactical operations, and manage IO.

m. **Support the Host Nation.** US forces committed to supporting COIN are there to assist a HN government. The long-term goal is to leave a government able to stand by itself, which is also normally the goal even if the US begins COIN in an area that does not have a HN government. Regardless of the starting conditions, the HN ultimately has to win on its own. Achieving this requires development of viable local leaders and institutions. US forces and agencies can help, but HN elements must accept responsibilities to achieve real victory. While it may be easier for joint forces to conduct operations themselves, it is better to work to strengthen local forces and institutions and then assist them. HN governments have the final responsibility to solve their own problems. Eventually all foreign armies are seen as interlopers or occupiers; the sooner the main effort can transition to HN institutions, without unacceptable degradation, the better.

Intentionally Blank

CHAPTER IV
UNITY OF EFFORT IN COUNTERINSURGENCY

> *"You cannot command what you do not control. Therefore 'unity of command' (between agencies or among government and non-government actors) means little in this environment. Instead, we need to create 'unity of effort' at best, and collaboration or deconfliction at least. This depends less on a shared command and control hierarchy, and more on a shared diagnosis of the problem, platforms for collaboration, information sharing and deconfliction."*
>
> **Dr. David J. Kilcullen**
> **Three Pillars of Counterinsurgency**

1. Unity of Effort and Unified Action

Unity of effort and unified action are essential for successful COIN operations. Unified action refers to the synchronization, coordination, and/or integration of military operations with the activities of governmental and nongovernmental entities to achieve unity of effort. Figure IV-1 depicts the joint military perspective of unified action. Unified action includes a "whole-of-government" or "comprehensive approach" that employs all instruments of national power. Achieving unity of effort is challenging in COIN due to the normally complex OE and its many potential actors—friendly, neutral, and adversarial. The military contribution to COIN must be coordinated with the activities of USG interagency partners, IGOs, NGOs, regional organizations, the operations of multinational forces, and activities of various HN agencies to be successful. Coordinating and integrating efforts between the joint force and USG interagency partners, IGOs, and NGOs should not be equated to the command and control (C2) of a military operation. Successful interagency, IGO, and NGO coordination helps enable the USG to build international support, conserve resources, and conduct coherent operations that efficiently achieve shared goals. All friendly and neutral actors should seek to coordinate, or at least deconflict, their activities with the activities of other organizations.

a. **Military.** While nonmilitary considerations are paramount for long-term success in COIN, the joint military contribution is essential to provide security that enables other COIN efforts. Joint forces contribute to unified action through unity of command and a solid C2 architecture that integrates strategic, operational, and tactical COIN. Services play a key role in both stability and countering insurgency and their efforts are most effective when synchronized. The JFC should coordinate with and draw on the capabilities of separate agencies as well as provide support, especially security, to other actors.

b. **Interagency.** Interagency coordination is conducted among agencies of the USG, including the DOD, for the purpose of accomplishing an objective. In COIN, interagency coordination between the joint force and USG interagency partners is fundamental. For US support to a HN's COIN efforts, the COM is the senior USG representative.

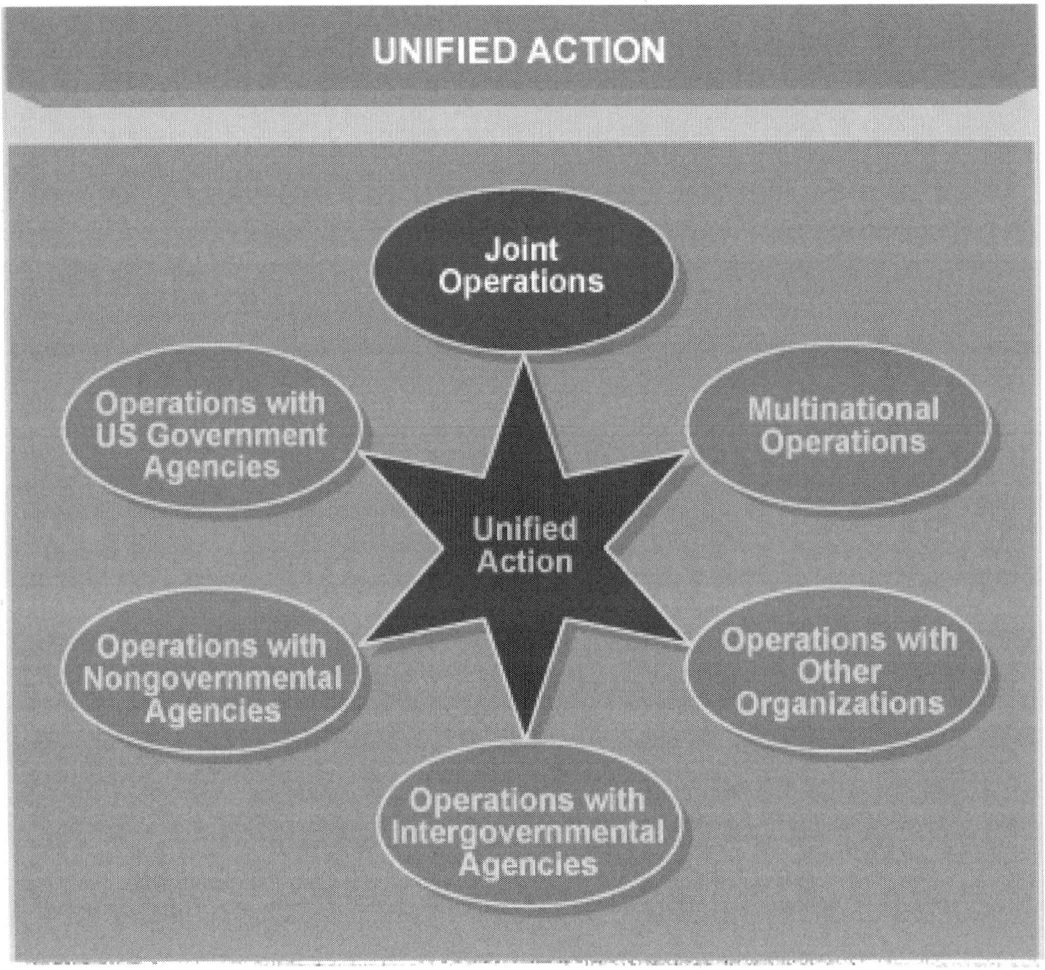

Figure IV-1. Unified Action

c. **Intergovernmental.** Intergovernmental coordination involves the USG, led by the DOS and implemented through the relevant COM and country team, working with one or more IGOs. When working with IGOs, the JFC should use existing mechanisms of the COM and country team, DOS, USAID, and other appropriate agencies. An IGO is created by a formal agreement between two or more governments. It may be established on a global, regional, or functional basis for wide-ranging or narrowly defined purposes. IGOs provide leadership, capabilities, and mandate; furthermore, they may lend legitimacy and credibility to governance, especially the HN.

d. **Multinational.** Multinational coordination involves the USG, led by the DOS and implemented through the relevant COM and country team, working with agencies and forces from other nations, and this coordination normally occurs within the framework of an alliance or coalition. When working with multinational organizations, the JFC should use existing mechanisms of the COM and country team, DOS, USAID, and other appropriate agencies. The HN is the most important entity for multinational coordination in COIN. As with any multinational efforts, trust and agreement bind the entities conducting COIN on common goals and objectives, which is especially important between the HN and the remainder of the multinational forces. Language and cultural differences often present the most immediate challenge, and all actors must strive to overcome these challenges through communication and improving cultural awareness. Liaisons and advisors can play a vital role in these areas. Multinational forces who support a HN's COIN effort must remember that they are present by the HN's request and that COIN is ultimately the HN's responsibility. Leaders of US contingents must work closely with their multinational counterparts to become familiar with agencies that may operate in their operational area. To the degree possible, military leaders should use military liaison personnel to establish appropriate relationships and awareness of their HN counterparts.

e. **Nongovernmental.** Nongovernmental coordination is between elements of the USG, led by the USAID and implemented through the relevant COM and country team, and NGOs, multinational corporations, private contractors, and private organizations of any kind to achieve an objective. When working with NGOs, the JFC should use existing mechanisms of the COM and country team, DOS, USAID, and other appropriate agencies. Absent a COM, a JFC may have to directly coordinate with NGOs, multinational corporations, private contractors, and private organizations until a US diplomatic mission is established. This can be facilitated by reachback through the GCC to relevant departments or agencies and through the use of civil-military operations centers (CMOCs). The preponderance of effort put forth by the JTF will continue to focus on creating the security conditions necessary to support the civilian administration of the host country government and establish the US diplomatic mission.

For official guidance on dealing specifically with humanitarian NGOs, see Guidelines for Relations Between US Armed Forces and Non-Governmental Humanitarian Organizations.

(1) **Nongovernmental Organizations.** An NGO is a private, self-governing, not-for-profit organization. Many NGOs will not wish to openly associate with the joint force, at all. Some NGOs are concerned with preserving the "humanitarian space" as open association with the military can give the perception that they are part of the COIN, thus potentially making them less effective or subject to insurgent attack. Collaborating and coordinating operations with these NGOs can be difficult. Establishing basic awareness of these groups and their activities may be the most commanders can achieve. NGOs, however, play important roles in resolving insurgencies. Many NGOs arrive before military forces and remain afterwards. They can support lasting stability. To the greatest extent possible, commanders try to complement and not override their capabilities. Building a complementary, trust-based relationship is vital. Regardless of the NGOs level of cooperation, the JFC and joint force have a moral obligation to do everything possible to ensure the security of NGOs to the extent that the NGO will allow. Commanders also must be aware that some illegal and potentially adversarial organizations will attempt to claim status as an NGO.

(2) **Multinational Corporations.** When working with multinational corporations, the JFC should use existing mechanisms of the COM and country team, DOS, USAID, and other appropriate agencies. Multinational corporations often engage in reconstruction, economic development, and governance activities. The joint force should provide support as required to the DOS economic counselor and the Foreign Commercial Service representative of the US Department of Commerce in the US mission to support the IDAD strategy. Even in the absence of USG civilian departments and agencies on the ground, the JFC should use reachback through the GCC to consult with the appropriate agencies in Washington prior to engagement with multinational corporations. At a minimum, commanders should seek to know which companies are present in their area and where those companies are conducting business. Such information can prevent fratricide and destruction of private property.

(3) **Government Contractors.** When contractors or other businesses are being paid to support military or USG interagency partners involved in COIN, the principle of unity of command applies.

(4) **Private Security Contractors.** Armed contractors may provide different security services to the USG, HN, NGOs, and private businesses. Many businesses market expertise in areas related to supporting governance, economics, education, and other aspects of civil society as well. Providing capabilities similar to some NGOs, these firms often obtain contracts through government agencies. When under a USG contract, private security contractors behave as an extension of the organizations or agencies for which they work. Commanders should identify private security contractors operating in their area and determine the nature of their contract, existing accountability mechanisms, and appropriate coordination relationships. Depending on the terms of their contract, the environment in which they operate and certain agreements the USG is a party to, private security contractors may be subject to the laws of the HN, US law, and international law. Any failure on the part of these actors will reflect negatively on counterinsurgent credibility and HN legitimacy.

f. **Other.** Some organizations that the joint force must coordinate with do not fit neatly into the previous five categories. Some organizations have the characteristics of more than one type of the previously mentioned five categories. Additionally, many other groups can play critical roles in influencing the outcome of a COIN effort yet are beyond the control of military forces or civilian governing institutions. These groups can include local leaders, informal associations, religious groups, families, and the media. Commanders must remain aware of the influence of such groups and be prepared to work with, through, or around them.

For more information, see JP 3-08, Intergovernmental Coordination During Joint Operations, *and JP 3-16,* Multinational Operations.

2. The Internal Defense and Development Strategy

When a HN is dealing with an insurgency and the US supports the HN, COIN is one aspect of a larger FID mission. The IDAD strategy is the overarching strategy in a FID mission; however, this is a joint military term and it is important to note that the HN and others may not use this term. **IDAD is the HN's plan that US FID supports; the HN does not support the US FID plan.** The purpose of the IDAD strategy is to promote HN growth and its ability to protect itself from subversion, lawlessness, and insurgency. IDAD programs focus on building viable political, economic, military, and social institutions that respond to the needs of society. The HN government mobilizes the population to participate in IDAD efforts. The ultimate goal is to prevent an insurgency or other forms of lawlessness or subversion by forestalling and defeating the threat; thus, IDAD is ideally a preemptive strategy. If an insurgency or other threat develops, IDAD becomes an active strategy to combat that threat. When dealing with an insurgency, IDAD programs focus on addressing the core grievances and dealing with the actual extant insurgency. JFCs and joint planners must understand the HN's IDAD strategy if they are to plan effectively to support it. In some cases, the joint force may need to assist the HN to formulate an appropriate IDAD strategy, especially if the joint force began operations in an area of weak or no HN governance. While IDAD is the overarching strategy; the HN's government below the national level needs to build the capability and capacity to support IDAD, which may necessitate civil-military support. Civil-military support may come in the form of organizations like national-level governmental assistance teams (GATs) or provincial reconstruction teams (PRTs).

a. **Concept. The IDAD strategy integrates all security force and development programs into a coherent, holistic effort.** Security actions provide a level of internal security that permits and supports growth through balanced development. This development often requires change to address core grievances. These changes may in turn promote temporary unrest; however, they are necessary for long-term success. The IDAD strategy must include measures to maintain conditions under which orderly development can take place. Similarly, addressing the core grievances of the insurgency often includes overcoming the HN government's inertia and shortcomings. It may be difficult for US leaders to convince the HN government to reform, but these reforms are often the best way to diffuse the core grievances of and support for the insurgency. An underlying assumption for the IDAD strategy is that the threat to the HN lies in insurgent political strength rather than military power. Although the counterinsurgents must contain violent insurgent actions, concentration on the military aspect of the threat does not address the real long-term danger. IDAD efforts must pay continuing, serious attention to the political claims and demands of the population and insurgents. Military and paramilitary programs are necessary for success, but are not sufficient alone.

b. **IDAD Functions.** The IDAD strategy blends four interdependent functions to prevent or counter internal threats. Figure IV-2 depicts the IDAD Strategy Model.

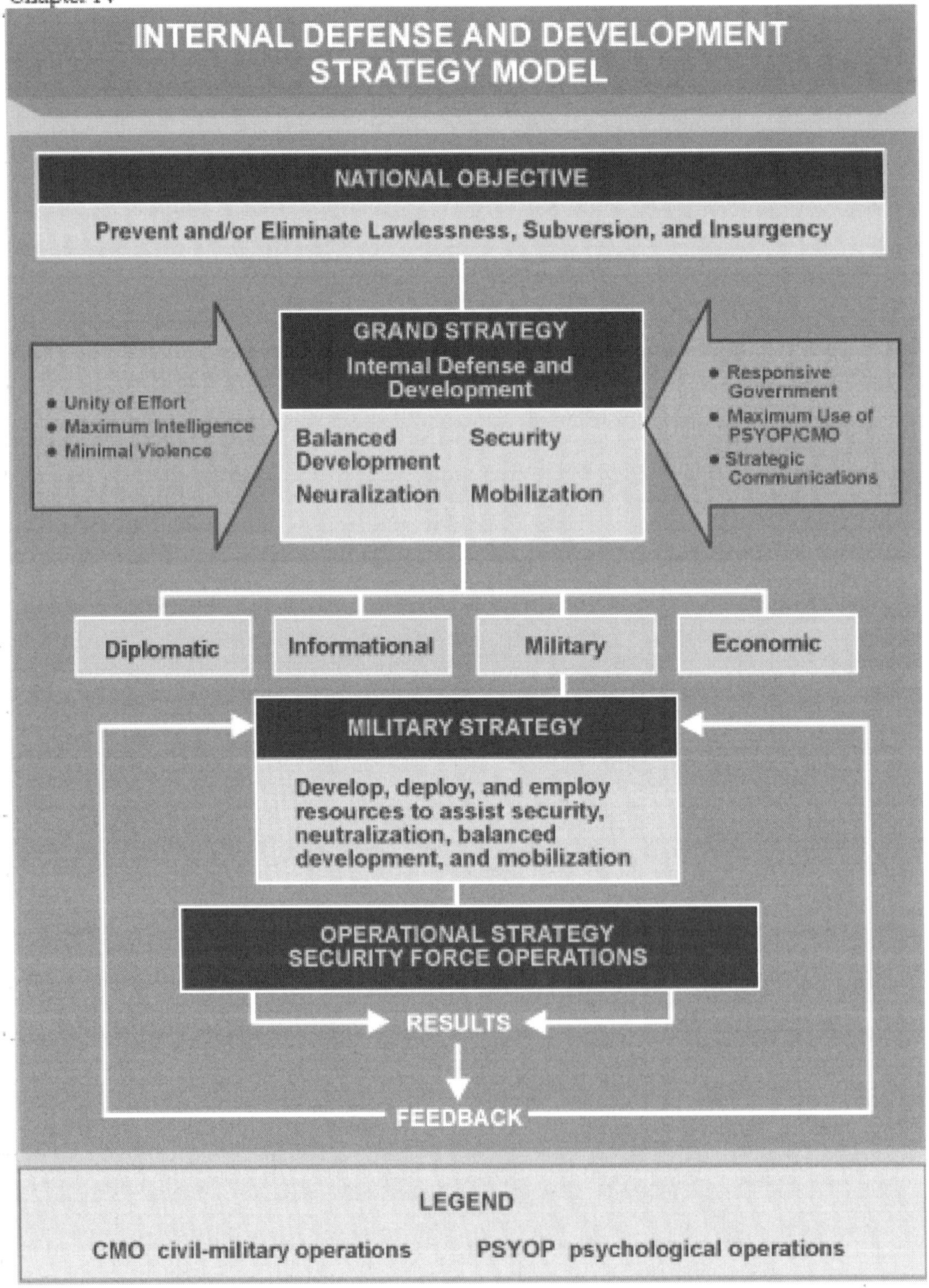
INTERNAL DEFENSE AND DEVELOPMENT STRATEGY MODEL
NATIONAL OBJECTIVE
Prevent and/or Eliminate Lawlessness, Subversion, and Insurgency
• Unity of Effort
• Maximum Intelligence
• Minimal Violence
GRAND STRATEGY
Internal Defense and Development
Balanced Development
Security
Neuralization
Mobilization
• Responsive Government
• Maximum Use of PSYOP/CMO
• Strategic Communications
Diplomatic
Informational
Military
Economic
MILITARY STRATEGY
Develop, deploy, and employ resources to assist security, neutralization, balanced development, and mobilization
OPERATIONAL STRATEGY
SECURITY FORCE OPERATIONS
RESULTS
FEEDBACK
LEGEND
CMO civil-military operations
PSYOP psychological operations

Figure IV-2. Internal Defense and Development Strategy Model

c. **Assessment.** The HN and any coalition partners must continually analyze the results of the IDAD strategy. Part of the assessment process is to establish measures of effectiveness (MOEs) and measures of performance, as well as having a methodology to provide feedback for future planning, refinement of strategy, and continued formulation of strategic national policy. While the HN should have input into all aspects of assessment, it should take the lead in determining MOEs. MOEs measure changes in system behavior, capability, or OE. MOEs in COIN predominately focus on the population. Although the HN has the best understanding of its own culture, its views have to be balanced with the views of other coalition partners to assist in providing other perspectives. Coalition perspectives are especially important if the HN government is slow to reform or has had a previous record of harsh treatment.

d. **Campaign Plan to IDAD Transition.** Some situations may require the joint force to occupy territory and to provide governance through a transitional military authority. However, this authority should transition to civilian authority as quickly as the situation allows. This civilian authority could be a provisional governing authority or an IGO such as the UN. Authority could also transfer from a provisional civilian authority to an IGO as an intermediate transition. Ultimately, authority will be transferred to a HN when either a government in exile or new government is ready, although this transition may be a lengthy process to ensure continued effective governance. As with transitions in governance, there may be several military transitions. When ready, the HN will first assume the lead and then eventually take over military operations. This transition may be phased over time.

e. **Internal Defense and Development Coordination.** Military assistance is often required to provide a secure environment enabling the activities of the COM and the country team in support of the HN's goals as expressed through the IDAD strategy. The US country team, led by the COM, is the cornerstone of US coordination with the HN. The COM, the US country team, the GCC, and other JFCs are responsible for ensuring that US plans and efforts are nested within the IDAD strategy. It is important to note that there are multiple supporting actors or echelons in both the JTF commanders' and coalition partners' FID programs. Figure IV-3 depicts the IDAD coordination.

(1) **Sovereignty.** The sovereignty of a HN must be respected. This means that the HN has the authority over the manner and pace of operations conducted within its borders. Sovereignty issues are among the most difficult for commanders conducting COIN. Multinational commanders—whether US, other nation, or specifically HN—are required to lead through coordination, communication, and consensus, in addition to traditional command practices. Political sensitivities must be acknowledged. Commanders and subordinates often act as diplomats as well as warriors. Within military units, legal officers and their staffs are particularly valuable for clarifying legal arrangements with the HN. To avoid adverse effects on operations, commanders should address all sovereignty issues through the chain of command to the US COM. As much as possible, sovereignty issues should be addressed before executing operations. Examples of sovereignty issues include: aerial ports of debarkation; basing; border crossings; collecting and sharing information; protection (tasks related to preserving the

(1) **Balanced Development.** Balanced development attempts to achieve HN goals through political, social, economic, and other developmental programs. Balanced development should allow all individuals and groups in the society to share in the rewards of development, thus alleviating frustration due to inequities. Balanced development should satisfy legitimate grievances that the opposition attempts to exploit. The government must recognize conditions that contribute to the internal threat and instability and take preventive measures. COIN must strive for balanced development as insurgents will take advantage of real or perceived development inequalities, especially with IO. All civil-military development should account for the IDAD balanced development function, including the integration of entities such as GATs and PRTs.

(2) **Security.** Security includes all activities implemented in order to protect the populace from the threat and to provide a safe environment for development. Security of the populace and government resources is essential to countering the threat. Protection and control of the populace permit development and deny the adversary access to popular support. The security effort should establish an environment in which the local government can provide for its own security with limited national government support; however, this security must adhere to the current legal framework. This function also includes any SFA functions that multinational forces, including the US, provide to the HN.

(3) **Neutralization.** Neutralization is a political concept that makes an organized force irrelevant to the political process. It is the physical and psychological separation of the threatening elements from the population, and includes all lawful activities to disrupt, preempt, disorganize, and defeat the insurgent organization. It may involve public exposure and the discrediting of centers of gravity (COGs) during a period of low-level unrest with little political violence, may involve arrest and prosecution when laws have been broken, or can involve combat action when the adversary's violent activities escalate. All neutralization efforts must be legal. They must scrupulously observe constitutional provisions regarding rights and responsibilities. The need for security forces to act lawfully is essential not only for humanitarian reasons but also because this reinforces government legitimacy while denying the adversary an exploitable issue. Special emergency powers may exist by legislation or decree. Government agents must not abuse these powers because they might well lose the popular support they need. Denying the adversary an opportunity to seize on and exploit legitimate issues against the government discredits their leaders and neutralizes their propaganda.

(4) **Mobilization.** Mobilization provides organized manpower and materiel resources and includes all activities to motivate and organize popular support of the HN government. This support is essential for a successful IDAD program. If successful, mobilization maximizes manpower and other resources available to the HN government while it minimizes those available to the insurgent. Mobilization allows the government to strengthen existing institutions, to develop new ones to respond to demands, and promotes the government's legitimacy. All mobilization efforts must have a plan for eventual demobilization or reintegration into the HN government and security apparatus.

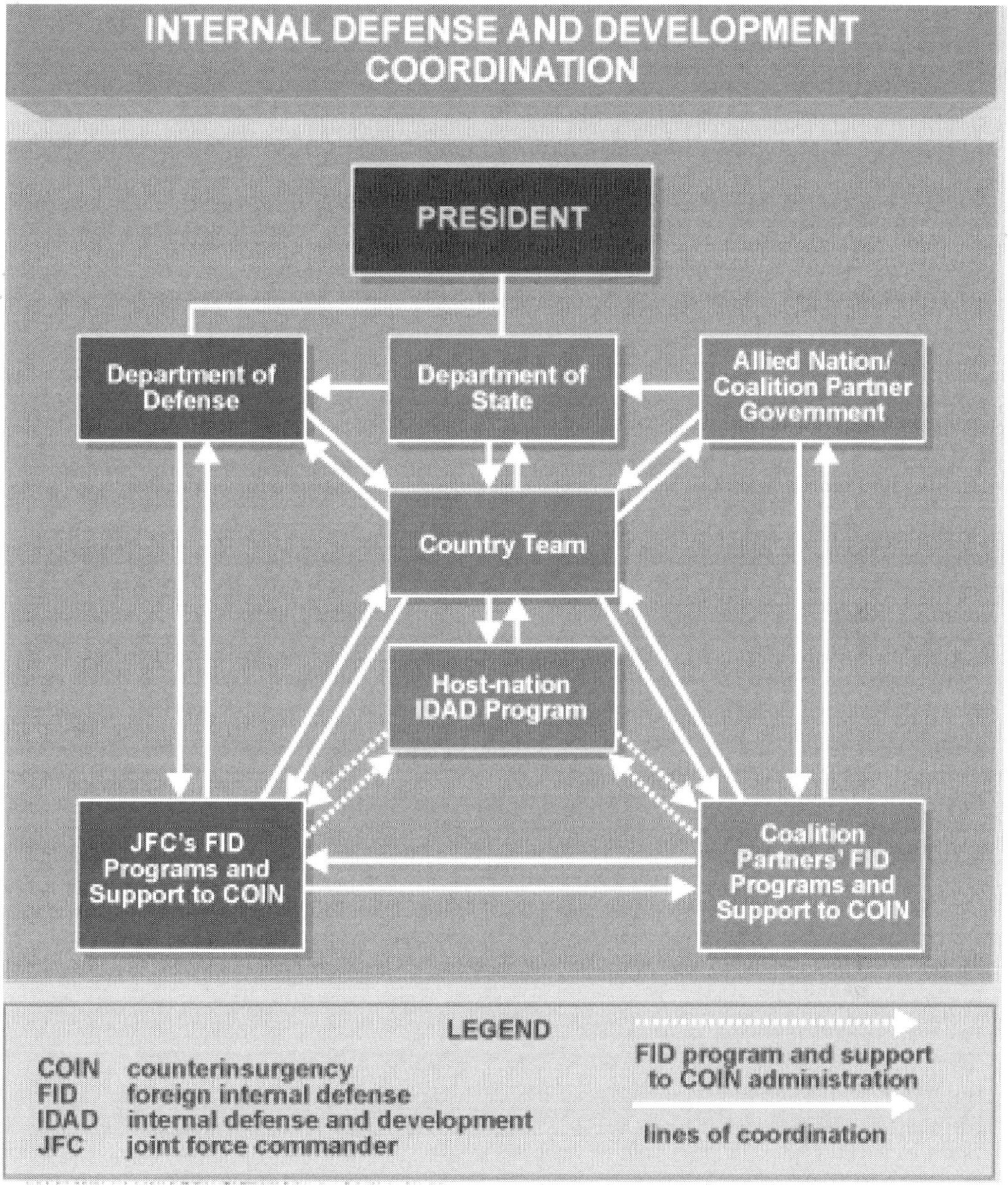

Figure IV-3. Internal Defense and Development Coordination

force); jurisdiction over members of the US and multinational forces; location and access; operations in the territorial waters, both sea and internal; overflight rights; police operations, including arrest, detention, penal, and justice authority and procedures; railheads; and seaports of debarkation. Counterinsurgents must be particularly respectful of HN sovereignty issues that cut to the heart of governance, rule of law, and the economy. Counterinsurgents must support the HN to find their own way, exercising extreme patience, rather than directing HN actions. This can be a point of friction between military commanders who tend to focus on short to midterm objectives and military end states, and country team personnel who tend to focus on long term issues.

(2) **Coordinating Mechanisms.** Commanders create coordinating mechanisms, such as committees or liaison elements, to facilitate cooperation and build trust with HN authorities. HN military or nonmilitary representatives should have leading roles in such mechanisms. These organizations facilitate operations by reducing sensitivities and misunderstandings while removing impediments. Sovereignty issues can be formally resolved with the HN by developing appropriate technical agreements to augment existing or UN Security Council resolution or status-of-forces agreement. In many cases, embassy security cooperation organizations, NGOs, and IGOs have detailed local knowledge and reservoirs of good will that can help establish a positive, constructive relationship with the HN.

(3) **Coordination and Support.** Coordinate and support down to the village and neighborhood level. All members of the joint force should be aware of the political and societal structures in their areas. Political structures usually have designated leaders responsible to the government and people. However, the societal structure may include informal leaders who operate outside the political structure. These leaders may be associated with economic, religious, informational, and family based institutions. Other societal leaders may emerge due to charisma or other intangible influences. Commanders should identify the key leaders and the manner in which they are likely to influence COIN efforts and attempt to build relationships and coordination mechanisms with them.

For more information see JP 3-22, Foreign Internal Defense.

3. United States Civil-Military Integration

COIN is normally only effective with a holistic approach that employs all HN and supporting nation instruments of national power. Joint military efforts to secure the population may initially dominate COIN, but the other instruments of national power are essential to achieve national strategic objectives. Interagency participants in COIN must know each others' roles, capabilities, cultures, and terminology. COIN planning at all levels should include indigenous representatives and other participants. Military participants should support civilian efforts, including those of NGOs, IGOs, USG interagency partners, IPI, and other friendly actors. Military participants, as required by the situation, conduct or participate in political, social, informational, and economic programs. Societal insecurity can trigger violence that discourages or precludes nonmilitary organizations, particularly external agencies, from helping the local populace. A more benign environment allows civilian agencies greater opportunity to provide their resources and expertise, thereby relieving joint forces of some of these responsibilities. Long-term development and therefore successful COIN depends on the joint force providing an environment in which civilian agencies can effectively operate, especially with respect to economic efforts. Many civilian humanitarian assistance (HA) providers view security differently than does the joint force. In fact, the HA community has an entirely different security paradigm than the joint force. For HA providers, security is based on belligerent perception of the neutrality of HA providers rather than on the lack of violence in an area or perceived strength of military forces. This security paradigm difference may impact military planning, execution, and assessment.

a. **Responsibilities and Leadership. Counterinsurgents are responsible for the population's well-being.** This includes security from insurgent intimidation and coercion, sectarian violence, and nonpolitical violence and crime. To succeed, counterinsurgents must ensure basic economic needs, essential services (such as sewage, water, electricity, sanitation, and health care), sustainment of key social and cultural institutions, and other aspects that contribute to a society's basic quality of life are provided. Informed, strong leaders must focus on the central problems affecting the local populace. Given the primacy of political considerations, military forces should support civilian efforts. The changing nature of COIN means that lead responsibility shifts among military, civilian, and HN authorities, and these transitions must be planned and managed at the highest levels. However, the joint force must prepare to assume local leadership for COIN efforts, as the situation and need dictate. The overall imperative is to focus on what needs to be done, not on who does it. While this imperative can be emphasized by senior civilian and military leaders, its practice must be based on positive interpersonal relationships and the IDAD strategy.

b. **Shared Understanding of the Operational Environment.** Countering an insurgency begins with understanding the complex environment and the numerous competing forces within it. Gaining an understanding of the environment—including the insurgents, affected population, and different counterinsurgent organizations—is essential to an integrated COIN operation. Various agencies acting to reestablish stability may differ in goals and approaches, based on their experience and institutional culture. When their actions are allowed to adversely affect each other, the populace suffers and insurgents identify grievances to exploit. Integrated actions are essential to defeat the ideologies professed by insurgents. A shared understanding of the operation's purpose provides a unifying theme for COIN efforts. Through a common understanding of that purpose, the COIN leaders can design an operation that promotes effective collaboration and coordination among all agencies and the affected populace.

c. **Preferred Division of Labor.** It is always preferable for civilians to lead the overall COIN effort, in addition to performing traditionally civilian tasks. Even where civilians' capability and capacity do not match their expertise, they should lead in the areas of governance, economics, rule of law, etc. as policy guides and decision makers who define the role the military should and will play to support the effort. Military leaders should avoid the temptation to take over the role of decision maker in these areas despite a lack of civilian capability and capacity. Their forces may play a significant role in executing actions in these areas, but should never proceed without the guidance of civilian agency personnel as to the course of action (COA) and the military role. It is important to note that civilian agencies often have the greatest capability and the joint force may have the greatest capacity; in this case the civilian agency should lead the overall effort with the joint force in a supporting role. Legitimate local authorities should receive special preference to lead or perform civilian tasks. There are many US agencies and civilian IGOs with more expertise in meeting the fundamental needs of a population than military forces have; however, the ability of such agencies to deploy to foreign countries in sustainable numbers and with ready access to necessary resources is often limited. The violence level in the area also can affect civilian agencies' ability to operate. The more violent the environment, the more difficult it is for civilians to operate effectively. Hence, the preferred or ideal division of labor is frequently unattainable. The more violent the insurgency, the more unrealistic is this preferred division of labor.

d. **Realistic Division of Labor.** Participants best qualified and able to accomplish nonmilitary tasks are not always available. The realistic division of labor does not always match the preferred division of labor. In those cases, military forces perform those tasks. Sometimes joint forces have the skills required; other times they learn them during execution.

(1) **Nonmilitary Contribution.** USG interagency partners and IGOs rarely have the resources and capabilities needed to address all COIN tasks. Success requires adaptable leaders who prepare to perform required tasks with available resources. These leaders understand that long-term security cannot be imposed by military force alone; it requires an integrated, balanced application of effort by all participants with the goal of supporting the local populace and achieving legitimacy for the HN government. Military forces can perform civilian tasks but often not as well as the civilian agencies with people trained in those skills. Further, military forces performing civilian tasks are not performing military tasks. Diversion from those tasks should be temporary and only taken to address urgent circumstances. Military forces should be aware that putting a military face on economics, politics, rule of law, etc., may do more harm than good in certain situations. The implications of the military role in these areas should be discussed at length with the country team.

(2) **Military Capability and Capacity.** In nonpermissive security situations, US and multinational military forces often possess the only readily available capability to meet many of the local populace's fundamental needs. Human decency, and even the law of war, may require joint forces to assist the populace in their operational areas. Leaders at all levels prepare to address civilian needs, including identifying people in their units with regional and interagency expertise, civil-military competence, and other critical skills needed to support a local populace and HN government. Even if lack of civilian capacity requires military forces to take on this mission, military leaders should consult with the country team on the proper COA to follow. Commanders should also seek awareness of NGOs that may be operating in the region and providing for the basic needs of the population. The joint force must strive to support the population and other partners that are supporting the population.

e. **Transitions.** Regardless of the division of labor, an important recurring feature of COIN is transitioning responsibility and participation. As consistently and conscientiously as possible, military leaders ensure continuity in meeting the needs of the HN government and local populace, which is best accomplished by all efforts supporting the IDAD strategy. The same general guidelines governing battle handovers apply to

COIN transitions. Whether the transition is between military units or from a military unit to a civilian agency, all involved must clearly understand the tasks and responsibilities being passed. Maintaining unity of effort is particularly important during transitions, especially between organizations of different capabilities and capacities. Relationships tend to break down during transitions. A transition is not a single event where all activity happens at once. It is a rolling process of little handoffs between different actors along several streams of activities. There are usually multiple transitions for any one stream of activity over time. Using the coordination mechanisms discussed below can help create and sustain the links that support effective transitions without compromising unity of effort.

f. **Coordination and Liaison.** COIN partners and other organizations have many interests and agendas that military forces cannot and should not try to control. Their local legitimacy is frequently affected by the degree to which local institutions are perceived as independent and capable without external support. Nevertheless, military leaders should make every effort to ensure that COIN actions are as well integrated as possible. Active leadership by civilian and military leaders is imperative to effect coordination, establish formal and informal liaison, and share information. Influencing and persuading groups outside a commander's authority requires skill and often subtlety. Commanders should also recognize that they will often be in a supporting role, and must realize that they may be on the receiving end of being influenced and persuaded by civilian agencies in charge. As actively as commanders pursue unity of effort, they should also be mindful of their prominence and recognize the wisdom of acting indirectly and in ways that allow credit for success to go to others—particularly local individuals and organizations. The joint force should remain in a supporting role to appropriate civilian agencies or groups, follow US policy and the COM's direction, and focus on supporting the IDAD strategy.

For more information see US Government Counterinsurgency Guide, *JP 3-16,* Multinational Operations, *and the* American, British, Canadian, Australian, and New Zealand Armies Program, Coalition Operations Handbook, *edition 4.*

4. United States Civil-Military Integration Mechanisms

There are several US civil-military integration mechanisms that facilitate unified action for COIN. Many of these structures exist and are often employed in other types of missions, such as peacekeeping or humanitarian relief, but they are fundamental for successful COIN. These mechanisms fall into two general areas: those that are located outside of the theater and those that are located in theater. It is important to note that these are options and may not always be present and their relationships can vary.

a. **Civil-Military Mechanisms in the United States.** Key civil-military integration mechanisms located outside of the GCC's area of responsibility (AOR) include the National Security Council (NSC), special missions established in Washington to provide policy guidance for a theater (e.g., Iraq Policy and Operations Group, and Afghanistan Interagency Operations Group), and appointed leaders focused on a particular COIN effort.

(1) **National Security Council.** At the strategic level, the NSC directs the creation of the interagency civil-military plan for COIN. When COIN substantially overlaps with and triggers the responsibilities given to the State Department's Coordinator for Reconstruction and Stabilization to direct interagency planning for countries at risk of, in, or in transition from conflict, the Interagency Management System (IMS) and accompanying USG Planning Framework for Reconstruction, Stabilization, and Conflict Transformation will be used to craft and implement the strategic whole-of-government plans. This will inform military and civilian planning in Washington, DC, at the GCC, at the embassy, and at the JTF level. Not all COIN operations will reach the threshold to activate the IMS, but commanders must be aware of the system and actively seek to find out if it has been stood up for the operation. The utilization of the USG Planning Framework does not require the establishment of the IMS. The NSC staff, guided by the deputies and principals, assists in integrating interagency processes to develop the plan for NSC approval. The country team, GCC, and department/agency country offices interact with the appropriate NSC policy coordinating committees/country groups (see Figure IV-4).

For more information on the IMS, see JP 3-08, Intergovernmental Coordination During Joint Operations, Volumes I and II.

(2) **Policy Operations Groups.** A policy operations group may be established to focus on a geographic region, state, or insurgency. For example, both Iraq and Afghanistan have a separate DOS mission to steer policy for the operations – The Iraq Policy and Operations Group and the Afghanistan Interagency Operations Group.

b. **Civil-Military Integration Mechanisms in Theater.** GCCs are charged with coordinating US military policy and operations within an assigned AOR. Subordinate JTFs are assigned to conduct joint military operations within a designated operational area which may be one or more countries suffering from an insurgency. The US country team, advance civilian team (ACT), JFC, executive steering committee, provincial authority, civil-military coordination board (CMCB), joint CMO task forces, joint interagency task forces (JIATFs), GATs PRTs, and CMOCs are key civil-military integration mechanisms that are normally located inside the designated operational area. The more extensive the US participation is in a COIN operation and the more dispersed US forces are throughout a country, the greater the need for additional mechanisms to extend civilian oversight and assistance. Operating with a clear understanding of the guiding political aims, members of the military at all levels must be prepared to exercise judgment and act without the benefit of immediate civilian oversight and control and ultimately to reinforce HN credibility and legitimacy. At each subordinate political level of the HN government, military and civilian leaders should establish the necessary integration mechanisms. These mechanisms should include military and civilian representatives of the HN and other coalition members. Commanders should be aware of the activities of IGOs and NGOs in the theater. However, JFCs should be aware that the IGO/NGO independent, impartial, and sometimes neutral status does not bind them to working as part of a USG or coalition team, or to support the IDAD strategy.

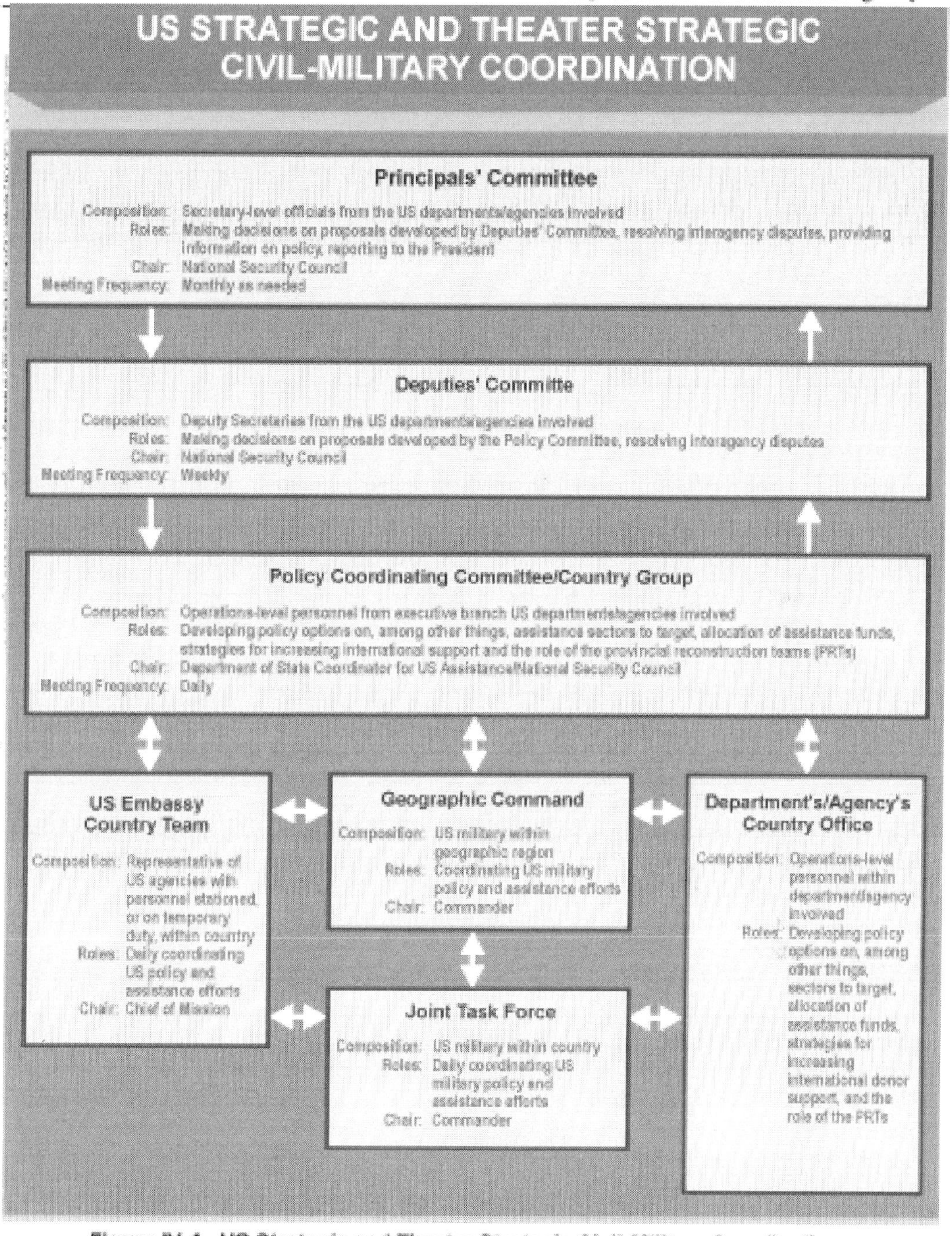
US STRATEGIC AND THEATER STRATEGIC CIVIL-MILITARY COORDINATION
Principals' Committee
Composition: Secretary-level officials from the US departments/agencies involved
Roles: Making decisions on proposals developed by Deputies' Committee, resolving interagency disputes, providing information on policy, reporting to the President
Chair: National Security Council
Meeting Frequency: Monthly as needed
Deputies' Committe
Composition: Deputy Secretaries from the US departments/agencies involved
Roles: Making decisions on proposals developed by the Policy Committee, resolving interagency disputes
Chair: National Security Council
Meeting Frequency: Weekly
Policy Coordinating Committee/Country Group
Composition: Operations-level personnel from executive branch US departments/agencies involved
Roles: Developing policy options on, among other things, assistance sectors to target, allocation of assistance funds, strategies for increasing international support and the role of the provincial reconstruction teams (PRTs)
Chair: Department of State Coordinator for US Assistance/National Security Council
Meeting Frequency: Daily
US Embassy Country Team
Composition: Representative of US agencies with personnel stationed, or on temporary duty, within country
Roles: Daily coordinating US policy and assistance efforts
Chair: Chief of Mission
Geographic Command
Composition: US military within geographic region
Roles: Coordinating US military policy and assistance efforts
Chair: Commander
Department's/Agency's Country Office
Composition: Operations-level personnel within department/agency involved
Roles: Developing policy options on, among other things, sectors to target, allocation of assistance funds, strategies for increasing international donor support, and the role of the PRTs
Joint Task Force
Composition: US military within country
Roles: Daily coordinating US military policy and assistance efforts
Chair: Commander

Figure IV-4. US Strategic and Theater Strategic Civil-Military Coordination

(1) **Joint Interagency Coordination Group (JIACG).** JIACGs help CCDRs support COIN by facilitating unified action in support of plans, operations, contingencies, and initiatives. The primary role of the JIACG is to enhance interagency coordination.

The JIACG is a fully integrated participant on the CCDR's staff with a daily focus on joint strategic planning. It provides a capability specifically organized to enhance situational awareness of interagency activities to prevent undesired consequences and uncoordinated activity. When activated, the JIACG will assist with the reception of the integration planning cell (IPC) of the IMS into the staff. The IPC is an interagency team that brings operation-specific capabilities to a regional military command, either a GCC or an equivalent multinational headquarters. The purpose of the IPC is to support civilian-military communication and integration of the civilian and military planning in order to achieve unity of effort. JIACGs include representatives from other federal departments and agencies and state and local authorities, as well as liaison officers from other commands and DOD components. **The JIACG provides the CCDR with the capability to collaborate at the operational level with other USG civilian agencies and departments.** Representatives and liaison officers are the subject matter experts for their respective agencies and commands. They provide the critical bridge between the CCDR and USG interagency partners; however, JIACGs can be called by different names in different combatant commands.

For additional information on JIACGs see JP 3-08, Intergovernmental Coordination During Joint Operations, Volumes I and II *and the* Commander's Handbook for the Joint Interagency Coordination Group.

(2) **US Country Team.** All USG COIN strategies, plans, programs, and activities that are undertaken to support a HN government are managed through the elements of the US country team, led by the COM. The US country team is the primary interagency coordinating structure that is the focal point for unified action in COIN. Figure IV-5 depicts a generic US country team's organization. The country team is the senior in-country coordinating and supervising body, headed by the US COM, who is normally the ambassador. Title 10, US Code, Section 3927, assigns the COM to a foreign country responsibility for the direction, coordination, and supervision of all government executive branch employees in that country except for Service members and employees under the command of a US JFC. Where a confirmed ambassador is not present, the charge d'affaires represents the Secretary of State as the senior diplomat accredited to the foreign government. The country team is composed of the senior member of each represented department or agency. In a foreign country, the COM is the highest US civil authority. As the senior USG official permanently assigned in the HN, the COM is responsible to the President for policy oversight of all USG programs. The COM leads the country team and is responsible for integrating US efforts in support of the HN. As permanently established interagency organizations, country teams represent a priceless COIN resource. They often provide deep reservoirs of local knowledge and interaction with the HN government and population.

For more information see JP 3-08, Interorganizational Coordination during Joint Operations, Volumes I and II.

(3) **Advance Civilian Team.** An ACT may be formed to implement the USG strategic plan for reconstruction and stabilization through development and management

of the interagency implementation plan (IIP), under the leadership of the COM. The ACT stands-up at the USG field headquarters, typically the embassy. When established, it is the integrating civilian counterpart of the JTF at the country level. The ACT is comprised of a combination of USG personnel already in-country and other agency personnel deployed to the country from agency headquarters or elsewhere.

(4) **Executive Steering Group (ESG).** The COM and a JTF commander can jointly form an ESG. The ESG may be composed of the principals from the JTF, the US embassy, NGOs/IGOs present in the operational area, and other organizations as appropriate. Lacking another similar forum, the ESG can provide high-level outlet for the exchange of information about operational policies as well as for resolution of difficulties arising among the various organizations. The ESG plays a policy role and is charged with interpreting and coordinating operational area aspects of strategic policy. A commander at any echelon may establish an ESG to serve as a conduit through which to provide information and policy guidance to participating agencies. The ESG may be charged with formulating, coordinating, and promulgating local and theater policies required for the explanation, clarification, and implementation of US policies. The ESG should either be co-chaired by the JFC and COM or assigned outright to either individual, depending on the nature of the US mission and possibly based on the security situation.

(5) **Regional Authority.** Direction and coordination of PRTs is conducted by a national-level interagency steering committee, under the supervision of the COM and JFC (for US-led PRTs) or a multinational executive committee (for coalition-led PRTs). This body will also conduct liaison with the HN national government to support PRT operations. Both embassy and JTF personnel staff the steering committee. Regional authorities may be established with regional commanders overseeing a number of PRTs to ensure coordination between provinces and with national level objectives. The regional authority coordinates the deployment and operations of all US PRTs in the operational area, including ensuring that PRTs have a long-term vision nested with either the campaign plan or the IDAD strategy, whichever is appropriate at the time. If an ACT has been established at the country level, a decision to deploy field advance civilian teams (FACTs) to sub-national regions or provinces may follow. FACTs, which are an element of the ACT and are managed by its headquarters, are responsible for implementing plans pertaining to their particular geographic AOR and for informing revisions of the overall USG strategic plan and IIP. They are also responsible for coordinating planning with any US military entities operating in their AOR, in order to achieve the objectives in the IIP. FACTs are primarily local, on-the-ground operational entities, but their role in assessments, plan revisions, and sub-national field level planning is also important.

For further detail on PRTs, see Appendix B, "Provincial Reconstruction Teams."

(6) **Civil-Military Coordination Board.** If established, a CMCB is the JTF commander's vehicle for coordinating CMO support. Membership is typically restricted to key representatives from the JTF staff sections. A senior member of the JTF staff, such as the JTF deputy commander or chief of staff, serves as chairperson of this board.

If a CMOC has been established at the JTF level, the CMOC director would be a key member of the board and also may serve as its chairperson. During COIN multinational operations, the JTF commander should normally include multinational partners on the board unless there are compelling reasons not to. The type of C2 structure and the level of staff integration in the JTF should drive the decision to establish a coordination board and determine its membership. Depending on the situation, the JTF commander should include selected members from the US country team on the board.

(7) **Joint Civil-Military Operations Task Force (JCMOTF).** The JTF commander may establish a JCMOTF to improve CMO in support of COIN operations. The JCMOTF can provide the JFC a subordinate command to exercise necessary control and coordinating support when the size and scope of the COIN mission is beyond organic CMO capabilities. The JCMOTF should be functionally organized around an existing command structure with augmentation. The JFC designates the JCMOTF commander. A JCMOTF is composed of units from more than one military department and is formed to carry out CMO. Although the JCMOTF is not a civil affairs (CA) organization, there may be a requirement for strong representation of CA. Because of their expertise in dealing with NGOs, IGOs, and USG interagency partners, they will greatly enhance the opportunity for success in COIN. By design, the US Army CA brigade, the maritime CA group, or the Marine Corps CA group can provide the structure to form a JCMOTF in support of the JTF commander. In rare instances, and depending on resources availability, a JCMOTF could be formed as a standing organization.

For more information see JP 3-57, Civil-Military Operations.

(8) **National-level Governmental Assistance Teams.** A national-level GAT supports governance and development at the national level in a semipermissive environment. GATs operate by combining civilian and military personnel for development and governance into one cohesive team. A DOS representative is the team leader and a military officer is normally the deputy commander. Personnel from appropriate USG agencies make up the elements focused on governance and development where DOD personnel comprise the civil security focused staffs. However, when civilian agencies lack the capacity, DOD personnel, especially reservists with civilian skills, may be used to mitigate a shortfall. GATs vary in structure, size, and mission to suit their situation; however, all GATs facilitate the campaign plan in a collapsed state setting or the IDAD strategy in COIN that directly supports a HN. GATs extend the reach, capability, and capacity of governance and facilitate reconstruction. While the GATs are primarily concerned with addressing national-level conditions, they also work on building and improving communication and linkages between the central government and regional/local agencies.

(9) **Provincial Reconstruction Teams.** A PRT is an interim interagency organization designed to improve stability in a given area by helping build the legitimacy and effectiveness of a HN local or provincial government in providing security to its citizens and delivering essential government services. PRTs vary in structure, size, and mission. PRTs extend the reach, capability, and capacity of governance and facilitate

reconstruction. While the PRTs are primarily concerned with addressing local conditions, they also work on building and improving communication and linkages among the central government, regional, and local agencies.

(10) **Civil-Military Operations Centers.** The CMOC is a mechanism for bringing a wide variety of civil, HN, and military elements together for coordination, and it serves as a meeting place for these elements. CMOCs coordinate the interaction of US and multinational military forces with a wide variety of civilian agencies. A CMOC is not a C2 element; it is useful for exchanging information and facilitating complementary efforts. Commanders build a CMOC around a nucleus of organic assets that typically includes CA, logistic, legal, and communications personnel. Commanders invite representatives from nonmilitary organizations. The size, structure, and location of the CMOC are situation dependent.

(11) **Joint Interagency Task Force.** Increasingly, JIATFs are being formed to achieve unity of effort and bring all instruments of national power to bear on COIN mission sets. JIATFs are often created to address problems such as militias, "bad neighbors," and foreign fighters, all of which complicate the COIN environment. JIATFs may be separate elements under the JFC, or they may be subordinate to a component command, a joint special operations task force, or a staff section such as the operations directorate of a joint staff. JIATFs are formal organizations usually chartered by the DOD and one or more civilian agencies and guided by a memorandum of agreement or other founding legal documents that define the roles, responsibilities, and relationships of the JIATF's members. JIATF members can coordinate with the country team, their home agencies, JIACGs in the area of interest (AOI), and other JIATFs in order to defeat complex networks. Because they utilize all instruments of national power, JIATFs are generally not a lethal COIN asset, but rather develop and drive creative nonlethal solutions and policy actions to defeat the insurgency.

(12) **Theater Example.** Figure IV-5 depicts a situation that uses a wide array of US civil-military integrating mechanisms in one theater. This example would be for a complex and difficult COIN situation. Some COIN efforts may not require all of these integrating mechanisms and other COIN efforts may require additional integrating mechanisms.

5. Military Unity of Command in Multinational Operations

Military unity of command is the preferred method for achieving unity of effort in any military operation. Military unity of command is achieved by establishing and maintaining formal command or support relationships. Unity of command should extend to all military forces engaged in COIN—US, HN, and other multinational forces. The purpose of these C2 arrangements is for military forces, police, and other security forces to establish effective control while attaining a monopoly on the legitimate use of violence within the society.

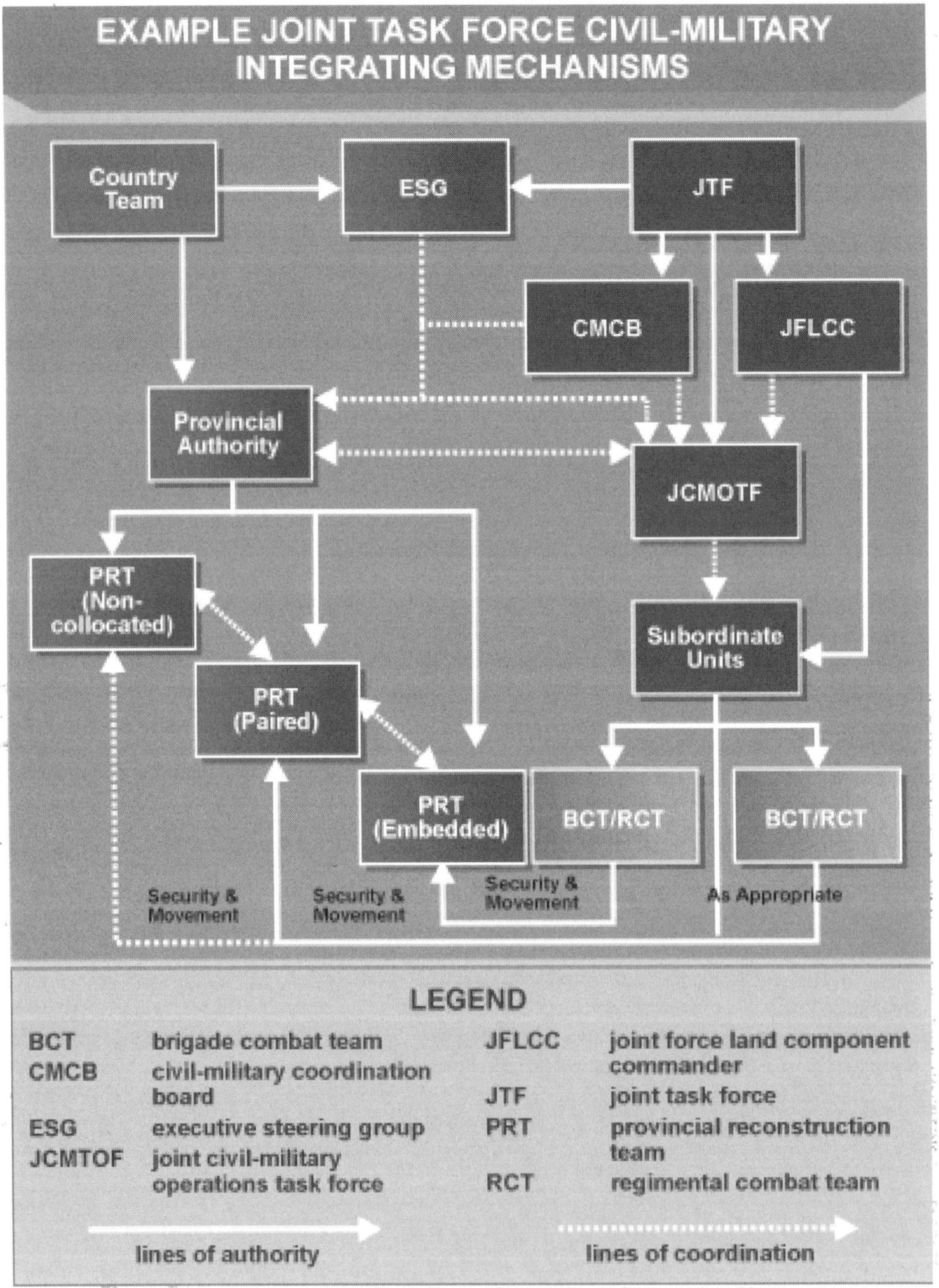

Figure IV-5. Example Joint Task Force Civil-Military Integrating Mechanisms

a. **Political Considerations.** As important as unity of command is to military operations, it is one of the most sensitive and difficult-to-resolve issues in COIN. Nations join coalitions for various reasons. Although the missions of multinational partners may appear similar to those of the United States, ROE, home-country policies, and sensitivities may differ among partners. Military leaders must have a strong cultural and political awareness of US, HN, and other multinational military partners. The participation of US and multinational military forces in COIN missions is inherently problematic, as it influences perceptions of the capacity, credibility, and legitimacy of local security forces. Although unity of command of military forces may be desirable, it may be impractical due to political considerations. Political sensitivities about the perceived subordination of national forces to those of other states or IGOs often preclude strong command relationships; however, the agreements that establish a multinational force provide a source for determining possible authorities and command, or other relationships. When operating under the control of a foreign commander, US commanders maintain the capability and responsibility to report separately to higher US authorities in addition to foreign commanders.

b. **National Mandates and Commitment.** Nations determine if and where they will expend their national resources. Nations also choose the manner and extent of their foreign involvement for reasons both known and unknown to other nations. The only constant is that a decision to join in a COIN effort is, in every case, a calculated political decision by each potential member of a coalition. The nature of their national decisions, in turn, influences the overall command structure. In most multinational operations, the differing degrees of national interest result in varying levels of commitment by alliance and coalition members. While some countries might authorize the full range of employment, other countries may limit their country's forces to strictly defensive or combat service support roles.

c. **Military Capabilities.** Numerous factors influence the military capabilities of nations. The operational level commander must be aware of the differences in the political constraints and capabilities of the forces of various nations, and consider these differences when assigning missions and conducting operations. Commanders at all levels may be required to spend considerable time working political issues related to the utilization of coalition troops; the requirement for diplomatic skills should not be underestimated. Commanders may routinely work directly with political authorities in the region, but should coordinate with the COM to ensure alignment with US foreign policy, to speak with one voice, and to avoid redundancy in engagements with key leaders. In the absence of a US diplomatic mission to the country, the commander should coordinate through the GCC to obtain guidance for any diplomatic engagements. The basic challenge in multinational operations is the effective integration and synchronization of available assets toward the achievement of common objectives. This goal may be achieved through unity of effort despite disparate and occasionally incompatible capabilities, ROE, equipment, and procedures. To reduce disparities among participating forces, minimum capability standards should be established and a certification process developed.

d. **Command Structure.** No single command structure meets the needs of every multinational command but one absolute remains constant; political considerations will heavily influence the ultimate shape of the command structure. This is especially important in COIN as the command structure may change depending on the overall political situation.

(1) **Lead Nation.** The best command structure in COIN is a lead nation structure wherein all member nations place their forces under the control of one nation. The lead nation command can be distinguished by a dominant lead nation command and staff arrangement with subordinate elements retaining strict national integrity. Regardless of the starting command structure, this is the goal—the HN must ultimately take the lead for COIN to be successful.

(2) **Integrated.** Multinational commands organized under an integrated command structure provide unity of effort in a multinational setting. This command structure often has a strategic commander designated from a member nation, but the strategic command staff and the commanders and staffs of subordinate commands are of multinational makeup. This is the second-best command structure in COIN. The structure is most effective when the HN is viable and has effective political and military establishments.

(3) **Parallel.** Under a parallel command structure, no single force commander is designated. The coalition leadership must develop a means for coordination among the participants to attain unity of effort. This can be accomplished through the use of coordination centers. Nonetheless, because of the absence of a single commander, the use of a parallel command structure should be avoided if at all possible. This may often be the initial conditions for supporting a HN's COIN efforts, although the least favored.

e. **Liaison Officers.** Regardless of the command structure, coalitions and alliances require a significant liaison structure, and liaisons are even more important in COIN in order to coordinate many disparate and highly politically sensitive efforts. For example, the success of COIN hinges upon timely and accurate information and intelligence sharing.

f. **Training.** Training of forces within the coalition for specific mission standards enhances unified action. The coalition should consider establishing common training modules or certification training to ensure assigned forces are trained for the missions assigned. Such training and certification of forces can occur prior to deployment to the theater or after deployment to the theater, although predeployment training is preferred.

For additional detail, see JP 3-16, Multinational Operations.

CHAPTER V
INTELLIGENCE SUPPORT TO COUNTERINSURGENCY

> *"Everything good that happens seems to come from good intelligence."*
>
> **General Creighton W. Abrams Jr., US Army**
> **1970**

1. Purposes of Joint Intelligence in a Counterinsurgency

a. **Inform the Commander.** In a COIN operation, the dynamic relationship between operations and intelligence is particularly important—intelligence drives COIN operations and successful COIN operations generate additional intelligence. The intelligence directorate of a joint staff (J-2) must gather and fuse intelligence and information from a multitude of sources (e.g., HN, multinational, interagency, intergovernmental, nongovernmental, and other sources) and keep all participants informed, often to an even greater degree than in other operations. Intelligence supports the JFC in COIN planning, operations, and assessment. In conjunction with the HN and coalition partners, the J-2 analyzes relevant aspects of the OE and assists the JFC in building a holistic view of the OE. The JFC and J-2 must focus on maintaining the initiative with respect to the insurgents, other adversaries, and the local population.

b. **Identify, Define, and Nominate Objectives.** Military planning is dependent on clearly defined, achievable, and measurable objectives. To do this, the JFC must understand IDAD strategy, the command's responsibilities, the overarching mission, and the means available. Intelligence should provide an understanding of the adversary's probable intention, objectives, strengths, weaknesses, critical vulnerabilities, and human factors. Objectives should be based on adversary critical factors (capabilities, requirements, and vulnerabilities), COGs, strategic approaches, campaign plans, and COAs. Objectives must be agreed upon by the HN, US, and coalition partners. **Once the objectives are agreed upon, the J-2 must continuously review them with respect to the population, the adversary, and the changing situation to determine whether they remain relevant.**

c. **Support the Planning and Execution of Operations.** After the objectives, nature, and scope of COIN operations are determined, intelligence is essential to plan, direct, conduct, and assess operations. Intelligence is crucial to identify and select specific objectives and targets. Intelligence will further enable analysis of desired and undesired effects, and determine means, operations, and tactics to most efficiently achieve overall mission objectives.

d. **Counter Adversary Deception and Surprise.** Despite the apparent weight of indicators and decision maker predisposition, intelligence analysts must remain sensitive to the possibility that they are being deceived. Intelligence analysts should therefore consider all possible adversary capabilities and intentions. For example, an absence of insurgent attacks or suicide bombings does not necessarily mean that the insurgency has been defeated. In fact, it may be that the insurgents have moved to another area, transitioned to an earlier phase of operations, or are preparing to change their focus of activity.

e. **Support Friendly Deception Efforts.** Misleading, deluding, or creating uncertainty in the mind of the adversary—including insurgents—helps achieve security and surprise; however, deception is difficult in COIN due to the need for transparency with the population. Intelligence also supports effective friendly IO, through human factors analysis of the adversary leadership. This analysis can assess insurgent leaders' beliefs, information environment, and decision-making processes. Intelligence personnel also conduct assessments to determine how the adversary is reacting to the friendly deception effort. **The process of identifying deception objectives to complement operational objectives should be an interactive process, with the HN, US, and coalition commanders in a central role orchestrating the efforts of operations and intelligence resources.**

f. **Assess the Effectiveness of Operations.** Intelligence assesses operations' impact on the population, insurgents, and other relevant aspects of the OE. Intelligence should assess whether operations are creating desired or undesired effects, when objectives have been attained, and when unforeseen opportunities can be exploited. **It is fundamental for HN representatives to participate in this process. There must be a balance of indigenous and outside participants to conduct a COIN assessment.**

2. Intelligence-Operations Dynamic and Intelligence Architecture

a. **Intelligence-Operations Dynamic.** As in any joint operation, intelligence and operations have a cyclical relationship. **This dynamic relationship is particularly important in COIN—intelligence drives operations and successful operations generate additional intelligence.** The reverse is also true. COIN efforts conducted without accurate intelligence may alienate the population, which results in their offering less information. Because intelligence and operations are so closely related, it is important for collectors to be linked directly to the analysts and operators they support. Similarly, analysts must remain responsive to their supported units' intelligence requirements. Collectors should not passively wait for operators to submit requirements; rather, they should closely monitor the OE and recommend requirements based on their understanding of operators' needs.

b. **Architecture.** An inclusive intelligence infrastructure must be created to provide the best possible intelligence. The joint force intelligence architecture required to support the COIN must be designed during the intelligence planning process and subsequently refined. The intelligence architecture must meet the demanding intelligence and operational requirements of COIN, especially the intelligence-operations dynamic. The same level of emphasis should be used on designing the intelligence architecture as traditionally has been done for other functions, such as task organization and C2. **Due to the imperative for operations-intelligence fusion in COIN, JTF commanders may consider fusion cells and other solutions that enable operations and intelligence to work more closely together in a dynamic relationship.**

(1) **Considerations.** There are many considerations for the intelligence architecture. Intelligence tasks and purposes must be defined, collection systems and sensors identified, an informational architecture established, and asset tasking authority determined. JFCs should address how to support their subordinate commanders with intelligence assets. All echelons must have the intelligence assets to properly analyze and understand their environment, including diagnosing key local system elements and how to best affect them. Subordinate commanders must have the capability to push their intelligence throughout the joint force, especially to higher echelons from those directly interacting with the population. All units in COIN are generating their own intelligence, and they must strive to effectively share it. Every participant in COIN should be viewed as a collector, and collectors and analysts must be tailored to meet the adversary. The hierarchy and reporting responsibilities of each intelligence organization should be clearly defined, and direction given to nontraditional collectors.

(2) **Interagency Considerations.** The compression of the strategic, operational, and tactical levels of war in COIN requires that control of strategic intelligence assets be pushed down or made easily accessible to the operational and tactical levels. Joint force intelligence and operations staffs should include representatives from the intelligence community. Tactical units in COIN benefit from direct connection to strategic intelligence community assets. Physical teaming of civilian and military intelligence assets in the field is preferable to traditional hierarchical reachback coordination, which is not responsive enough in a COIN environment.

(3) **Responsiveness.** Given the dynamic nature of COIN, the intelligence architecture must be responsive to the changing OE and resultant changes to intelligence requirements. The intelligence architecture should remain flexible as operations progress, especially to realign with any changes to the commander's intent and main effort. Regular liaison between all intelligence organizations should be conducted, and the frequency should reflect the tempo of operations.

(4) **Multinational Considerations.** Foreign disclosure guidelines could be a significant constraint to intelligence sharing with allies. Intelligence staffs should sanitize collected intelligence and downgrade material so that it is releasable to coalition partners in accordance with the foreign disclosure policy. This is important in maintaining the integrity of a common holistic understanding of the OE. Other nations are also likely to have access to their own national intelligence and should be encouraged to share across coalition elements.

3. Principles of Intelligence Operations in Counterinsurgency

Intelligence efforts in COIN must assist with fighting insurgency as well as developing the intelligence needed to address the root causes and grievances fueling the insurgency. Intelligence must be "fought" actively. Intelligence gaps and information requirements determined during joint intelligence preparation of the operational environment (JIPOE) may range from insurgent leaders' locations, to the populace's perceptions of insurgents, to HN political parties' status. In general, collection focuses on the populace, insurgents, and HN. Several factors are particularly important for ISR operations in COIN environments, including: a focus on the local population, collection occurring at all echelons, localized nature of insurgencies, all counterinsurgents prepared to function as potential collectors, and insurgent use of complex terrain. Given the potential challenges faced by intelligence assets in collecting information against insurgent networks, counterinsurgents must effectively employ all available intelligence collection capabilities.

a. **Bottom-Up Intelligence Flow.** The fact that all units collect and report information, combined with the mosaic nature of insurgencies, means that the intelligence flow in COIN is more bottom up than top down. Conducting aggressive ISR operations and pushing intelligence collection assets and analysts to the lowest tactical level possible benefits all echelons. It strengthens local intelligence, enhances regional and national reporting, and bolsters operations at all levels.

b. **Collection.** Collection may occur in any unit and collectors may be pushed to the lowest levels, which is essential in COIN. Nonetheless, the overall intelligence plan must remain synchronized so that all echelons receive the intelligence they require. There are several means of ensuring this happens. One is to ensure that priority intelligence requirements (PIRs) are nested at all echelons. PIRs must be articulated clearly by the commander to ensure limited assets are employed against the right efforts and focused on the insurgent dynamics. Headquarters monitor requests for information from lower echelons and taskings from higher echelons to get information to requestors when they need it.

c. **Feedback.** Feedback from analysts and intelligence consumers to collectors is important to synchronizing the ISR effort in COIN. Responses tell collectors that a report is of interest and that they should follow it up. Such feedback may come from any unit at any echelon but often comes from the bottom up in COIN. Also affecting intelligence synchronization is the requirement to work closely with USG agencies, HN security and intelligence organizations, and multinational intelligence organizations.

d. **Intelligence Collection Considerations.** Because all counterinsurgents are potential collectors, the collection plan addresses all day-to-day tactical operations. This means every patrol or mission should be given intelligence collection requirements as well as operations requirements. There are two types of reconnaissance and surveillance: overt and covert. Overt and covert reconnaissance and surveillance are excellent means to learn more about the OE; however, covert these types of reconnaissance and surveillance operations are often ineffective in places where the populace is alert and suspicious of outsiders. Therefore, using a HUMINT network or aerial imagery platforms is often preferable to ground reconnaissance and surveillance. Persistent aerial surveillance can often identify people, vehicles, and buildings—even when they are hidden under heavy growth. Manned and unmanned aircraft can patrol roads to locate the emplacement activities of insurgent ambushes and IEDs.

e. **Nontraditional ISR Assets.** Commanders should consider use of assets not traditionally used for ISR to fill gaps in ISR coverage; however, using assets for missions they were not intended must be weighed against any negative impact on their primary mission. Assets not traditionally used for ISR can fulfill intelligence requirements in denied areas or provide real-time imaging allowing platforms to directly communicate with ground forces in order to engage targets based on this real-time intelligence. Commanders should ensure intelligence from nontraditional assets is fused with other analytical efforts in order to maintain the appropriate situational awareness. Open-source intelligence (OSINT) is often more useful than any other discipline for understanding public attitudes and public support for insurgents and counterinsurgents. OSINT is also an important means of determining the effectiveness of IO. Monitoring all available media, e.g., radio, television (TV), Internet, in multiple languages benefits the COIN effort. Each echelon should submit collection requirements to monitor open source material that satisfies their requirements. Reporting by major news networks often provides information pertinent to the combatant command level; in contrast, local newspapers or radio stations may be more relevant to tactical units. OSINT must be evaluated for bias, including who owns and/or controls a specific media (government, pro-insurgent, foreign-owned).

For more information on OSINT, see JP 2-0, Joint Intelligence, *Appendix B,* Intelligence Disciplines.

4. Intelligence Disciplines

Intelligence disciplines are core competencies of the intelligence community involved in intelligence planning, collection, processing, exploitation, analysis, production, and dissemination using a specific category of technical or human resources. While the JP 2-0 series provides a comprehensive discussion of intelligence doctrinal fundamentals and principles this paragraph will highlight some issues specific to COIN.

a. **Geospatial Intelligence (GEOINT).** GEOINT can be crucial to successful COIN operations. GEOINT is the combination of imagery, the intelligence derived from imagery, and geospatial information. Together, they provide the ability to visualize the OE and establish a shared situational awareness picture. It aids in identifying facilities and structures, finding and fixing potential adversaries, and warning of possible hostile action. The National Geospatial-Intelligence Agency (NGA) is a national asset in this area, and is a civil-military agency. NGA analysts frequently deploy in support of military operations with support teams or individuals embedded in both intelligence and operations staff sections at JTFs.

(1) **Imagery.** Imagery is a likeness or presentation of any natural or man-made feature or related object or activity and the positional data acquired at the same time the likeness or representation was acquired. Imagery platforms are vital for surveillance and detection of insurgent activities and locales. Static imagery, such as aerial photos of facilities, is useful for detecting long-term changes in structures or activities. Similarly, full motion video, in concert with other sensors, are critical to assessing whether

particular locations are likely sites of insurgent activity. This capability may also be used to track insurgents during operations. If flown high enough that insurgents cannot hear the platform, real-time video provides surveillance in areas where it is difficult or impossible to use observation posts.

(2) **Imagery Intelligence (IMINT).** IMINT is the technical, geographic, and intelligence information derived through the interpretation or analysis of imagery and collateral materials. IMINT provides the who, what, and why of facilities, buildings, or equipment identified on imagery.

(3) **Geospatial Information.** Geospatial information identifies the geographic location and characteristics of natural or constructed features and boundaries on the Earth. Geospatial information is the basic data used to produce maps and charts, which facilitate spatial visualization of the OE. It also includes social and cultural data for characterization of the population occupying the OE.

GEOINT is addressed in detail in JP 2-03, Geospatial Intelligence Support to Joint Operations.

b. **Human Intelligence.** HUMINT is a category of intelligence derived from information collected and provided by human sources. HUMINT operations often collect information that is difficult or sometimes impossible to obtain by other, more technical, means. **During COIN operations, actionable intelligence is often based on information gathered from people. Analysts and HUMINT collectors should work closely with operations staffs and other personnel to ensure sources are properly exploited and that potential new sources are identified. Although any counterinsurgent can provide intelligence information from observations, only trained and certified HUMINT collectors can conduct HUMINT collection operations.**

(1) **Source Operations.** Designated and fully trained DOD HUMINT collection personnel may develop information through the elicitation of sources. Establishing a reliable source network is an effective collection method. Source operations provide the COIN equivalent of the reconnaissance and surveillance conducted by scouts in conventional operations. People are a significant source of intelligence information during COIN operations. The urban populace, in particular, should be a focus of HUMINT operations. HUMINT sources serve as "eyes and ears" on the street and provide an early warning system for tracking insurgent activity. All counterinsurgents should report information given to them by walk-up contacts (one time voluntary sources), including liaison relationships, but they may not develop recurring HUMINT sources or networks. Biometric data and intelligence from technical intelligence (TECHINT) sources such as signals intelligence (SIGINT) may be used to verify HUMINT source identification. Sources include:

(a) **"Walk-in" sources,** who without solicitation make the first contact with HUMINT personnel.

(b) **Developed sources** that are met over a period of time and provide information based on operational requirements.

(c) **Unwitting persons**, with access to sensitive information.

(d) **Protecting Sources.** The lives of people offering information on insurgents are often in danger as insurgents try to defeat collection operations. Careless handling of human sources can result in murder or intimidation of sources. Not only will this result in the loss of a source, but a perception among the population that counterinsurgent forces are careless or callous about protecting sources, whether or not based in truth, will lead to a dramatic reduction in HUMINT. HUMINT collectors are trained in procedures that limit the risk to sources and handlers. HUMINT reporting may increase if counterinsurgents protect the populace from insurgents. Analysts and leaders must remain aware of the fragile state of HUMINT sources; especially when involving media, interagency organizations, and NGOs during COIN operations.

(e) **Inaccuracies.** People may provide inaccurate and conflicting information to counterinsurgents. They may be spreading rumors or providing inaccurate information purposefully for their own reasons. Sources from the general population should be vetted to determine how trustworthy they may be; then the accuracy of information should be verified before being used to support operations. This means that reported information should be verified with information gained from other intelligence disciplines and fused into all-source intelligence products. Examples of reasons for giving false information include: using counterinsurgents to settle tribal, ethnic, or business disputes; leading counterinsurgents into ambushes; enticing counterinsurgents into executing operations that upset the populace; learning about US planning time and tactics; and stretching COIN forces thin by causing them to react to false reports.

(2) **Interrogation.** Interrogation is the systematic direct and indirect questioning of a person in the custody of joint or HN COIN forces to procure information to answer specific collection requirements. Proper questioning of guerrillas, insurgents, or other detainees by trained and certified DOD interrogators may obtain information, provided voluntarily or inadvertently.

There are important legal restrictions on interrogation and source operations. Federal law and Department of Defense policy require that these operations be carried out only by specifically trained and certified personnel. Violators may be punished under the Uniform Code of Military Justice.

(3) **Debriefing.** Debriefing is the process of interviewing cooperating human sources to satisfy intelligence requirements, consistent with applicable law. Through debriefing, face-to-face meetings, conversations, and elicitation, information may be obtained from a variety of human sources, including the general populace, friendly forces, dislocated civilians (DCs), detainees, defectors, and repatriated forces.

(4) **Interrogation of Detainees and Debriefing of Defectors.** Both detainees and defectors should be thoroughly questioned on all aspects of an insurgency discussed in Chapter II, "Insurgency." Their answers should be considered along with information obtained from captured equipment, pocket litter, and documents to build a better understanding of the insurgency. Properly trained personnel can conduct immediate tactical questioning of detainees or defectors. However, only trained HUMINT personnel are legally authorized to conduct interrogations. A trained debriefer should be used for questioning a defector. All questioning of detainees is conducted to comply with US law and regulation, international law, execute orders, and other operationally specific guidelines.

(5) **Collection of Evidence.** Procedures that ensure captured equipment and documents are tracked accurately and attached to the correct insurgents are necessary. Evidence needs to be enough to justify using operational resources to apprehend the individuals in question; however, it does not necessarily need be enough to convict in a court of law. Assigning HUMINT or law enforcement personnel to the lowest possible echelons can improve target, document, and media exploitation by tactical units. Tactical units must receive intelligence collected and exploited from the documents, equipment, and personnel they capture in a timely manner.

(6) **Document and Media Exploitation.** Captured documents and media, when properly processed and exploited, may provide valuable information for COIN. These sources may provide insight into insurgent plans and intentions, force locations, equipment capabilities, and logistical status. This category includes all media capable of storing fixed information to include computer storage material. This operation can provide critical information that analysts need to evaluate insurgent organizations, capabilities, and intentions, as well as provide a great benefit to HUMINT collectors in substantiating what detainees know and whether they are telling the truth.

(7) **Human Intelligence Teams.** Dedicated HUMINT teams with appropriate cultural and linguistic skills and/or interpreters are vital to successful COIN. This is especially true if COIN efforts involve large multinational forces operating amongst the population in support of a HN's COIN efforts. These teams are normally low density and have a large impact, so their use must be carefully planned and managed. HUMINT teams and other similar groups often have force protection and sustainment requirements that must be addressed.

(8) **Interpreters.** In many environments, HUMINT collectors without the proper language skills and/or cultural knowledge are severely constrained and require the support of interpreters. Properly trained and cleared interpreters can identify language and culturally based clues that can help confirm the validity of information from sources as well as assist the collector with cultural issues.

(9) **Human Intelligence and Geospatial Intelligence.** HUMINT and GEOINT information may be combined to produce accurate population information. Local law

enforcement officials are crucial sources of information regarding criminal organizations, individuals, activities, areas, and methods. Combining HUMINT and GEOINT intelligence from multiple sources can produce network analysis diagrams and corresponding geospatial products that are particularly important for successful COIN operations. Figure V-1 depicts a notional example of one of these products.

HUMINT is addressed in detail in JP 2-01.2, Counterintelligence and Human Intelligence Support to Joint Operations.

c. **Signals Intelligence.** SIGINT is intelligence produced by exploiting foreign communications systems and noncommunications emitters. SIGINT collection is a good

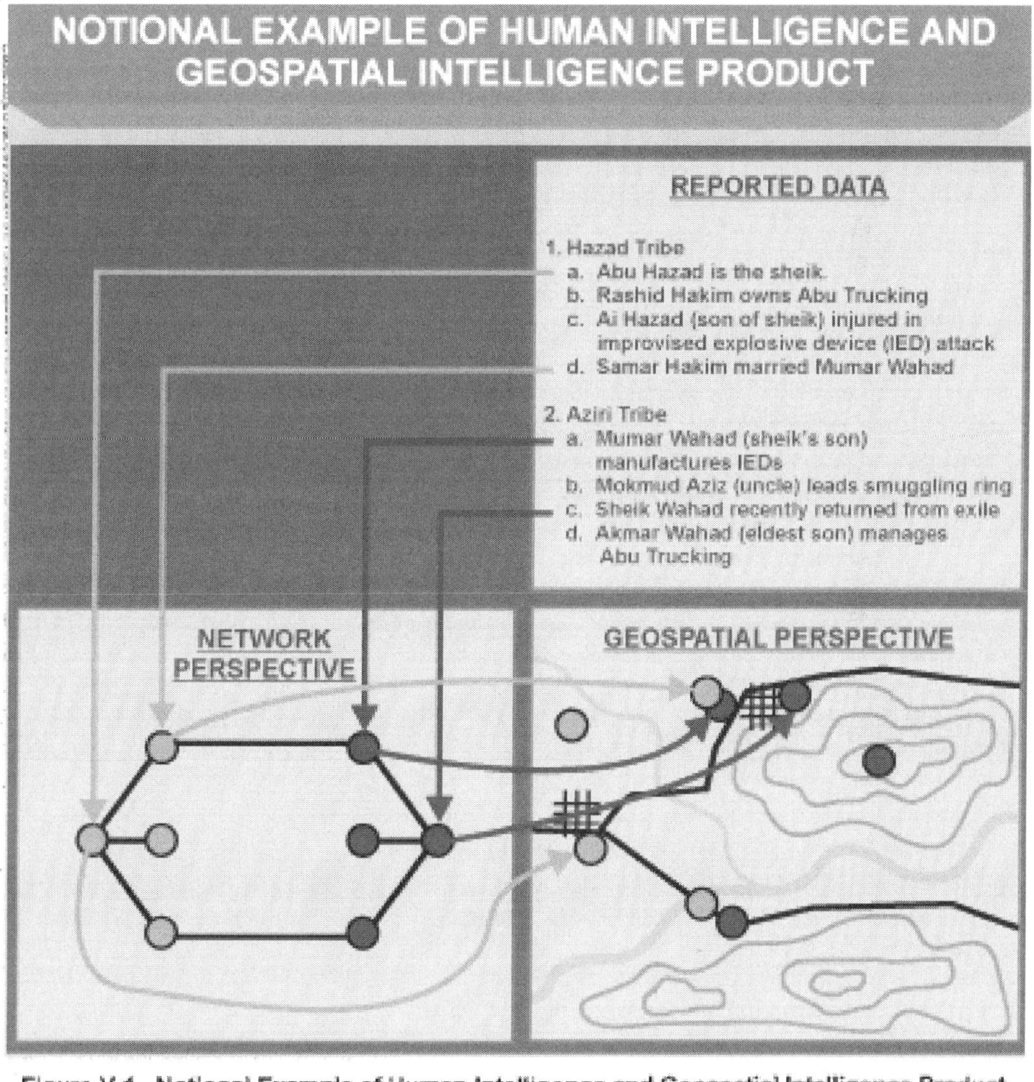
NOTIONAL EXAMPLE OF HUMAN INTELLIGENCE AND GEOSPATIAL INTELLIGENCE PRODUCT
REPORTED DATA
1. Hazad Tribe
a. Abu Hazad is the sheik.
b. Rashid Hakim owns Abu Trucking
c. Ai Hazad (son of sheik) injured in improvised explosive device (IED) attack
d. Samar Hakim married Mumar Wahad
2. Aziri Tribe
a. Mumar Wahad (sheik's son) manufactures IEDs
b. Mokmud Aziz (uncle) leads smuggling ring
c. Sheik Wahad recently returned from exile
d. Akmar Wahad (eldest son) manages Abu Trucking
NETWORK PERSPECTIVE
GEOSPATIAL PERSPECTIVE

Figure V-1. Notional Example of Human Intelligence and Geospatial Intelligence Product

source for determining adversary locations, intentions, capabilities, and morale. This is especially important if an area is under insurgent control. SIGINT is often helpful for confirming or denying HUMINT reporting and may be the primary source of intelligence in areas under insurgent control. SIGINT provides unique intelligence information, complements intelligence derived from other sources, and is often used for cueing other sensors to potential targets of interest. The conduct of SIGINT operations against US persons or in the US raises substantial policy and legal concerns and should be vetted by legal personnel.

(1) **Communications Intelligence (COMINT).** COMINT is intelligence and technical information derived from collecting and processing intercepted foreign communications passed by radio, wire, or other electromagnetic means. COMINT can also include computer network exploitation, which is gathering data from target or adversary automated information systems or networks. COMINT also may include imagery, when pictures or diagrams are encoded by a computer network/radio frequency method for storage and/or transmission. The imagery can be static or streaming, to include transmission of messages embedded in pictures sent across computer networks via electronic mail (i.e., steganography).

(2) **Electronic Intelligence (ELINT).** ELINT is intelligence derived from the interception and analysis of noncommunications emitters such as radar. ELINT provides locational data by emitter type and can be useful in conducting nodal analysis.

(3) **Foreign Instrumentation Signals Intelligence (FISINT).** FISINT involves the technical analysis of data intercepted from foreign equipment and control systems such as telemetry, electronic interrogators, tracking/fusing/arming/firing command systems, and video data links.

d. **Measurement and Signature Intelligence (MASINT).** MASINT is scientific and TECHINT obtained by quantitative and qualitative analysis of data (metric, angle, spatial, wavelength, time dependence, modulation, plasma, and hydromagnetic) derived from specific technical sensors for the purpose of identifying any distinctive features associated with the target, source, emitter, or sender. MASINT is also derived from imagery to detect spatial change over time or movement using infrared or other forms of technical means. MASINT sensors can provide remote monitoring of avenues of approach or border regions for smugglers or insurgents. They can also be used to locate insurgent safe havens and cache sites and determining insurgent activities and capabilities. MASINT can also contribute to targeting.

For more information on MASINT, see JP 2-0, Joint Intelligence, *Appendix B,* Intelligence Disciplines.

e. **Civil Information Management (CIM).** Civil information is information developed from data about civil areas, structures, capabilities, organizations, people, and events (ASCOPE) that can be fused or processed to increase interagency, IGO, and NGO situational awareness. It is a CA planning consideration. CIM is the process whereby civil information is collected, entered into a central database, and fused with the supported JFC, higher headquarters, DOD and joint intelligence organizations, other USG and DOD agencies, NGOs, and the private sector to ensure the timely availability of information for analysis and the widest possible dissemination of the raw and analyzed civil information to military and nonmilitary partners. With the rise of the importance of CMO to HUMINT and the concept of "cultural intelligence," the role of CMO in the JIPOE process has likewise accelerated. Through civil-military liaison activities such as key leader engagement and its CMOC and CIM functions, CA can contribute significantly as an information source for JIPOE.

For more discussion on CIM, see JP 3-57, Civil-Military Operations.

f. **Technical Intelligence.** TECHINT assesses the capabilities and vulnerabilities of captured military materiel and provides detailed assessments of foreign technological threat capabilities, limitations, and vulnerabilities. Insurgents often adapt their tactics, techniques, and procedures (TTP) rapidly. TECHINT on insurgent equipment can help understand insurgent capabilities. These may include how insurgents are using IEDs, homemade mortars, and other pieces of customized military equipment.

For more information on TECHINT, see JP 2-0, Joint Intelligence, *Appendix B,* Intelligence Disciplines.

g. **Counterintelligence.** CI counters or neutralizes intelligence collection efforts through collection, CI investigations, operations, analysis and production, and functional and technical services. CI is especially important in COIN to prevent insurgent infiltration into HN and other areas. CI includes all actions taken to detect, identify, exploit, and neutralize the multidiscipline intelligence activities of competitors, opponents, adversaries, and enemies.

(1) **Vetting.** Background screenings should include collection of personal and biometric data and a search through available reporting databases to determine whether the person is an insurgent. Biometric concerns the measurement and analysis of unique physical or behavioral characteristics such as fingerprints or voice patterns. Identification badges may be useful for providing security and personnel accountability for local people working on US and HN government facilities. Biometric data is preferable, when available, because identification badges may be forged or stolen and insurgents can use them to identify people working with the HN government.

(2) **Insurgent Intelligence.** Insurgents place heavy emphasis on gathering intelligence. They use informants, double agents, reconnaissance, surveillance, open-source media, and open-source imagery. Insurgents can potentially use any person interacting with HN, US, or multinational personnel as informants. These include the same people that US forces use as potential HUMINT sources. OPSEC is thus very important; US personnel must carefully screen personnel working with them. Failure to do so can result in infiltration of US facilities and deaths of US personnel and their partners.

(a) **Insurgent Reconnaissance and Surveillance.** Insurgents have their own reconnaissance and surveillance networks. Because they usually blend well with the populace, insurgents can execute reconnaissance without easily being identified. They also have an early warning system composed of citizens who inform them of counterinsurgent movements. Identifying the techniques and weaknesses of enemy reconnaissance and surveillance enables commanders to detect signs of insurgent preparations and to surprise insurgents by neutralizing their early warning systems. Thus, sophisticated counter ISR efforts may be required.

(b) **Insurgent Signals Intelligence.** Insurgents may also have a SIGINT capability based on commercially available scanners and radios, wiretaps, or captured counterinsurgent equipment. Counterinsurgents should not use commercial radios or phones because insurgents can collect information from them. If counterinsurgents must use commercial equipment or unencrypted communications, they should employ authorized brevity codes to reduce insurgents' ability to collect on them. However, joint forces conducting CMO will likely require commercial equipment as their primary means of communicating with representatives of the HN or NGOs in the conduct of their day to day activities. Severely limiting this capability will result in a degraded CMO effort. Counterinsurgents must be careful to exercise OPSEC protocols when utilizing commercial equipment to communicate.

CI is addressed in detail in JP 2-01.2, Counterintelligence and Human Intelligence Support to Joint Operations.

5. All-Source Intelligence

The multidisciplinary (HUMINT, IMINT, GEOINT, SIGINT, FISINT, MASINT, OSINT) fusion of information by intelligence organizations at all echelons results in the production of all-source intelligence products. Analysis for COIN operations is very challenging, due in part to the need to understand perceptions and culture, the need to track hundreds or thousands of personalities, the local nature of insurgencies, and the tendency of insurgencies to change over time.

a. **Analysts at the Tactical Level.** Intelligence requirements supporting COIN require staffing tactical units with intelligence analysts. This is necessary due to the requirement to collect and analyze large amounts of information on the local population and insurgents. Pushing analysts to the lowest tactical level places analysts closer to collectors and improves holistic understanding of the OE. Intelligence analysis at the tactical level supports operational-level intelligence. This is due to the bottom-up flow of intelligence. Tactical units develop intelligence for their operational areas and higher echelons fuse this information into theater-wide intelligence analysis of the insurgency. Operational-level intelligence also fuses relevant strategic intelligence from national-level intelligence organizations.

b. **Current Operations Analysis.** Current operations intelligence supports a commander's understanding of what insurgents are currently doing. The basic tasks of analysts working in current operations are to analyze past and current enemy actions to look for changes in the insurgents' approach, operation or campaign plan, or tactics; track the impact of friendly operations on the populace and insurgents; provide intelligence support to ongoing operations; and disseminate immediate threat warnings to appropriate consumers. Intelligence for current operations comes from a variety of sources, but operations reports are particularly important. This is because current enemy activities are more often reported by patrols, units conducting raids, or observation posts than they are by dedicated intelligence collectors. Current operations analysis depends on the insurgent actions database for determining changes in insurgent tactics and techniques.

c. **Comprehensive Insurgency Analysis.** Accurate and thorough intelligence on insurgent organizations, leadership, financial support networks, and the OE contribute to more effective friendly operations. Comprehensive insurgency analysis integrates a range of analytic tools to develop this intelligence. These tools include automated software which can aid in link, time, and pattern analysis. Comprehensive insurgency analysis provides information for the commanders and staffs. Effective development and the integration of information from a range of intelligence and operations sources provides the detailed knowledge and insights required to exploit insurgents' vulnerabilities, as well as mitigate their strengths.

(1) **Time and Level of Detail.** Developing knowledge and using network analytic tools requires an unusually large investment of time compared to conventional analytic problem-solving methods. Comprehensive insurgency analysis may not provide immediately usable intelligence. Analysts may have to spend weeks or months analyzing numerous all-source intelligence reports before providing an accurate picture of insurgent groups, leaders, and activities.

(2) **Comprehensive Insurgency Analysis Teams.** It is essential that commanders designate a group of analysts to perform comprehensive insurgency analysis. This team must be insulated from the short-term demands of current operations and day-to-day intelligence demands. These analysts focus on long-term intelligence development. It is ultimately the commander's responsibility to ensure that comprehensive and basic insurgent network analysis still occurs despite high-profile demands and time-sensitive requirements.

d. **Reachback.** Reachback refers to the process of obtaining products, services, applications, forces, equipment, or material from organizations that are not forward-deployed. This is vital for COIN as it leads to an improved understanding of the OE, especially the population, its core grievances, and insurgents. Deployed or deploying units should use reachback capabilities to "outsource" time-intensive aspects of analysis.

e. **Analytic Continuity.** The complexity and difficulty of analyzing the COIN OE, especially insurgents, means it often requires months to understand the nuances of the OE holistically. The most productive analysts and action officers generally have more than a year focused on an aspect of the insurgency problem. Commanders should therefore try to maintain continuity among their analysts.

6. Factors Effecting Intelligence Collaboration

Effective intelligence collaboration organizes the collection and analysis actions of counterinsurgent organizations into a coherent, mutually supportive intelligence effort. The intelligence portion of understanding the OE and other supporting intelligence for COIN operations is complex. It is important not to oversimplify an insurgency.

a. **Complexity.** Insurgencies are often localized; however, most have national or international aspects to them. This characteristic complicates intelligence collaboration between adjacent units and among various echelons. A common database based on intelligence reporting is a prerequisite for effective intelligence fusion. Also complicating collaboration is that COIN involves many government agencies and foreign security forces. Analysts must establish good working relationships with various agencies and elements to ensure they can fuse intelligence.

b. **Intelligence Cells and Working Groups.** Intelligence officers form working groups or boards to synchronize COIN collection, analysis, and targeting efforts. Cells and working groups conduct regular meetings to establish and maintain a shared understanding of the OE and situational awareness, share collection priorities, deconflict activities and operations, discuss target development, and share results of operations.

c. **Intelligence Sharing.** The effective use and sharing of intelligence information in a COIN environment is key to successful operations. The commander must establish and maintain reliable networks with which to share critical operational intelligence among all echelons and partners. However, information about sources and methods for obtaining that intelligence is extremely sensitive and should not be shared with allies and coalition partners unless cleared to do so by the appropriate national level agency. In many cases, the commander uses a tiered approach to information sharing; involving two or more levels of intelligence cleared for release to coalition allies and partners, according to the level of trust involved.

d. **Host-Nation Integration.** COIN operations require US personnel to work closely with the HN. Sharing intelligence with HN security forces and government personnel is an important and effective means of supporting their COIN efforts. HN intelligence should be considered useful but definitely not the only intelligence available. It is essential for US intelligence personnel to evaluate HN intelligence capabilities and offer training as required.

e. **Infiltration of Host-Nation Intelligence.** Infiltration of HN security forces by insurgents or foreign intelligence services can create drawbacks to intelligence sharing. Insurgents may learn what is known about them, gain insight into COIN intelligence sources and capabilities, and get early warning of targeting efforts. When sharing intelligence with the HN, it is important to understand the level of infiltration by insurgents or foreign intelligence services. Insofar as possible, intelligence should be tailored so required intelligence still gets to HN consumers but does not give away information about sources and capabilities. In addition, care is needed when providing targeting information; it should be done such that insurgents do not receive early warning of an upcoming operation. As trust develops between HN and US personnel, the amount of intelligence shared should grow. This will make the COIN effort more effective.

Intentionally Blank

CHAPTER VI
SUPPORTING OPERATIONS FOR COUNTERINSURGENCY

> *"It's not necessarily the insurgent, the individual, that you focus on, but what the insurgents are doing – their means to accomplish their ends. That's what you are really going after. Some insurgents cloak themselves in a noble cause, but their objective is more about power and control. As information warriors, we have to expose the façade. We need to understand what is sensitive to our adversary, and work that to discredit their means."*
>
> **Deirdre Collings and Rafal Rohozinski**
> **Shifting Fire, Conference Report, 2006**

SECTION A. INFORMATION OPERATIONS

1. General

a. **Overview.** IO employ capabilities that will significantly contribute to the achievement of the end state. A strong IO plan when integrated effectively in military operations will (1) assist the HN government in acquiring control of legitimate social, political, economic and security institution; (2) marginalize or separate both physically and psychologically insurgency and its leaders from the population; and help demobilize and reintegrate armed insurgents forces into the political, economic and social structures of the population. Specifically, IO focuses on influencing the population's perception of events and the HN's legitimacy, as well as insurgent decisions and decision-making processes.

b. **Information Environment.** The information environment is made up of three interrelated dimensions: physical, informational, and cognitive. All of the dimensions are important for COIN, but the cognitive dimension is vital for COIN. **The cognitive dimension is normally where COIN success is determined—in the HN population's perception of legitimacy.** It is also vital to understand that the information environment in COIN is dynamic. The free flow of information present in all theaters via television, telephone, and Internet, can present conflicting messages that quickly defeat the intended effects. To preclude unintended effects, continuous synchronization and coordination between IO, PA, public diplomacy (PD), and our allies are imperative. This effort will allow information themes employed during operations involving neutral or friendly populations to remain consistent.

For more information on the information environment and its dimensions, see JP 2-01.3, Joint Intelligence Preparation of the Operational Environment, *and JP 3-13,* Information Operations.

For more discussion on IO, see JP 3-13, Information Operations.

c. **Information Superiority and Its Advantages**

(1) The forces possessing better information and using that information to more effectively gain understanding have a major advantage over their adversaries. Counterinsurgents who gain this advantage can use it to accomplish missions by affecting perceptions, attitudes, decisions, and actions. However, information superiority is not static; during COIN, all sides continually attempt to secure their own advantages and deny useful information to adversaries. **IO have a direct impact on the population's perceptions of COIN credibility and legitimacy; consequently, the struggle between counterinsurgents and insurgents will be centered on the population's perception of information.**

(2) Information superiority can be difficult to attain during an insurgency. When it exists, the information available to counterinsurgents allows them to accurately visualize the situation, anticipate events, and make appropriate, timely decisions more effectively than adversary decision makers. In essence, information superiority enhances counterinsurgents' freedom of action and facilitates maintaining the initiative. **However, counterinsurgents must recognize that without continuous IO designed to achieve and maintain information superiority, adversaries may counter those advantages and possibly attain information superiority themselves.** Counterinsurgents can achieve information superiority by maintaining accurate situational understanding while controlling or affecting the adversaries' or TA's perceptions. The more counterinsurgents shape this disparity, the greater the friendly advantage.

d. **Dominant Narrative.** Counterinsurgent leaders must compose a unified message that exploits the negative aspects of the insurgent efforts and reinforces the credibility and legitimacy of the counterinsurgent efforts, which can be referred to as the dominant narrative. The dominant narrative counters insurgent narrative and propaganda. It is vital for counterinsurgents to analyze, advertise, and exploit the differences between accepted cultural norms and the insurgent narrative and propaganda. The dominant narrative must be the result of a painstaking and detailed effort using a comprehensive approach. While the dominant narrative should appeal to a wider audience, it must be shaped and adaptable to appeal to the cultural perspective of the population. The dominant narrative must strike a balance between simplicity for ease of understanding and explain an often complex situation. The dominant narrative also must be adaptive, or it will fail or even be counterproductive. Finally, it assists in managing both expectations and information.

2. Employing Information Operations Capabilities

a. Insurgencies typically succeed or fail based on the support of the population. IO provide COIN with capabilities to influence the population's perceptions of the insurgents' activities and leadership.

b. **Core Capabilities.** IO core capabilities are PSYOP, military deception (MILDEC), OPSEC, and electronic warfare (EW), and computer network operations (CNO). These capabilities are integrated into the planning and execution of operations in the information environment. All capabilities must be synchronized and coordinated to create the effects needed to establish successful conditions of COIN.

(1) **Psychological Operations.** PSYOP has a central role in the achievement of IO objectives in support of COIN. PSYOP must be coordinated with CI, MILDEC, and OPSEC to ensure deconfliction and synchronization. There also must be close cooperation and coordination between PSYOP and PA efforts to maintain credibility with their respective audiences.

For more discussion on PSYOP, JP 3-13.2, Psychological Operations *and JP 3-13,* Information Operations.

(2) **Military Deception.** MILDEC is fundamental to successful IO, but can be difficult in a COIN environment, as COIN efforts need to be transparent to the population. Successful deception of the insurgents that causes resentment amongst the population is counterproductive for long-term success. MILDEC relies upon understanding how insurgent leaders support and plan and how both use information management to support their efforts. This requires a high degree of coordination with all elements of friendly forces' activities in the information environment as well as with physical activities. Each of the core, supporting, and related capabilities has a part to play in the development of successful MILDEC and in maintaining its credibility over time. While PA should not be involved in the provision of false information, it must be aware of the intent and purpose of MILDEC in order not to inadvertently compromise it.

For more discussion on MILDEC, see JP 3-13.4, Military Deception.

(3) **Operations Security.** OPSEC is critical for COIN as insurgent intelligence efforts can be pervasive, substantial, and effective. Good OPSEC denies the insurgent the information needed to correctly assess counterinsurgent capabilities and intentions. To be effective, other types of security must complement OPSEC.

For more discussion on OPSEC, see JP 3-13.3, Operations Security, *and JP 3-13,* Information Operations.

(4) **Electronic Warfare.** EW and other countermeasures are very important in countering IEDs and disrupting insurgent communication networks. EW and related electronic countermeasures alone do not necessarily mean IEDs will be successfully countered.

For more discussion on EW, see JP 3-13.1, Electronic Warfare, *and JP 3-13,* Information Operations.

(5) **Computer Network Operations.** The network infrastructure supporting insurgents and their reliance to disseminate information determine the importance of CNO in IO plans and activities. Insurgents' use of computers and supporting networks offers both opportunities to attack and exploit information and vulnerabilities. To

prevent a similar attack to friendly computer networks, requirements for protection are identified and resolved through computer network defense actions.

For more discussion on CNO or any of the core IO capabilities, see JP 3-13, Information Operations.

c. **Supporting Capabilities.** Capabilities supporting IO include information assurance (IA), physical security, physical attack, CI, and combat camera (COMCAM). These are either directly or indirectly involved in the information environment and contribute to effective IO for COIN. **They must be integrated and coordinated with the core capabilities, but can also serve other wider COIN purposes.**

(1) **Information Assurance.** IA and IO have an operational relationship in which IO are concerned with the coordination of COIN activities in the information environment, while IA protects the electronic and automated portions of the information environment.

(2) **Physical Security.** The physical security process includes determining vulnerabilities to known threats (including insurgent threats), applying appropriate deterrent, control, and denial safeguarding techniques and measures, and responding to changing conditions.

(3) **Physical Attacks.** Physical attacks disrupt, damage, or destroy insurgent targets. Physical attacks can also be used to create or alter insurgent perceptions or drive an adversary to use certain exploitable information systems. Physical attacks can be employed in support of IO as a means of attacking insurgent leaders or other C2 nodes to affect enemy ability to exercise C2. IO capabilities, for example PSYOP, can be employed in support of physical attacks to maximize the effect of the attack on the morale of an insurgency. The integration and synchronization of other COIN efforts with IO through the targeting process is fundamental to long-term success.

(4) **Counterintelligence.** CI analysis offers a view of the insurgent's information-gathering methodology. From this, CI can develop the initial intelligence target opportunities that provide access to the adversary for MILDEC information, PSYOP products, and computer network attack or computer network exploitation efforts.

For more discussion on CI, see Chapter V, "Intelligence Support to Counterinsurgency," *JP 3-13,* Information Operations, *and classified JP 2-01.2,* Counterintelligence and Human Intelligence Support to Joint Operations.

(5) **Combat Camera.** COMCAM is responsible for rapid development and dissemination of products that support strategic and operational IO and COIN objectives.

For more discussion on IO supporting capabilities see JP 3-13, Information Operations.

d. **Related Functions.** There are three related functions, PA, CMO, and defense support to public diplomacy (DSPD), specified as related capabilities for IO in COIN. **These capabilities make significant contributions to IO and COIN and must always be coordinated and integrated with the core and supporting IO capabilities.**

(1) PA's principal focus during COIN operations is to inform domestic and international audiences of COIN to support public information needs. PA and IO must be coordinated and synchronized to ensure consistent themes and messages are communicated to avoid credibility losses. While intents differ, PA and IO ultimately support the dissemination of information, themes, and messages adapted to their audiences. PA contributes to the achievement of objectives, for instance, by countering insurgent misinformation and disinformation through the publication of accurate information. PA also assists OPSEC by ensuring that the media are aware of the implications of a premature release of information.

(2) **Civil-Military Operations.** CMO may include performance by joint forces of activities and functions that are normally the responsibility of local, regional, or national government. The CMO staff has an important role to play in the development of broader IO plans and objectives. Given the accessibility of information to the widest public audiences and the conduct of COIN in open environments, the linkage between CMO and IO objectives is vital.

For more discussion on CMO, see JP 3-57, Civil-Military Operations, *and JP 3-13,* Information Operations.

(3) **Defense Support to Public Diplomacy**. DOD contributes to PD, which includes those overt international information activities of the USG designed to promote US foreign policy objectives by seeking to understand, inform, and influence foreign audiences and opinion makers and by broadening the dialogue between American citizens and institutions and their counterparts abroad. This is a vital USG function for COIN that DOD supports. When approved, PSYOP assets may be employed in support of DSPD as part of security cooperation initiatives or in support of US embassy PD programs. Much of the operational level IO activity conducted in any theater will be directly linked to PD objectives. DSPD requires coordination with both the interagency and among DOD components.

For more discussion on DSPD, see DODD 3600.1, Information Operations (IO), *and JP 3-13,* Information Operations.

3. Planning Information Operations in Counterinsurgency

a. COIN planning should specify a visualization of the IO tasks to be executed in order to create effects necessary to achieve objectives. This includes effects that other planned tasks have in order to support IO and how to sustain unity of the messages. **Planners must also understand the insurgents' IO capabilities and objectives.**

Insurgents will attempt to seize or hold information superiority while striving to undermine COIN IO.

b. **Release and Execution Authority.** IO may involve complex legal and policy issues requiring careful review and national-level coordination and approval; however, it is vital that IO planning in COIN be as rapid and flexible as the insurgent IO, and the population's perception of events is vital.

c. **Vision.** The vision of IO's role in an operation should begin before the specific planning is initiated; it is a vital component of operational art and design for COIN. COIN relies on IO capabilities and must ensure that IO related PIRs and requests for information are given priority for the intelligence products to be ready in time to support the COIN planning, execution, and assessment.

d. **Logical Lines of Operations and Information Operations.** IO must be considered in any COIN plan, and IO are often depicted as a logical lines of operations (LOOs). If IO is a separate logical LOO, the plan must emphasize that the other logical LOOs and the IO LOO are interdependent. Any objective of one of the other LOOs (such as a security logical LOO) must be considered in conjunction with the IO LOO. Some of these other LOOs' objectives will support the IO LOO, IO LOO will support the other LOOs' objectives, and in some cases it will be both. Planners must integrate IO and other efforts to change the conditions necessary to reach the objective. Commanders should ensure that the IO function is not placed within the staff in such a way as to be inaccessible to the intelligence, operations, plans, and CMO staff elements in particular. IO staff officers must work closely with intelligence, plans, operations, and CMO staff to integrate IO into every aspect of the campaign plan and its execution.

e. **Effective Information Operations in COIN.** There are three key considerations when planning IO in COIN.

(1) **Factually Based.** Effective IO and related activities are tailored to the TA's frame of reference utilizing consistent themes, which are based on policy and program guidance. PSYOP manage the local populace's expectations regarding what counterinsurgents can achieve. Themes must be reinforced by actions along all logical LOOs. Making unsubstantiated claims can undermine the long-term credibility and legitimacy of the HN government. Counterinsurgents should never knowingly commit themselves to an action that cannot be completed. However, to reduce the negative effects of a broken promise, counterinsurgents should publicly address the reasons expectations cannot be met before insurgents can take advantage of them. It should be noted that the need to be factually based is a consideration when considering MILDEC operations in COIN.

(2) **Countering Insurgent Propaganda.** Insurgents are not constrained by truth; they create propaganda that furthers their aims. Insurgent propaganda may include lying, deception, and creating false causes. Historically, as the environment changes, insurgents change their message to address the issues that gain them support. IO should

point out the insurgency's propaganda and lies to the local populace. Doing so creates doubt regarding the viability of the insurgents' short- and long-term intentions among the uncommitted public and the insurgency's supporters. In countering insurgent propaganda, the counterinsurgent risks could give validity to insurgent claims or inadvertently provide information to insurgents.

(3) **Impartiality.** Impartiality is a common theme for information activities when there are political, social, and sectarian divisions in the HN. Counterinsurgents should avoid taking sides, when possible. Perceived favoritism can exacerbate civil strife and make counterinsurgents more desirable targets for sectarian violence.

For more discussion on IO, see JP 3-13, Information Operations.

4. Influencing the Population's Perspective Through Psychological Operations

a. By lowering insurgent morale and reducing their efficiency, PSYOP can also discourage aggressive actions and create dissidence and disaffection within insurgent ranks. **When properly employed, PSYOP can reduce the insurgent's will to fight; consequently saving the lives of civilians, friendly forces, and the insurgents themselves.**

b. **Purpose.** The purpose of PSYOP in COIN is to influence foreign audiences in order to induce or reinforce attitudes and behavior that support HN legitimacy and are favorable to the end state, including addressing perceived core grievances, drivers of conflict, and the illegitimacy of the insurgents. PSYOP efforts in COIN are most effective when personnel with a thorough understanding of the language and culture of the TA are included in the review of PSYOP materials and messages. The dissemination of PSYOP includes print, broadcast, Internet, facsimile messaging, text messaging, and other emerging media. However, face-to-face communications are the most effective and preferred method of communicating with local audiences, especially in COIN.

c. **Categories.** There are three categories of military PSYOP: strategic, operational, and tactical, which are used to establish and reinforce foreign perceptions of counterinsurgent credibility and HN legitimacy. Strategic PSYOP are international information activities conducted by USG agencies to influence foreign attitudes, perceptions, and behavior in favor of US goals and objectives during peacetime and in times of conflict. These programs are conducted predominantly outside the military arena but can utilize DOD assets. **Operational PSYOP are in a defined operational area to promote the effectiveness of COIN, and tactical PSYOP are conducted in the area assigned to a tactical commander for COIN tactical efforts.** Tactical PSYOP forces are vital in COIN. They build rapport for US/coalition forces, enhance legitimacy and populace support for the HN, and support ongoing CMO, as well as reduce combat effectiveness of the insurgents.

d. **The Psychological Operations Program.** The PSYOP program forms the legal authority to integrate PSYOP in SecDef approved missions in a theater of operation. The program establishes the parameters for the execution of PSYOP. The components of a PSYOP program provide the necessary guidelines from which to develop and approve PSYOP series to target foreign audiences. The program is staffed and coordinated through the Joint Staff and interagency process and approved by the SecDef to ensure PSYOP products reflect national and theater policy, strategy, and also receive the broadest range of policy considerations.

e. **PSYOP Product Approval.** Under US policy and the PSYOP Supplement to the Joint Strategic Capabilities Plan, PSYOP product approval authority may be sub-delegated by the Under Secretary of Defense for Policy to the GCC and further to the JFC through official message traffic. When required or requested, the SecDef can authorize PSYOP product approval authority to be delegated down to the brigade combat team in order to facilitate responsive PSYOP support. Current policy facilitates decentralized PSYOP execution and allows for continuous data recordings with product approval authority to develop a streamlined time sensitive product approval process. **A JFC must have an approved PSYOP program, execution authority, and delegation of product approval authority before PSYOP execution can begin.**

For more discussion on PSYOP see JP 3-13.2, Psychological Operations, *and JP 3-13,* Information Operations.

f. **Key Leader Engagement.** Commanders often interact directly with local populations and stakeholders through face-to-face meetings, town meetings, and community events highlighting counterinsurgent community improvements. These interactions give commanders additional opportunities to assess their efforts' effectiveness, address community issues and concerns, and personally dispel misinformation. These events often occur in the CMOC. Leader engagement must be included in the overall plan. Dissemination of information by leaders can be vital and help build credibility and HN legitimacy. These meetings should include the media and key leaders within the population. **This interaction should be an ongoing process, it may increase to support certain COIN efforts or to counter insurgent efforts.**

5. Planning Psychological Operations in Counterinsurgency

a. **PSYOP Responsibilities**

(1) Preparing key audiences for USG activities can directly assist the HN in establishing a friendly environment that promotes internal stability and security. PSYOP increase HN support for programs that provide positive populace control and protection from adversary activities. PSYOP forces advise, train, and assist HN counterparts and government agencies to develop and implement effective information activities. In COIN, a PSYOP goal is the development of a HN ability to conduct information activities in support of achieving and maintaining internal security.

(2) Providing the cultural, linguistic, and social expertise required to analyze populations influenced by adversary information. As part of strategic communication

(SC), PSYOP mitigate the effects of adversary information, thus reducing their credibility and access to resources and safe havens.

(3) Integrating with civil affairs operations (CAO) activities to increase support for the HN government and reduce support to destabilizing forces. PSYOP can publicize the existence and successes of CAO to enhance the positive perception of US and HN actions. PSYOP inform and direct civilians concerning safety and welfare to reduce civilian casualties, suffering, and interference with military operations.

(4) Providing personnel to conduct IO staff functions to coordinate, synchronize, and deconflict core, supporting, and related capabilities. PSYOP and IO capabilities are mutually supporting, however, both can be conducted independently. SOF and conventional forces working within the same AOR must synchronize IO activities to prevent duplication of effort and information inconsistencies.

(5) PSYOP can be employed as an economy of force or main effort with a capacity to create effects not possible by physical force alone. In this capacity, PSYOP can increase friendly relative combat power and decrease enemy relative combat power.

b. **PSYOP Officer.** The senior PSYOP officer in the operational area, normally the joint PSYOP task force commander, may also serve as the de facto joint force PSYOP officer. Working through the various component operations staffs, the joint force PSYOP officer ensures continuity of psychological objectives and identifies themes to stress and avoid.

c. **Planning Concepts.** There are four general planning concepts for PSYOP.

(1) **Persuasive Communications.** All communications that systemically convey information with the intent of affecting the perceptions and behaviors of the foreign TA are persuasive communications. These communications are conducted to influence individual beliefs that will change or reinforce attitudes and behaviors. **Persuasive communications are important in COIN as they reinforce counterinsurgent credibility and HN legitimacy.**

(2) **Command Disruption.** Disruption of C2 systems not only directly interferes with the capabilities of an insurgency to succeed in combat but also can have serious impact upon the morale, cohesion, discipline, and public support essential to efficient operations. The effectiveness of these efforts against insurgencies depends upon the accurate analysis of core grievances of the insurgency and the motivation of insurgents. An ideological insurgency will often be a more difficult target for command disruption.

(3) **Counterinformation.** Competing parties systematically can deny opponents information they require to formulate decisions. The DOD Information Security Program establishes procedures to protect classified information, and the

OPSEC program establishes measures to deny unclassified but sensitive indicators of friendly activities, capabilities, and intentions.

(4) **Intelligence Shaping.** It is possible to systematically convey or deny data to opposing intelligence systems with the objective of causing opposing analysts to derive desired judgments. These judgments interact with the perceptions of opposing planners and decision makers to influence estimates upon which capabilities, intentions, and actions are based.

d. **Key Support Roles.** PSYOP can be vital for COIN in support of detainee, civilian internee, and DC operations. In many cases in COIN, joint forces come into close contact with and, in some cases, control people who are demoralized, desperate, apprehensive, and distrustful. These emotions can create a volatile atmosphere that is dangerous to counterinsurgents and those civilians and detainees being managed, handled, or interned. **PSYOP can be used to dispel rumors, create dialogue, and pacify or inform detainees, civilian internees, or DCs to minimize violence, facilitate efficient camp operations, and ensure safe and humane conditions persist.** PSYOP forces also may use this function to facilitate other PSYOP tasks. These tasks include testing informational PSYOP materials, assessing the culture of potential audiences, collecting intelligence, and recruiting key communicators, informants, and collaborators.

e. **Target Groups.** PSYOP TAs are approved by the SecDef. Messages are tailored to specific TAs each addressing a specific behavior.

(1) **Insurgents.** PSYOP should aim to create dissension or exploit existing divisions, disorganization, low morale, subversion, and defection within insurgent forces, as well as help discredit them internally and externally. These efforts must be closely planned and coordinated with amnesty and defector programs. Insurgent defection or desertion can be devastating to the morale and effectiveness of the insurgents who remain.

(2) **Host-nation Civilian Population.** PSYOP can gain, preserve, and strengthen civilian support for the HN government and its COIN programs. This may include projecting a favorable image of the HN government and the United States. These PSYOP efforts may also include supporting HN programs that protect the population from insurgent activities and strengthening HN support of programs that provide positive population control and protection from insurgent activities. **These efforts can be vital to help gain and maintain a perception of HN legitimacy.**

(3) **Military Forces.** PSYOP can strengthen military support, with emphasis on building and maintaining the morale of the HN forces. **This can be vital to SFA efforts, including retention and recruitment.** It can include providing close and continuous support to CMO.

(4) **Neutral Elements.** PSYOP can gain the support of uncommitted groups inside and outside the HN. This includes discrediting the insurgent forces with neutral

groups and informing the international community of HN and US intent and goodwill. **These PSYOP efforts also undermine external support for the insurgency.**

(5) **External Hostile Powers.** PSYOP can convince hostile foreign TAs that the insurgency will fail. This often includes bordering powers that are actively supporting the insurgency. Diminishing this support can have a significant impact on the insurgency. **This is especially true when PSYOP are combined with strategic physical isolation of the insurgency.**

SECTION B. PUBLIC AFFAIRS AND MEDIA SUPPORT TO COUNTERINSURGENCY

6. General

a. Public opinion, perceptions, media, public information, and rumors influence how the populace perceives the HN legitimacy. PA shapes the information environment through public information activities and facilitates media access to preempt, neutralize, or counter adversary disinformation efforts.

b. To effectively communicate with the intended audience, it is necessary to understand the cognitive dimension of the insurgency and how it pervades the OE's social, political, informational, and other systems that support its success.

7. Public Affairs Focus

a. PA activities are critical for informing and influencing the populace's understanding and perceptions of events. Insurgents and counterinsurgents know that popular perception and support, both locally and globally are important considerations for success. Consequently, open and honest communication with the population is desirable during COIN operations.

b. In their planning, the public affairs officer (PAO) supports the commander's COIN objectives through the communication of truthful, timely, and factual unclassified information about joint military activities within the operational area to foreign, domestic, and internal audiences.

c. PA provides public information targeting audiences to influence their perceptions. The timely and accurate release of factual information helps to deter propaganda, misinformation and disinformation.

d. The primary emphasis of the PA assessment is identifying, measuring, and evaluating the implications of the information environment that the commander does not control, but can influence through a coherent, comprehensive strategy and early integration in the planning and decision-making process. Analyzing the relevant information (media coverage, Internet content, polls, intelligence products, etc.) will also determine the success of PA activities.

(1) The PA staff collaborates with pertinent members of the joint force staff (SC, CA, PSYOP, intelligence, etc.) on assessment development.

(2) The PAO must provide the JFC with an assessment of public support within the operational area and provide timely feedback on trends in public opinion based on media analysis, published polling data, and professional assessments.

(3) Based on assessments, the PAO advises the commander on the implications of command decisions on public perception and operations, media events and activities, and the development and dissemination of the command information message.

8. Public Affairs Relationships with Related Functions

a. **Actions, Images, and Words.** The information environment is influenced by a combination of actions, images and words. PA must coordinate with other stakeholders that influence the information environment to ensure consistency in actions, images and words. Coordination and synchronization of themes and messages for both strategic and operational approaches to COIN is essential.

b. **Coordination and Synchronization.** Consistency, accuracy and dissemination of information, themes, and messages adapted to various audiences require close planning, coordination and deconfliction with other related functions such as IO, CMO and DSPD.

(1) **Information Operations.** As a related function, IO themes and messages should be synchronized with PA activities. In that both IO and PA shape the information environment, through their own capabilities, close coordination must occur during COIN planning to preclude unintended effects.

(2) **Civil Military Operation and Community Engagement.** PA provides specialized skills in planning and developing relationships and interaction within local communities while conducting operations. PA should be involved in the planning, preparation and execution of engagements within the local/HN communities to support the CMO plan.

(3) **Defense Support to Public Diplomacy.** PA activities should be planned and coordinated with any other DSPD activities to ensure unity of effort and maximum effect. DSPD can entail the use of a military information support team (MIST), to support a US embassy within a HN. The MIST prepares information products, based on the guidance of the country team to communicate country-specific themes and messages. It could also involve the deployment of a joint public affairs support element (JPASE) team to a contingency location where JPASE representatives work out of the US embassy and coordinate military PA activities with embassy goals and objectives.

9. Media Engagement

a. The embedding of media in combat units offers new opportunities, as well as risks, for the media and the military; the PA staff has a key role in recommending ground rules for embedding media. Many adversaries rely on limiting their population's knowledge to remain in power; PA and IO provide ways to get the joint forces' messages to the populations.

b. **Media Relations.** Well-planned, properly coordinated, and clearly expressed themes and messages can significantly clarify confusing situations often associated with countering an insurgency. Clear, accurate portrayals can improve the effectiveness and morale of counterinsurgents, reinforce the will of the US public, and increase popular support for the HN government. The right messages can reduce misinformation, distractions, confusion, uncertainty, and other factors that cause public distress and undermine COIN efforts. **Constructive and transparent information enhances understanding and support for continuing operations against the insurgency.**

c. **Embedded Media.** Embedded media representatives experience the joint force perspective of operations in the COIN environment. Media representatives should be embedded for as long as practicable. Representatives embedded for weeks become better prepared to present informed reports. Short-term media embedding risks media representatives not gaining a full understanding of the context of operations. Such short exposure may actually lead to unintended misinformation.

d. **Press Conferences.** Commanders may hold periodic press conferences to explain operations and provide transparency to the people most affected by COIN efforts. Ideally, these sessions should include the HN media and HN officials. **Such events provide opportunities to highlight the accomplishments of the HN government and counterinsurgent efforts.**

e. **Media Outlets and Communications.** Commanders should apply resources to establish the proper combination of media outlets and communications to transmit the repetitive themes of HN government accomplishments and insurgent violence against the population. This may require counterinsurgents to be proactive, alerting the media to news opportunities and perhaps providing transportation or other services to ensure proper coverage. Helping establish effective HN media is another important COIN requirement. **However, counterinsurgents must strive to avoid the perception of attempting to manipulate the population or media. Even the slightest appearance of impropriety can undermine the credibility of the COIN force and HN legitimacy.**

f. **Working Relationships.** Good working relationships between counterinsurgent leaders and members of the media are vital. When they do not understand COIN efforts, media representatives portray the situation to their audience based on what they know. Such reports can be incomplete, if not incorrect. **Through professional relationships, military leaders should strive to ensure that the media's audiences understand the counterinsurgents' efforts from the counterinsurgents' perspective.**

For more discussion on PA, see JP 3-61, Public Affairs, *and JP 3-13,* Information Operations.

SECTION C. DETAINEE OPERATIONS IN COUNTERINSURGENCY

10. General

a. How counterinsurgents treat captured insurgents has immense potential impact on insurgent morale, retention, and recruitment. Humane and just treatment may afford counterinsurgents many short-term opportunities as well as potentially damaging insurgent recruitment. Abuse may foster resentment and hatred; offering the enemy an opportunity for propaganda and assist potential insurgent recruitment and support. It is important that all detainees or other persons captured in any conflict, regardless of how it is characterized, shall be treated, at a minimum, in accordance with Common Article 3 of the Geneva Conventions of 1949, unless they are entitled to another standard based on status.

b. **Detainees.** Counterinsurgents must carefully consider who will be detained, and the manner and methods that will be used to detain them. Detainees can be vital sources of information. Counterinsurgents detaining people who are not part of the insurgency or do not support insurgency damages the counterinsurgents' credibility and legitimacy; thus, poor detainee operations can prolong the war, increase resentment, and undermine any efforts to ameliorate grievances or discredit the insurgents' narrative.

c. **Detention.** The methods and infrastructure for detention of insurgents is complex and important. The exact chain of custody and responsibility is vitally important and must be carefully planned, prepared, and conducted. The infrastructure and sustainment effort must be able to cope with the volume of people in detention. The methods and perception of credibility and legitimacy for the release of personnel in detention is also important. **Fairness may help the counterinsurgent cause while any negative perceptions will hurt efforts in the long term.** For those in custody, reintegration efforts should begin as soon as possible. Detention should protect and empower moderate detainees.

11. Voluntary Detainee Programs

It is vital that detainees have voluntary access to a wide array of programs. These programs help protect and empower moderate detainees from extremist influence, prepare detainees for release, and encourage them to not rejoin the insurgency when released. While the programs must be tailored for each area and insurgency, they can include vocational, educational (especially reading and writing), and religious programs.

12. Release Authority

For transfer or release authority of US-captured detainees during COIN, the SecDef or designee shall establish criteria for transfer or release and communicate those criteria to all commanders operating within the operational area. How to reintegrate released detainees is of vital importance and requires careful planning. Coordination is required with respect to the local governmental and security forces of the area that the detainee will be released to, especially if this was the same area where the individual was detained. Release procedures and policy must be closely coordinated with disarmament, demobilization, and reintegration (DDR).

For more information on detainee operations, see JP 3-63, Detainee Operations.

SECTION D. SECURITY SECTOR REFORM OPERATIONS IN COUNTERINSURGENCY

13. General

National defense and internal security are the traditional cornerstones of state sovereignty. Security is essential to legitimate governance and participation, effective rule of law, and sustained economic development. The security sector comprises the individuals and institutions responsible for the safety and security of the HN and the population. This often includes the military and any state-sponsored paramilitary forces; national and local police; the justice and corrections systems; coastal and border security forces; oversight bodies; and militia and private military and security companies employed by the state. The security sector represents the foundation of effective, legitimate governance and the potential of the state for enduring viability. **An effective security sector is essential to deal with an ongoing insurgency and other destabilizing elements or external support and is vital in accomplishing US objectives for HN stability and self-sufficiency.**

14. Security Sector Reform Operations

a. **Security Sector Reform.** Security sector reform (SSR) is the set of policies, plans, programs, and activities that a government undertakes to improve the way it provides safety, security, and justice. SSR aims to provide an effective and legitimate public service that is transparent, accountable to civilian authority, and responsive to the needs of the public. It may include integrated activities in support of defense and armed forces reform; civilian management and oversight; justice, police, corrections, and intelligence reform; national security planning and strategy support; border management; DDR; and concurrent reduction of armed violence. **SSR must be part of any COIN plan, including the IDAD strategy, from the outset.**

(1) **Institutions.** SSR involves the reestablishment or reform of the institutions and key ministerial positions that maintain and provide oversight for the safety and security of the HN and its people. Through unified action, individuals and institutions

assume an effective, legitimate, and accountable role that provides external and internal security for their citizens under the civilian control of a legitimate state authority. Effective SSR enables a state to build its capacity to provide security and justice. SSR promotes stability, fosters democratic reform processes, and enables economic development. The desired outcome of SSR programs is an effective and legitimate security sector firmly rooted within the rule of law.

(2) **Reform.** SSR includes reform efforts targeting the individuals and institutions that provide a nation's security and promote and strengthen the rule of law. By recognizing the inherently interdependent aspects of the security sector and by integrating operational support with institutional reform and governance, SSR promotes effective, legitimate, transparent, and accountable security and justice. SSR captures the full range of security activities under the broad umbrella of a single, coherent framework—from military and police training to weapons destruction; from community security to DDR of former combatants; and to security sector oversight and budgeting. Cultural sensitivities, political concerns, or apprehensions within neighboring states can become obstacles to reform.

(3) **Unified Action.** In SSR, the USG and its agencies, including the DOD, pursue an integrated approach to SSR based on unified action. With the support of the HN, military forces collaborate with interagency representatives and other civilian organizations to design and implement SSR strategies, plans, programs, and activities. DOS leads and provides oversight for these efforts through its bureaus, offices, and overseas missions. The DOD provides coercive and constructive capability to support the establishment; to restructure or reform the armed forces and defense sector; and to assist and support activities of other USG agencies involved in SSR. Joint forces participate in and support SSR activities as directed by the JFC.

b. **Program Implementation.** Effective SSR requires coordinated assessment, planning, training, implementation, and monitoring and evaluation. The following guidelines are designed to assist with the execution of this statement, which is resource-neutral.

(1) **Assessment.** Ideally, interagency analysis should be the basis for USG-wide programming decisions. Interagency SSR assessments may be initiated by the COM in country or by any of the contributing USG agencies. Where possible and appropriate, an interagency team comprised of relevant USG agencies and offices should conduct the assessment. A thorough assessment will combine desktop study with field work and will map institutions and actors, identify capacity strengths and gaps, and prioritize entry points for SSR programs and activities. Assessment teams should consider US foreign policy objectives; partner government capabilities, requirements, and resources; the possible contribution of other members of the international community; and community and individual security needs. Wherever possible, assessment teams should consider vulnerable groups and the security and justice issues that affect them.

(2) **Planning.** Coordinated interagency planning is required to ensure balanced

development of the entire security sector. Imbalanced development can actually undermine the long-term success of SSR efforts. Coordination of US strategic and operational objectives through integrated planning that synchronizes USG program and budget execution will help to prioritize and sequence the activities of each contributing agency into a coherent SSR strategy. Interagency planning should be conducted both in the field and at the appropriate Washington and regional headquarters level to ensure adequate resources are made available to support the effort. All departments and agencies of the USG engaged in security or justice activities in a given country and should be included in planning efforts. Equally important, other donors are likely to be engaged in security and justice programs, and should be consulted early in the planning process to avoid duplication of effort. Through unified action, the various actors consider the unique capabilities and contributions of each participant. The ensuing plan aims for a practical pace of reform and accounts for the political and cultural context of the situation. The plan accounts for available resources and capabilities while balancing the human capacity to deliver change against a realistic timeline. The SSR plan reflects HN culture, sensitivities, and historical conceptions of security. As with the broader campaign plan, the SSR plan seeks to resolve the underlying sources of conflict while preventing new or escalating future security crises. The level of HN development—especially as it pertains to poverty and economic opportunity—is an important consideration in SSR planning. Planning for SSR includes building or rebuilding culturally appropriate security forces, judicial systems, law enforcement, and corrections. SFA builds or improves security forces.

(3) **Implementation**. SSR strategies, plans, and programs should incorporate the guiding principles of:

(a) Support HN ownership.

(b) Incorporate principles of good governance.

(c) Respect for human rights.

(d) Balance operational support with institutional reform.

(e) Link security and justice.

(f) Foster transparency.

(g) Do no harm.

(4) **Monitoring and Evaluation.** SSR programs should be monitored throughout implementation to ensure they deliver sustainable results while minimizing unintended negative consequences. Program evaluation at key decision points, and at the close of specific projects, will provide important measures of effectiveness to adjust ongoing programs and to provide lessons for future SSR programs.

c. **Security Sector Elements.** The security sector consists of both uniformed forces—police and military—and civilian agencies and organizations operating at various levels within the OE. Elements of the security sector are interdependent; the activities of one element significantly affect other elements. The four core elements of the security sector consist of state security providers, government security management and oversight bodies, civil society and other nonstate actors, and nonstate security sector providers. State security providers are those bodies authorized by the state to use or support the use of force. Government security management and oversight bodies are those bodies, both formal and informal, authorized by the state to manage and oversee the activities and governance of armed and public security forces and agencies. The third core element of the security sector consists of the civil society and other nonstate actors. Nonstate security sector providers are nonstate providers of justice and security.

d. **Host Nation Ownership.** Successful SSR is a HN effort supported by USG and other donors. Nonmilitary SSR partners, focus on all SSR activities, including the transition from external to HN responsibility for security and public safety should be planned based on the initial assessment. SSR activities may also transition to new HN institutions, groups, and governance frameworks as part of the peace process. As the transition proceeds, US military primacy recedes and other civilian agencies and organizations come to the forefront.

e. **Agency Guidance and Policy.** Participants in SSR help develop the program using their own policy guidance and policy implementation mechanisms. For example, UN Security Council resolutions define the mandates of UN peacekeepers and UN-integrated missions. National policy guidance; national justice systems; and relevant national legislation, treaties, and agreements—both bilateral and multilateral— provide a framework for HN and military forces. US security assistance, in particular, must proceed within the framework of legislated provisions governing the delivery of foreign assistance by US agencies, both military and civilian. While SSR integrates these influences, ultimately, it reflects the HN institutions, laws, and processes.

f. **Planning.** Sustainable SSR depends on thorough planning and assessment. Through unified action, the various actors consider the unique capabilities and contributions of each participant. The ensuing plan aims for a practical pace of reform and accounts for the political and cultural context of the situation. The plan accounts for available resources and capabilities while balancing the human capacity to deliver change against a realistic timeline. The SSR plan reflects HN culture, sensitivities, and historical conceptions of security. It does not seek to implement a Western paradigm for the security sector, understanding that a Western model may not be appropriate. As with the broader campaign plan, the SSR plan seeks to resolve the underlying sources of conflict while preventing new or escalating future security crises. The level of HN development—especially as it pertains to poverty and economic opportunity—is an important consideration in SSR planning. Planning for SSR includes building or rebuilding culturally appropriate security forces, judicial systems, law enforcement, and corrections. SFA builds or improves security forces.

For more discussion on security sector reform and SFA, see JP 3-22, Foreign Internal Defense, *and Army Field Manual (FM) 3-07,* Stability Operations.

SECTION E. DISARMAMENT, DEMOBILIZATION, AND REINTEGRATION IN COUNTERINSURGENCY

15. General

DDR attempts to stabilize the OE by disarming and demobilizing insurgents and by helping return former insurgents to civilian life. DDR has cultural, political, security, humanitarian, and socioeconomic dimensions. DDR can potentially provide incentives for insurgent leaders and combatants to facilitate political reconciliation, dissolve belligerent force structures, and present opportunities for former insurgents and other DDR beneficiaries to return to their communities. A successful DDR program helps establish sustainable peace. A failed DDR effort can stall COIN or reinforce drivers of conflict.

16. Disarmament, Demobilization, and Reintegration Elements

a. **Purpose.** The objective of the DDR process is to contribute to security and stability in post-conflict environments so that recovery and development can begin. The DDR of former combatants is a complex process, with political, military, security, humanitarian and socioeconomic dimensions. It aims to deal with the post-conflict security problem that arises when former combatants are left without livelihoods or support networks, other than their former comrades, during the vital transition period from conflict to peace and development. Disarmament and demobilization refers to the act of releasing or disbanding an armed unit and the collection and control of weapons and weapons systems. Reintegration helps former combatants return to civilian life through benefit packages and strategies that help them become socially and economically embedded in their communities.

b. **Disarmament.** Disarmament is the collection, documentation, control, and disposal of small arms, ammunition, explosives, and light and heavy weapons of former insurgents and the population. Disarmament also includes the development of responsible arms management programs. Ideally, disarmament is a voluntary process carried out as part of a broader peace process to which all parties accede. Disarmament functions best with high levels of trust between those being disarmed and the forces overseeing disarmament. Some groups may hesitate to offer trust and cooperation or even refuse to participate in disarmament efforts. In these circumstances, disarmament may occur in two stages: a voluntary disarmament process followed by more coercive measures. The latter will address individuals or small groups refusing to participate voluntarily. In this second stage, disarmament of combatant factions can become a contentious and potentially very destabilizing step of DDR. **The HN and coalition partners manage DDR carefully to avoid disarmament becoming a catalyst for renewed violence. Disarmament may be a slow process in an ongoing COIN and realistic goals must be set.**

c. **Demobilization.** Demobilization is the process of transitioning a conflict or wartime military establishment and defense-based civilian economy to a peacetime configuration while maintaining national security and economic vitality. **Demobilization for COIN normally involves the controlled discharge of active combatants from paramilitary groups, militias, and insurgent forces that have stopped fighting.** Demobilization under these circumstances may include identifying and gathering ex-combatants for demobilization efforts. Demobilization involves deliberately dismantling insurgent organizations and belligerent group loyalties, replacing those with more appropriate group affiliations, and restoring the identity of former fighters as part of the national population. **The demobilization of insurgents enables the eventual development of value systems, attitudes, and social practices that help them reintegrate into civil society.**

d. **Reintegration.** Reintegration is the process through which former combatants, belligerents, and DCs receive amnesty, reenter civil society, gain sustainable employment, and become contributing members of the local population. **It encompasses the reinsertion of individual former insurgents into HN communities, villages, and social groups.** Reintegration is a social and economic recovery process focused on the local community; it complements other community-based programs that spur economic recovery, training, and employment services. It includes programs to support their resettlement in civilian communities, basic and vocational education, and assistance in finding employment in local economies. It accounts for the specific needs of women and children associated with insurgent and other armed groups.

(1) **Insurgent Reintegration.** Former insurgents, when properly protected, reintegrated, and well treated, can become positive members of their community. Conversely, unprotected, poorly prepared, or poorly treated former insurgents will become powerful IO opportunities for the insurgents. The reintegration process and programs, such as HN led moderate ideological or religious education and job training, should be started early in the reintegration process.

(2) **Amnesty and Reconciliation.** Reintegration also addresses the willingness of civilian communities to accept former fighters into their midst; amnesty and reconciliation are key components to successful reintegration. In this context, reintegration cannot be divorced from justice and reconciliation programs that are part of the broader transition process. Successful reintegration programs tend to be long term and costly, requiring the participation of multiple external and HN participants. The Chinese philosopher Sun Tzu wrote that a commander must: "Build your opponent a golden bridge to retreat across." While Sun Tzu intended this remark to illustrate how a cornered enemy will often fight more intensely than one with an escape route, this admonition can apply in a COIN context as well. **Counterinsurgents must leave a way out for insurgents who have lost the desire to continue the struggle.** Effective amnesty and reintegration programs provide the insurgents this avenue; amnesty provides the means to quit the insurgency and reintegration allows former insurgents to become part of greater society. Rifts between insurgent leaders, if identified, can be exploited in

this fashion. Offering amnesty or a seemingly generous compromise can also cause divisions within an insurgency and present opportunities to split or weaken it. COIN can also act to magnify existing rifts.

(3) **Amnesty Programs.** Amnesty programs provide a means for members of the insurgency to stop fighting. **The essential part of an amnesty program is that insurgents believe they will be treated well and protected from their erstwhile comrades' potential reprisal.** Thus, the counterinsurgents must have detailed IO plans to get insurgents to know about the program, to turn themselves in, and to support subsequent amnesty efforts. Pragmatism must be the first consideration of amnesty programs, not ideology or vendetta. Counterinsurgents also must have methods to protect the former insurgents. Incentives for disaffected insurgents or their supporters are important, especially modest monetary rewards.

(4) **Defector Programs. Turning former insurgents against their erstwhile comrades can prove invaluable to COIN efforts.** Defectors can provide vital intelligence and even become valuable allies and combatants. Incentives and a sense of fair treatment by counterinsurgents are vital to effective defector programs, which are also dependent on effective IO so insurgents are aware of their options. Insurgents may be prone to defect when conflict has been prolonged, the broad population is weary of conflict, or if the insurgents have an uneven sense of purpose or drive. Defector knowledge of how the insurgents are led, organized, and operate can prove invaluable. This can include personality profiles of insurgent leaders, current communication procedures, plans, and TTP. This detailed intelligence is difficult to gain without defector operations.

(5) **Reinsertion.** Reinsertion is the assistance offered to former insurgents and belligerents prior to the long-term process of reintegration. Reinsertion is a form of transitional assistance intended to provide for the basic needs of reintegrating individuals and their families; this assistance includes transitional safety allowances, food, clothes, shelter, health services, short-term education, training, employment, and tools. While reintegration represents enduring social and economic development, reinsertion is a short term material and financial assistance program intended to meet immediate needs.

(6) **Repatriation.** The repatriation of foreign nationals to their country of citizenship is governed by complex US and international legal standards, legal standards that likely apply differently in each case of proposed repatriation. Any program of repatriation is likely to raise important legal issues that must be reviewed by US legal personnel.

(7) **Resettlement.** Resettlement is the relocation of refugees to a third country, which is neither the country of citizenship nor the country into which the refugee has fled. Resettlement to a third country is granted by accord of the country of resettlement. It is based on a number of criteria, including legal and physical protection needs, lack of local integration opportunities, health needs, family reunification needs, and threat of

violence and torture. Resettlement can also mean the relocation of internally displaced persons to another location within the country.

(8) **Return.** The return of refugees and internally displaced persons to their homes is one of the most difficult aspects of COIN. If their dislocation was originally caused by ethnic or sectarian cleansing, their return risks a return to ethno-sectarian violence. Often abandoned homes are occupied by squatters, who must be removed in order to return the home to the rightful owner. Poor real estate records and immature judicial systems and laws exacerbate the return process, as ownership must be legally established prior to return. Counterinsurgents can play a key role in transporting and providing security for returnees, and often play a role in establishing temporary legal mechanisms to resolve property disputes.

17. Planning a Disarmament, Demobilization, and Reintegration Program

a. **Importance to COIN.** The promise and nature of DDR to insurgents often plays a crucial role in undermining insurgent recruitment, increasing insurgent desertion or defection, and even achieving a peace agreement. The success of DDR depends on integrating strategies and planning across all the sectors.

(1) For example, the employment opportunities extended to former insurgents depend on an effectively governed, viable economy with an active market sector. If the DDR program ends without providing alternative economic opportunities to the former combatants, the likelihood of a return to violence substantially increases.

(2) DDR closely coordinates with reform efforts in all sectors to ensure an integrated approach that synchronizes activities toward a common end state. DDR planning directly ties to SSR, determining the potential size and scope of military, police, and other security structures.

b. **DDR Planning.** Planning for a successful DDR program requires an understanding of both the situation on the ground and the goals, political will, and resources in which actors and other donor organizations are willing to support. Effective DDR planning relies on analysis of possible DDR beneficiaries, power dynamics, and local society as well as the nature of the conflict and ongoing peace processes. Assessments are conducted in close consultation with the local populace and with personnel from participating agencies who understand and know about the HN. Joint forces and other actors may enter the DDR process at many different stages; therefore, assessment is a continuous process used to guide decision-making throughout the DDR program.

c. **Unified Action.** Governmental and NGOs from the international community and the HN cooperate to plan and execute DDR programs. External and HN military forces and police working together in a peace support role may facilitate DDR. Former insurgents must develop confidence in DDR and the organizations charged with implementing it. To build this confidence, the DDR program focuses on restoring the society, the government, and the economy at all levels. This leads to the HN taking responsibility for DDR processes.

d. **Joint Contribution.** Generally, the joint force does not lead the planning and execution of the DDR program. However, joint forces must be integrated in the planning of DDR from its inception and may be involved more directly in the disarmament and demobilization stages. Security forces and police, whether from external sources or the HN, are fundamental to the broad success of the program, providing security for DDR processes. Successful DDR programs use many approaches designed for specific security environments. Each program reflects the unique aspects of the situation, culture, and character of the state.

Intentionally Blank

CHAPTER VII
COMPONENT CONTRIBUTIONS TO COUNTERINSURGENCY

> *"As long as the insurgent has failed to build a powerful regular army, the counterinsurgent...needs infantry and more infantry, highly mobile and lightly armed."*
>
> **David Galula**
> ***Counterinsurgency Warfare, Theory, and Practice***

1. Joint Counterinsurgency is Team Counterinsurgency

All components of the joint force are essential for the overall military contribution to COIN. Joint warfare is a team effort and air, land, maritime, and special operations components of the joint force make vital contributions in support of all instruments of national power in achieving national security objectives. Military operations must address counterguerrilla operations, which include securing the populations and neutralizing the insurgent military wing. Neutralizing the insurgent military wing includes killing or capturing irreconcilable insurgents and securing the population from insurgent terrorism. While the land component is normally the supported component during COIN, this can change due to external threats or if an insurgency has developed a conventional military threat, such as in the Chinese Communist Revolution in 1948-9. In this case, all components of the joint force are involved in both COIN and combat operations. This is also true if an external power has sent conventional military forces to assist the insurgents.

2. Host-Nation Land Contribution to Counterinsurgency

Much of securing or protecting the population is done by deploying land forces within the population and with an enduring presence. Normally, US land forces will operate in designated contiguous operational areas that coincide with HN national political boundaries. However, HN forces should provide most of this enduring presence. The current COIN operational approach—direct, balanced, or indirect—will determine the size, footprint, roles, and relationship of HN, US, and coalition partner land forces.

See JP 3-31, Command and Control for Joint Land Operations.

a. **Host-Nation Military Forces.** HN military forces will be unique to their particular culture and location. This includes their quantity, quality, and effectiveness. There may or may not be a professional standing army, navy, air force, marine corps, coast guard, police, or other security force. Regardless of their situation at the outset of COIN, indigenous forces will be indispensable in terms of execution of COIN and, more importantly, creating enduring solutions. When the US is supporting a HN COIN, professional HN military forces will be invaluable for ISR collection, assessment, and/or collaboration and understanding the OE, particularly when the joint force is new to the OE.

(1) **Host-Nation Military Forces and Legitimacy.** If US or external coalition elements are working with or training HN security forces, care must be taken to ensure that the population perceives their nation's security forces as capable, competent, and professional—failure to do so will generally undermine the HN government's legitimacy.

(2) **Security Sector Reform.** The training and development of HN security forces is a key part of SSR, which is covered in Chapter VI, "Supporting Operations for Counterinsurgency." SSR requires unified action to develop not only military forces, but other aspects of security and governance, such as border police, prison services, and the judiciary.

b. **Host-Nation Law Enforcement.** HN law enforcement plays an indispensable role in COIN, if they are competent and trustworthy. If they are legitimate in the eyes of the population, they are likely to have access to detailed intelligence on insurgent leaders, networks, and links to criminal elements. The presence of indigenous law enforcement elements, particularly if they are perceived to be leading operations, will have a stabilizing and normalizing impact on the population.

(1) **Coordination between Law Enforcement and the Military.** Military COIN forces coordinate closely with law enforcement. Military forces will support law enforcement to provide security and protection for police in their routine duties when the security situation requires. Law enforcement may support the military as well. For example, police may arrest insurgents captured and detained by military forces and cooperate in site exploitation to gather evidence to prosecute the insurgents. Law enforcement and military forces may be collocated to conduct joint operations and to afford the police additional protection, based on the security situation. This coordination will often provide valuable intelligence sources, and law enforcement and military intelligence should be shared within prudent classification restrictions. As security improves, law enforcement should assume a greater role and profile amongst the population, thus allowing military forces to focus on subsequent operations. Increasing HN law enforcement presence while simultaneously decreasing military presence enhances HN legitimacy, which is essential to successful COIN.

(2) **Proficiency.** The role of law enforcement in the HN and the level of employment of those law enforcement forces are often dependent on the proficiency of the police force and judiciary and the population's perception of them. For example, if a police force or judiciary is regarded as corrupt, the population will have little trust that the police will have the best interests of the people in mind or that the force can provide real security.

For more details on HN security forces, see FM3-24/Marine Corps Warfighting Publication (MCWP) 3-33.5, Counterinsurgency, *FM 3-07,* Stability Operations, *and FM 3-07.1,* Security Force Assistance.

(3) **Training Police Forces.** Military forces may have to be used in some instances to train HN law enforcement, especially civilian police. Ideally, this

responsibility will be assumed by supporting police forces so that they receive proper mentoring and training in all aspects of police duties. However, the military will continue to work closely with police forces and mentor them when necessary.

(4) **Corruption.** Some law enforcement forces are not organized or controlled in a manner common to responsible governance. Law enforcement may be corrupt or have been poorly organized, trained, and equipped. In fact, corrupt law enforcement or other security forces may have been a root cause of the insurgency or may be a driver of continuing conflict. One must also understand the potential ramification of using former combatants as police. Efforts must be made to rectify any issues with corruption, especially as it is unlikely that a nation will be stable without a competent, professional law enforcement apparatus. Commanders and their staffs must ensure they fully understand the cultural differences in what constitutes corruption in the affected population. Western value systems do not carry equal implications in many non-Western cultures.

c. **Host-Nation Auxiliary Forces.** When the security situation requires, counterinsurgents should organize and mobilize the local population to protect themselves by forming auxiliary forces. This is a key, but potentially dangerous policy decision that the HN must make. These auxiliary forces will need to be demobilized and disarmed when hostilities cease. Resentments between local groups may make disarming them difficult. These forces may augment military and/or law enforcement efforts.

(1) **Training and Roles.** Well organized, equipped, trained, and led auxiliary forces can play a decisive role in COIN. They can augment and assist professional military and law enforcement forces, especially with providing a permanent presence within the population. A permanent presence within the population is vital to security, but is manpower intensive. Auxiliary forces are best used to augment or execute defensive or stability operations.

(2) **Advantages.** Auxiliary forces are often based on local family, tribal, clan, ethnic, or religious affiliations, so they have inherent cultural and linguistic advantages. In this capacity, they can be invaluable intelligence assets; their understanding of the local OE is far superior to that of any outsider. Auxiliary forces may also have specialized skills developed as part of their culture that may complement other more professional forces. These skills can include tracking, patrolling, understanding of the terrain and wildlife, and local communications methods.

(3) **Disadvantages.** Auxiliary forces can have disadvantages, but these can generally be overcome with oversight. Auxiliary forces may be more prone to insurgent infiltration, and they may provide informational, operational, and security challenges. Counterinsurgents should realize that some nominally counterinsurgent auxiliaries may be simultaneously working for insurgents offering services for immediate monetary or material advantage. It is also common for auxiliaries to shift sides when they perceive an opportunity or which side may have gained the advantage. Members of auxiliaries or their friends and family may be subject to insurgent coercion and violence. The overall

context will determine how vulnerable and therefore how useful the auxiliary forces may be.

3. Air Contribution to Counterinsurgency

Air forces and capabilities play a vital role in the military contribution to COIN. These forces and capabilities are especially critical for successful counterguerrilla, intelligence, combating weapons of mass destruction (CWMD), humanitarian, and informational efforts. Air contributions include close air support, precision strikes, armed overwatch, personnel recovery, air interdiction, ISR, communications, EW, combat support, and air mobility. Air forces and capabilities provide considerable asymmetric advantages to counterinsurgents, especially by denying insurgents secrecy and unfettered access to bases of operation. If insurgents assemble a conventional force or their operating locations are identified and isolated, air assets can respond quickly with joint precision fires or to airlift ground forces to locations to accomplish a mission. Airpower enables counterinsurgents to operate in rough and remote terrain, areas that insurgents traditionally have used as safe havens. The air component may be the supported component in COIN when attacking approved insurgent sanctuaries that are outside land or maritime forces operational areas.

a. **Air Command and Control.** The C2 relationships established for engagement operations should consider both the need for flexibility and the training level of forces to be employed. For example, the training and competency required for precision strikes in COIN are more demanding than for traditional warfare. Consequently, JFCs and component commanders must consider the C2 architecture that best suits the situation.

(1) **Command and Control Architecture.** The joint structure applies to more than just US forces; it involves coordinating air assets of multinational partners and the HN. COIN planners must establish a joint and multinational airpower C2 system and policies, with HN and interagency, on the rules and conditions for employing airpower in the theater. In the same manner, COIN planning must account for and incorporate interagency capabilities and functions.

(2) **Planning.** During COIN operations, most planning occurs at lower echelons. Air planners require visibility of actions planned at all echelons to provide the most effective air support so coordination should occur at all levels. Furthermore, COIN planning is often fluid and develops along short planning and execution timelines, necessitating some degree of informal coordination and integration for safety and efficiency.

b. **Air Mobility.** Cargo mobility aircraft provide the important support with intertheater and intratheater transport. This transport can include deployment to remote regions to deliver resources and personnel and can be used to rapidly deploy, sustain, and reinforce ground forces as part of security and counterguerrilla operations. Air mobility can be used to support political goals by extending effective governance to remote areas and delivering highly visible humanitarian aid. Sustainment tasks are enabled through airland, airdrop, and aerial extraction of equipment, supplies, and personnel. Fixed-wing and vertical-lift airlift provide a crucial capability in COIN. In the military realm, fixed-wing transports are best suited for carrying ground forces into forward staging areas. Vertical-lift platforms are ideal for carrying ground forces to remote sites that are unable to support fixed-wing operations. Lift capable of moving small units around the battlefield have proven very valuable in assisting COIN forces. The ability to maneuver while engaged with an adversary is extremely powerful in managing the battle and insuring that the adversary is unable to disengage at a time and place of their choosing. Casualty evacuation is integral to any operation involving the employment of personnel in hostile-fire situations, with vertical-lift assets best suited for this task. While land forces can execute these basic missions alone, airlift bypass weaknesses insurgents have traditionally exploited. However, airlift is more costly than surface or maritime transportation and in some circumstances may be inhibited by terrain, weather, and threats such as man portable surface-to-air missiles and rocket-propelled grenades. Also, requesting airlift may be subject to limitations due to availability and other priority requirements. It is usually a small percentage of the overall transportation network during major combat operations; however, in particularly challenging situations, airlift may become the primary transportation mode for sustainment and repositioning.

c. **Precision Engagement.** The joint force air component can provide close air support, armed overwatch, air interdiction, and strategic attack that in COIN often includes the use of precision-guided munitions with a full spectrum of capabilities (lethal and nonlethal). These precision strikes are often based on corroborated HUMINT and are an effective means of destroying the insurgent military wing, leaders, or assets with minimal collateral damage or risk to land forces. The use of lethal fires, regardless of source, against insurgents must be carefully considered and targets confirmed in terms of their authenticity and value. Additionally, insurgents may have signature reduction methods, deception methods, and man-portable air defense systems that must be considered and addressed.

(1) **Airpower.** The impact on the population from using strike operations against insurgents must be carefully considered. In determining the appropriate capability to create the desired effects, planners should look at the desired objectives and end state, duration, and consequences to ensure that not only the direct but the longer-term indirect effects that may result are anticipated. Collateral damage and civilian casualties can do much to undermine indigenous, domestic, and international support. Additionally, insurgents will exploit such incidents especially through IO and propaganda, using international media coverage when possible.

(2) **Intelligence.** Just as in traditional warfare, attacks on key nodes usually reap greater benefits than attacks on dispersed individual targets. For this reason, effective strike operations are inextricably tied to the availability of actionable intelligence, effective ISR, and detailed systems analysis that identifies and fully characterizes the potential targets of interest (networks, nodes, and links). Persistence is critical as it is often not known in advance how long a particular node will remain stationary.

(3) **Host-nation Precision Engagement.** If US or coalition forces conduct the strike, there may be the perception that the HN government is dependent for its survival on foreign forces. This may have the indirect effect of delegitimizing the HN government in the public's perception. Precision engagement should be designed to employ HN airpower resources to the greatest extent possible. Properly trained and structured teams of airpower advisors, ranging from planning liaison to tactical operations personnel, offer potential for HN unilateral and combined actions against high-value targets. Use of these options serves to enhance the legitimacy of the HN government while achieving important coalition security objectives. Use of assets controlled by US agencies outside the DOD, but not directly affiliated with it, may also prove useful in providing precision strike capability.

d. **Interoperability Between Ground and Air.** Video downlink and datalink technology have revolutionized real-time air to ground employment allowing air assets to seamlessly integrate into and support the ground commander's scheme of maneuver. Armed overwatch missions provide ground forces with the critical situational awareness, flexibility, and immediate fire support necessary to succeed in the dynamic COIN environment. Airpower's ability to quickly support ground forces can lower the need for mutual support between ground units and therefore decrease overall manpower density. This allows counterinsurgents to further disperse ground forces in areas and in numbers that would not be feasible without air power—mutual support can come from the air rather than from other ground forces or indirect ground fire. Dispersion of ground forces facilitates the actual and perceived level of security. However, joint planners must carefully balance the risk of catastrophic tactical surprise of dispersed ground forces with the benefits gained from dispersion.

e. **Personnel Recovery (PR) Operations.** The part of PR that plays the largest role in COIN and combating terrorism is combat search and rescue (CSAR). The availability of dependable CSAR and casualty evacuation, especially at night, has dramatically improved the willingness and ability of HN ground combatant forces to engage in operations they may otherwise be less motivated to perform.

f. **Basing.** US and multinational air units, along with HN forces, will likely use expeditionary airfields. COIN planners must consider where to locate airfields, including those intended for use as aerial ports of debarkation and other air operations. US air forces frequently build and provide infrastructure to HN air services as part of performing COIN operations. Airpower operating from remote or dispersed airfields may present a smaller signature than large numbers of land forces, possibly lessening HN sensitivities to foreign military presence. Employment of long-range bombers for COIN operations has increased due to advances in Global Positioning System-guided weapons and carriage of advanced targeting pods. Often these platforms are free from the basing limitations of shorter range tactical platforms. Commanders must properly protect their bases and coordinate their defense among all counterinsurgents.

g. **Building Host-Nation Airpower Capability.** US and multinational aviation SFA operations strive to enable the HN to provide its own internal and external defense. Developing an air force is a foundational initiative for unifying, advancing, or developing a nation. Airpower capability is a catalyst for government legitimacy, projecting national sovereignty, and accelerating the nation's overall internal stability as well as regional security. Rebuilding HN air capability will require long lead times. Planners, therefore, need to establish a long-term program to develop a HN airpower capability. The HN air force should be appropriate for that nation's requirements and sustainment base. For conducting effective COIN operations, a HN air force may be able to provide aerial reconnaissance and surveillance, air transport, close air support and interdiction for land forces, helicopter troop lift, medical evacuation, and counterair. Likewise, airlift supports essential services, governance, and economic development by providing movement of personnel and supplies, particularly in a COIN operation with IEDs and other dangers on the roads. HN security forces thus should include airlift development as the HN's first component of airpower. Frequently, the majority effort of air forces centers on providing combat support and combat service support, such as train and equip services, to HN air forces. Infrastructure to include airfields and a viable air traffic control system construction and development are also frequently required. Development of supporting services (maintenance, logistics and planning) often requires the most extensive timelines when working with HN air services. HN air services often include a mixture of civil and military aviation assets that provides unique challenges to air force efforts at engagement.

For additional information, see JP 3-17, Air Mobility Operations, *Air Force Doctrine Document (AFDD) 2-3,* Irregular Warfare, *AFDD 2-6,* Air Mobility Operations; *AFDD 2-7,* Special Operations; *AFDD 2-3.1,* Foreign Internal Defense, *and FM 3-24/MCWP 3-33.5,* Counterinsurgency.

4. Maritime Contribution to Counterinsurgency

For COIN, the maritime component plays a critical role in controlling the seas, which may be vital to isolating an insurgency physically and psychologically. The expeditionary character and versatility of maritime forces provide an advantage in areas where access is denied or limited. The maritime contribution to COIN will continue to be vital because much of the world's population lives in littoral areas, including large coastal cities. Demographic projections also indicate that the population of these areas will continue to grow in overall numbers and in relative terms to inland populations. Much of this burgeoning population may live in poverty, which may be a key root cause leading to insurgency. Due to the rise in population and potential unrest, the likelihood of COIN's being conducted in the littoral areas also increases. COIN in littoral areas has important maritime considerations. Maritime forces may provide direct support to the JTF that does not include combat operations, to include CMO, logistic support, intelligence/communication sharing, humanitarian relief, maritime civil affairs (MCAG), and expeditionary medical aid and training.

a. **Maritime Security Operations (MSO).** As discussed in Chapter II, "Insurgency" the OE may affect the insurgent's planning considerations and objectives, whether they are lethal or nonlethal. If the insurgency is dependent on external support for material resources, in the form of funding, weapons, equipment, fighters, or intelligence, COIN planning should include MSO as part of its efforts. MSO counters terrorism, insurgency and crime, while complimenting the effort to protect the HN, its sovereignty, the people, and critical infrastructure from insurgent efforts of subversion or violence. It also assures access to HN ports, and free-flow of commerce and sustained logistic support through the waterways. MSO is vital as a force multiplier to isolating insurgent dependent upon external support along inland waterways especially with respect to the littorals. Riverine units provide security along inland waterways, which helps to isolate insurgents within the affected area or, if the river is an international border, from external support. Since insurgent funding requirements may require reliance on criminal activities, piracy and smuggling are common sources to secure funds. Piracy threatens freedom and safety of maritime navigation, undermines economic security, and contributes to the destabilization of governance and the security situation. Because maritime forces conduct MSO in open ocean and the littorals, MSO can be applied towards negating piracy which may guarantee the HN's access to sea lines of communications, while eliminating a source of funding used for sustaining insurgent operations.

b. **Intelligence, Surveillance, and Reconnaissance.** Naval forces provide the joint force with expeditionary ISR capabilities with global reach and persistence. These capabilities can support any of the intelligence disciplines discussed in Chapter V, "Intelligence Support to Counterinsurgency."

c. **Deterrence and Patrols.** Naval support to COIN may consist of deterrence, escort operations, presence, patrols, and defending critical infrastructure. Maritime intercept operations are used to enforce sanctions or blockades, support law enforcement operations, and provide a means to extend situational awareness in the maritime domain. The presence of maritime forces can be adjusted as conditions dictate to enable flexible approaches to escalation, de-escalation, and deterrence. A visible presence just offshore demonstrates support for an ally or coalition partner, which may send a strong message to insurgents and their sympathizers. Naval forces' ability to loiter over the horizon reduces the appearance of a large US footprint while still maintaining the ability to influence events ashore.

d. **Sustainment and Transport.** Maritime forces can provide land-based forces with key sustainment capabilities. This includes commercial vessels' provision of the majority of bulk supplies. The expeditionary nature of naval forces, however, may transport forces within the theater as well. Naval forces can also provide a forced entry capability for insurgent-controlled areas or bases bordering waterways or in the littorals.

e. **Naval Aircraft.** Like ground-based aircraft, as part of a carrier airwing, are multi-mission platforms which provide rapid response capabilities, and are capable of conducting precision strikes, C2, EW, and CSAR. Naval aircraft have the added flexibility in that aircraft carriers are self-sustaining, secure bases that can be quickly repositioned within theater. Theater based maritime patrol aircraft further complement the flexibility with their endurance and multi mission capability. Naval aviation can thus provide the JFC with a source of airpower without increasing the coalition footprint ashore.

f. **Precision Strikes and Naval Fires.** Naval aircraft execute maritime interdiction and precision strikes, complementing land based aircraft close air support and precision strike missions. However, naval forces also are capable of launching precision-guided munitions from surface or subsurface platforms, while surface combatants can conduct naval surface fire support for expeditionary forces ashore. Like the air-launched precision-guided munitions, precise targeting, and quality, continuous and actionable ISR is required for these munitions to be effective. As with any use of force in COIN, all of the potential desired and undesired effects – fratricide and collateral damage, must be considered.

g. **Building Host-Nation Maritime Capability.** SFA also applies to assisting the HN with building or improving its maritime capability and capacity. The maritime component of security forces includes HN navy, marine, coast guard elements, and interagency organizations which may be loosely affiliated with the HN maritime organization. These may include fishery patrols, interior security, port authority, customs, and immigration. Further considerations to enhance the HN maritime capability is to introduce or expand existing maritime domain awareness efforts. Development of a robust automated identification system, tied into an interagency maritime operations center, will increase the HN's ability to track and identify vessels of interest, potentially involved in illegal or illicit activities. SFA planners must develop a long-term plan to assist the HN in these areas. As with the land and air, assistance to the maritime elements of a HN must be appropriate for that nation's requirements and sustainment base.

h. **Maritime Civil Affairs.** The maritime component may also contribute to the HN rebuilding effort with a dedicated MCAG. MCAG skill sets are uniquely tailored to those areas most likely to influence HNs rebuilding efforts in maritime and naval affairs. These are:

(1) Maritime law.

(2) Marine fisheries and resource management.

(3) Port administration and port operations.

(4) Maritime interagency coordination.

(5) Port/waterborne security.

(6) Customs and logistics.

(7) Port/intercoastal surveys.

(8) Control of maritime immigration.

5. Special Operations Forces Contribution to Counterinsurgency

a. **Special Operations Forces and Counterinsurgency Approaches.** SOF are vitally important to successful COIN operations. Their capacity to conduct a wide array of missions, working by, with, and through HN security forces or integrated with US conventional forces make them particularly suitable for COIN campaigns. They are particularly important when the joint force is using an indirect approach to COIN. In a more balanced or direct approach to COIN, however, they should be used to complement rather than replace conventional forces in traditional warfare roles.

b. **Special Operations Forces' Core Tasks and COIN.** SOF are specifically organized, trained, and equipped to accomplish the following nine core tasks: direct action (DA), special reconnaissance (SR), UW, FID, CT, CAO, PSYOP, IO, and CWMD, which embraces many tenets of the aforementioned core tasks, as well as discrete CWMD tasks. Any of these SOF core tasks may be involved in COIN. SOF must adhere to the same principles of COIN as conventional joint forces. Even if focused on DA missions, SOF must be cognizant of the need to win and maintain popular support.

(1) **Direct Action.** DA missions may be required in COIN to capture or kill key insurgent leaders or other vital insurgent targets. The specific types of DA are raids, ambushes, and direct assaults; standoff attacks; terminal attack control and terminal guidance operations; personnel recovery operations; precision destruction operations; and anti-surface operations.

(2) **Special Reconnaissance.** SOF may conduct SR into insurgent strongholds or sanctuaries. Activities within SR include environmental reconnaissance, armed reconnaissance, target and threat assessment, and poststrike reconnaissance.

(3) **Foreign Internal Defense.** Both conventional and SOF units have a role and capability to conduct FID missions. SOF's primary role in this interagency activity is to assess, train, advise, and assist HN military and paramilitary forces with the tasks that require their unique capabilities. The goal is to enable these forces to maintain the HN's internal stability, to counter subversion, lawlessness and insurgency in their country, and to address the causes of instability. Internal stability forms the shield behind which a nation assistance campaign can succeed.

For more information on FID, see JP 3-22, Foreign Internal Defense.

(4) **Unconventional Warfare.** These are operations that involve a broad spectrum of military and paramilitary operations, normally of long duration, predominantly conducted by, with, or through indigenous or surrogate forces who are organized, trained, equipped, supported, and directed in varying degrees by an external source.

(5) **Counterterrorism.** CT consists of actions taken through approaches applied directly against terrorist networks and indirectly to influence and render global environments inhospitable to terrorist networks. Indirect and direct approaches to CT are mutually supporting and integrate the capabilities to concurrently disrupt violent extremist organizations operating today and to influence the environment in which they operate to erode their capability and influence in the future. Both approaches are integrated globally from the strategic national to tactical levels. Either or both approaches may be conducted within the scope of a broader campaign or in conjunction with COIN as directed by a JFC.

For additional information, see JP 3-26, Counterterrorism, *JP 3-05,* Joint Special Operations, *JP 3-22,* Foreign Internal Defense, *and AFDD, 2-3.1,* Foreign Internal Defense. *For detailed discussion of integrating conventional forces and SOF, see US Special Operations Command Publication 3-33,* Conventional Forces and Special Operations Forces Integration and Interoperability Handbook and Checklist.

c. **Army Special Operations Forces (ARSOF) Capabilities.** ARSOF elements (special forces, rangers, and aviation) can support COIN operations by HN forces and conducting combat or other operations as required. ARSOF also has CAO and PSYOP elements that can support COIN.

d. **Marine Corps Special Operations Forces (MARSOF) Capabilities.** MARSOF can support COIN operations by providing a foreign military training unit that provides tailored military combat skills training and advisor support for identified foreign forces. It can also execute DA and other operations in support of COIN as required.

e. **Navy Special Operations Forces (NAVSOF) Capabilities.** NAVSOF can support COIN operations by providing sea-air-land and special boat teams to train HN forces or conduct combat or other operations as required. They generally operate in maritime, littoral, and riverine areas.

f. **Air Force Special Operations Forces (AFSOF) Capabilities.** AFSOF support COIN operations by working by, with, and through HN aviation forces from the ministerial level to the tactical unit. When required, AFSOF provide persistent manned and unmanned ISR, mobility, and precision engagement to support COIN operations. AFSOF maintain specially trained combat aviation advisors to assess, train, advise, and assist HN aviation capability thereby facilitating the availability, reliability, safety, and interoperability of these forces into COIN operations. Additionally, AFSOF special tactics teams enhance the air-to-ground interface, synchronizing conventional and special operations during COIN operations.

For additional information on SOF capabilities, see JP 3-05.1, Joint Special Operations Task Force Operations.

Intentionally Blank

CHAPTER VIII
OPERATIONAL ENVIRONMENT

> *"Counter-insurgency intelligence must cover a wide field and deal not only with the operational organization and capabilities of the insurgents, but must try also to expose and to understand their minds, their mentality and their motives. The influence that they are likely to exert over the populace must also be anticipated so that their efforts at subversion and intimidation can be thwarted."*
>
> **Julian Paget**
> ***Counter-Insurgency Campaigning***

1. Holistic Counterinsurgency Operational Environment

The OE for all joint operations is the sum of the conditions, circumstances, and influences that affect how the commander uses the available capabilities and makes decisions. The OE encompasses physical domains, nonspatial environments and other factors. The OE includes the information environment, sociocultural considerations, and civil considerations. A holistic understanding of the OE includes all of these aspects and helps the commander to understand how the OE constrains or shapes options, how the OE affects capabilities, and how friendly, adversary, and neutral actors' actions affect or shape the OE. While all aspects of the OE are important, COIN is a battle of will and ideas that is often determined by the population. Consequently, JIPOE must conduct a thorough analysis of population for COIN. Because individuals and groups are the foundation of the COIN OE and because human behavior is multifaceted, shifting, and difficult to predict, the COIN OE as a whole is shifting, dynamic, and complex. **Understanding of the COIN environment begins with understanding the population, then the insurgents, and finally the counterinsurgents.**

a. **Physical Domains.** Physical domains are composed of physical geography, both natural and man-made, and include the air, land, maritime, and space domains. While insurgents tend to operate primarily on land and inland waterways, some advanced insurgencies have used aircraft and operated offshore. As the insurgents primarily operate in the land domain and operate weakly in the other domains, the joint force has advantages it can exploit given its capabilities in air, maritime, and space domains. **The physical domains are also important aspects to consider for isolating and restricting the insurgent.**

b. **Information Environment.** The information environment both transcends and resides within the four physical domains and is the aggregate of individuals, organizations, and systems that collect, process, disseminate, or act on information. The information environment is made up of three interrelated dimensions: physical, informational, and cognitive. Cyberspace is a global domain within the information environment consisting of the interdependent network of information technology infrastructures, including the Internet, telecommunications networks, computer systems, and embedded processors and controllers. All actors in the OE affect the information environment. In fact, any attempt to interact with the information environment, including attempts to merely measure it, change or affect it. Increasingly, disproportionally small actors in this environment can gain asymmetric advantage in the information environment. **The information environment is paramount in COIN, as it is a medium that greatly influences the population.**

(1) **Physical Dimension.** The physical dimension consists of the physical infrastructure and means of transmission of command, control, and communication systems. The physical dimension makes up a significant portion of cyberspace as well.

(2) **Informational Dimension.** The informational dimension is where information is collected, processed, stored, disseminated, displayed, and protected. It consists of the content and flow of information. The informational dimension also makes up a significant portion of cyberspace.

(3) **The Cognitive Dimension.** The cognitive dimension encompasses how people think, perceive, visualize, and decide. How people think is affected by a myriad of factors such as propaganda, education, training, experience, personal motivations, religion, leadership, morale, cohesion, emotion, state of mind, public opinion, perceptions, media, and rumors. For COIN the cognitive dimension extends to US and international public opinion. **Because COIN battles and campaigns are struggles of will and ideas, they are ultimately won and lost in the cognitive dimension.** When trying to contemplate the cognitive dimension, it is imperative that counterinsurgents understand that it is not only how the populace views the counterinsurgents, but how counterinsurgents view the populace.

c. **Systems Perspective.** A systems perspective of the OE provides an understanding of relationships within interrelated political, military, economic, social, information, and infrastructure (PMESII) and other systems relevant to a specific joint operation without regard to geographic boundaries. This perspective helps facilitate understanding of the complex COIN OE, including the continuous and complex interaction of friendly, adversary, and neutral systems.

d. **Other Factors.** Other factors that help comprise a holistic view of the OE include intangible aspects such as the electromagnetic spectrum, weather and climate, time, and cultural and country characteristics. **While in traditional warfare sociocultural and civil factors were secondary considerations, these factors are critically important for COIN.**

(1) **Civil Factors.** An analysis of civil factors determines who, what, when, where, why, and how with respect to civilians, what activities those civilians are engaged in that might affect the military operation, what operations the military are engaged in that might affect the civilians' activities, and what the commander must do to support and interact with those civil actions. **There are six key civil considerations: ASCOPE.** Complex adaptive systems remain coherent under pressure and during change. Adversarial systems such as insurgencies will not acknowledge defeat without first attempting to adapt and change. Insurgencies tend to be less regimented and hierarchical, often allowing them to adapt quickly. The insurgent ability to adapt requires counterinsurgents to learn as well. The COIN environment is itself a complex adaptive

system as it potentially includes multiple unique insurgencies, a larger combination of adversaries, and a diverse population with varied sociocultural and civil factors. The population also consists of multiple complex adaptive systems that have inherent internal and external tensions and divisions. As a result, COIN is a complex adaptive problem. Because adversaries and other elements in the OE have adapted to earlier COIN efforts, those leading COIN may discover that the original understanding of a problem is no longer valid.

(2) **Sociocultural Factors.** While outsiders can gain an understanding of the OE, this understanding is still second-hand. Only someone from the indigenous population can truly understand the OE and all of its nuances. Thus, the HN representatives must be involved in every facet of COIN operations—from JIPOE to assessment. **There are five sociocultural factors for the COIN environment: society, social structure, culture, power and authority, and interests.**

e. **Holistic View.** The holistic view of the OE provides a detailed and comprehensive perspective on the OE. **The OE constrains and shapes the options that counterinsurgents can perform. Planning COIN operations is based first on the perspective of the people, accounts for the insurgency second, and then attempts to plan COIN operations or, in other words, shape the OE.**

For more detail on the holistic view of the OE see JP 2-01.3, Joint Intelligence Preparation of the Operational Environment.

2. Joint Intelligence Preparation of the Operational Environment Overview

Initial JIPOE must focus on having enough detail to complete mission analysis of the joint operation planning process (JOPP). JIPOE in COIN follows the process described in JP 2-01.3, *Joint Intelligence Preparation of the Operational Environment,* with an emphasis of sociocultural and civil factors. The joint force should include HN representatives if possible in the JIPOE process.

For more detail on JIPOE, see JP 2-01.3, Joint Intelligence Preparation of the Operational Environment.

SECTION A. STEP ONE

3. Define the Operational Environment

The first step of the JIPOE process is defining the OE by identifying those aspects and significant characteristics that may be relevant to the joint force's mission. Defining the OE must include the many military and nonmilitary organizations involved in the COIN effort. Knowledge of nonmilitary organizations is needed to establish working relationships and procedures for sharing information. These relationships are critical to developing a holistic, common operational picture.

a. **Identify the Joint Force's Operational Area.** HN and coalition partner policy determine theater level operational area considerations. Below the theater level, additional considerations are conducted like any joint operation: there are several choices to define the operational area, these areas may be contiguous or noncontiguous, and higher headquarters are responsible for the area between noncontiguous areas.

b. **Analyzing the Mission and Joint Force Commander's Intent.** The JFC's stated intent and all characteristics of the mission are of special significance to the JIPOE process for any mission, including COIN. The sociocultural and civil factors that are involved in COIN will expand the OE far beyond the designated limits of the operational area. Similarly, the HN, other multinational coalition partners, and the international community impact a COIN OE.

c. **Determine the Significant Characteristics of the Operational Environment.** This JIPOE step consists of a *cursory* examination of each aspect of the OE in order to identify those characteristics of *possible* significance or relevance to the joint force and its mission. A more *in-depth* evaluation of the impact of each relevant characteristic of the OE takes place during step two of the JIPOE process. Specific adversary capabilities and possible COAs are evaluated *in detail* during the third step of the JIPOE process. Other significant characteristics of the OE include: geographical features and meteorological and oceanographic (METOC) characteristics, complex relationships between PMESII systems, civil considerations, sociocultural considerations, infrastructure, ROE or legal restrictions, all friendly and adversary conventional, unconventional, and paramilitary forces and their general capabilities and strategic objectives, environmental conditions, psychological characteristics of adversary decision making, all locations of foreign embassies, and NGOs. **For COIN this step should pay special attention to the sociocultural factors, civil factors, root causes of the insurgency, insurgent desired end state, and insurgent narratives.**

d. **Counterinsurgency Operational Environment Framework.** Four important groups comprise the COIN OE: the population, adversaries, friendly elements, and neutral actors. **Subsequent steps of JIPOE—especially development of a PMESII systems perspective—add depth and clarity to understanding the COIN environment.**

(1) **Groups.** Effective analysis requires a framework with which to look at and examine the behaviour and motivation of actors within the population that may be involved, as the population is not a homogeneous, single group (see Figure VIII-1). There are four main categories based on their attitude towards the government. In addition to the four main groups it is inevitable that there will be 'spoilers', who have an interest in maintaining that level of local instability that enables them to achieve their own, often criminal ends. They may be disinterested in involvement in the political settlement, but will seek to maintain freedom of action through corruption, coercion, and undermining the rule of law. They will attempt to frustrate progress or to prevent any change that could adversely affect their activities. The four main categories are:

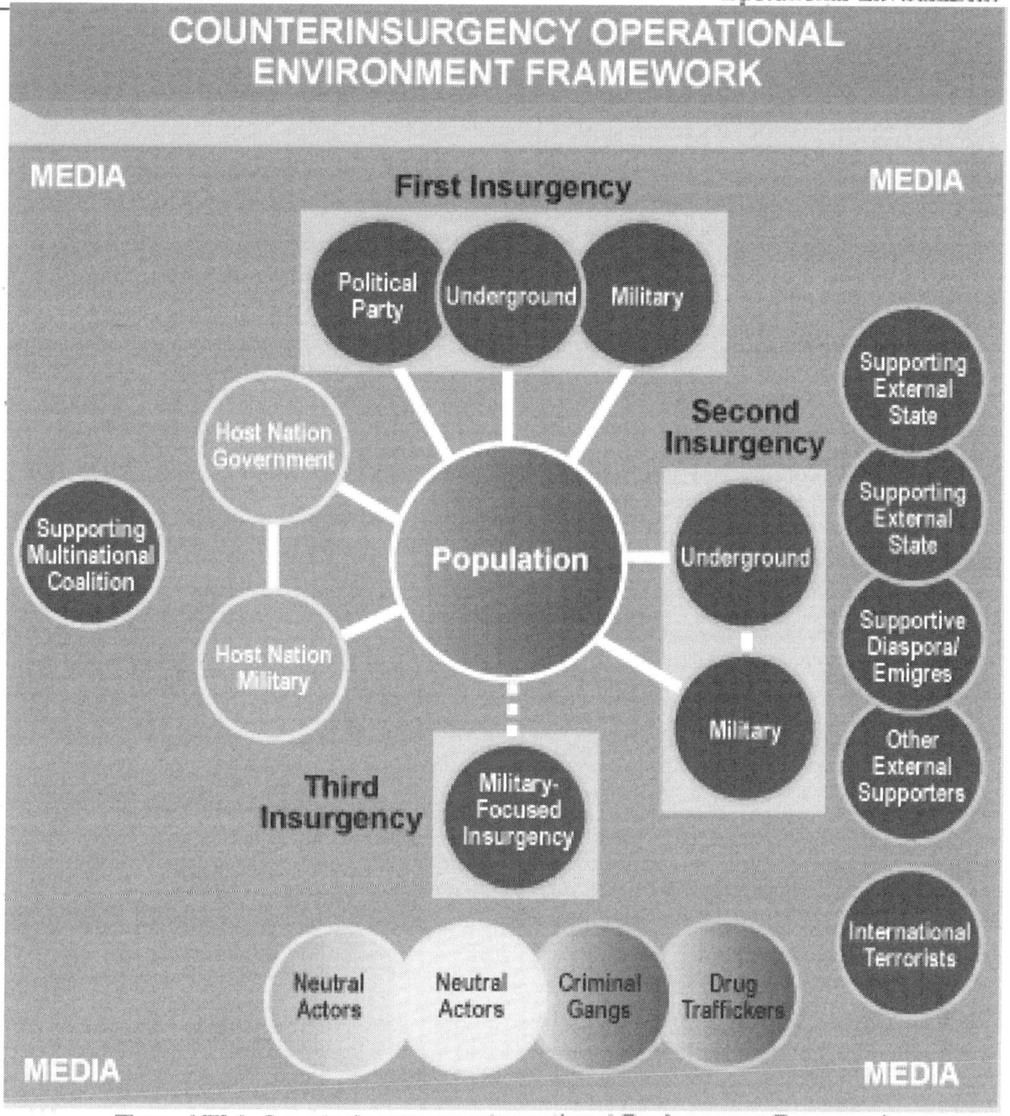

Figure VIII-1. Counterinsurgency Operational Environment Framework

(a) **Positive.** Those in this category will generally see the HN government as both legitimate and beneficial and will be supportive of their actions. They would be expected to include members of the HN government and its institutions including the judiciary, police, army and other internal security forces. These institutions are liable to infiltration by groups opposed to either the HN government or US intervention.

(b) **Neutral.** Some groups will ally themselves neither with hostile nor positive groups. The conflict produces uncertainty as to where their best interests. Nevertheless, neutral groups may play a critical role in any campaign especially if they constitute a large proportion of the population. They may offer potential and unseen support. When analyzing neutral groups, to develop means of engagement, it will be crucial to understand their aims, objectives and needs in order that at a minimum the status quo of their involvement in the conflict remains consistent with the wider political end state. The support of formerly neutral groups has historically proven to be vital to the success of either the HN or hostile groups.

(c) **Negative.** Those in this category oppose the HN authority but their day-to-day behaviour stops short of violence against that authority. Those who adopt a negative stance will do so for a variety of reasons, often based on core grievances and cycles of violence. Guarding against these individuals becoming the next generation of insurgents will be as much to do with our behaviour as that of the hostile groups.

(d) **Hostile.** Those in this category are actively and violently opposed to the HN government and joint forces. They will view violence as a legitimate means to their ends. However, even amongst those who are in this category there will be reconcilable and irreconcilable elements.

(2) **Population.** The population is the most important group in the COIN environment. Portions of the population will be pro-insurgent, pro-government, and neutral; however, the majority will most likely be neutral. COIN efforts seek to decrease the support for insurgents while increasing the neutral and the pro-government support. Physical and psychological links between the insurgents and counterinsurgents are important to determine who succeeds in the overall struggle.

(3) **Adversaries.** Some adversaries in a COIN environment directly challenge the HN, while others merely cause instability. **Competent insurgencies seek to strengthen their physical and psychological links with the population while breaking the HN's links with the population.** The adversaries in the example COIN OE in Figure VIII-1 consist of three distinct insurgencies, the external support for insurgencies, and other destabilizing actors.

(a) **Insurgencies.** The most advanced of the three insurgencies depicted in Figure VIII-1 has an associated political party to legitimize the insurgents, delegitimize the HN, and propagate the narrative. The political party and the underground are attempting to provide the population with a political alternative by building a shadow government. The military wing conducts sabotage, assassinations, and attacks in support of these efforts. Overall, this insurgency has strong physical and psychological links with the population. The second example insurgency does not have an associated political party but has an underground and military component. This insurgency is not as advanced as the previous one, but it enjoys much external support and has strong links with the population. The third insurgency is employing a military-focused strategy and is not providing a strong alternative to the HN. Due to its focus, it has weak linkages to the population.

(b) **Other Major Adversaries.** There are two other major adversaries depicted in Figure VIII-1: drug traffickers and international terrorists. Drug traffickers are members of powerful organization that present destabilizing influences but are typically contained by the HN law enforcement apparatus. The drug trafficking organization could begin efforts to nullify the HN's control in two HN provinces to counter successful law enforcement efforts; therefore, transforming the organization's criminal ends into an insurgency. International terrorists could exploit destabilizing situations in the HN to undermine the credibility of select HN leaders and/or coalition members. However, international terrorists do not function as irregular units in the open, nor are they interested in the population, holding terrain, or forming a shadow government.

(4) **Friendly Actors.** US and multinational efforts should focus on working by, with, and through the HN elements whenever possible and to the maximum extent possible. The more the HN does, the more likely it is to gain legitimacy. Figure VIII-1 depicts a coalition, including the US, supporting the HN's COIN efforts. Some of these multinational efforts are directly aimed at the population and the insurgents, although in consonance with the IDAD. As the HN capabilities and capacities increase, coalition efforts take on a more supporting role instead of a lead role. **HN elements are linked physically and psychologically to the population, and COIN efforts should strive to protect and strengthen these links with the population while breaking the links between the insurgents and the population.**

(5) **Neutral Actors.** Neutral actors in the COIN environment may be completely neutral or they may be friendly or adversarial by degree. For example, the media are neutral actors that may have elements that are biased towards either the friendly or the adversarial side. Overall, neutral actors play an important role in COIN.

e. **Establish the Limits of the Joint Force's AOI.** The AOI is the area of concern for the JFC. People and information flow through the operational area continuously, so the AOI may be quite large due to their impact. The AOI must include the impacts of media influence on the local population, the US population, and multinational partners. External financial, moral, and logistic support for the insurgents must be considered in determining the AOI as well.

f. **Determine the Level of Detail Required.** The time available for JIPOE may not permit each step to be detailed. Overcoming time limitations requires focusing JIPOE on what is most important. COIN is normally protracted, so large databases can and should be built.

g. **Determine Intelligence Gaps and Priorities.** There will be gaps in existing databases and these gaps must be identified in order to initiate appropriate intelligence collection efforts. **The IDAD strategy, stated intent, and PIRs establish priorities for intelligence collection, processing, production, and dissemination.**

h. **Collect Material and Submit Requests for Information.** Collecting data and incorporating it into JIPOE is a continuous effort. The intelligence staff initiates collection operations and issues requests for information to fill intelligence gaps to the level of detail required. When new intelligence confirms or repudiates previously made assumptions, the intelligence staff must inform the HN, COM, JFC, and other appropriate actors. When this occurs, all COIN participants should reexamine any evaluations and decisions that were based on those assumptions.

For more detail on defining the OE see JP 2-01.3, Joint Intelligence Preparation of the Operational Environment.

SECTION B. STEP TWO

4. Describe the Impact of the Operational Environment

This JIPOE step continues to develop a holistic view of the OE by analyzing the non-physical and physical aspects of the OE, developing a systems perspective of relevant PMESII links and nodes. The JIPOE process for evaluating the physical aspects of the OE is generally the same as in any other operation, but must pay attention to how the physical aspects relate to the population and the insurgency. **COIN operations require a detailed understanding of sociocultural factors and civil factors from three perspectives: the population, the insurgent, and the counterinsurgent.**

5. Sociocultural Factors

To understand the population the following five sociocultural factors should be analyzed: society, social structure, culture, power and authority, and interests.

a. **Society.** JIPOE must consider societies or societal links to groups outside the operational area and the impact of society on the overall OE.

b. **Social Structure.** Understanding social structure provides insight into how a society functions and how to attempt to build HN legitimacy, address core grievances, conduct successful IO, and undermine insurgent popular support. Social structures are often described by racial and ethnic groups, tribes, institutions and organizations, and other groups and networks.

(1) **Groups.** Tensions or hostilities between groups may destabilize a society, be a root cause of an insurgency, or provide opportunities for insurgents. It is vital to identify major groups inside and outside the operational area, to include their formal relationships, informal relationships, divisions and cleavages between groups, and cross-cutting ties.

(2) **Races and Ethnic Groups.** Of special note, racial or ethnic groups are often key sources of friction within societies and may be a root cause of insurgency or be a destabilizing influence.

(3) **Tribes.** Social roles, status, and norms form the foundation of the social structure affecting the populace and its perceptions. Tribes, clans, and kinship groups form another layer of identity for the population in COIN. In some cultures, loyalty to this layer of identity is the most powerful explanation for behavior.

c. **Culture.** Once the social structure has been thoroughly assessed, the JIPOE effort should identify and analyze the culture of the society as a whole and of each major group within the society. Culture is a system of shared beliefs, values, customs, behaviors, and artifacts that members of a society use to cope with their world and with one another. Where social structure comprises the relationships within a society, culture provides meaning within the society.

(1) **Identity.** Primary identities can be national, racial, and religious (specific examples could be tribe and clan affiliation). Secondary identities include past times or personal preferences. Individuals belong to multiple social groups which determine their cultural identities. Furthermore, people tend to rank order these identities depending on the importance they place on different groups. As a result, an individual's cultural identities may conflict with one another, such as when tribe loyalty may conflict with political affiliation.

(2) **Values and Attitudes.** A value is an enduring belief that a specific mode of conduct or end state of existence is preferable. Values may be in conflict within a society. Attitudes are affinities for, or aversions to, groups, persons, and objects. Attitudes affect perception, which is the process by which an individual selects, evaluates, and organizes information from the external environment. Counterinsurgents must understand how values and attitudes impact core grievances, public opinion, HN legitimacy, and support for insurgents.

(3) **Belief Systems.** Not only must counterinsurgents understand relevant belief systems, but they must avoid making arbitrary assumptions regarding what a society considers right and wrong, good and bad.

(4) **Cultural Forms.** Cultural forms are the outward expressions of the relevant culture. While not strictly dogmatic, cultural forms help define a culture, both for members and observers. Cultural forms include language, rituals, symbols, ceremonies, myths, and the cultural narrative. Understanding cultural forms of the relevant population (which may include several different cultures or combinations of cultures, each with their own forms) can be key to understanding the OE in COIN. The most important cultural form for counterinsurgents to understand is the narrative.

(a) **Language.** Communication requires more than just grammatical knowledge; it requires understanding the social setting, appropriate behaviors towards people of different statuses, and nonverbal cues.

(b) **Rituals.** It is vital for counterinsurgents to understand not only rituals, but the context in which they take place and the associated meaning or message.

(c) **Symbols.** Counterinsurgents should pay careful attention to the meaning of common symbols and how various groups use them.

(d) **Ceremonies.** These are a formal act or set of formal acts established by customs, or authority, or just over time and can be associated with religious or state occasion. The behavior can follow rigid etiquette or a prescribed formality. Just as for rituals, it is vital to understand not only the ceremonies, but also their context and its meaning.

(e) **Myths.** Myths are traditional stories of unknown origin passed on from generation to generation which serve to explain some phenomenon. They often greatly influence a given population's perception of truth. The counterinsurgent must understand that some myths are as resilient as the truth, and can influence the TA either negatively or positively.

(f) **Narratives.** A cultural narrative is a story recounted in the form of a linked set of events that explains an event in a group's history and expresses the values, character, or identity of the group. Narratives are the means through which ideologies are expressed and absorbed by members of a society.

d. **Power and Authority.** There are four major forms of power in a society: coercive force, social capital, economic resources, and authority. There are formal and informal power holders in a society and neither can be neglected during COIN operations. **JIPOE should analyze each group to identify its type of power, what it uses power for, and how it acquires and maintains power.**

(1) **Coercive Force.** Insurgents and other nongovernmental groups may possess considerable means of coercive force and often use it to gain power over the population.

(2) **Social Capital.** In a system based on patron-client relationships, an individual in a powerful position provides goods, services, security, or other resources to followers in exchange for political support or loyalty, thereby amassing power. Counterinsurgents must take these relationships into account when dealing with the population and their centers of influence.

(3) **Economic Power.** In weak or failed states, the formal economy may not function well. The informal economy refers to such activities as smuggling, black market activities, barter, and exchange. JIPOE must analyze how groups use economic power with the OE and how that power can be exploited during COIN operations.

(4) **Authority.** Understanding authority is vital to working with leaders to address core grievances, build HN legitimacy, and undermine insurgency.

e. **Interests.** Interests refer to the core motivations that drive behavior, which is a key issue during COIN operations. These include physical security, essential services, economic well-being, political participation, and core grievances. During times when the government does not function, groups and organizations to which people belong satisfy some or all of their interests that the government does not. **Reducing support for**

insurgents and gaining support for the HN government requires that the joint force understand the population's interests.

(1) **Physical Security.** During periods of instability people's primary interest is physical security for themselves and their families. When HN forces fail to provide security or threaten the security of civilians, the population is likely to seek alternative security measures, which may include guarantees from insurgents, militias, or other armed groups. JIPOE should therefore determine whether the population is safe from harm; whether there is a law enforcement system which is fair and nondiscriminatory and which provides security for each group when no effective government security apparatus exists.

(2) **Essential Services.** Essential services provide those things needed to sustain life. Examples of these essential needs are food, water, clothing, shelter, and healthcare. Stabilizing a population requires meeting these needs. If the HN government provides reliable essential services, the population is more likely to support it.

(3) **Economic Well-Being.** A society's individuals and groups satisfy their economic interests by producing, distributing, and consuming goods and services. Economic root causes of an insurgency may include the following: disenfranchisement, exploitative arrangements, and significant income disparity that creates or allows for intractable class distinctions. Operations or insurgent actions can adversely affect the economy, which can generate resentment against the HN government. Conversely, economic efforts can energize the economy and positively influence local perceptions.

(4) **Political Participation.** Many insurgencies begin because groups within a society believe that they have been denied political rights. JIPOE determines whether all members of the civilian population enjoy political participation; if ethnic, religious, or other forms of discrimination exist; and if legal, social, or other policies are creating grievances that contribute to the insurgency.

(5) **Grievances.** Resentment or frustration—real or perceived—may grow to become grievances. These grievances may become vulnerable to the insurgent narrative and exploitation. If the other two prerequisites for insurgency—leadership available for direction and lack of governmental control—are present, conditions exist for insurgency. A key point for COIN is consensus amongst all counterinsurgents on grievances and how to address them. JIPOE must determine the grievances of the population and the insurgents, and accurately distinguish between the two. The next step is to determine if these grievances are reasonable using subjective and objective criteria.

For more detail on sociocultural factors see JP 2-01.3, Joint Intelligence Preparation of the Operational Environment, *and FM 3-24/MCWP 3-33.5,* Counterinsurgency.

6. Civil Factors

Civil factors include ASCOPE. **ASCOPE analysis will help determine COIN impact on neutral, adversarial, and friendly systems.**

a. **Areas.** Areas are localities or physical terrains that have direct impact on the population and its activities. Examples include tribal regions, police districts, political boundaries, religious boundaries, territorial boundaries, military boundaries, polling stations, and government centers. **Areas are where the population congregates.**

b. **Structures.** Structures are existing important infrastructure. Examples include hospitals, bridges, communications towers, power plants, dams, jails, warehouses, schools, television stations, radio stations, and print plants. For COIN, some cultural structures may be even more vital, such as churches, mosques, national libraries, and museums. **Analysis of these structures includes determining why they are important with respect to their location, functions, capabilities, and application.**

c. **Capabilities.** Capabilities are key functions and services. They include, but are not limited to, administration, safety, emergency services, food distribution, agricultural systems, public works and utilities, health, public transportation, electricity, economics, and commerce. Sewage, water, electricity, academic, trash, medical, and security (SWEAT-MS) are the essential services local authorities must provide. Failure to provide essential services may give credibility to insurgents' grievances, reduce HN credibility, and ultimately undermine COIN. **This analysis must include who is officially and unofficially responsible for these functions and services.**

d. **Organizations.** Organizations can be religious, fraternal, criminal, media, patriotic or service, and community watch groups. They include media, IGOs, NGOs, merchants, squatters, and other groups. **Counterinsurgents must understand what organizations are important.**

e. **People.** People include all nonmilitary personnel in the AOI. Analysts must consider historical, cultural, ethnic, political, economic, and humanitarian factors when examining a given population. Any affiliations may have tremendous effect on the local population's support to an insurgency, including areas where people and insurgents may transit, retreat, evade, or hide. Populations such as squatters, the homeless, refugees, displaced persons, and outcast groups can also have an immense impact on the OE, and can be exploited by insurgents. **In addition to sociocultural factors, JIPOE must determine how people communicate, who are key communicators, and other formal and informal processes used to influence the population.**

f. **Events.** Events are routine, cyclical, planned, or spontaneous activities that significantly affect the OE. Some examples are planting and harvest seasons, elections, changes in government, key leader succession, economic reforms, political reforms, holidays, observances, anniversaries of key historical events, riots, and trials. Events may spur an increase or decrease in insurgent attacks. For example, insurgents may escalate violence to prevent an election, or insurgent activity may decrease during a harvest season as they assist the population. Combat operations, including indirect fires, deployments and redeployments, also affect the OE. **JIPOE must determine when events are occurring and analyze the events for their political, economic, psychological, environmental, and legal implications.**

7. Core Grievances, Prerequisites, and Drivers of Conflict

a. **Core Grievances.** JIPOE must determine the sources of frustration or anger within the population, from their perspective. These are the core grievances of the insurgency. Chapter II, "Insurgency," discussed the five general categories of core grievances for insurgencies, although there often are multiple core grievances. These core grievances can be the basis of grievances among the population, and these grievances are key contributors to what makes a population vulnerable (one of the three prerequisites for insurgency). Additional core grievances may appear or the original core grievances may change over time, especially if the HN government's actions further alienate the population. The general categories of core grievances are: identity, religion, economy, corruption, repression, foreign exploitation or presence, occupation, and essential services. Insurgents use grievances to communicate their cause through their narrative.

b. **Prerequisites.** JIPOE also must determine if the three prerequisites for insurgency are present: a vulnerable population, leadership available for direction, and lack of government control. When all three exist in an area, insurgency can operate with some freedom of movement, gain the support of the people, and become entrenched over time.

For more detail on core grievances and prerequisites, please see Chapter II, "Insurgency."

c. **Drivers of Conflict.** Although core grievances, or prerequisites, all play a role in insurgency and conflict overall, other factors can perpetuate, exacerbate, and escalate conflict. These dynamic factors are drivers of conflict and may or may not be directly associated with insurgency. Drivers of conflict fall into several categories, including but not limited to: sectarian, political, religious, external pressure, criminal, terrorist, revenge, and extremist ideology.

8. Develop a Systems Perspective of the Operational Environment

a. The development of a systems perspective of the COIN OE will require cross-functional participation by other joint force staff elements and collaboration with all other participants in COIN efforts.

For detail on a systems perspective, see JP 2-01.3, Joint Intelligence Preparation of the Operational Environment.

b. **Identifying relevant nodes.** While most of individual nodes (people) and their links are not relevant at the strategic and operational levels, some individual nodes have tactical importance during COIN operations. Thus, the level of the systems analysis will affect what is a node and what is a system.

(1) **Political Nodes.** Due to the primacy of politics in COIN, these nodes are often the most important nodes. Competent insurgents will strive to gain influence and control of these nodes. Counterinsurgents strive to work with these nodes to address the core grievances of insurgency and build the legitimacy of the HN while simultaneously degrading or breaking links between insurgency and political nodes.

(2) **Military Nodes.** Insurgents purposely distribute and network these military nodes to protect them, especially from infiltration. The exception to dispersing its military nodes occurs when an insurgency becomes powerful enough relative to the COIN security forces that it can openly conduct operations with irregular, traditional forces, or a fusion of the two. Counterguerrilla efforts must focus on destroying or neutralizing insurgent military nodes as well as breaking or degrading links between insurgent military nodes.

(3) **Economic Nodes.** Economic nodes may be targeted by the insurgency to gain power, secure funding, and delegitimize the HN. Insurgents normally have covert control of economic assets, as open control of any economic nodes requires holding terrain. COIN focuses on protecting and developing economic systems and degrading or destroying insurgent economic systems, although the effect on the population must be considered when attacking insurgent economic systems.

(4) **Social Nodes.** Social nodes, like political nodes, are vitally important to successful COIN. Competent insurgents will strive to gain influence and control of these nodes. Counterinsurgents must always strive to work with these nodes to address the core grievances of insurgency and build the legitimacy of the HN.

(5) **Infrastructure Nodes.** Like economic nodes, infrastructure nodes may be targeted by the insurgency to gain power and delegitimize the HN, although covertly. COIN focuses on protecting and developing infrastructure systems and degrading or destroying insurgent infrastructure systems, although the effect on the population must be considered when attacking insurgent infrastructure systems.

(6) **Information Nodes.** The control or use of information nodes is another key struggle in COIN. Insurgents will attempt to use these nodes for subversion. They will also attempt to destroy or degrade information nodes that support the HN. Counterinsurgents must strive to support and maintain freedom of the information network (press, radio, TV, etc.) while building and protecting HN legitimacy.

For more information on determining and analyzing node-link relationships, see JP 2-01.3, Joint Intelligence Preparation of the Operational Environment.

SECTION C. STEP THREE

9. Evaluate the Adversary

JIPOE uses the eight dynamics as a framework to analyze insurgencies. While each dynamic is important, analyzing their overarching interaction is essential to understand the insurgency holistically. The following paragraphs focus on JIPOE considerations for the eight dynamics:

a. **Leadership.** Insurgent leaders exploit the grievances of a vulnerable population to their end state. Leaders of insurgencies provide vision, direction, guidance, coordination, and organization. As discussed in Chapter II, "Insurgency," insurgent leadership may be distributed, collective, or charismatic. Because the leaders' personalities and decisions often determine whether the insurgency succeeds, JIPOE must identify them and analyze their individual beliefs, intentions, capabilities, and vulnerabilities. Important leader characteristics include the role in the organization; known activities; known associates; background and personal history; beliefs, motivations, and ideology; education and training; temperament; importance of the organization; and popularity outside the organization. It is also important to know if the insurgency has few leaders or if there is redundant leadership.

(1) **Senior Leaders.** Effective insurgent senior leaders provide cohesion and direction for the insurgency as a whole. Senior leaders in some insurgencies must communicate directly with insurgents for significant action, which leaves the insurgency vulnerable to penetration. Effective use of covert or clandestine communications, on the other hand, is the mark of effective insurgent senior leadership, as are decentralized but coordinated operations. Similarly, leaders who instill cohesion and discipline are also indicators of a capable insurgency.

(2) **Subordinate Leaders.** Subordinate leaders may include senior staff members, spokesmen, political leaders, guerrilla leaders, auxiliary leaders, underground leaders, and leaders of individual cells. Subordinate leaders in advanced insurgencies are organized and indoctrinated to act without constant guidance from the key insurgent leaders. If these individuals possess a high level of discipline and indoctrination, it is an indicator of an advanced insurgency.

b. **Objectives.** Insurgents have political objectives and are motivated by ideology, grievances, or power. Identifying insurgent objectives and motivations assists counterinsurgents in addressing both the conflict's core grievances as well as the insurgency itself. There may be multiple insurgent groups with differing goals and motivations, which require separate monitoring of each insurgency's objectives. Additionally, insurgent leaders may have different motivations from their followers, and insurgent leaders may change as well as the insurgency's goals. Insurgents may also hide their true motivations to portray their efforts in a way that the population will be more supportive. JIPOE must identify insurgent strategic, operational, and tactical objectives.

c. **Ideology.** Ideology drives many facets of the insurgency. Most importantly, ideology drives the insurgent end state. The insurgency normally uses an ideological alternative to which the government cannot or does not provide. Insurgent ideology often explains the population's grievances and how the insurgency will provide a resolution to those grievances. Ideology also provides justification for the insurgents' actions.

(1) **Addressing Core Grievances.** What the insurgency says about its ability to address root causes is a key indicator of its end state, methods, and level of sophistication. This can help the counterinsurgent understand the core grievances in the area and people's perception of their problems. Counterinsurgents should work with local leaders and the HN to address core grievances, increase HN legitimacy, and to pre-empt insurgent efforts to address the core grievances.

(2) **Insurgent Perception.** Ideology influences the insurgent's perception of the OE and shapes its organization and methods. It acts as a prism or lens for the insurgency's view of actors and activities. Insurgents may also work to reinforce or create false perceptions. An example is the perception that the government does not support a specific ethnic group. Counterinsurgents should use IO to address these insurgent efforts and ensure COIN actions do not reinforce false perceptions. Coalition partners should arrange for local leaders and the HN government to work together and allow legitimate leaders a voice in the government. Every action the counterinsurgent takes should be accompanied with an IO message with special emphasis on publicizing HN efforts and neutralizing the insurgent IO.

(3) **Internal Ideological Conflict.** Conflicting ideologies among the insurgents can create exploitable fracture points between different insurgent factions. Similarly, "external" ideologies can be exploited by working with the HN government using nationalist sentiments to expose the insurgents as "puppets of foreigners."

d. **Physical Environment.** This dynamic is the holistic view of the OE from an insurgent perspective. Considerations of METOC and terrain should include how the current weather and aspects of the terrain affects operations as well as how climate, weather, seasons, and terrain affect the local inhabitants and the insurgent. Additionally, JIPOE must account for the different aspects of rural and urban areas. The OE in these areas will greatly influence the insurgent organization and tactics due to terrain, density of people, and location of government forces. An urban environment is a dynamic mosaic where insurgent objectives and tactics may vary by neighborhood and the insurgents can easily blend in to the population. Proximity to international borders may provide an insurgency with sanctuary or support. Rugged, inaccessible terrain with populations hostile to outsiders may provide sanctuary or support for insurgents as well.

e. **External Support.** External support to insurgency can provide political, psychological, and material resources that might otherwise be limited or unavailable. External support for an insurgency can be provided by a state, organization, or non-state actor. JIPOE must consider what type of support is being provided, how much support is being provided, and who is providing the support and why. Two key indicators of external support are the presence of advisors with insurgents and supporters actively promoting the insurgent cause or strategic goals in international forums.

f. **Internal Support.** Internal support is essential for insurgencies. Insurgents recruit from and exploit vulnerable populations, and they often co-opt, coerce, deter, or marginalize other segments of the population. Internal support can be active or passive, open or hidden. This support may come from a small or large segment of the population. Internal support is especially important when insurgencies are latent or incipient, as they are attempting to grow and consequently are vulnerable.

g. **Phasing and Timing.** There are three basic phases to insurgencies: strategic defense, strategic equilibrium, and strategic offensive. There are several considerations with respect to phasing and timing. The insurgent leaders' ability to shift the insurgent organization from one phase to another to support political-military goals is a key consideration. More capable leaders will be able to rapidly shift to adjust to the current situation in the concerned area. Another consideration is the insurgent ability to shift personnel geographically, often in response to counterinsurgent pressure. Advanced insurgencies will be able to shift rapidly and effectively. Finally, the insurgent ability to consolidate and reorganize is an indicator of how capable the insurgency is; however, the lack of guerrilla activity does not necessarily mean there are no insurgents. Leaders and other elements may temporarily remain underground but will reappear when conditions are favorable. During periods like this, counterinsurgents must continue to address core grievances.

h. **Organizational and Operational Patterns.** Every insurgency's organization is unique; however, the type and level of organization are indicators of which approach it employs. Analyzing the organizational and operational patterns help the counterinsurgent to model and predict insurgent TTP. Understanding their organization also helps us to understand their capabilities and their potential targets. As discussed in Chapter II, "Insurgency," insurgents have a military wing and a political wing as well as several elements. These elements include leaders, the underground, combatants, cadre, auxiliary, and a mass base.

(1) **Insurgent Structure.** Insurgencies can be structured in several ways, and each structure has its own strengths and limitations. The structure used balances the following: security, efficiency and speed of action, unity of effort, survivability, geography, and social structures and cultures of the society. An insurgency's structure often determines whether it is more effective to target enemy forces or enemy leaders. Understanding an insurgent organization's structure requires knowing if the insurgency is hierarchical or nonhierarchical, structured or unsystematic, centralized or decentralized, independent or part of a larger organization, and emphasizes political or violent action. Additionally, it is important to ascertain if the insurgency's members are specialists or generalists. Organizations also vary greatly by region and time. Insurgent organizations are often based on existing social networks—familial, tribal, ethnic, religious, professional, or others.

(2) **Insurgent Error.** It should be noted that insurgents may be inept at the use of a given strategic approach. Alternatively, they may misread the OE and use an inappropriate approach. Knowledge of misapplication of approach or the use of different approaches by different insurgent groups may provide opportunities for counterinsurgents to exploit. It is imperative not only to identify insurgent approaches but also to understand their strengths and weaknesses in the context of the OE.

10. Evaluating Insurgent Activities

JIPOE must carefully examine insurgent activities. Not only are insurgent activities indicators of what approach or approaches an insurgency is using, they will help determine what counters can be used.

a. **Popular Support.** Developing support early in an insurgency is often critical to an insurgent organization's long-term survival and growth. As an insurgent group gains support, its capabilities grow. New capabilities enable the group to gain more support. Insurgencies that strive for acquiescence from the population desire freedom of movement and, consequently, the ability to expand their operations. Insurgents generally view popular support or acquiescence as a zero-sum commodity; that is, a gain for the insurgency is a loss for the government, and a loss for the government is a gain for the insurgency.

(1) **Forms of Popular Support.** Popular support can originate internally or externally and this support can be active or passive in nature. External support can take the form of finances, logistics, training, fighters, and safe havens. A state can provide passive external support as well. A foreign state passively supports an insurgency through inaction. Active internal support is usually the most important to an insurgent group. Passive internal support allows insurgents to operate and includes not providing information to counterinsurgents.

(2) **Methods of Generating Popular Support.** Insurgents generate popular support through persuasion, coercion, and encouraging overreaction.

(a) **Persuasion.** Insurgents can use persuasion to obtain either internal or external support. Forms of persuasion include charismatic attraction to a leader or group, appeal to an ideology, promises to address core grievances, and demonstrations of potency. Demonstrations of potency could be large-scale attacks or social programs for the poor.

(b) **Coercion.** Insurgents use coercion to either force people to support them or to acquiesce to insurgent activities. Insurgents can use violence or the threat of violence. Coercion is often very effective in the short term; however, coercion can undermine long-term insurgent efforts by alienating the population.

(c) **Encouraging Overreaction.** Encouraging overreaction refers to insurgents' enticing counterinsurgents to use brutal and repressive tactics. This is especially harmful to COIN if the counterinsurgents focus the reaction on the population rather than the elusive insurgents, thus alienating the population.

(3) **Critical Information.** Unbiased analysis of the relative levels of popular support of the insurgency and the HN are critical to understanding the OE and planning COIN. This analysis must extend to specific segments of the population. The relative levels of support of other states, non-state actors, and criminal organizations are also important.

b. **Support Activities.** Support activities often make up the majority of insurgent efforts. These activities are often tied to an insurgency's ability to generate popular support or external support. Safe havens, logistical areas, and training areas are key facilities for insurgent support activities. Logistics, finances, communications, recruiting, training, intelligence, and CI are key functions for insurgencies.

c. **Information and Media Activities.** Information and media activities are often an insurgency's main effort, with violence used in support of IO. This is one effective asymmetric tactic in that it minimizes the insurgency's materiel weakness and accentuates its potential sociocultural strengths, including the core grievances. Insurgents use information activities for several purposes—undermining HN legitimacy, undermining COIN forces' credibility, excusing insurgent transgressions, generating popular support, and garnering external support. Insurgents try to broadcast their successes, counterinsurgent failures, HN failures, and illegal or immoral actions by counterinsurgents or the HN. Insurgent efforts need not be factual; they need only appeal to the intended audience. Additionally, insurgents often seek to influence the global audience by directly attacking international and US public support for the COIN effort. Overall, insurgent media efforts can use forms or mediums such as: word of mouth, speeches, handouts, newspapers, periodicals, books, audio recordings, video recordings, radio, TV, web sites, e-mail, blogs, mobile telephones, and text messaging.

d. **Political Activities.** Insurgents use political activities to achieve their goals and enhance their cause's legitimacy. Competent insurgents link their political activities, IO, and acts of violence to achieve their goals. Political parties affiliated with an insurgent organization may negotiate or communicate on behalf of the insurgency, thereby serving as its public face. However, links between insurgents and political parties may be weak or easily broken by disputes between insurgents and politicians. In such cases, political parties may not be able to keep promises to end violent conflict. Some political parties may have much stronger ties to insurgencies. These ties can be hidden or overt. It is important to understand not only the links between insurgent groups and political organizations but also the amount of control each exerts over the other.

e. **Violent Activities.** Violent actions by insurgents include guerrilla warfare, terrorism, and conventional warfare, all of which may occur simultaneously. Terrorism and guerrilla warfare are usually planned to achieve the greatest political and informational impact with the lowest amount of risk to insurgents. JIPOE must analyze insurgent tactics, insurgent targeting, how the insurgent organization uses violence to achieve its goals, and how violent actions are linked to political and informational efforts.

(1) **Guerrilla Warfare.** Guerrilla tactics feature hit-and-run attacks by lightly armed irregular forces. The primary targets are HN government activities, security forces, and other COIN elements. Guerrillas usually avoid decisive confrontations unless they know they can win. Instead, they focus on harassing counterinsurgents. Guerrilla tactics are neither mindless nor random, but focused on attrition of enemy capabilities and erosion of enemy will.

(2) **Terrorism.** Terrorism is a tool the insurgents often use to strike fear into the civilian and military populace. Terrorism is sometimes not a tactic unto itself but supports the insurgent's strategic goals. Terror attacks generally require fewer personnel than guerrilla warfare or conventional warfare. They allow insurgents greater security and have relatively low support requirements. Insurgencies often rely on terrorist tactics early in their formation due to these factors. Terrorist tactics do not involve mindless destruction nor are they employed randomly. Insurgents choose targets that produce the maximum informational and political effects.

(3) **Conventional Warfare.** While insurgents may use conventional warfare, it is rare and not always necessary for success. These operations normally follow after the insurgency develops extensive popular support and sustainment capabilities. Only then can insurgents generate a traditional military force that can engage HN government forces. Building up a force capable of conducting conventional warfare usually requires significant external support as well.

f. **Exploiting Insurgent Vulnerabilities.** JIPOE should focus on insurgent vulnerabilities to exploit and strengths to mitigate. It is important to identify divisions between the insurgents and the populace as well as between the HN government and the people. Determining such divisions identifies opportunities to conduct operations that expand splits between the insurgents and the populace or lessen divides between the HN government and the people.

For more information on insurgent vulnerabilities, see Chapter II, "Insurgency."

11. Identify Adversary Centers of Gravity

Thorough and detailed COG analysis helps commanders and staffs to understand the systemic nature of the OE and the actions necessary to shape the conditions that define the desired end state. A thorough understanding of the insurgent ends, scopes, dynamics, approach, and activities are required to begin an insurgent COG analysis. The nature of the insurgent strategic ends is predominantly political and often more intangible than in traditional warfare. **As a source of power or strength, COGs are inherently complex and dynamic; they can change over time.** COGs consist of certain critical factors that may include intrinsic weaknesses. These critical factors help commanders identify and analyze COGs, formulate methods to neutralize or isolate them, and prevent them from influencing events. Insurgent COGs and critical factors also tend to be conceptual and moral, although an advanced insurgency that is able to engage in a war of movement and has a shadow government will have more tangible COG and critical factors.

a. **Insurgent Centers of Gravity.** The insurgent strategic COG is likely to be conceptual or moral, although the core grievances of the insurgency may well be physical. A strategic COG analysis will therefore highlight the insurgent's ideology, motivations, and cause. Critical strengths and weaknesses are predominantly tactical and intangible in their nature. This also makes it difficult to determine which of the enemy's critical strengths represent the true COG. The insurgent leaders or the underground might comprise a COG. In some cases, ideology should be considered an important part of the COG. The individual insurgent commanders and their forces in the countryside may in exceptional cases constitute an operational COG. At the operational level, insurgents rarely mass large forces to constitute a tangible operational COG.

b. **Operational Level Example.** A notional insurgency's propaganda apparatus could represent an operational-level COG. The critical capabilities (CCs) necessary for the COG to function might include information collection, internal communications, key leaders of the apparatus, and dissemination methods. Without those capabilities, the propaganda apparatus has no potential for action and would not represent a COG. For those CCs to function, they in turn require certain conditions, resources, and means (critical requirements [CRs]) to be fully operational, such as internet access, radio stations, television stations, printing facilities, and collectors. Critical factors analysis identifies systemic vulnerabilities that, if attacked, influence the COG through the loss of CCs. The critical vulnerabilities (CVs), which the counterinsurgents could locate and gain control, could be the radio stations, television stations, and printing facilities. While efforts can be made against insurgent internet access and collectors, these would be much more difficult, if not impossible, to consistently deny the insurgent.

c. **Using Critical Requirements and Vulnerabilities.** CRs and CVs are interrelated. The loss of one CR may expose vulnerabilities in other CRs; the loss of a CR may initiate a cascading effect that accelerates the eventual collapse of a COG. The analysis of a COG and its critical factors will reveal these systemic relationships and their inherent vulnerabilities. In situations where a COG possesses multiple CVs, critical factors analysis helps commanders and staffs prioritize the vulnerabilities. Due to the complex nature of the insurgency and OE, CRs and CVs are often more difficult to identify and target.

d. **Tactical Critical Requirements.** The CRs that sustain a strategic or operational COG function are independent of the respective level of war. This exposes CVs to actions generated at any echelon. For example, an operational COG may rely upon certain CRs that are vulnerable at the tactical level of war.

SECTION D. STEP FOUR

12. Determine Adversary Courses of Action

The first three steps of the JIPOE process help to provide JFCs, subordinate commanders, and their staffs with a holistic view of the OE by analyzing the impact of the OE, assessing adversary approaches and tactics, and identifying adversary COGs. The fourth step of the JIPOE process builds upon this holistic view to develop a detailed understanding of the adversary's plan and probable COAs. The insurgency's overall approach, or combination of approaches, the insurgent senior leaders have selected to achieve their goals and their recent tactics are key indicators of their plan. From these indicators a model of the insurgent plan can be constructed. The final step is determining the COAs the insurgency may use.

a. **Insurgent Plan.** The insurgent plan is the way that the strategic approach is applied to create the conditions necessary to achieve the desired end state. Insurgents can accomplish this goal by maintaining preexisting adverse conditions or by creating those conditions. While the insurgents normally do not have a campaign plan in the same sense that US and multinational forces do, constructing a model of their actions in this form adds to understanding the insurgency, predicting insurgent COAs, planning a COIN operation, seizing the initiative in COIN, executing the overall COIN, and assessing a COIN operation.

(1) **Collaborative Effort.** Constructing a model of the insurgents' plan requires participation and input from the HN, JFC, outside agencies, and the entire staff. Cultural understanding as well as judgment, experience, education, intelligence, boldness, perception, and character are required to effectively cooperate. It is imperative that the entire process be based on open discussion and intellectual honesty. Mirror imaging or biasing this process will result in not only a skewed enemy campaign plan, but it will skew all friendly efforts based on it.

(2) **Model-Making.** The process of constructing a model of the insurgents' plan is an inductive and intuitive one. Constructing a model of the insurgents' plan requires intelligence products and the previous steps of the JIPOE to build and subsequently update the model. The intelligence products and JIPOE are based on the insurgents' actions, and building the model requires analyzing these products holistically and then inductively determining the insurgents' logical LOOs. For example, insurgents that rely heavily on terrorism to gain the population's acquiescence will have a terrorism logical LOO, or another insurgency may focus on propaganda and therefore may merit having a propaganda logical LOO that is separate from just subversion.

(3) **Graphic Example.** Figure VIII-2 graphically depicts two examples of an insurgent's plans. The population can include the HN, coalition partners, and even the international community. Guerrilla warfare normally focuses on the military and law enforcement elements of the opposition. The insurgent end state is the sum of several conditions that the insurgents must change from current conditions. The insurgency does

this though activities that successfully cause effects. The logical LOOs are the insurgency's operational ways to cause effects to change the current conditions. Insurgents execute tactical actions simultaneously or sequentially along these logical LOOs. These tactical actions hope to cause effects in the overall OE. The effects or an accumulation of effects may occur simultaneously or sequentially, depending on the situation and the effectiveness of insurgent and counterinsurgent efforts. When tactical actions and their cumulative effects have successfully translated to the operational level to change all of the conditions, the insurgency will have reached its end state. The COIN OE is extremely dynamic, requiring flexible planning and execution and continuous analysis of desired conditions.

(4) **Multiple Threats.** If there are multiple insurgencies, this process of model making must be done for each insurgency or adversary. Once the models have been made for each adversary, they must be accounted for holistically or cumulatively. Thus, the intelligence community will incorporate this comprehensive view of adversarial end states, conditions, and logical LOOs into the intelligence estimate. The comprehensive view must be accounted for in the IDAD strategy and other subordinate COIN plans.

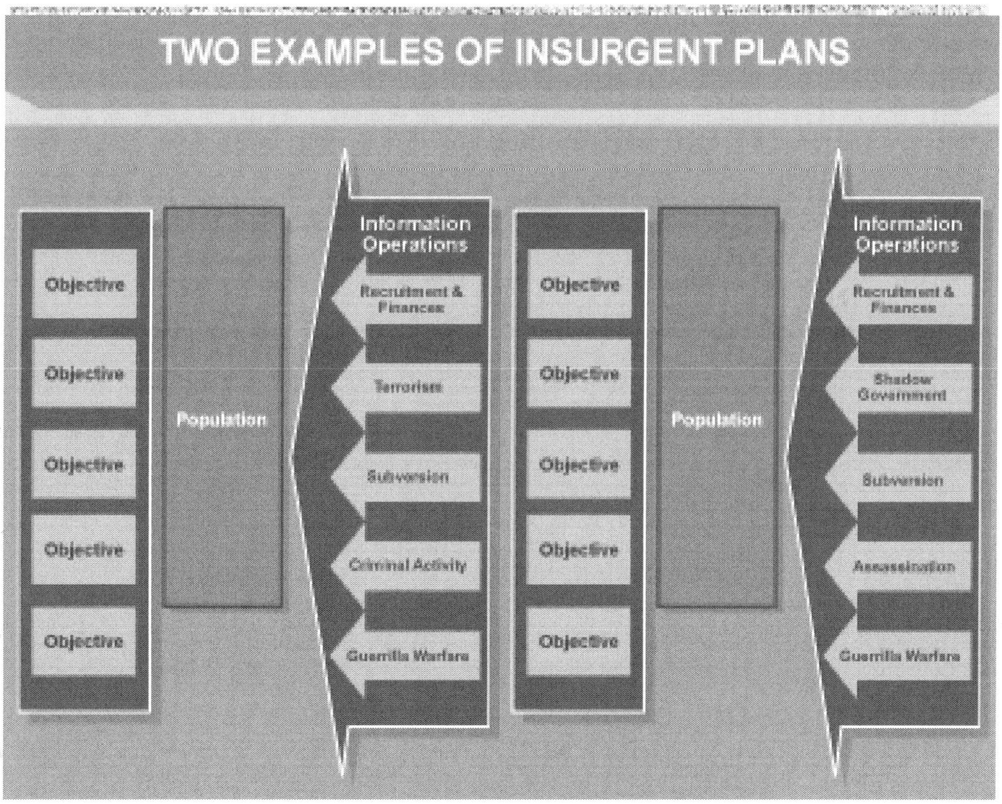

Figure VIII-2. Two Examples of Insurgent Plans

(5) **Assessment and Adjustment.** Once an initial model is constructed, it must be evaluated during the continuous assessment of operations. If necessary, the model should be updated, which could potentially cause the IDAD strategy and subordinate friendly plans to be modified accordingly. The dynamic nature of the COIN environment will often require tactical adjustments. Similarly, the operational level may require changes, although major changes in this area will normally be less frequent or sweeping. The strategic level, specifically the strategic approach, will normally change even less frequently than the operational level.

b. **Insurgent Courses of Action.** The insurgency plan model provides a disciplined methodology for analyzing the set of potential adversary COAs in order to identify the COA the adversary is most likely to adopt. However, insurgents may pursue many different tactical COAs within an operational area at any time, although these efforts will support the broader plan, and their tactical COAs change with both time and location. Insurgent tactics are the means to achieve tactical objectives in support of the plan. Insurgents base their tactical COA on their capabilities and intentions. Evaluating the support, information, political, and violent capabilities of insurgent organizations was discussed previously. The intentions come from goals, motivations, approach, culture, perceptions, and leadership personalities. However, insurgent tactical actions can have operational and strategic effects. This is because insurgent propaganda and media reporting can reach a wide and even global audience, multiplying the effects of insurgent tactical actions.

CHAPTER IX
PLANNING IN COUNTERINSURGENCY

> *We need to stop planning operationally and strategically as if we were going to be waging two separate wars, one with tanks and guns on a conventional battlefield, the other with security and stabilization of the population… we should do extensive planning on how we will establish [or support] an indigenous host government, to include military and police forces, and how we will provide protection and essential services to the conflict population. The most critical initial problem in such a campaign will not be how to form [or support] a central indigenous government, but how to 'clear, hold, and build.'*
>
> **John J. McCuen, Colonel (Ret), US Army**
> ***Hybrid Wars*, March-April Military Review 2008**

1. Counterinsurgency Planning

a. **Influencing the Future.** Planning involves thinking about ways to influence the future rather than responding to events. This involves evaluating potential decisions, actions, and shaping conditions in advance. Planning involves integrating these individual decisions and tasks together into creating potential effects, as well as examining the implications of these decisions, tasks, and effects. Planning involves thinking through the conditions and, through operational art and design, understanding how achieving the objectives will cumulatively reach the end state.

b. **Planning Horizons.** In general, a planning horizon refers to a future time or event associated with a specific planning effort. The farther into the future that plans reach, the wider the range of possibilities and the more uncertain the forecast of the future conditions. **Because COIN operations require comprehensive solutions, planning horizons in COIN are normally longer than other operations, despite increased uncertainties associated with these longer planning horizons.** During COIN, JFCs may plan in months and years, and subordinate units' time horizons are similarly expanded in duration. Careful oversight of planning efforts must be maintained to avoid planning in too detailed a fashion too far into the future, which wastes time and effort.

c. **Planning for Unified Action.** Although there are many specific ways to counter insurgency, comprehensive planning efforts are essential for successful long-term COIN. While the joint force primarily contributes to the military instrument of national or coalition power, the joint force supports the other instruments. More specifically, the joint force supports the HN's military COIN efforts, which is primarily the counterguerrilla effort (destruction or neutralization of the insurgent's military wing), and this support to the overall counterguerrilla effort is vital to short- and long-term success of COIN. The unified action required to achieve the comprehensive solutions that will bring success during COIN operations, in turn requires interorganizational planning efforts among all interagency, intergovernmental, and nongovernmental partners involved. The level of unity of effort in planning will vary from close coordination of operational plans to informal collaboration to sharing of information through third parties. Additionally, planning horizons for the partners that the JFC is supporting tend to be significantly longer than military planning horizons. The JFC must ensure that military planning complements planning conducted by interagency and other partners. This will require liaison and the nesting of operational plans to accommodate supported interagency objectives and longer planning horizons

For more information on joint planning, see JP 3-0, Joint Operations, *and JP 5-0,* Joint Operation Planning.

2. Levels of War and Counterinsurgency

a. The levels of war remain the same for any form of warfare, regardless of whether it is traditional, irregular, or a combination. The levels of war in COIN may be compressed and difficult to define. The tactical and operational levels in COIN may be compressed due to the protracted nature of the conflict and the complexity of the OE. The levels of war are not closely associated with echelons in COIN as they have tended to be in traditional warfare. For example, a Marine expeditionary force may be the basis of the operational-level headquarters in one theater while an Army corps may be the basis of the operational-level headquarters in another. Time horizons for COIN are extended at every level of war; it takes longer to achieve the objectives in COIN.

b. A COIN operation or campaign normally consists of a series of major tactical actions and operations of long duration. Tactical action in COIN is the direct link with the relevant population and gaining counterinsurgent credibility and HN legitimacy. The cumulative effect of tactical action translates to changing conditions. The operational and strategic levels in COIN are extremely sensitive to tactical actions. Tactical commanders should be empowered with the authority and capabilities they need. They must also understand their role in supporting the non-security LOOs led by civilian agencies, and the effects their security actions may have on those LOOs. Tactical COIN efforts are normally decentralized with a centralized vision and message. However, JFCs must avoid having a "strategy of tactics." In other words, JFCs must have a plan within which tactical efforts nest. Additionally, JFCs must ensure that tactics are not used that win in combat but prevent operational or strategic success.

c. The COIN environment presents complex problems that have incomplete, contradictory, and changing requirements. The solutions to these problems are often difficult to recognize because of complex interdependencies. While attempting to solve a complex problem, the solution of one of its aspects may reveal or create another complex problem.

3. Joint Operation Planning and Operational Design

a. **Joint operation planning blends two complementary processes.** The first is the JOPP. JOPP is an orderly, analytical planning process, which consists of a set of logical steps to analyze a mission, develop, analyze, and compare alternative COAs, select the best COA, and produce a plan or order. JOPP underpins planning at all levels and for missions across the full range of military operations. Although the JFC can compress or extend JOPP steps in response to the urgency of the situation and complexity of assigned tasks, each planning step is relevant to any mission. The steps of JOPP facilitate interaction between the JFC, staff, and subordinate and supporting organizations, regardless of strategic objectives, the nature of the OE, and the type of operation (such as COIN).

b. The second process is **operational design**, the use of various design elements in the conception and construction of the framework that underpins a joint operation plan and its subsequent execution. Operational design helps expand and synthesize the intuition and creativity of the commander with the methodical and logical planning process.

c. While operational design is continuous throughout planning and execution, the process plays a particularly important early role in helping commanders and staffs visualize a broad approach to a solution rather than jumping prematurely to consideration of detailed, alternative COAs. A COIN operation can be more complex and its operational and strategic objectives more difficult to achieve than those of traditional, force-on-force military operations. The initial observable symptoms of an insurgency often do not reflect the true nature and core grievances of the insurgency, so the JFC and staff must devote sufficient time and effort early in planning to correctly frame the problem and design a broad approach to a solution. *Line of operations, objective, center of gravity*, and *end state* are design elements that are particularly important in the early design effort to help commanders and staffs visualize a joint operation's framework.

d. Through early and continuous assessment during COIN execution, the staff and JFC monitor the OE and progress toward accomplishing tasks and achieving objectives. Assessment helps the JFC ensure that the design concept, concept of operations, and tasks to subordinate and supporting commands remain feasible and acceptable in the context of higher policy, guidance, or orders. If the current approach is failing to meet these criteria, or if aspects of the OE change significantly, the JFC may decide to revisit earlier design conclusions and decisions that led to the current design concept. This could result in small adjustments to current operations or in a significant reorientation involving new objectives and organizational realignments. The challenge in COIN, more than in traditional combat operations, is that changes in the OE are often more subtle and difficult to assess. Likewise, when the JFC revisits and changes the design decisions that drove the original plan's concept of operations, execution of a new design and CONOPS typically will evolve slowly. See Chapter X, "Execution in Counterinsurgency," for more information on assessment during COIN.

e. **Elements of Operational Design.** Operational design for COIN should reflect a comprehensive approach applicable to the phase or stage of the campaign. Because there is only one IDAD strategy or campaign, there should only be one operational design. This single design should incorporate all actors, with particular attention placed on interagency partners and HN participants, if there is a legitimate HN present. The elements of operational design for COIN are superficially the same as for any joint planning effort, but the context and therefore their application are different. During execution, commanders and planners continue to consider design elements. Reframing may become necessary due to friendly, adversary, or other effects changing the OE significantly. This may be to adjust both current operations and future plans to capitalize on tactical and operational successes as the joint operation unfolds.

(1) **Termination.** If the joint force is supporting a HN's COIN efforts, termination will depend on political discourse between the HN, the US, and other coalition members. This discourse is normally based on the projected security environment. The ends, core grievances, drivers of conflict, and leadership of an insurgency are also important factors. Insurgencies based on interest-based root causes, such as economic disparity or political corruption, may be persuaded or coerced back into a political process. Insurgencies based on ideology, ethnicity, or religious or cultural identities are value-based and their demands are more difficult to negotiate. Some insurgencies or groups of insurgencies will be both value- and interest-based. The drivers of conflict also impact the conditions necessary for termination.

(2) **End State and Objectives.** The end state normally will represent a point in time or circumstance beyond which the President does not require the military instrument of national power to achieve remaining objectives of the national strategic end state. **The combined political and military nature of COIN, however, make the overall military end state very close or even the same as the national end state.** Aside from its obvious role in accomplishing strategic objectives, clearly defining the conditions of the end states promotes unified action, facilitates synchronization, and helps clarify (and may reduce) the risk associated with the joint campaign or operation. In COIN, commanders should include both the national end state and the military end state in their planning guidance and commander's intent statement.

(3) **Effects.** Identifying desired and undesired effects within the OE connects military strategic and operational objectives to tactical tasks. Combined with a systems perspective of the COIN environment, the identification of desired and undesired effects informs a holistic view of the OE. Counterinsurgents plan joint COIN operations by developing strategic and operational objectives supported by measurable strategic and operational effects and assessment indicators. **Effects are useful in planning COIN; however, effects can be difficult to accurately predict given their highly sociocultural and political nature. The difficulty in predicting these effects reinforces the need for wide participation and lengthy discourse when planning COIN.**

(a) **Direct and Indirect.** A direct effect is the first-order consequence of an action, and an indirect effect is a delayed consequence associated with an action. **Indirect effects are often more important in COIN, which is one of the factors that tend to make COIN both protracted and difficult.** These effects establish conditions, and counterinsurgents should determine the best sequence of actions to create these effects. **Discourse should develop and refine the necessary conditions for success in COIN.**

(b) **Intelligence, Discourse, and Effects.** Determining required effects requires a clear understanding of the desired end state and the current conditions, both of which require appropriate discourse to develop. JIPOE informs discourse and helps provide a holistic view of the current OE or, in other words, the current conditions.

(4) **Centers of Gravity.** COGs are inherently complex and dynamic in that they change depending on each belligerent's objectives and the OE. Changes to COGs must be carefully planned for and analyzed. Changes to COGs often indicate a change in the nature of operations. JFCs consider not only the insurgents' COGs, but also identify and protect their own COGs. Counterinsurgents must similarly determine the friendly strategic and friendly operational COGs. Critical factors analysis provides commanders with a detailed, systemic understanding of friendly and adversary COGs, and the knowledge to balance resources accordingly to protect them as the situation requires.

See Chapter VIII, "Operational Environment," *for more information on COG and critical factors analysis.*

(5) **Decisive Points.** Decisive points are a logical extension of COGs critical factors. Counterinsurgents should identify decisive points to leverage friendly capabilities to exploit insurgent vulnerabilities. **A decisive point is a node, system, or key event that allows a marked advantage over an insurgent and greatly influences the outcome of COIN.** Decisive points are not COGs; they are keys to attacking or protecting COG CRs. **In COIN, this can be influential individuals in the population, and leader engagement and providing them security may provide the counterinsurgents an advantage over the insurgents.** When it is not feasible to attack a COG directly, commanders focus operations to weaken or neutralize the CRs—therefore critical vulnerabilities—upon which it depends. These critical vulnerabilities are decisive points, providing the indirect means to weaken or collapse the COG. Decisive points at the operational level provide the greatest leverage on COGs, where tactical decisive points are directly tied to task and mission accomplishment.

(a) **Prioritization.** COIN typically presents more decisive points than the joint force can control, destroy, or neutralize with available resources. Through critical factors analysis, commanders identify the decisive points that offer the greatest leverage on COGs. They designate the most important decisive points as objectives and allocate enough resources to create the desired results on them. Decisive points that enable commanders to seize, retain, or exploit the initiative are crucial. Controlling these decisive points during operations helps commanders gain freedom of action, maintain momentum, and dictate tempo. If the adversary maintains control of a decisive point, it may exhaust friendly momentum, force early culmination, or facilitate an adversarial counterattack.

(b) **Stability Decisive Points.** Decisive points assume a different character during stability operations, which are a key part of COIN. These decisive points may be less tangible and more closely associated with critical events and conditions. For example, they may include repairing a vital water treatment facility, establishing a training academy for HN security forces, securing a major election site, or quantifiably reducing crime. While most of these decisive points are physical, all are vital to establishing the conditions for defeating an insurgency, addressing core grievances, and building HN capabilities, capacity, and ultimately legitimacy.

(6) **Direct Versus Indirect.** In theory, direct attacks against enemy COGs resulting in their neutralization or destruction is the most direct path to victory. **It is often difficult or impossible to attack an insurgency's strategic COG or operational COG; thus, COIN often requires an indirect approach.** As a result, the insurgent's CVs can offer indirect pathways to gain leverage over the insurgent's COGs. In this way, JFCs employ a synchronized combination of operations to weaken insurgent COGs indirectly and over time by attacking CRs that are sufficiently vulnerable.

(7) **Lines of Operations.** Logical LOOs are a key tool for counterinsurgents to visualize the operational design as positional reference to insurgent forces may have little operational relevance. **Each logical LOO represents a conceptual category along which the HN government and COIN force commander intend to "attack" the insurgent strategy and build HN government legitimacy.** Logical LOOs describe the linkage of various actions on nodes and decisive points with an operational or strategic objective and the conditions of the end state. They also connect tasks and effects to nodes and decisive points related in time and purpose with an objective. **COIN requires the synchronization of activities along multiple and complementary logical LOOs in order to work through a series of tactical and operational objectives to attain the military end state.** The JFC should not organize the staff around LOOs. Figure IX-1 depicts a set of example logical LOOs, some working through the population and others focused on the insurgents.

(a) **Main Effort.** Commanders may specify a logical LOO as the main effort. In this case the other LOOs shape the OE for the main effort. **This prioritization may change as COIN creates or exploits insurgent vulnerabilities, insurgents react or adjust their activities, or the environment changes.** In this sense, commanders adapt their operations not only to the state of the insurgency, but also to the OE.

(b) **Interdependence.** Success in one logical LOO reinforces successes in the others. **Progress along each LOO contributes to attaining a stable and secure environment for the HN.** Stability is reinforced by popular recognition of the HN government's legitimacy, improved governance, and progressive, substantive reduction of the core grievances of the insurgency. **There is no list of logical LOOs that applies in all COIN or all phases of COIN.** Logical LOOs should be based on the holistic understanding of the OE and what must be done to achieve the end state.

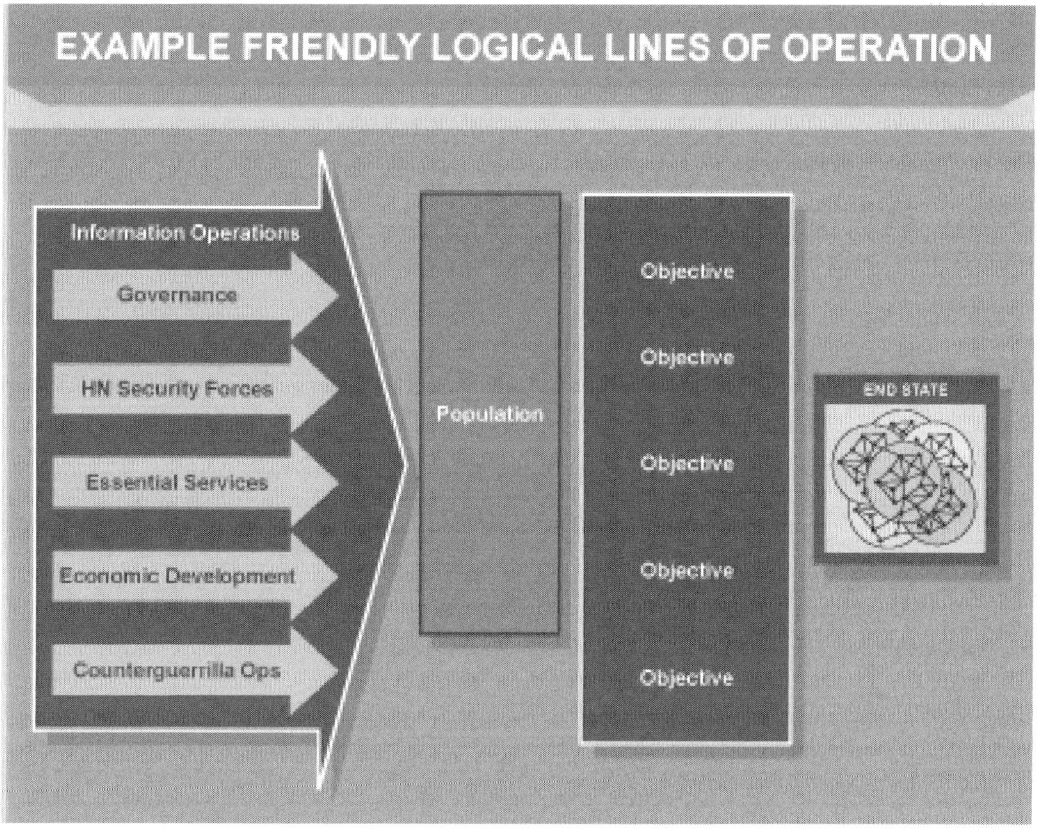

Figure IX-1. Example Friendly Logical Lines of Operations

(8) **Operational Reach.** Operational reach is the distance and duration over which a joint force can successfully employ military capabilities. Operational reach may be a factor in COIN if there are limitations set on the number, type, or general footprint of forces that can support a HN's COIN efforts. Operational reach can also be a factor if the joint force faces insurgency when there is no HN.

(9) **Simultaneity and Depth.** Simultaneity refers to the simultaneous application of military and nonmilitary power against the adversary's key capabilities and sources of strength. **Simultaneity in COIN contributes directly to an insurgency's erosion and ultimate collapse by addressing core grievances and placing more demands on insurgent military forces and functions than can be handled.** Simultaneity also refers to the concurrent conduct of operations at the tactical, operational, and strategic levels. **For COIN, depth applies to time as well as to space.** This reflects that most insurgencies protract the conflict by design. **Because of the inherent tight interrelationships between the levels of war in COIN, commanders cannot be concerned only with events at their respective echelon, but must understand how their actions contribute to the military end state and the overall end state.**

(10) **Timing and Tempo.** The joint force should conduct operations at a tempo and point in time that best exploits friendly capabilities and inhibits the enemy. **However, the COIN intelligence-operations dynamic ultimately determines the tempo that the counterinsurgents can maintain. Good intelligence will allow for successful operations that may in turn result in more usable intelligence.** Given actionable, reliable intelligence and proper timing, counterinsurgents can dominate the action, remain unpredictable, and operate ahead of the insurgency's ability to react.

(11) **Forces and Functions.** COIN should focus on addressing the core grievances and drivers of conflict in addition to defeating the insurgency as a military force (counterguerrilla operations). Defeating the insurgency as a military force consists largely of the counterguerrilla aspect of neutralizing or destroying the insurgent military wing.

(12) **Leverage.** Leverage is gaining, maintaining, and exploiting advantages across all domains and the information environment. Leverage can be achieved through asymmetrical actions that pit joint force strengths against insurgent vulnerabilities and the concentration and integration of joint force capabilities. Leverage allows counterinsurgents to impose their will on the insurgency, increase the enemy's dilemma, and maintain the initiative.

(13) **Balance.** Balance is the maintenance of the force, its capabilities, and its operations in such a manner as to contribute to freedom of action and responsiveness. **Balance refers to the appropriate mix of forces and capabilities within the overall counterinsurgent force as well as the nature and timing of operations conducted.** Balance is particularly challenging to achieve in an interagency campaign, where the mix of capabilities includes civilian agencies, and time horizons differ widely between the shorter-term focus of the JTF and the longer-term focus of the US embassy. Balance also refers to a proper balance of offense, defense, and stability operations.

(14) **Anticipation.** Anticipation is essential to effective planning and execution for COIN. Counterinsurgents must use intelligence to ascertain the insurgents' approach and campaign plan, which will assist in anticipating insurgent activities. A shared, common holistic view of the OE aids counterinsurgents in anticipating opportunities and challenges. **Knowledge of the population, friendly capabilities, insurgent and other adversarial capabilities, intentions, and likely COAs allows COIN to focus efforts on where they can best impact the situation.** However, anticipation is not without risk, especially if insurgent deception is effective.

(15) **Synergy.** Counterinsurgents integrate and synchronize operations, forces, and capabilities in a manner that addresses the core grievances of insurgency, deals with the drivers of conflict, and neutralizes and defeats insurgents. This includes combining forces and actions to achieve concentration throughout the OE, culminating in achieving the objectives. Synergy in COIN consists of physical and psychological aspects. In the complex COIN environment, it is impossible to accurately view the contributions of any

individual organization, capability, or the area in which they operate in isolation from all others. Each may be critical to success, and each has certain capabilities that cannot be duplicated. Commanders and JTF staff must work with the COM and embassy staff to develop mechanisms to synchronize the campaign plan and achieve civil-military synergy in operations.

(16) **Culmination.** Culmination has both an offensive and a defensive application and can occur at any level of war. Culmination may, during COIN or stability operations, form the erosion of national will, or the decline of popular support, pose questions concerning legitimacy or restraint, or create lapses in protection leading to excessive casualties. A well-developed assessment methodology is crucial to supporting the commander's determination of culmination, both for insurgent and friendly actions.

(17) **Arranging Operations.** Counterinsurgents must determine the best arrangement of COIN operations to accomplish the assigned tasks and joint force mission. This arrangement often will be a combination of simultaneous and sequential operations to achieve the end state conditions. **A variety of factors must be considered when determining this arrangement for COIN operations, including the population's current view of counterinsurgent credibility, HN legitimacy, and the insurgents in general.** The arrangement of COIN operations impacts the tempo of activities in time, space, and purpose.

(a) **Phases. Reaching the end state for COIN requires the conduct of a wide array of operations over a protracted period.** Consequently, the design of COIN operations normally provides for related phases implemented over time. **Phasing helps visualize and think through the entire COIN effort and to define requirements in terms of forces, resources, time, space, and purpose.** The primary benefit of phasing is that it assists in systematically achieving objectives that cannot be attained all at once by arranging smaller, related operations in a logical sequence. Each phase should represent a natural subdivision of the campaign or operation's intermediate objectives. **Transitions between phases are designed to be distinct shifts in focus by the counterinsurgent force, often accompanied by changes in command relationships.** The need to move into another phase normally is identified by assessing that a set of objectives are achieved or that the insurgent has acted in a manner that requires a major change in focus for the joint force and is therefore usually event driven, not time driven. Changing the focus of the operation takes time and may require changing priorities, command relationships, force allocation, or even the design of the operational area. While the phasing construct is a helpful planning tool, phases are not linear nor represent a clear-cut distinction in reality. Conditions in the operating environment may force returning or regressing to earlier phases, and various geographic areas within the theater may be in different phases at any given time, even within a single city. JFCs and joint forces must be agile in recognizing how conditions affect phasing. Similarly, they must be prepared to shift from military to civilian control based on the operating environment.

(b) **Branches and Sequels. Many COIN operation plans require adjustment beyond the initial stages of the operation.** Consequently, plans should be flexible by having branches and sequels. Both branches and sequels are plans associated with the base plan, all of which are created using the initial problem frame. **When transitioning to a branch or a sequel, counterinsurgents should examine if reframing the problem is required by the current conditions.**

1. **Branches.** Branches are options built into the basic plan. Branches may include shifting priorities, changing unit organization and command relationships, or changing the very nature of COIN itself. Branches add flexibility to plans by anticipating situations that could alter the basic plan. Such situations could be a result of insurgent action, availability of friendly capabilities or resources, or many other potential situations. It is vital to prioritize COIN branch planning efforts with respect to the most likely and most dangerous branch plans.

2. **Sequels.** Sequels are subsequent operations based on the possible outcomes of the current operation — victory, defeat, or stalemate. **In COIN, sequels can focus on different phases or shifting the overall approach.** For example, unanticipated success might allow for a more indirect US approach, or defeat might require a more direct US approach to shore up HN security forces.

See JP 3-0, Joint Operations, *and JP 5-0,* Joint Operation Planning, *for more detail on the elements of operational design.*

CHAPTER X
EXECUTION IN COUNTERINSURGENCY

> ***"Learn and adapt.** Continually assess the situation and adjust tactics, policies, and programs as required. Share good ideas (none of us is smarter than all of us together). Avoid mental or physical complacency. Never forget that what works in an area today may not work in that same area tomorrow."*
>
> **David Petraeus, General, US Army**
> **Multinational Force-Iraq Commander's Guidance**

1. Introduction

a. **The Nature of Counterinsurgency Operations.** COIN operations require synchronized application of military, paramilitary, political, economic, psychological, and civic actions. Successful counterinsurgents support or develop local institutions with legitimacy and the ability to provide basic services, economic opportunity, public order, and security. The political issues at stake are often rooted in culture, ideology, societal tensions, and injustice. As such, they defy nonviolent solutions from the parties involved. Joint forces can compel obedience and secure areas; however, they cannot by themselves achieve the political settlement needed to resolve the situation. Successful COIN efforts include civilian agencies, US military forces, and multinational forces. These efforts purposefully attack the basis for the insurgency rather than just its fighters, and comprehensively address the HN's core problems. HN leaders must be purposefully engaged in this effort and ultimately must take lead responsibility for it.

b. **Executing Counterinsurgency.** There are many ways to achieving success in COIN. The components of each form of execution are not mutually exclusive. In fact, several are shared by multiple forms. These forms are not the only choices available and are neither discrete nor exclusive. They may be combined, depending on the environment and available resources, and they have proven effective. However, the approaches must be adapted to the demands of the local environment. Three examples are: clear-hold-build, combined action, and limited support.

c. **General Patterns.** COIN efforts normally require the joint force to create the initial secure environment for the population. Ideally, HN forces hold cleared areas. As the HN security forces' capabilities are further strengthened, the joint force may shift toward combined action and limited support. As HN forces assume internal and external security requirements, US forces can redeploy to support bases, reduce force strength, and eventually withdraw. SOF and conventional forces continue to provide support as needed to achieve IDAD objectives.

d. **Insurgency and Counterinsurgency Conflict.** COIN is fundamentally a counterstrategy for insurgency. While a counter effort, COIN does not concede the initiative. In fact, insurgency (which may include multiple individual insurgent groups) and COIN are in a constant struggle. Figure X-1 depicts with logical LOOs how the two sides conflict. The insurgents on the right attempt to work towards their end state from right to left. The counterinsurgents work towards their end state from left to right. Much

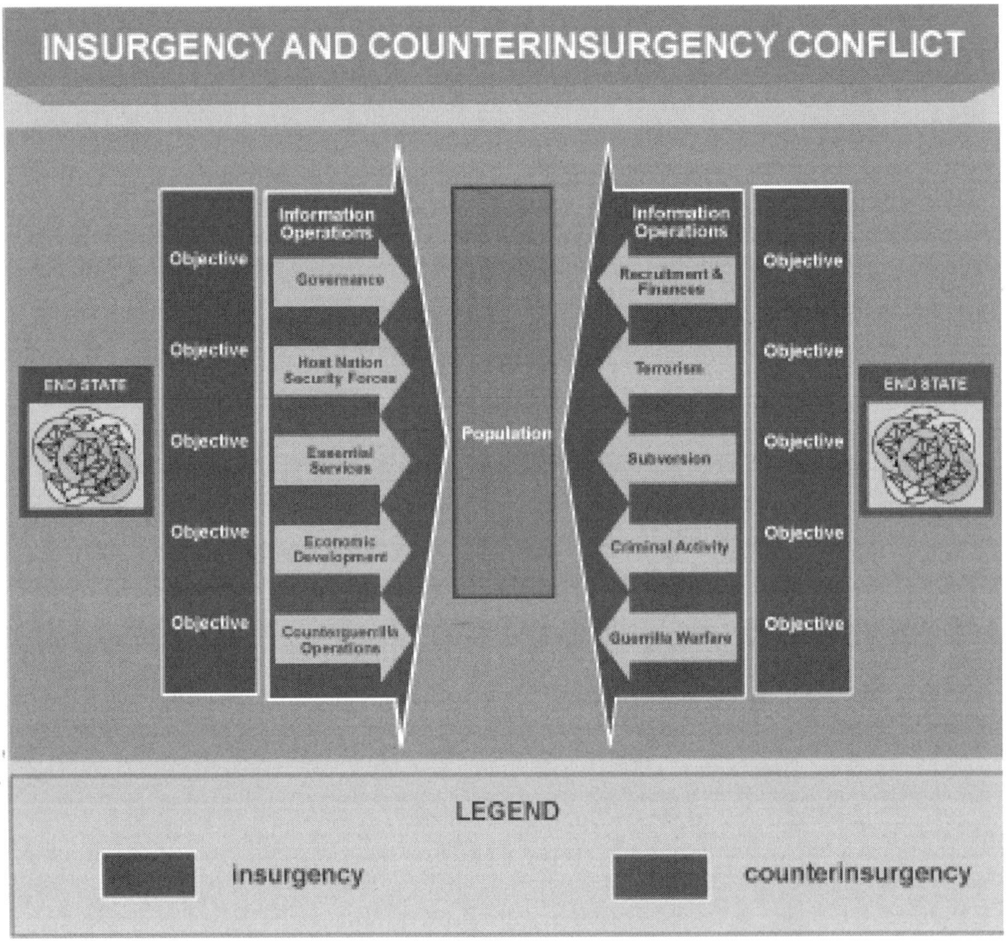

Figure X-1. Insurgency and Counterinsurgency Conflict

of these efforts are focused on winning popular support or, in the insurgents' case, forcing the population's acquiescence. The population is depicted in the middle, although the size of the diagram does not indicate its importance.

2. Clear-Hold-Build

A clear-hold-build operation is executed in a specific, high-priority area experiencing overt insurgent operations (see Figure X-2). It has the following objectives: create a secure physical and psychological environment, establish firm government control of the populace and area, and gain the populace's support. Popular support can be measured in terms of local participation in HN programs and political systems to counter the insurgency and whether people give counterinsurgents usable information about insurgent locations and activities.

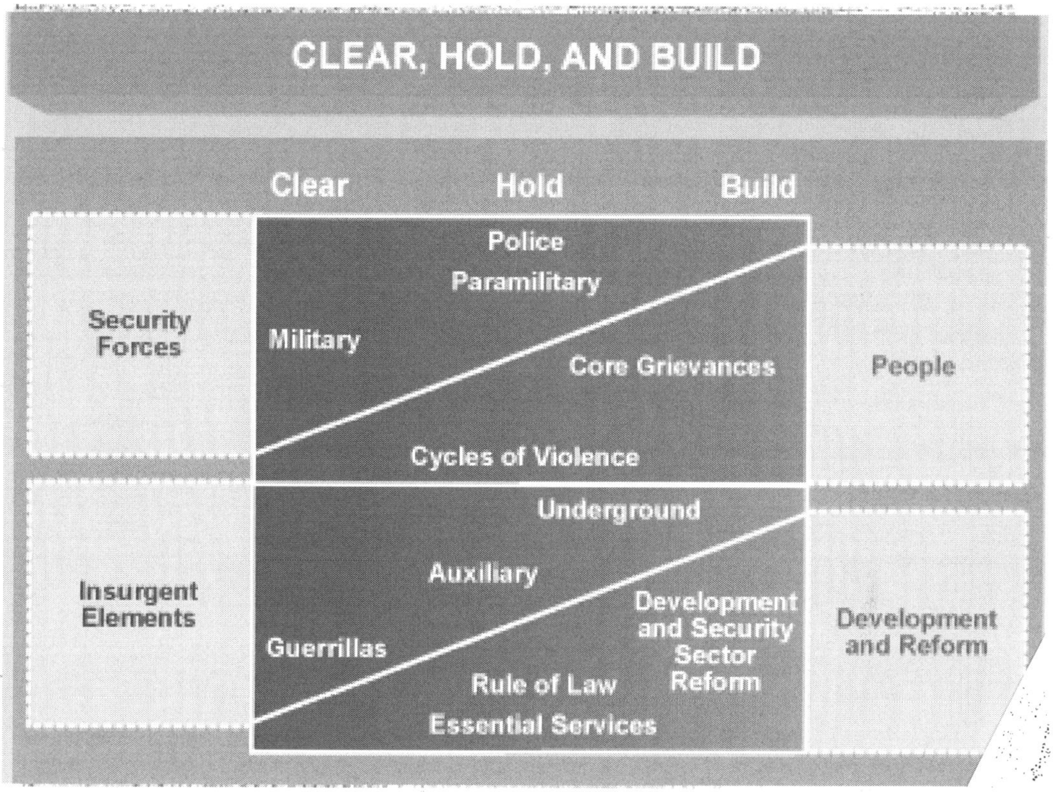

Figure X-2. Clear, Hold, and Build

a. **Key Areas.** COIN efforts should begin by controlling key areas. S influence then spread out from secured areas. The pattern of this approac hold, and build one village, area, or city—and then reinforce success by other areas. This approach aims to develop a long-term, effective framework and presence that secures the people and facilitates meeting Success reinforces the HN government's legitimacy. The primary t during clear-hold-build are:

(1) Provide continuous security for the local populace.

(2) Eliminate insurgent presence.

(3) Reinforce political primacy.

(4) Enforce the rule of law.

(5) Rebuild local HN institutions.

b. **Initial Focus.** To create success that can spread, a clear-hold-build operation should not begin by assaulting the main insurgent stronghold. However, some cases may require attacks to disrupt such strongholds, even if counterinsurgents cannot clear and hold the area. "Disrupt and leave" may be needed to degrade the insurgents' ability to mount attacks against cleared areas. Clear-hold-build objectives require considerable resources and time. US and HN commanders should prepare for a long-term effort. All operations require unity of effort by civil authorities, intelligence agencies, and security forces. Coherent IO are also needed.

c. **Expansion.** Clear-hold-build operations should expand outward from a secure base where the population supports the government effort and where security forces are in firm control. No population subjected to the intense organizational efforts of an insurgent organization can be won back until certain conditions are created:

(1) The counterinsurgent forces are clearly superior to forces available to the insurgents.

(2) Enough nonmilitary resources are available to effectively carry out all essential improvements needed to provide basic services and control the population.

(3) The insurgents are cleared from the area.

(4) The insurgent organizational infrastructure and its support have been neutralized or eliminated.

(5) A HN government presence is established to replace the insurgents' presence, and the local populace willingly supports this HN presence.

3. Clear

The following discussion describes some examples of activities involved in the clear-
old-build approach (see Figure X-2). Its execution involves activities across all logical
OOs. There can be overlap between steps—especially between hold and build, where
levant activities are often conducted simultaneously. For COIN, clear is a task that
uires the commander to remove all guerrilla forces and eliminate organized resistance
an assigned area. The force does this by destroying, capturing, or forcing the
drawal of guerrilla combatants. This task is most effectively initiated by a clear-in-
or cordon-and-search operation. This operation's purpose is to disrupt insurgent
s and force a reaction by major insurgent elements in the area. Commanders employ
bination of offensive small-unit operations. These may include area saturation
ing that enables the force to defeat insurgents in the area, interdiction ambushes,
geted raids. Counterinsurgents must take great care in the clear stage to avoid
ion or disruption of civilian homes and businesses. Collateral damage,
inate targeting, or driving people out of their homes and business in order to
military headquarters in preparation for the hold stage, even when accompanied

by compensation, can have negative second and third order effects, particularly when not accompanied by an effective SC strategy.

a. **Initial Effort.** Clear is an offensive operation that is only the beginning, not the end state. Eliminating insurgent forces does not remove the entrenched insurgent infrastructure. While their infrastructure exists, insurgents continue to recruit among the population, attempt to undermine the HN government, and try to coerce the populace through intimidation and violence. After insurgent forces have been eliminated, removing the insurgent infrastructure begins. This should be done so as to minimize the impact on the local populace. Rooting out such infrastructure is essentially a police action that relies heavily on military and intelligence forces until HN police, courts, and legal processes can assume responsibility for law enforcement within the cleared area.

b. **Isolation and Pursuit.** If insurgent forces are not eliminated but instead are expelled or have broken into smaller groups, they must be prevented from reentering the area or reestablishing an organizational structure inside the area. Once counterinsurgents have established their support bases, security elements cannot remain static. They should be mobile and establish a constant presence throughout the area. Offensive and stability operations are continued to maintain gains and set the conditions for future activities. These include isolating the area to cut off external support and to kill or capture escaping insurgents; conducting periodic patrols to identify, disrupt, eliminate, or expel insurgents; and employing security forces and government representatives throughout the area to secure the populace and facilitate follow-on stages of development.

c. **Information Operations.** Operations to clear an area are supplemented by IO focused on two key audiences: the local populace and the insurgents. The message to the populace focuses on gaining and maintaining their overt support for the COIN effort. This command theme is that the continuous security provided by US and HN forces is enough to protect the people from insurgent reprisals for their cooperation. Conversely, the populace should understand that actively supporting the insurgency will prolong combat operations, creating a risk to themselves and their neighbors. The command message to the insurgents focuses on convincing them that they cannot win and that the most constructive alternatives are to surrender or cease their activities.

4. Hold

Ideally HN forces or combined HN and coalition forces execute the hold portion of clear-hold-build approach (see Figure X-2). Establishment of security forces in bases among the population furthers the continued disruption, identification, and elimination of the local insurgent leadership and infrastructure. The success or failure of the effort depends, first, on effectively and continuously securing the populace and, second, on effectively reestablishing a HN government presence at the local level. Measured offensive operations continue against insurgents as opportunities arise, but the main effort is focused on the population.

a. **Protecting Key Infrastructure.** Key infrastructure must be secured. Since resources are always limited, parts of the infrastructure vital for stability and vulnerable to attack receive priority for protection. These critical assets should be identified during planning. For instance, a glassmaking factory may be important for economic recovery, but it may not be at risk of insurgent attack and therefore may not require security.

b. **Target Audiences.** There are four key TAs during the hold stage:

(1) Population.

(2) Insurgents.

(3) COIN force.

(4) Regional and international audiences.

(a) **Population-Focused Themes and Messages.** IO should also emphasize that security forces will remain until the current situation is resolved or stated objectives are attained. This message of a persistent presence can be reinforced by structuring contracts with local people for supply or construction requirements. Themes and messages to the population should affirm that security forces supporting the HN government are in the area to accomplish the following:

1. Protect the population from insurgent intimidation, coercion, and reprisals.

2. Eliminate insurgent leaders and infrastructure.

3. Improve essential services where possible.

4. Reinstate HN government presence.

(b) **Insurgent-Focused Themes and Messages.** The IO message to the insurgents is to surrender or leave the area. IO emphasizes the permanent nature of the government victory and presence. The HN government might try to exploit success by offering a local amnesty. Insurgent forces will probably not surrender in great numbers, but they may temporarily cease hostile actions against the HN government agencies in the area. The insurgents will fade into the population when not actively operating, thus making them difficult to detect.

(c) **Counterinsurgent-Focused Themes and Messages.** The commander's message to the COIN force should explain changes in missions and responsibilities associated with creating or reinforcing the HN government's legitimacy. The importance of protecting the populace, gaining people's support by assisting them, and using measured force when fighting insurgents should be reinforced and understood.

c. **Purpose of Hold Operations.** Operations during this stage are designed to:

(1) Continuously secure the people and separate them from the insurgents.

(2) Establish a firm government presence and control over the area and populace.

(3) Recruit, organize, equip, and train local security forces.

(4) Establish a government political apparatus to replace the insurgent apparatus.

(5) Develop a dependable network of sources by authorized intelligence agents.

d. **Execution.** Major actions occurring during this stage include:

(1) Designating and allocating area-oriented counterinsurgent forces to continue offensive operations. Other forces that participated in clearing actions are released or assigned to other tasks.

(2) A thorough population screening to identify and eliminate remaining insurgents and to identify any lingering insurgent support structures.

(3) In coordination with USAID or other USG civilian agencies, conducting area assessment to determine available resources and the populace's needs. Local leaders should be involved.

(4) Environmental improvements designed to convince the populace to support the HN government, participate in securing their area, and contribute to the reconstruction effort.

(5) Engaging local paramilitary security forces to seek their cooperation and inclusion in the HN security structure. From the outset, counterinsurgents must consider implications for DDR to avoid arming a group that may return to the insurgency if counterinsurgent support ends without a viable alternative for the group.

(6) Establishing a communications system that integrates the area into the HN communications grid and system.

5. Build

Progress in building support for the HN government requires protecting the local populace (see Figure X-2). People who do not believe they are secure from insurgent intimidation, coercion, and reprisals will not risk overtly supporting COIN efforts. The populace decides when it feels secure enough to support COIN efforts.

a. **Protecting the Population.** To protect the populace, HN security forces continuously conduct patrols and use measured force against insurgent targets of opportunity. Contact with the people is critical to the local COIN effort's success. Actions to eliminate the remaining covert insurgent political infrastructure must be continued; an insurgent presence will continue to threaten and influence people.

b. **Tasks.** Tasks that provide an overt and direct benefit for the community are key, initial priorities. Special funds (or other available resources) should be available to pay wages to local people to do such beneficial work. Accomplishing these tasks can begin the process of establishing HN government legitimacy. Sample tasks include:

(1) Collecting and clearing trash from the streets.

(2) Removing or painting over insurgent symbols or colors.

(3) Building and improving roads.

(4) Digging wells.

(5) Preparing and building an indigenous local security force.

(6) Securing, moving, and distributing supplies.

(7) Providing guides, sentries, and translators.

(8) Building and improving schools and similar facilities in coordination with the local population, HN, and other actors.

(9) Providing essential health services.

(10) Developing of local and regional markets.

c. **Population Control Measures.** Population control includes determining who lives in an area and what they do. This task requires determining societal relationships—family, clan, tribe, interpersonal, and professional. Establishing control normally begins with conducting a census and issuing identification cards and family records. A census is an extremely complex evolution. Conducting a census can be complicated by the fear of the population of being identified with a certain group and/or a history of ethnic or religious oppression from a previous government. Census records can provide information regarding real property ownership, relationships, and business associations. The COM/country team can be requested to assist with appropriate tasks such as advertising and a detailed plan for execution.

(1) Other population control measures include:

(a) Curfews.

(b) A pass system (for example, one using travel permits or registration cards) administered by security forces or civil authorities.

(c) Limits on the length of time people can travel.

(d) Limits on the number of visitors from outside the area combined with a requirement to register them with local security forces or civil authorities.

(e) Checkpoints along major routes to monitor and enforce compliance with population control measures.

(2) **Explanation.** The HN government should explain and justify new control measures to the affected population. People need to understand what is necessary to protect them from insurgent intimidation, coercion, and reprisals. Once control measures are in place, the HN government should have an established system of punishments for offenses related to them. These should be announced and enforced. The HN should establish this system to ensure uniform enforcement and conformity with the rule of law throughout its territory. The HN government must be able to impose fines and other punishments for such civil infractions.

(3) **Insurgent Counterefforts.** Insurgents may try to force people to destroy their identification cards. The benefits of retaining identification cards must be enough to motivate people to resist losing them. Insurgents may participate in the census to obtain valid identification cards. Requiring applicants to bring two men from outside their family to swear to their identity, for instance, can reduce this probability. Counterinsurgents must use all assets at their disposal – sociocultural experts, intelligence, etc. – to ensure that the witnesses are not members of the insurgency swearing to the identity of a fellow insurgent. Those who affirm the status of an applicant are accountable for their official statements made on behalf of the applicant. Identification cards should have a code that indicates where the holders live.

d. **Increasing Popular Support.** Counterinsurgents should use every opportunity to help the populace and meet its needs and expectations. Projects to improve economic, social, cultural, and health needs can begin immediately. Actions speak louder than words. Once the insurgent political infrastructure is destroyed and local leaders begin to establish themselves, necessary political reforms can be implemented. These aspects of COIN should ideally be led by civilian agencies, IGOs, or NGOs, with the military in a supporting role. The JFC should coordinate actions in these areas with the COM and the country team. Other important tasks include the following:

(1) Establishing HN government agencies to perform routine administrative functions and begin improvement programs.

(2) Providing HN government support to those willing to participate in reconstruction. Selection for participation should be based on need and ability to help. People should also be willing to secure what they create.

(3) Beginning efforts to develop regional and national consciousness and rapport between the population and its government. Efforts may include participating in local elections, making community improvements, forming youth clubs, and executing other projects.

(4) Providing systems for safely reporting adversary or friendly acts of intimidation, violence, crime, and corruption.

e. **Information Operations.** Commanders can use IO to increase popular support. Command messages are addressed to the populace, insurgents, and counterinsurgents.

(1) **Population-Focused Messages.** The IO message to the population has three facets:

(a) Obtaining the understanding or approval of security force actions that affect the populace, such as control measures or a census. Tell the people what forces are doing and why they are doing it.

(b) Establishing HUMINT sources that lead to identification and destruction of any remaining insurgent infrastructure in the area.

(c) Winning over passive or neutral people by demonstrating how the HN government is going to make their life better.

(2) **Insurgent-Focused Messages and Themes.** The IO message to insurgents should aim to create divisions between the movement leaders and the mass base by emphasizing failures of the insurgency and successes of the government. Success is indicated when insurgents abandon the movement and return to work with the HN government.

(3) **Counterinsurgent-Focused Messages and Themes.** Commanders should emphasize that counterinsurgents must remain friendly towards the populace while staying vigilant against insurgent actions. Commanders must ensure all forces understand the ROE, which become more restrictive as peace and stability return.

(4) **Timeliness of Messages and Themes.** Commanders should afford sufficient latitude to subordinates to enable them to generate IO messages in a timely manner that is ahead of insurgent propaganda.

f. **Key Tasks.** The most important activities during the build stage are conducted by nonmilitary agencies. HN government representatives reestablish political offices and normal administrative procedures. National and international development agencies rebuild infrastructure and key facilities. Local leaders are developed and given authority. Life for the area's inhabitants begins to return to normal. Activities along the combat operations/civil security operations logical LOO and HN security force LOO become secondary to those involved in essential services and good governance LOOs.

6. Combined Action

Combined action is a technique that involves joining US and HN ground troops in a single organization, usually a platoon or company, to conduct COIN operations. This technique is appropriate in environments where large insurgent forces do not exist or where insurgents lack resources and freedom of maneuver. Combined action normally involves joining a US rifle squad or platoon with a HN platoon or company, respectively. Commanders use this approach to hold and build while providing a persistent counterinsurgent presence among the populace. This approach attempts to first achieve security and stability in a local area, followed by offensive operations against insurgent forces now denied access or support. Combined action units are not designed for offensive operations themselves and rely on more robust combat units to perform this task. Combined action units can also establish mutual support among villages to secure a wider area.

a. **Security Situation.** A combined action program can work only in areas with limited insurgent activity. The technique should not be used to isolate or expel a well-established and supported insurgent force. Combined action is most effective after an area has been cleared of armed insurgents.

b. **Influencing Factors.** The following geographic and demographic factors can also influence the likelihood of success:

(1) Towns relatively isolated from other population centers are simpler to secure continuously.

(2) Towns and villages with a limited number of roads passing through them are easier to secure than those with many routes in and out. All approaches must be guarded.

(3) Existing avenues of approach into a town should be observable from the town. Keeping these areas under observation facilitates interdiction of insurgents and control of population movements.

(4) The local populace should be small and constant. People should know one another and be able to easily identify outsiders. In towns or small cities where this is not the case, a census is the most effective tool to establish initial accountability for everyone.

(5) Combined action or local defense forces must establish mutual support with forces operating in nearby towns. Quick reaction forces (ground maneuver or air

assault), fires, close air support, and medical evacuation should be quickly available. Engineer and explosive ordnance disposal assets should also be available.

c. **Relationships.** Combined action unit members must develop and build positive relationships with their associated HN security forces and with the town leadership. By living among the people, combined action units serve an important purpose. They demonstrate the commitment and competence of counterinsurgents while sharing experiences and relationships with local people. These working relationships build trust and enhance the HN government's legitimacy. To build trust further, US members should ask HN security forces for training on local customs, key terrain, possible insurgent hideouts, and relevant cultural dynamics. HN forces should also be asked to describe recent local events.

d. **Command and Control Architecture.** Combined action units are integrated into a regional scheme of mutually supporting security and influence; however, they should remain organic to their parent unit. Positioning reinforced squad-sized units among HN citizens creates a dispersal risk. Parent units can mitigate this risk with on-call reserve and reaction forces along with mutual support from adjacent villages and towns.

e. **Integration.** Thoroughly integrating US and HN combined action personnel supports the effective teamwork critical to the success of each team and the overall program. US members should be drawn from some of the parent unit's best personnel. Designating potential members before deployment facilitates the training and team building needed for combined action unit success in theater. Preferably, team members should have had prior experience in the HN. Other desirable characteristics include:

(1) The ability to operate effectively as part of a team.

(2) Strong leadership qualities, among them:

(a) Communicating clearly.

(b) Maturity.

(c) Leading by example.

(d) Making good decisions.

(3) Ability to apply the commander's intent in the absence of orders.

(4) Possession of cultural awareness and understanding of the HN environment.

(5) The absence of obvious prejudices.

(6) Mutual respect when operating with HN personnel.

(7) Experience with the HN language, the ability to learn languages, or support of reliable translators.

(8) Patience and tolerance when dealing with language and translation barriers.

f. **Tasks.** Appropriate tasks for combined action units include, but are not limited to, the following:

(1) Helping HN security forces maintain entry control points.

(2) Providing reaction force capabilities through the parent unit.

(3) Conducting multinational, coordinated day and night patrols to secure the town and area.

(4) Facilitating local contacts to gather information in conjunction with local HN security force representatives. (Ensure information gathered is made available promptly and on a regular basis to the parent unit for timely fusion and action.)

(5) Training HN security forces in leadership and general military subjects so they can secure the town or area on their own.

(6) Conducting operations with other multinational forces and HN units, if required.

(7) Operating as a team with HN security forces to instill pride, leadership, and patriotism.

(8) Assisting HN government representatives with civic action programs to establish an environment where the people have a stake in the future of their town and nation.

(9) Protecting HN judicial and government representatives and helping them establish the rule of law.

7. Limited Support

Not all COIN efforts require large combat formations. In many cases, US support is limited, focused on missions like advising security forces and providing fire support or sustainment. The longstanding US support to the Philippines is an example of such limited support. The limited support approach focuses on building HN capability and capacity. Under this approach, HN security forces are expected to conduct combat operations, including any clearing and holding missions. This is an indirect approach to COIN and is COIN in support of FID.

See JP 3-22, Foreign Internal Defense, *for more information.*

8. Targeting in Counterinsurgency

Targeting is the process of selecting and prioritizing targets and matching the appropriate response to them, considering operational requirements and capabilities. The targeting process facilitates achieving effects that support the logical LOOs in a COIN campaign plan. **Targeting is conducted for all COIN efforts, not just attacks against the insurgent military wing** (counterguerrilla operations). The targeting process can support IO, CMO, and even meetings between commanders and HN leaders. Targeting also links intelligence, plans, and operations across all levels of command. Targeting encompasses many processes, all linked and logically guided by the joint targeting cycle, that continuously seek to analyze, identify, develop, validate, assess, and prioritize targets for engagement in order to achieve the commander's objectives and end state.

a. **Purpose.** The purpose of targeting is to integrate and synchronize efforts. Targeting provides an iterative methodology for the development, planning, execution, and assessment in supporting objectives. Targeting in COIN is a unified action that involves participation from all appropriate elements.

b. **Focus.** The focus for COIN targeting is on people, both insurgents and civilians. There are several different potential targets that can link objectives with effects in COIN. These can include, but are not limited to, insurgents, insurgent internal support structure, insurgent external support systems, and, when directly supporting insurgent operations, HN governance, HN security forces, and other HN functions. Effective targeting identifies the targeting options, both lethal and nonlethal, to create effects that support the commander's objectives. Some targets are best addressed with lethal means, while other targets are best engaged with nonlethal means. Having nonlethal weapons available during CMO, FID, and humanitarian operations when dealing with crowd control and individuals with unknown intent, can be beneficial. Other nonlethal options include IO, negotiation, political programs, economic programs, social programs, and other noncombat methods. Creating effects with nonlethal weapons and other means in COIN will discourage, delay, and prevent hostile actions; limit escalation of violence; provide force options when lethal force in not preferred or authorized; enhance long term force protection; and reduce collateral damage that will help decrease post-conflict costs of reconstruction.

c. **Targeting Cycle.** The joint targeting cycle is an iterative process that is not time-constrained, and steps may occur concurrently, but it provides a helpful framework to describe the steps that must be satisfied to successfully conduct joint targeting (see Figure X-3). An effective, disciplined joint targeting cycle helps minimize undesired effects and reduces inefficient actions during COIN.

For more information on targeting, see JP 3-60 Joint Targeting.

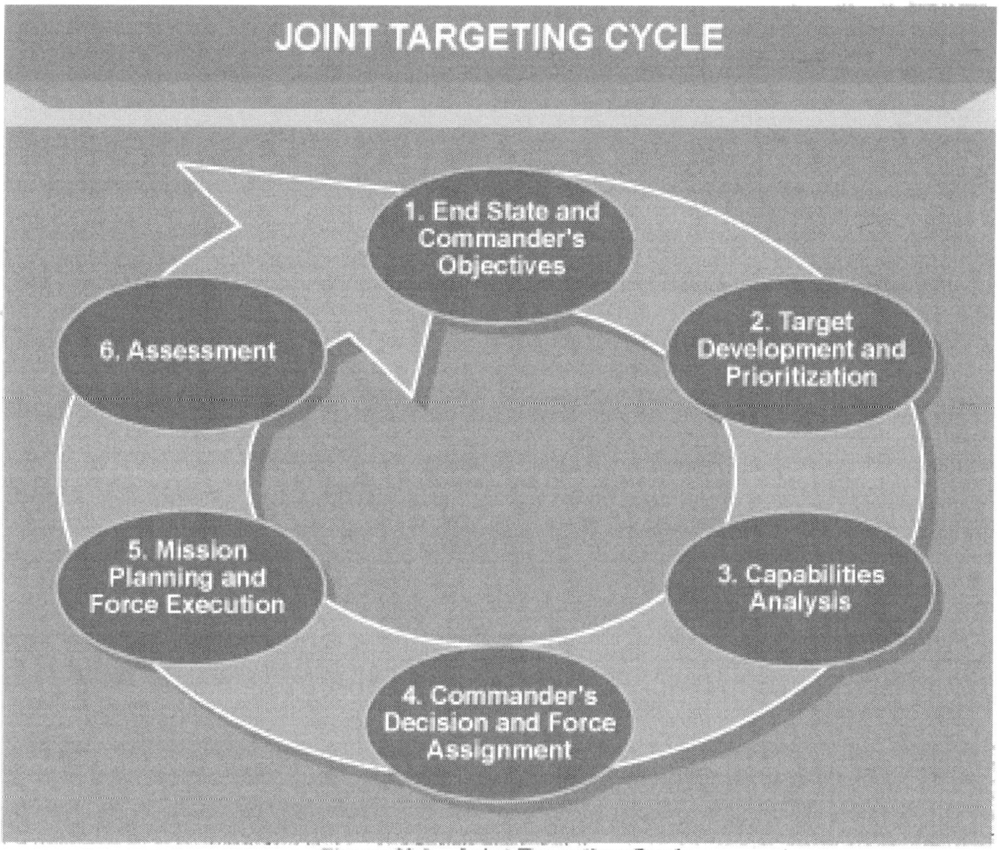

Figure X-3. Joint Targeting Cycle

9. Joint Assessment and Counterinsurgency

Effective assessment in COIN operations is necessary for counterinsurgents to recognize changing conditions and determine their meaning. It is crucial to successfully adapt to the changing situation. A continuous discourse among counterinsurgents at all echelons provides the feedback the senior leadership needs to refine the design (see Figure X-4).

a. **Reframing.** In an ideal world, the commander of military forces engaged in COIN operations would enjoy clear and well-defined goals for the operation or campaign from the very beginning. However, the reality is that many goals emerge only as the operation or campaign develops. For this reason, counterinsurgents usually have a combination of defined and emerging goals toward which to work. Likewise, the complex problems encountered during COIN operations can be so difficult to understand that a clear design cannot be developed initially. Often, the best choice is to create iterative solutions to better understand the problem. In this case, these iterative solutions allow the initiation of intelligent interaction with the environment.

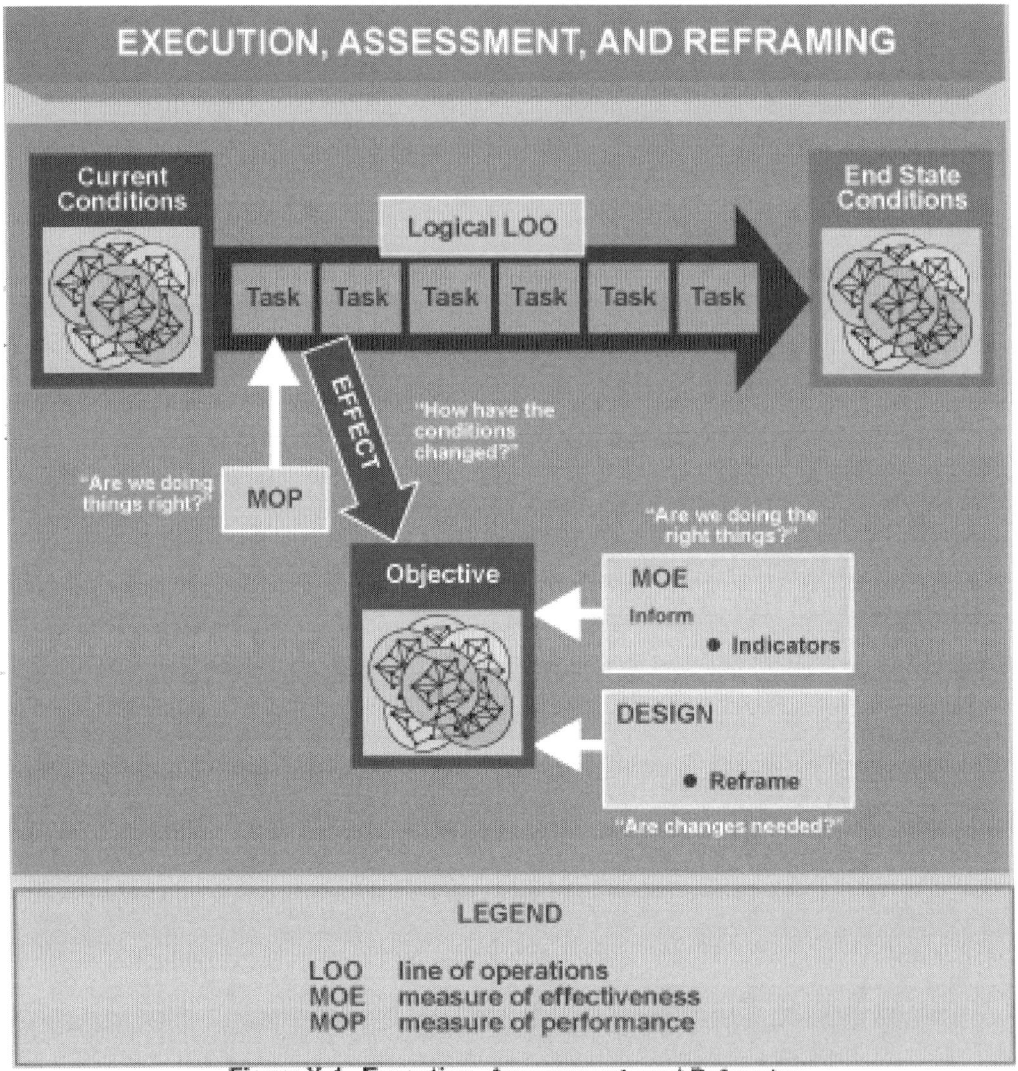

Figure X-4. Execution, Assessment, and Reframing

b. **Assessing Insurgencies.** The following measures can be useful in assessing insurgencies:

(1) Changes in local attitudes (friendliness towards US and HN personnel).

(2) Changes in public perceptions.

(3) Changes in the quality or quantity of information provided by individuals or groups.

(4) Changes in the economic or political situation of an area.

(5) Changes in insurgent patterns.

(6) Captured and killed insurgents.

(7) Captured equipment and documents.

c. **Detainees, Defectors, and Captured Documents and Equipment.** Critical and vital information may be obtained from detainees, captured documents and other forms of media, and captured equipment. Its exploitation and processing into intelligence often adds to the overall understanding of the enemy. This understanding can lead to more targeting decisions. In addition, the assessment of the operation should be fed back to collectors. This allows them to see if their sources are credible. In addition, effective operations often cause the local populace to provide more information, which drives future operations.

d. **Learning and Adapting.** When an operation is executed, counterinsurgents may develop the situation to gain a more thorough situational understanding. This increased environmental understanding represents a form of operational learning and applies across all logical LOOs. counterinsurgents and staffs adjust the operation's design and plan based on what they learn.

(1) **Cycles of Adaptation.** COIN operations involve complex, changing relations among all the direct and peripheral participants. These participants adapt and respond to each other throughout an operation. A cycle of adaptation usually develops between insurgents and counterinsurgents; both sides continually adapt to neutralize existing adversary advantages and develop new (usually short-lived) advantages of their own. Success is gained through a tempo or rhythm of adaptation that is beyond the other side's ability to achieve or sustain. Therefore, counterinsurgents should seek to gain and sustain advantages over insurgents by emphasizing the learning and adaptation that this publication stresses throughout.

(2) **Complexity.** Learning and adapting in COIN is very difficult due to the complexity of the problems counterinsurgents must solve. Generally, there is not a single adversary that can be singularly classified as the enemy. Many insurgencies include multiple competing groups. Success requires the HN government and counterinsurgents to adapt based on understanding this very intricate environment. But the key to effective COIN design and execution remains the ability to adjust better and faster than the insurgents.

e. **Developing Measurement Criteria.** Assessment requires determining why and when progress is being achieved along each logical LOO. Traditionally, counterinsurgents use discrete quantitative and qualitative measurements to evaluate progress. However, the complex nature of COIN operations makes progress difficult to measure. Subjective assessment at all levels is essential to understand the diverse and complex nature of COIN problems. It is also needed to measure local success or failure against the overall operation's end state. Additionally, counterinsurgents need to know how actions along different logical LOOs complement each other; therefore, planners evaluate not only progress along each logical LOO but also interactions among logical LOOs.

f. **Assessment Tools for COIN.** Assessment tools help counterinsurgents and staffs determine:

(1) Completion of tasks and their impact.

(2) Level of achievement of objectives.

(3) Whether a condition of success has been established.

(4) Whether the operation's end state has been attained.

(5) Whether the leader's intent was achieved.

g. For example, planning for transition of responsibility to the HN is an integral part of COIN operational design and planning. Assessment tools may be used to assess the geographic and administrative transfer of control and responsibility to the HN government as it develops its capabilities. Assessments differ for every mission, task, and logical LOO, and for different phases of an operation. Leaders adjust assessment methods as insurgents adapt to counterinsurgent tactics and the environment changes.

h. Assessment is a process that measures progress of the counterinsurgent team toward mission accomplishment. It is important for the commander to understand the larger context of the assessment as it relates to the OE and the principles guiding the USG response. A USG framework for assessment whose principles have been approved is the Interagency Conflict Assessment Framework (ICAF). It is a tool that enables an interagency team to assess conflict situations systematically and collaboratively and supports interagency planning for conflict prevention, mitigation, and stabilization. The purpose of the ICAF is to develop a commonly held understanding across relevant USG departments and agencies of the dynamics driving and mitigating violent conflict within a country that informs US policy and planning decisions. It may also include steps to establish a strategic baseline against which USG engagement can be evaluated. It is a process and a tool available for use by any USG agency to supplement interagency planning.

i. **Measuring Progress in Conflict Environments.** A metrics framework for assessing conflict transformation and stabilization is being field tested in Afghanistan, Haiti, Kosovo, and Sudan. It is focused on developing an overarching framework of indicators that measure outcomes over time and across five sectors (governance, economics, security, rule of law and social well-being). It also provides sample metrics and a methodology for collecting data involving statistical, polling, expert opinion.

APPENDIX A
INSURGENCY AND CRIME

1. General

There often is a nexus between insurgency and crime, and this problem continues to grow in the twenty-first century. Crime is often necessary for insurgents to fund their operations, control the population, and erode counterinsurgent efforts. Some insurgents and criminals can form temporary coalitions when it is in their collective interests. Paradoxically, some criminals may oppose insurgencies that threaten criminal goals. The most powerful criminal organizations can also grow into insurgencies in their own right.

2. Criminal Evolution

Left unchecked, criminal violence often grows worse over time. Criminal activity can develop from low-level "protection," "gangsterism", and brigandage; to drug trafficking, piracy, smuggling people, body parts, armament, and other lucrative "items" associated with the global criminal activity; to taking political control of ungoverned space or areas governed by corrupt politicians and functionaries. Most criminal organizations, however, never move beyond protectionism and "gangsterism." As small criminal organizations expand their activities to compete with or support long-established criminal organizations, they expand their geographical and commercial parameters. Criminals may seek areas of political nullification that allow them sufficient latitude to operate and that discourage rival criminal enterprises. They can generate more and more violence and instability over wider sections of the political map. Some criminal organizations can generate substate, state, and suprastate instability and insecurity; they can become partners of a kind with insurgents in order to further their criminal ends. Some criminal organizations may seek to co-opt political power through corruption and intimidation. The more they seek freedom of action, the more they inhibit state sovereignty. However, the criminal organizations may not want to take direct control of the government, yet they may take indirect control. Thus, some criminal organizations can become an insurgency unto themselves. As criminal organizations evolve through these developmental and functional shifts, three generations emerge.

3. First-Generation

The first-generation, or traditional, street gangs are primarily turf-oriented. They have loose and unsophisticated leadership that focuses on turf protection to gain petty cash. They often focus on gang loyalty within their immediate environs such as designated city blocks or neighborhoods. When first-generation criminal organizations engage in criminal enterprise, it is largely opportunistic and individual in scope, tends to be localized, and operates at the lower end of extreme societal violence. Most gangs stay firmly within this first generation of development, but some evolve into and beyond the second generation of criminal organizations. First-generation gangs are not insurgents; however, they certainly can be a local destabilizing factor and can work, either actively or accidentally, to assist insurgents. They can also further degrade conditions in a generic and unaffiliated manner or even actively oppose insurgencies that degrade their criminal enterprises. Increasing the law enforcement capabilities of a HN as a part of FID can help a HN deal with this form of criminal activity (see JP 3-22, *Foreign Internal Defense*).

4. Second-Generation

This generation is organized for illicit business and commercial gain. The leaders of these organizations are more centralized and tend to focus on trafficking and market protection. These criminal organizations operate in a broader area than first-generation criminal organizations, which may include neighboring cities and countries. Second-generation criminal organizations are known to expand their activities to smuggling people, body parts, weapons, and cars; associated intimidation, murder, kidnapping and robbery; money laundering; home and community invasion; intellectual property theft to include the production of pirated goods; and other lucrative activities. These criminal organizations use the level of violence necessary to protect their markets and control their competition. They seek to control or incapacitate state security institutions, and they often begin to dominate vulnerable community life within large areas of the nation-state. As second-generation criminal organizations develop broader, market-focused, and sometimes overtly political agendas to improve their market share and revenues, they often more overtly challenge state security and sovereignty. When these criminal organizations use subversion and violence as political interference to negate law enforcement efforts directed against them, they become insurgents. Al Capone's organization during Prohibition is a good example of a second-generation criminal organization.

5. Third-Generation

Some criminal organizations develop into sophisticated transnational criminal organizations with ambitious economic and political agendas. These third-generation criminal organizations often begin to control ungoverned territory within a nation-state, acquire political power in poorly-governed space, and eventually vie for HN controlled space. This political action is intended to provide security and freedom of movement for the criminal organization's activities. As a result, the third-generation criminal organization and its leadership challenge the legitimate state monopoly on the exercise of political control and the use of violence within a given geographical area. In this case, a third-generation criminal organization is an insurgency, although its ends are materially focused and not ideological. In some cases, these criminal organizations may have the objectives to neutralize, control, depose, or replace an incumbent government. In other cases, they may wish to control parts of a targeted country or sub-regions within a country and create autonomous enclaves that are sometimes called "criminal free-states" or "parastates."

APPENDIX B
PROVINCIAL RECONSTRUCTION TEAMS

"Do not try to do too much with your own hands. Better the Arabs do it tolerably than that you do it perfectly. It is their war, and you are to help them, not to win it for them. Actually, also, under the very odd conditions of Arabia, your practical work will not be as good as, perhaps, you think it is."

- T.E. Lawrence

1. General

The focus of the PRT is on the provincial government and local infrastructure in the area assigned. Normally, PRTs are assigned by province, but may be assigned to local governments within a province or to more than one province. Both the effectiveness and legitimacy of provincial governments will vary widely from country to country and even from province to province within a country; as such, the focus of the PRT's effort will largely depend on the needs of the government in place. In an area where the government lacks legitimacy (possibly because it has not existed previously or is perceived as corrupt and ineffective), it may be necessary for the PRT to take on initial stabilization activities without the presence of the HN government until initial trust can be established and relationships built that will help enhance the legitimacy of the provincial government as progress continues. In another area where the government enjoys some measure of legitimacy, but is largely ineffective (and therefore in danger of losing legitimacy as well), the PRT will focus on helping HN government institutions develop the capacity to govern.

2. Organization

a. The organization and size of the PRT will vary largely depending on the OE and required tasks. In addition to size, PRTs differ in roles, contractor participation, interagency participation, staff organization, and even the chain of command. Military participation, which will be driven by the operational requirements among other considerations, is often the driving factor in PRT size.

b. The PRT leader is normally a DOS official but may be a DOD official. Personnel serving in a PRT continue to work for their parent agency and are subject to operating guidelines of their original chain of command for performance, discipline, etc., but are expected to follow the PRT leader's directions, rules, policies, and procedures. Although the agency providing the PRT leader may differ from one PRT to the next, the DOS, DOD, and USAID senior members generally form a command group. Maintaining consensus within this command group is key to the integration of all the organization's elements.

c. Functional groups within the PRT will also vary, but are generally similar to JTF directorates (administration, operations, service support, etc.). The operations group (or groups) may be organized by LOOs (rule of law, economic development, etc.), by capabilities (engineer, USAID office, security, etc.), or by a combination thereof. When multinational partners are included in a PRT, they may function as a distinct organization within the PRT. The PRT organization may include a CMOC to coordinate and share information with NGOs and IGOs operating in the area.

d. Agencies participating in addition to DOD, DOS, and USAID may include, but are not limited to, Department of Agriculture, Department of Justice, Department of Health and Human Services, and Department of Commerce as well as HN national government agencies (such as the interior ministry). Interagency (and possibly international) memoranda of agreement may be required in the establishment of PRTs to define roles, responsibilities, command relationships, and funding lines. When possible, PRT members should receive their training as a unit prior to deployment to facilitate unity of effort upon arrival in country.

e. Military support to a PRT normally includes CA representation and other forces for CMO. Additionally, the military may provide a security element as well as a quick reaction force. Military support may also include, but is not limited to, mobility, sustainment, administration and communication. The PRT may contract for many of these functions, including security, rather than drawing on direct military support; this will be most prevalent as the security environment becomes more stable. Alternatively, when the security environment dictates the location of the PRT on a forward operating base, the local military commander may provide some of these support capabilities.

3. Command and Control

a. The nature of command and coordinating relationship is complex and should be addressed early and continuously. Direction and coordination of PRTs can be conducted by a national level interagency steering committee, under the supervision of the COM, a multinational executive committee, or JFC.

b. Funding is perhaps the most difficult issue for PRT management. Funding will come from several different sources, even within a single executive department. PRT leaders carefully track and should understand sources of funding lines and legal restrictions on their use. The success of interagency coordination at the highest levels will be reflected in the ability of the PRT to coordinate interagency funding lines in the field.

4. Employment

a. Participation in planning by the core PRT staff should begin as early in this process as possible to build coordinating relationships. Although PRTs are employed primarily for the purpose of stability operations (which can occur in each phase), PRTs typically focus their efforts on achieving objectives in the *stabilize* phase of a joint operation, facilitating the transition to *enable civil authority* phase. It should be noted that the stabilize phase may come at different times for different provinces or operational areas based on the design of the operation. The PRT should enter the operational area not later than when the joint force begins the transition from *dominate* to *stabilize*.

b. As HN civil authority is established and the environment is stabilized, military support decreases, and eventually the PRT will dissolve; the other components of the PRT may transition to more traditional means of providing development assistance.

c. **Governance.** The primary focus of a PRT in any area of operations is to improve the provincial government's ability to provide democratic governance and essential services. Improving the provincial government is important given the decentralization of authority often associated with COIN.

(1) **Assistance Specialists.** USAID typically contracts a three-person team of civilian specialists to provide training and technical assistance programs for PRTs. The program aims to improve the efficiency of provincial governments by providing policy analysis, training, and technical assistance to national ministries, their provincial representatives, provincial governors, and provincial councils. The team of civilian specialists works directly with provincial officials to increase competence and efficiency. For example, they assist provincial council members with the conduct of meetings, budget development, and oversight of provincial government activities. The team also encourages transparency and popular participation by working with citizens and community organizations, hosting conferences, and promoting public forums.

(2) **Other Expertise.** The USAID team contains members with expertise in local government, financial management, and municipal planning. Up to seventy percent of the contracted staff members come from regional countries and include local professionals. Additional contracted experts are on call from regional offices. The USAID requires that contract advisors speak the HN language and possess extensive professional experience. USAID-trained instructors present training programs based on professionally developed modules in the HN language. The training and technical assistance programs emphasize practical application with focus areas in computers, planning, public administration, and provision of public services.

d. **Security.** The absence of security impacts the effectiveness of PRT operations and efforts to develop effective local governments.

(1) **Security Impacts.** Provincial governors and other senior officials may be intimidated, threatened, and assassinated in limited or unsecure areas. Provincial councils may potentially reduce or eliminate regular meetings if security deteriorates. Additionally, provincial-level ministry representatives could become reluctant to attend work because of security concerns. PRT personnel and local officials may lose the ability to meet openly or visit provincial government centers and US military installations in limited security environments. During security alerts, PRT civilian personnel may be restricted to base, preventing interaction with HN counterparts. Unstable security situations limit PRT personnel from promoting economic development by counseling

local officials, encouraging local leaders and business owners, and motivating outside investors.

(2) **Secure Movement and Presence.** Heavily armed and armored personnel have more difficulty connecting with the population than those who can move more naturally amongst the population. A dismounted soldier not wearing full body armor is more approachable than a mounted soldier or one in full body armor. Military commanders must balance force protection and approachability. In nonpermissive environments PRT personnel move with armed military escorts, which contributes to the overall security presence. However, the PRT does not conduct military operations, nor do they assist HN military forces. The only security role assigned to a PRT is force protection by providing armored vehicles and an advisor to escort PRT personnel to meetings with local officials. US military assigned to escort civilian PRT members receive training in providing PRT civilian personnel protection under an agreement with DOS. The training is designed to reinforce understanding of escort responsibilities and to prevent endangerment to PRT civilian personnel. US military escorting PRT personnel should not combine this responsibility with other missions. The problem of providing PRT civilian personnel with security is compounded by competing protection priorities, precluding dedicated security teams in most situations and limiting security teams to available personnel.

e. **Reconstruction.** The USAID representative of the PRT has the primary responsibility for developing the PRT economic development work plan including its assistance projects. The PRT emphasizes the construction of infrastructure including schools, clinics, community centers, and government buildings. The PRT also focuses on developing human capacity through training and advisory programs.

5. Fundamental Guidelines

a. **Objective.** The mission of a PRT is to stabilize the OE, creating conditions for development, laying the foundations for long-term stability, and enabling the civil authorities. PRT planners for a particular area must define decisive and achievable goals for that province that meet the objective of stability, giving direction to all PRT operations. These goals will define the lifespan of the PRT, facilitating its transition to more traditional development mechanisms.

b. **Unity of Effort.** The success of the PRT depends on its ability to operate as a composite unit. When unity of command is not possible, members nonetheless must lay aside interagency differences to focus on the common objective. Additionally, members of the PRT must ensure higher agency organizations understand and support the unified effort required. Beyond interagency integration, the PRT must also work with IGOs and NGOs in the area to share information, reduce duplication of work (or counterproductive efforts), and communicate about civil-military sensitivities.

c. **Promotion of Legitimacy and Effectiveness.** The key to achieving long-term stability and development is the establishment of the local government as the legitimate and effective governing authority. To achieve this, the PRT will often need to "lead from behind and underneath," building capacity and working behind the scenes to ensure HN ownership and promoting HN primacy and legitimacy. This will often mean accepting local government solutions rather than imposing expertise. Legitimacy may be partly achieved by facilitating the visibility of HN presence in the province by assisting official visits to remote districts and villages (e.g., by providing transportation or communications). Another key element will be the engagement of HN officials, the local communities, and the population through established and traditional bodies.

d. **Restraint.** PRTs establish realistic objectives and balance the tempo of operations to maintain the primacy of HN legitimacy and effectiveness. SC efforts must be aimed at managing expectations – promising only what can be delivered. Planning for all programs and projects must include long-term sustainability. Additionally, efforts at the local level must be coordinated with national level processes to ensure the legitimacy and effectiveness of the entire HN government.

Intentionally Blank

APPENDIX C
INSURGENT APPROACHES INDICATORS

1. Analyzing Insurgent Approaches

It is important to analyze what approach an insurgency is using. Understanding an insurgency's approach provides insight into their campaign plan and potential COAs. There are indicators for each insurgent approach.

2. Indicators of Urban Terrorist Approach

In this strategy the insurgents attack government targets with the intention of causing government forces to over-react against the population. This strategy can be initiated without popular support and its success relies almost exclusively on spontaneous uprising sparked by rage at government oppression. The urban terrorist approach actions are often predictable. Some indicators that the insurgents are using this approach are:

a. Insurgent actions calculated to provoke harsh government or counterinsurgent response.

b. Terrorist attacks which are high-visibility and produce high casualties.

c. Propaganda focuses on government brutality, calling attention to specific harsh government actions such as massacres, torture of political prisoners, "disappearances," brutal responses to peaceful demonstrations.

d. In this strategy there normally is little political organization or sustained effort to indoctrinate political cadre or the masses.

e. Little or no effort to subvert the government from within.

f. Insurgency may have popular sympathy if government is particularly brutal or corrupt, but very limited committed support.

3. Indicators of a Military-Focused Approach

Insurgents using a military-focused approach are focused on causing the government to lose legitimacy, and inspiring a vulnerable population to join the insurgents against the government. This approach is vulnerable to effective counterguerrilla operations. Its success depends upon successful military action and popular uprising. Like the urban terrorist approach, a military-focused strategy can be predictable. Some indicators of this approach are:

a. Attacks on government targets, accompanied by propaganda inciting people to join the insurgency and rise up against the government.

b. IO focused on HN government weakness and illegitimacy.

c. Little evidence of long-term efforts at building a political base.

d. Few efforts along other lines of operations such as creating a political wing or infiltrating legitimate organizations.

4. Indicators of a Protracted Popular War Approach

Although other insurgent strategies have phases as discussed in the phasing and timing dynamic, the protracted popular war approach is based upon the three distinct phases: latent and incipient, guerrilla warfare, and war of movement. Each phase's activities build upon those of the previous; the insurgents generally continue activities from previous phases. There are a number of variations to this strategy, with different emphasis along different lines of operations. This approach has a political wing and a military wing. This approach is characterized by its high level of organization and indoctrination, actions along multiple lines of operations, and ability of leadership to direct shifting of phases according to circumstances. Due to its flexibility, the protracted popular war approach is difficult and time consuming to effectively counter. Some indicators of this approach are:

a. Continuous, long-term efforts to build popular support, infiltrate legitimate government organizations, and establish and maintain a clandestine organization.

b. Highly-indoctrinated leadership, political cadre, and guerrillas.

c. Extensive, well-organized auxiliary and underground.

d. Leadership that is able to exert control over the insurgency.

e. Able to shift phases at the direction of its leadership; including return to previous phase when necessary.

f. Repeated attacks on infrastructure and attacks designed to wear down the government and allies.

g. Continuous operations along multiple lines of operations, although some will be emphasized more than others in different phases.

5. Indicators of a Subversive Approach

An insurgency using a subversive approach uses part of its illegal political wing to become a legitimate political party and enter the government. It then attempts to subvert and destroy the government from within. The insurgents' purpose is not to integrate into the national government, but to overthrow the government. This is a difficult approach to counter due to its highly political nature. Indicators of this approach are:

a. Insurgents' seeking meetings with government or coalition forces to discuss ceasefires.

b. Repeated attacks on infrastructure; designed to wear down and reduce credibility of government.

c. Public statements denouncing violence, distancing itself from the insurgency while still operating under control of insurgent leadership.

d. An apparent breach between militant and political elements of the insurgency.

e. Formation of new alliances, sometimes with groups that seem to have little in common with the insurgency or its ideology.

f. End or reduction in guerrilla activity; increase in political activity.

g. Intensive efforts to gain international moral and political support.

h. Sophisticated IO aimed at specific TAs with appropriate messages.

i. Emergence of insurgent political wing that seeks recognition and entry into national politics or election to local, district, department, regional, or national offices.

6. Shifting Approaches

Insurgents will change approaches, using different approaches in different phases or in different geographical areas. These decisions are based on the current state of the OE, insurgent objectives, and counterinsurgent pressure. Significant changes in approach may indicate a shift from one approach to another. Insurgencies move to some form of the protracted popular war approach or the subversive approach after other approaches have proved to be unsuccessful. Insurgencies are most vulnerable while they shift between approaches or phases. These shifts may be due to fractures among the leadership or key losses. Other reasons for a shift include changes in external support, changes in leadership, or counterinsurgent action. These shifts will often occur quickly, so counterinsurgents must be prepared to exploit them. Indicators of a shift in approach are:

a. Changes in IO content or methods.

b. Sudden increase in internal communications.

c. Unexplained and sudden pauses in guerrilla attacks or increases in attacks.

d. Shift of insurgent effort from urban to rural or vice versa.

e. Apparent disappearance of insurgents in specific areas to reappear elsewhere.

f. Statements of support for insurgency from external actors.

g. Evidence of increasing organization, indoctrination of followers, and more secure means of communications.

h. Evidence of new efforts to infiltrate legitimate organizations.

i. New insurgent advocacy for rights of peasants, farmers, or other groups.

j. Change in focus of attacks, such as targeting a different, specific sector.

For more detail on insurgent approaches, see Chapter II, "Insurgency."

APPENDIX D
REFERENCES

The development of JP 3-24 is based upon the following primary references:

1. Strategic Guidance and Policy

a. *The National Security Strategy of the United States of America.*

b. *National Defense Strategy of the United States of America.*

c. *National Military Strategy.*

d. National Security Presidential Directive (NSPD)-44, *Management of Interagency Efforts Concerning Reconstruction and Stabilization.*

e. DODD 3000.05, *Military Support for Stability, Security, Transition and Reconstruction (SSTR) Operations.*

f. DODD 3000.07, *Irregular Warfare.*

2. Joint Publications

a. JP 1, *Doctrine for the Armed Forces of the United States.*

b. JP 2-0, *Joint Intelligence.*

c. JP 2-01.3, *Joint Intelligence Preparation of the Operational Environment.*

d. JP 3-0, *Joint Operations.*

e. JP 3-05, *Joint Special Operations.*

f. JP 3-05.1, *Joint Special Operations Task Force Operations.*

g. JP 3-07.3, *Peace Operations.*

h. JP 3-08, *Intergovernmental Coordination During Joint Operations,* Volumes I and II.

i. JP 3-13, *Information Operations.*

j. JP 3-13.2, *Psychological Operations.*

k. JP 3-13.3, *Operations Security.*

l. JP 3-16, *Multinational Operations.*

m. JP 3-22, *Foreign Internal Defense.*

n. JP 3-26, *Counterterrorism.*

o. JP 3-40, *Combating Weapons of Mass Destruction.*

p. JP 3.57, *Civil-Military Operations.*

q. JP 4-0, *Joint Logistics.*

r. JP 4-02, *Health Service Support.*

s. JP 5-0, *Joint Operation Planning.*

3. Allied Joint Publications

a. Allied Joint Pub – 3.4.4, Allied Joint Publication for Counterinsurgency.

b. Allied Joint Pub – 5, Allied Joint Doctrine Operational Planning.

c. Allied Joint Pub – 9, NATO Civil-Military Cooperation (CIMIC) Doctrine.

4. Service Publications

a. AFDD 2-3, *Irregular Warfare.*

b. AFDD 2-3.1, *Foreign Internal Defense.*

c. FM 3-05.40, *Civil Affairs Operations.*

d. FM 3-05.201, *Special Forces Unconventional Warfare Operations.*

e. FM 3-05.202, *Special Forces Foreign Internal Defense Operations.*

f. FM 3-24/MCWP 3-33.5, *Counterinsurgency.*

g. FM 7-98, *Operations in a Low-Intensity Conflict.*

h. FM 90-8, *Counterguerrilla Warfare.*

i. Marine Corps Doctrine Publication (MCDP) 1-2, *Campaigning.*

j. MCDP 5, *Planning.*

5. Department of State Publications

a. United States Government Interagency Counterinsurgency initiative, *US Government Counterinsurgency Guide,* January 2009.

b. DOS publication, *Post-Conflict Reconstruction Essential Tasks,* April 2005.

6. General

a. Byman, Daniel, *Understanding Proto-Insurgencies.* Santa Monica: RAND Corporation, 2007.

b. Cassidy, Robert M. *Counterinsurgency and the Global War on Terror: Military Culture and Irregular Warfare.* Westport: Greenwood Publishing Group, INC., 2006.

c. Celeski, Joseph D. JSOU Report 05-2: *Operationalizing COIN.* Hurlburt Field: Joint Special Operations University, 2005.

d. Fishel, John T. and Max G. Manwaring. *Uncomfortable Wars Revisited.* Norman: University of Oklahoma Press, 2006.

e. Gray, Colin S. *Another Bloody Century.* London: Weidenfeld & Nicholson, 2005.

f. Hoffman, Frank G. *Conflict in the 21st Century: The Rise of Hybrid Wars.* Arlington: Potomac Institute for Policy Studies, 2007.

g. Kilcullen, David J. *The Accidental Guerrilla.*

h. Mackinlay, John and Alison Al-Baddawy. *Rethinking Counterinsurgency.* Santa Monica: RAND Corporation, 2008.

i. Manwaring, Max G. *A Contemporary Challenge to State Sovereignty: Gangs and Other Illicit Transnational Criminal Organizations In Central America, El Salvador, Mexico, Jamaica, and Brazil.* Carlisle: Strategic Studies Institute, 2007.

j. McCormick, Gordon H., Steven B. Horton, and Laruen A. Harrison. *Things Fall Apart: the endgame dynamics of internal wars.* Third World Quarterly, Vol. 28, No. 2, 2007, pp 321-367.

k. Metz, Steven. *Rethinking Insurgency.* Carlisle: Strategic Studies Institute, 2007.

l. Mockaitis, Thomas R. *The Iraq War: Learning from the Past, Adapting to the Present, and Planning for the Future.* Carlisle: Strategic Studies Institute, 2007.

m. McCuen, John J. *The Art of Counter-Revolutionary War.* Mechanicsburg, Stackpole Books, 1966.

n. Rosenau, William. *Subversion and Insurgency*. Santa Monica: RAND Corporation, 2007.

APPENDIX E
ADMINISTRATIVE INSTRUCTIONS

1. User Comments

Users in the field are highly encouraged to submit comments on this publication to: Commander, United States Joint Forces Command, Joint Warfighting Center, ATTN: – Doctrine and Education Group, 116 Lake View Parkway, Suffolk, VA 23435-2697. These comments should address content (accuracy, usefulness, consistency, and organization), writing, and appearance.

2. Authorship

The lead agent for this publication is the US Army. The Joint Staff doctrine sponsor for this publication is the Strategic Plans and Policy Directorate (J-5).

3. Change Recommendations

a. Recommendations for urgent changes to this publication should be submitted:

TO: DA WASHINGTON DC// G35-SSP//
INFO: JOINT STAFF WASHINGTON DC//J-7-JEDD//
CDRUSJFCOM SUFFOLK VA//JT10//

Routine changes should be submitted electronically to Commander, Joint Warfighting Center, Doctrine and Education Group and info the Lead Agent and the Director for Operational Plans and Joint Force Development J-7/JEDD via the CJCS joint electronic library (JEL) at http://www.dtic.mil/doctrine.

b. When a Joint Staff directorate submits a proposal to the CJCS that would change source document information reflected in this publication, that directorate will include a proposed change to this publication as an enclosure to its proposal. The Military Services and other organizations are requested to notify the Joint Staff J-7 when changes to source documents reflected in this publication are initiated.

c. Record of Changes:

CHANGE NUMBER	COPY NUMBER	DATE OF CHANGE	DATE ENTERED	POSTED BY	REMARKS

4. Distribution of Publications

Local reproduction is authorized and access to unclassified publications is unrestricted. However, access to and reproduction authorization for classified joint publications must be in accordance with DOD 5200.1-R, *Information Security Program.*

5. Distribution of Electronic Publications

a. Joint Staff J-7 will not print copies of JPs for distribution. Electronic versions are available on JDEIS at https://jdeis.js.mil (NIPRNET) and https://jdeis.js.smil.mil (SIPRNET) and on the JEL at http://www.dtic.mil/doctrine (NIPRNET).

b. Only approved joint publications and joint test publications are releasable outside the combatant commands, Services, and Joint Staff. Release of any classified joint publication to foreign governments or foreign nationals must be requested through the local embassy (Defense Attaché Office) to DIA Foreign Liaison Office, PO-FL, Room 1E811, 7400 Pentagon, Washington, DC 20301-7400.

c. CD-ROM. Upon request of a JDDC member, the Joint Staff J-7 will produce and deliver one CD-ROM with current joint publications.

GLOSSARY

PART I – ABBREVIATIONS AND ACRONYMS

ACT	advance civilian team
AFDD	Air Force doctrine document
AFSOF	Air Force special operations forces
AOI	area of interest
AOR	area of responsibility
ARSOF	Army special operations forces
ASCOPE	areas, structures, capabilities, organizations, people, and events
C2	command and control
CA	civil affairs
CAO	civil affairs operations
CBRN	chemical, biological, radiological, and nuclear
CC	critical capability
CCDR	combatant commander
CI	counterintelligence
CIM	civil information management
CJCS	Chairman of the Joint Chiefs of Staff
CMCB	civil-military coordination board
CMO	civil-military operations
CMOC	civil-military operations center
CNO	computer network operations
COA	course of action
COG	center of gravity
COIN	counterinsurgency
COM	chief of mission
COMCAM	combat camera
COMINT	communications intelligence
CR	critical requirement
CSAR	combat search and rescue
CT	counterterrorism
CV	critical vulnerability
CWMD	combating weapons of mass destruction
DA	direct action
DC	dislocated civilian
DDR	disarmament, demobilization, and reintegration
DOD	Department of Defense
DODD	Department of Defense directive
DOS	Department of State
DSPD	defense support to public diplomacy
ELINT	electronic intelligence
ESG	executive steering group
EW	electronic warfare

FACT	field advance civilian team
FID	foreign internal defense
FISINT	foreign instrumentation signals intelligence
FM	field manual (Army)
GAT	governmental assistance team
GCC	geographic combatant commander
GEOINT	geospatial intelligence
HA	humanitarian assistance
HN	host nation
HUMINT	human intelligence
IA	information assurance
ICAF	Interagency Conflict Assessment Framework
IDAD	internal defense and development
IED	improvised explosive device
IGO	intergovernmental organization
IIP	interagency implementation plan
IMINT	imagery intelligence
IMS	Interagency Management System
IO	information operations
IPC	integration planning cell
IPI	indigenous populations and institutions
ISR	intelligence, surveillance, and reconnaissance
IW	irregular warfare
J-2	intelligence directorate of a joint staff
JCMOTF	joint civil-military operations task force
JFC	joint force commander
JIACG	joint interagency coordination group
JIATF	joint interagency task force
JIPOE	joint intelligence preparation of the operational environment
JOPP	joint operation planning process
JP	joint publication
JPASE	Joint Public Affairs Support Element
JTF	joint task force
LOO	line of operations
MARSOF	Marine Corps special operations forces
MASINT	measurement and signature intelligence
MCDP	Marine Corps doctrine publication
MCAG	maritime civil affairs group
MCWP	Marine Corps warfighting publication
METOC	meteorological and oceanographic

MILDEC	military deception
MIST	military information support team
MOE	measure of effectiveness
MSO	maritime security operations
NAVSOF	Navy special operations forces
NGA	National Geospatial-Intelligence Agency
NGO	nongovernmental organization
NSC	National Security Council
OE	operational environment
OPSEC	operations security
OSINT	open-source intelligence
PA	public affairs
PAO	public affairs officer
PB	peace building
PD	public diplomacy
PEO	peace enforcement operations
PIR	priority intelligence requirement
PKO	peacekeeping operations
PM	peacemaking
PMESII	political, military, economic, social, information, and infrastructure
PO	peace operations
PR	personnel recovery
PRT	provincial reconstruction team
PSYOP	psychological operations
ROE	rules of engagement
SC	strategic communication
SCA	support to civil administration
SecDef	Secretary of Defense
SFA	security force assistance
SIGINT	signals intelligence
SOF	special operations forces
SR	special reconnaissance
SSR	security sector reform
TA	target audience
TECHINT	technical intelligence
TTP	tactics, techniques, and procedures
TV	television

UGA	ungoverned area
UN	United Nations
USAID	United States Agency for International Development
USG	United States Government
UW	unconventional warfare
WMD	weapons of mass destruction

PART II — TERMS AND DEFINITIONS

Unless otherwise annotated, this publication is the proponent for all terms and definitions found in the glossary. Upon approval, JP 1-02, *Department of Defense Dictionary of Military and Associated Terms*, will reflect this publication as the source document for these terms and definitions.

civil-military operations. The activities of a commander that establish, maintain, influence, or exploit relations between military forces, governmental and nongovernmental civilian organizations and authorities, and the civilian populace in a friendly, neutral, or hostile operational area in order to facilitate military operations, to consolidate and achieve operational US objectives. Civil-military operations may include performance by military forces of activities and functions normally the responsibility of the local, regional, or national government. These activities may occur prior to, during, or subsequent to other military actions. They may also occur, if directed, in the absence of other military operations. Civil-military operations may be performed by designated civil affairs, by other military forces, or by a combination of civil affairs and other forces. Also called CMO. (JP 1-02. SOURCE: JP 3-57)

civil-military operations center. An organization normally comprised of civil affairs, established to plan and facilitate coordination of activities of the Armed Forces of the United States with indigenous populations and institutions, the private sector, intergovernmental organizations, nongovernmental organizations, multinational forces, and other governmental agencies in support of the joint force commander. Also called CMOC. See also civil-military operations. (JP 1-02. SOURCE: JP 3-57)

counterguerrilla operations. Operations and activities conducted by armed forces, paramilitary forces, or nonmilitary agencies against guerrillas. (Approved for inclusion in JP 1-02.)

counterguerrilla warfare. None. (Approved for removal from JP 1-02.)

counterinsurgency. Comprehensive civilian and military efforts taken to defeat an insurgency and to address any core grievances. Also called COIN. (This term and its definition modify the existing term and its definition and are approved for inclusion in JP 1-02.)

counterintelligence. Information gathered and activities conducted to protect against espionage, other intelligence activities, sabotage, or assassinations conducted by or on behalf of foreign governments or elements thereof, foreign organizations, or foreign persons, or international terrorist activities. Also called CI. (JP 1-02. SOURCE: JP 2-0)

country team. The senior, in-country, US coordinating and supervising body, headed by the chief of the US diplomatic mission, and composed of the senior member of each represented US department or agency, as desired by the chief of the US diplomatic mission. (JP 1-02. SOURCE: JP 3-07.4)

foreign internal defense. Participation by civilian and military agencies of a government in any of the action programs taken by another government or other designated organization to free and protect its society from subversion, lawlessness, and insurgency. Also called FID. (JP 1-02. SOURCE: JP 3-22)

governance. The state's ability to serve the citizens through the rules, processes, and behavior by which interests are articulated, resources are managed, and power is exercised in a society, including the representative participatory decision-making processes typically guaranteed under inclusive, constitutional authority. (Approved for inclusion in JP 1-02.)

host nation. A nation which receives the forces and/or supplies of allied nations and/or NATO organizations to be located on, to operate in, or to transit through its territory. Also called HN. (JP 1-02. SOURCE: JP 3-57)

indicator. In intelligence usage, an item of information which reflects the intention or capability of an adversary to adopt or reject a course of action. (JP 1-02. SOURCE: JP 2-0)

information operations. The integrated employment of the core capabilities of electronic warfare, computer network operations, psychological operations, military deception, and operations security, in concert with specified supporting and related capabilities, to influence, disrupt, corrupt or usurp adversarial human and automated decision making while protecting our own. Also called IO. See also psychological operations. (JP 1-02. SOURCE: JP 3-13)

instruments of national power. All of the means available to the government in its pursuit of national objectives. They are expressed as diplomatic, economic, informational and military. (JP 1-02. SOURCE: JP 1)

insurgency. The organized use of subversion and violence by a group or movement that seeks to overthrow or force change of a governing authority. Insurgency can also refer to the group itself. (This term and its definition modify the existing term and its definition and are approved for inclusion in JP 1-02.)

insurgent. None. (Approved for removal from JP 1-02.)

intelligence operations. The variety of intelligence and counterintelligence tasks that are carried out by various intelligence organizations and activities within the intelligence process. Intelligence operations include planning and direction, collection, processing and exploitation, analysis and production, dissemination and integration, and evaluation and feedback. (JP 1-02. SOURCE: JP 2-01)

intelligence, surveillance, and reconnaissance. An activity that synchronizes and integrates the planning and operation of sensors, assets, and processing, exploitation, and dissemination systems in direct support of current and future operations. This is an integrated intelligence and operations function. Also called ISR. (JP 1-02. SOURCE: JP 2-01)

internal defense and development. The full range of measures taken by a nation to promote its growth and to protect itself from subversion, lawlessness, and insurgency. It focuses on building viable institutions (political, economic, social, and military) that respond to the needs of society. Also called IDAD. See also foreign internal defense. (JP 1-02. SOURCE: JP 3-22)

irregular forces. Armed individuals or groups who are not members of the regular armed forces, police, or other internal security forces. (JP 1-02. SOURCE: JP 3-24)

irregular warfare. A violent struggle among state and non-state actors for legitimacy and influence over the relevant population(s). Irregular warfare favors indirect and asymmetric approaches, though it may employ the full range of military and other capacities, in order to erode an adversary's power, influence, and will. Also called IW. (JP 1-02. SOURCE: JP 1)

measure of effectiveness. A criterion used to assess changes in system behavior, capability, or operational environment that is tied to measuring the attainment of an end state, achievement of an objective, or creation of an effect. Also called MOE. (JP 1-02. SOURCE: JP 3-0)

measure of performance. A criterion used to assess friendly actions that is tied to measuring task accomplishment. Also called MOP. (JP 1-02. SOURCE: JP 3-0)

multinational operations. A collective term to describe military actions conducted by forces of two or more nations, usually undertaken within the structure of a coalition or alliance. (JP 1-02. SOURCE: JP 3-16)

operational art. The application of creative imagination by commanders and staffs — supported by their skill, knowledge, and experience — to design strategies, campaigns, and major operations and organize and employ military forces. Operational art integrates ends, ways, and means across the levels of war. (JP 1-02. SOURCE: JP 3-0)

operational design. The conception and construction of the framework that underpins a campaign or major operation plan and its subsequent execution. (JP 1-02. SOURCE: JP 3-0)

operational environment. A composite of the conditions, circumstances, and influences that affect the employment of capabilities and bear on the decisions of the commander. Also called OE. (This term and its definition modify the existing term and its definition and are approved for inclusion in JP 1-02and sourced to JP 3-0.)

paramilitary forces. Forces or groups distinct from the regular armed forces of any country, but resembling them in organization, equipment, training, or mission. (JP 1-02. SOURCE: JP 3-24)

peace building. Stability actions, predominately diplomatic and economic, that strengthen and rebuild governmental infrastructure and institutions in order to avoid a relapse into conflict. Also called PB. See also peace enforcement; peacekeeping; peacemaking; peace operations. (JP 1-02. SOURCE: JP 3-07.3)

peace enforcement. Application of military force, or the threat of its use, normally pursuant to international authorization, to compel compliance with resolutions or sanctions designed to maintain or restore peace and order. See also peace building; peacekeeping; peacemaking; peace operations. (JP 1-02. SOURCE: JP 3-07.3)

peacekeeping. Military operations undertaken with the consent of all major parties to a dispute, designed to monitor and facilitate implementation of an agreement (cease fire, truce, or other such agreement) and support diplomatic efforts to reach a long-term political settlement. See also peace building; peace enforcement; peacemaking; peace operations. (JP 1-02. SOURCE: JP 3-07.3)

peacemaking. The process of diplomacy, mediation, negotiation, or other forms of peaceful settlements that arranges an end to a dispute and resolves issues that led to it. See also peace building; peace enforcement; peacekeeping; peace operations. (JP 1-02. SOURCE: JP 3-07.3)

peace operations. A broad term that encompasses multiagency and multinational crisis response and limited contingency operations involving all instruments of national power with military missions to contain conflict, redress the peace, and shape the environment to support reconciliation and rebuilding and facilitate the transition to legitimate governance. Peace operations include peacekeeping, peace enforcement, peacemaking, peace building, and conflict prevention efforts. Also called PO. See also peace building; peace enforcement; peacekeeping; and peacemaking. (JP 1-02. SOURCE: JP 3-07.3)

propaganda. Any form of communication in support of national objectives designed to influence the opinions, emotions, attitudes, or behavior of any group in order to benefit the sponsor, either directly or indirectly. (JP 1-02. SOURCE: JP 3-13.2)

psychological operations. Planned operations to convey selected information and indicators to foreign audiences to influence their emotions, motives, objective reasoning, and ultimately the behavior of foreign governments, organizations, groups, and individuals. The purpose of psychological operations is to induce or reinforce foreign attitudes and behavior favorable to the originator's objectives. Also called PSYOP. (JP 1-02. SOURCE: JP 3-13.2)

public affairs. Those public information, command information, and community relations activities directed toward both the external and internal publics with interest in the Department of Defense. Also called PA. (JP 1-02. SOURCE: JP 3-61)

reachback. The process of obtaining products, services, and applications, or forces, or equipment, or material from organizations that are not forward deployed. (JP 1-02. SOURCE: JP 3-30)

security sector reform. The set of policies, plans, programs, and activities that a government undertakes to improve the way it provides safety, security, and justice. Also called SSR. (Approved for inclusion in JP 1-02.)

strategic communication. Focused United States Government efforts to understand and engage key audiences to create, strengthen, or preserve conditions favorable for the advancement of United States Government interests, policies, and objectives through the use of coordinated programs, plans, themes, messages, and products synchronized with the actions of all instruments of national power. (JP 1-02. SOURCE: JP 5-0)

strategy. A prudent idea or set of ideas for employing the instruments of national power in a synchronized and integrated fashion to achieve theater, national, and/or multinational objectives. (JP 1-02. SOURCE: JP 3-0)

subversion. Actions designed to undermine the military, economic, psychological, or political strength or morale of a governing authority. (This term and its definition modify the existing term and its definition and are approved for inclusion in JP 1-02).

support to counterinsurgency. None. (Approved for removal from JP 1-02.)

support to insurgency. None. (Approved for removal from JP 1-02.)

terrorism. The calculated use of unlawful violence or threat of unlawful violence to inculcate fear; intended to coerce or to intimidate governments or societies in the pursuit of goals that are generally political, religious, or ideological. See also terrorist; terrorist group. (JP 1-02. SOURCE: JP 3-07.2)

terrorist. An individual who commits an act or acts of violence or threatens violence in pursuit of political, religious, or ideological objectives. See also terrorism. (JP 1-02. SOURCE: JP 3-07.2)

terrorist group. Any number of terrorists who assemble together, have a unifying relationship, or are organized for the purpose of committing an act or acts of violence or threatens violence in pursuit of their political, religious, or ideological objectives. See also terrorism. (JP 1-02. SOURCE: JP 3-07.2)

theater of operations. An operational area defined by the geographic combatant commander for the conduct or support of specific military operations. Multiple theaters of operations normally will be geographically separate and focused on different missions. Theaters of operations are usually of significant size, allowing for operations in depth and over extended periods of time. Also called TO. (JP 1-02. SOURCE: JP 3-0)

theater strategy. Concepts and courses of action directed toward securing the objectives of national and multinational policies and strategies through the synchronized and integrated employment of military forces and other instruments of national power. See also strategy. (JP 1-02. SOURCE: JP 3-0)

unconventional warfare. A broad spectrum of military and paramilitary operations, normally of long duration, predominantly conducted through, with, or by indigenous or surrogate forces who are organized, trained, equipped, supported, and directed in varying degrees by an external source. It includes, but is not limited to, guerrilla warfare, subversion, sabotage, intelligence activities, and unconventional assisted recovery. Also called UW. (JP 1-02. SOURCE: JP 3-05)

unified action. The synchronization, coordination, and/or integration of the activities of governmental and nongovernmental entities with military operations to achieve unity of effort. (JP 1-02. SOURCE: JP 1)

5732192R00138

Printed in Great Britain
by Amazon.co.uk, Ltd.,
Marston Gate.

OBSERVATIONS ON LIFE

BY

GRAHAM ROBINSON

Acknowledgments

I would like to acknowledge and thank the following people for their help, guidance, mentoring, understanding and friendship given to me whilst writing this book over the past few years:

Mrs Ali Lavelle
Liverpool Bards
Ms Celia Gentles
The Wirral Alliance of Poets
City Talk FM Radio Station in Liverpool
Mr James Hollingworth – A Fine Illustrator
Lesley and Staff at Greasby Library on The Wirral
Mrs Judy Ugonna – Poets a'hoy and all other members
Mrs Peggy Poole – Greasby Poets and all other members
All staff at Hoylake Library where I have spent many hours
Mr Charles McIntyre – Countyvise and all other members of staff
PITWR (Poets In The Waiting Room) of Kew Gardens in London
Richard and Linda Palmer of The Firkin House in Hoylake for their unstinting friendship

First Published 2011 by Appin Press, an imprint of Countyvise Ltd
14 Appin Road, Birkenhead, CH41 9HH

British Library Cataloguing in Publication Data.
A catalogue record for this book is available from the British Library.

ISBN 978 1 906205 73 7

Illustrations

Warning

This book contains explicit language
and adult content which some readers
may find offensive.

Dedication

In the first instance I would like to dedicate this book to the memory of my dear long suffering mother Mrs Pearl Doreen Blake (deceased) the nicest woman I have ever met.
My brother Mr Clifford Dennis Robinson...
I am pleased to say is alive and well in Surrey.
My three lovely daughters Abigail, Beverley and Cara...
plus my grandson Callum.
And to all other family members (I love you all and owe you so much) I dedicate this book to them for their unconditional love and support over the years.

Foreword by the Author

A bit of background about me first.

I was born in the draconian 1950s to an alcoholic, violent, disciplinarian father and a kind, loving, caring, artistic mother. We lived for 15 years in a Prefabricated (asbestos prefab) bungalow on a tough West London council estate which was purposely built after the Second World War to create homes for returning soldiers.

My education was initially gained at Dormers Wells School (which resembled a prison). I have not been back there for some years now and it has probably become a mosque or a railway museum.

Growing up was not very pleasant as you may read from two of my poems ('The Pain of a Child' and 'The Early Years'). Enough said I think.

Sometimes no matter how hard we all work and strive, things do not work out as we imagined or planned they would do. I met my now ex-wife (Carol) in Spain and we married in 1973. We spent the next 13 years having extensive infertility treatment under a Mr Robert Winston of Hammersmith Hospital (now of TV fame and a Lord to boot) a truly great man! (Other couples had to get married as the woman got pregnant – not us!)

In 1986 our first daughter Cara Ami was born (it was surely a miracle). Two years later in July 1988 we were blessed with twin daughters Beverley and Abigail (more miracles) after much elation and those sleepless nights, plus a house move and I had started my own Travel Agency, having worked for British Airways, The Sheraton Hotel Group, Air Malta, Europcar at Heathrow and Spurs Travel I had become ABTA and IATA trained. But Carol had been diagnosed with Post Natal Depression (PND – sounds like a political party) and we moved back to Carol's birthplace on the Wirral Peninsular near Liverpool with our 3 lovely daughters all aged under 3 (to be near Carol's family). My own family was left 250 miles behind and I sold the business, and looked forward to a new happier life together.

I am not going to turn this 'Note from The Author' in to an autobiography (I tried that and could not get it published – not PC enough) so I think I will ask you to read my poem 'Unfortunate', which will explain much of my life in the North West which indirectly led to me writing, following my business failure in 1997 and the loss of our home (my fault) and subsequent divorce from Carol in 2002.

Following this I moved into a charming 2 bedroomed flat built in 1888 in Hoylake where I still live today.

I had joined a few local reading clubs and poetry groups and attended lots of readings and read lots of books, as I had always liked words and had written a couple of school plays.

I wrote *My Life in Verse* as Sir John Betjeman had done with 'Summoned by Three Bells' but it was too sad (I thought bad news sold newspapers? Obviously this doesn't apply to books of poetry).

By this time I had read all the masters and had gained quite a lot of life experiences in the business sector, plus marriage and divorce and watching my three daughters grow up.

I had become ever 'observant' probably following my 'depression' and decided to write a different type of poetical book, based on my life observations and changing morals, views and values, which led to the birth of *Observations On Life* which has taken me many years to live and just over 8 years to write and re-write, and which I hope you will enjoy.

A lot of my work was read out on *City Talk FM* radio in Liverpool and has been published by United Press under their National Anthology banner in books entitled *Summer Daze* and *A Guiding*

Light. My work has also been selected for the soon to be introduced 'Poets in The Waiting Room' for the NHS and GP waiting rooms for patients to read.

In addition to my 'Acknowledgements' and 'Dedications' may I also thank all friends and fellow (tormented) poets and writers who either know me or whom I have met.

Before I finish, may I just say that I write what I feel, see and hear and that I wear my heart on my sleeve (wrongly or rightly) and like everybody I am affected by what happens to us and around us in today's changed, materialistic, selfish and capitalistic needy and greedy society. (Sorry folks, the truth hurts.)

I do use very strong words in certain poems which I feel are in line with both the depth of my feelings and reflect the seriousness of the subject matter and that I do not swear wantonly or on a whim. I am also not a racist or activist of any kind, more a humorist.

My book has not been written to offend, but as a realist in today's society I may not have observed a certain degree of 'political correctness' but I am a poet and a writer for which I make no apology.

I will cover many contentious and thought-provoking issues in my poetry, which I have tried to write in a passionate yet understandable fashion with a degree of humour and a lot of life experience.

At the end of each poem I have included a 'Note to the Reader' (i.e. you) so that you can not only enjoy my poetry but also appreciate why I have written it.

Thank You

Graham Robinson (Author)

Contents

Observations On Life

OBSERVATIONS ON LIFE

Love the way you would like to be loved –
Kiss the way you would like to be kissed.

Notice people the way you want to be noticed –
Miss people the way you want to be missed.

Sing from the diaphragm, as if there is nobody to listen –
Smile so that it makes one's eyes glisten.

Try and be positive in all you say and do –
Don't behave as if you haven't got a clue.

Don't smoke it is bad for others and your own health –
There are many cheaper ways of losing your wealth.

Don't worry too much it puts lines upon your face –
Don't try and find fault with the whole human race.

Don't become a workaholic –
Try not to become an alcoholic.

Dance vigorously as if there is nobody looking –
Put plenty of oil and vegetables in one's cooking.

Do smile and laugh - keep fit and look after yourself –
Take regular exercise and maintain your health.

Don't place too much emphasis on material objects –
And the trappings of wealth.

Please try and find happiness with a loving partner –
Don't get left upon life's shelf.

Note to the reader – Well this is the way I try and see life – how about you?

BEAUTIFUL AND FORBIDDING

Beautiful and Forbidding as a –
Storm lashed Hebridean Isle – as a
Lion growling in its lair – as a
Scorned woman's smile – as an
Eagle hunting in the air.

Beautiful and Forbidding as a –
Great white shark – as a
Grisly bear with open claw showing – as a
Sexual encounter after dark – as a
Rapids white water flowing.

Beautiful and Forbidding as a –
Hunting Tawny Owl – as a
Car skidding in a chicane – as a
Leopard's scowl – as an
Advancing hurricane.

Beautiful and Forbidding as a –
High up falling waterfall – as a
Freefall skydive from a plane – as a
Raging bull in pain – in an arena – as a
Cry from a wolf or – laughing hyena.

Beautiful and Forbidding as a –
Woman out to get a man – as a
Man who knows he can – as a
Soldier with a loaded gun – as a
Hunted animal on the run.

Note to the reader – That's life folks – beautiful, scary and sometimes forbidding.

WHEN

When you are down and feeling ill.
When the road you are travelling seems all uphill.
When those clouds of doubt are all about.
When you need to smile but want to shout.
When your income is low and you wonder why.
When your bills are far too high.
When you want to travel up through the sky.
When you want to laugh but have to cry.
When you feel like living but hope to die.
When you feel so low but want to be high.
When you need to be brave.
When you have that 'close shave'.
When you want to quit just sit and chill.
When you are panic stricken stay calm and still.
When you want to play but feel too tired.
When you are feeling bad and need to be wired.
When you are hungry but have no food.
When you keep getting in those moods.
When you feel sad and negative.
When you need to be happy and positive.
When you are living on bread and honey.
When you want to spend but have no money –

Hey there don't worry –
Just call Graham because he is very funny...

Note to the reader – We all have highs and lows in life, but as the luxury car salesman said 'That's the way the Mercedes – Benz' (bends) Ha ha. Positive attitude in life is a must I feel sure you will agree with me... please read my poem – Smile and Laugh.

WET AND WINDY WIRRAL

I have woken to The Wirral Wind with strong driving rain –
Again, on this dark and grey November morn' –
The sort of wind that cuts through you like a Viking knife –
with pain.
With a persistent soaking rain that fills one full of dampened scorn.
It was this wind that drove those Viking invaders upon our shores –
O'er Thurstaston Common all those many, years before.
They did not know where they had come to,
or what peninsular of – land – ho!

In the Winter I call 'Wet and Windy Wirral',
but it also has an immeasurable beauty.
The Vikings didn't care – they were just invaders blown off course –
bound for Ireland.
We will never really know what they were looking for,
those many years ago?
But they came ashore from their longboats,
battle dressed ready to do their duty.

The warlike Vikings soon overran the millers and farmers
of Cows and Sheep.
With quiet stealth, and great strength –
of both the sword, and axe, they attacked –
Wet and Windy Wirral – raping, killing and pillaging all,
whilst asleep.
It was clear these fighting men had not come for a holiday,
this is indeed a fact.
But historians will have us all believe the Vikings –
taught us many things.

Of how to sail and flail, and fight or flight, and things –
and suffer the arrows and slings.
Had those historians not read of –
The Roman Empire and Hadrian or Caesar –
Our rulers who had visited us from Italy,
some hundreds of years earlier –
And of Londinium, Bath, Winchester, Chichester, Leicester and –
Chester?
Building walls and ever straight roads –
and hot baths with central heating underground.
Of nearly 2000 years ago, evidence of which to this very day –
can still be found.

Note to the reader – Oh! How I love my green England and 'My Wet and Windy Wirral.' Long to rain o'er us in peace and happiness – never less.

NATURE

A kestrel hovering on high –
In a cloudy, windy sky.
Field mouse wondering why –
Bloodhounds give a warring cry.
Fox must find a hole or die –
Or up in a bush or tree must hide.

Hunting eagles swooping down –
Rabbits grasped off the ground.
Seagulls, squawking – looking –
Sitting – waiting for a crab.
Hoping, wishing for a dab –
Either one - with claw and beak will grab.

Kingfisher upon a tree – in wait at river's bend –
No rods or hooks, but a fisherman's friend –
Tells them when the fish are coming.
Colourful bird, not hovering or humming.
Fishes through the reeds a swimming –
Unaware of their impending end.

Busy buzzing honey bees –
Collecting pollen on their hairy knees –
Hiding from the hot sun under cooling leaves –
High up in the branches of trees.
Flowers open wide, inviting in
Allowing pollination to begin.

Aphids, insects, wasps and flies
Climbing, biting, clinging –
Arriving from out of blue skies.
Flying, crawling, gnawing, stinging –
Blissfully unaware of armour plated ladybirds wanting filling –
Eating, chewing, munching, consuming and killing.

Note to the reader – Well it's only nature after all!

SOME FACTS OF LIFE

A few hard hitting facts for you all folks –
No I am not telling a joke –
There is no real goodness in an egg yolk.
There is no fun to poke.
Smoking is a selfish, stupid and costly thing to do –
One feels worse when one smokes – with a cold or flu –
It's horrible for people around you – it makes them feel rough.
And as with an injury to a sportsman – early in game –
you will get carried off!

Massaging oil of Keratin or Melanin in to a man's hair –
Will only make people stop and stare.
It will also make his hair all sticky up and smelly –
One might as well rub it in his shoulders or on his bulging belly.
Or forget it – for the good that it will do –
One might as well use super glue!
I do think it strange that most women
do not lose their hair when ageing –
No! There is certainly nothing guaranteed
to stop a man from balding?

Yes ! – we all know that one must eat plenty –
of fruit and fibre during our lives –
If one is to avoid painful itching –
from those much unwanted Chalfont St. Giles.
Plus swimming or jogging and riding a bike –
Or mountain climbing or trampolining –
will help reduce one's stress.
Why not a regular walk in the fresh air – or go for a hike?
Any of these – are good for your knees –
and will stop one getting fat, or in a mess.

But sometimes it makes me laugh when you just watch what –
and how people eat.
It really is quite a feat – not a treat.
It's like a race – to stuff one's face and become a mess.
Who are they trying to beat – or defeat?
When quite simply, the answer to staying fitter and trimmer,
is to eat slowly and less.

Note to the reader – Well, come on folks it's not rocket science is it? – No I am not being patronising at all – I am just trying to give you another fact of life, that's all!

SMOKING

Smoking makes your clothes and breathe both stink –
Smoking makes your health sink.

Smoking makes you and others cough and choke –
Smoking takes your money and leaves you broke.

Smoking now is not PC and very not OK –
Smoking will give you tooth decay.

Smoking makes your lungs all wheezy and black –
Smoking will help to give you a heart attack.

Smoking can give aged – wrinkled skin
Smoking gives you cancer and makes you thin.

Smoking upsets other fellows –
Smoking makes your teeth and paintwork yellow.

Smoking really is a mugs game –
Smoking gives you arterial sclerosis and can make you lame.

Smoking is not really for the thrilling –
Smoking is really for the killing.

Note to readers who smoke – Please don't, you will feel better and have more money for your pension and funeral costs!

BIRDS

I love all birds that can fly – and the freedom they represent.
It is a true wonder where they came from – and why?
Have they evolved from their prehistoric cousins,
or are birds heaven sent?
No! – Please don't say from out of the sky.

If one could be a bird for day – which one would you like to be?
A carnivorous bird of prey I hear you say,
one who likes to eat fresh meat.
Why not an albatross or puffin?
Whose friends are the oceans and seas.
Or a swan or a pelican, or a flamingo –
or even an ostrich with oversized feet?

I would dearly love to be a bird for a day,
to soar up high in the sky.
There are however, a few feathered friends –
I would much prefer not to be.
Now I can hear you all – asking me why?
Well my list would include a chicken, a duck, a turkey, a pheasant –
Or any bird with an unnatural enemy –
who is decidedly not very pleasant!

They say that 'birds of a feather, stick together' –
Whatever the weather.
Which to be honest is entirely wrong.
Birds of prey – are not found in flocks –
Although arctic penguins do huddle and throng.
Mind you they don't sing the same song.
But I think I am like a domesticated falcon –
And have reached the end of my tether.

Note to the reader – I would have loved to have been an ornithologist – wouldn't you?

WARM NIGHTS

Warm Nights – No sheets and no lights.
Warm Nights – Too many drinks and fights.
Warm Nights – Went out but should've stayed at home.
Warm Nights – Can't get to sleep all on my own.
Warm Nights – There's nothing good on the telly.
Warm Nights – Drinking beer with swollen belly.
Warm Nights – Out walking with a sweaty face.
Warm Nights – Got bloody gnat bites all over the place.
Warm Nights – Spent out mowing the lawn.
Warm Nights – Getting up before dawn.
Warm Nights – Too many spent alone.
Warm Nights – Nobody calls or texts or phones.
Warm Nights – Can't laugh or talk with my ex.
Warm Nights – Would be nice to have some sex.
Warm Nights – Wanting someone to love or care.
Warm Nights – Needing to share or be a pair.

...Warm Nights – Spent in sadness and despair...

Note to the reader – I think this one is self-explanatory – too much wine, too warm and too lonely – Just call me Tony, if only?

SMILE AND LAUGH

You can work very hard and long –
You can give of your best always.
But –
People won't like you if you don't smile and laugh.

You can take all the stress that comes your way –
You can take all the hardships and the low pay.
But –
People won't like you if you don't smile and laugh.

You can take hatred, racism, loneliness and redundancy –
You can take divorce, separation, sadness and fear.
But –
People won't like you if you don't smile and laugh.

You can put up with death, destruction, depression and
desperation.
You can put up with needless wars, struggle and strife –
You can put up with the loss of a husband, or even that of a wife.
But –
People won't like you if you don't smile and laugh.

You can take the pain of ill health –
You can take the lack of real wealth –
You don't even have to show any stealth.
But –
People won't like you if you don't smile and laugh.

You can take all the rubbish that comes your way –
You can put up with a few rainy days on one's holiday –
You can leave although you really want to stay.
But –
People won't like you if you don't smile and laugh.

Note to the reader – It is hard but no matter what life throws at you please try to smile and laugh, it can help, and others are not living your life and don't realise why you are sad – laughing releases valuable endorphins and may increase one's serotonin levels.

DOS AND DON'TS IN LIFE

Do get the best education you can.
Don't take the first job you are offered.
Do start a Pension Plan as soon as finances allow.
Don't rely on somebody else's pension or savings.
Do have children if you have lots of patience.
Don't have somebody else's children.
Do have sex as regularly as you can.
Don't have anal sex it can represent a major health risk to you both.
Do brush your teeth properly at least twice every day.
Don't use Dentifloss too often it will wear your gums away.
Do have self-belief and trust yourself.
Don't trust anybody else, especially banks, or lenders.
Do get a mortgage and buy a house.
Don't steal anything of anybody.
Do change your underwear every day.
Don't wear anybody else's underwear, ever.
Do care about all things and people close to you.
Don't worry too much it will put lines upon your face.
Do start your own business if you can ultimately afford to lose it.
Don't go into a partnership situation unless you are 100% sure.
Do give yourself a luxury each week, however small or large.
Don't expect gifts or luxuries from others.
Do have aims, goals and ambitions in life.
Don't be lazy and expect somebody else to provide for you.
Do get married for the right reasons.
Don't expect your marriage to last indefinitely.
Do drink plenty of water and eat fruit and vegetables.
Don't become addicted to anything.
Do love and respect your parents if they deserve it.
Don't expect your parents to be there forever.
Do try and make people smile and laugh as much as you can.
Don't be sarcastic and laugh at people, try and laugh with them.
Do love and help your children in all things for as long as you can.
Don't expect your children to love you and help you.

Do learn to drive if you have good road sense and can afford the costs.
Don't drive if you have been drinking alcohol and never take drugs.
Do work to live – but not more than 45 hours per week.
Don't live to work – have other hobbies and interests.
Do try and always see your cup as half full.
Don't see your cup as half empty.
Do be positive in all dealings with people.
Don't be negative, try to smile and laugh.
Do enjoy your life – remember life is a very special gift!

Note to the reader – Well do you? – or don't you? It's up to you.

LIFE CONCERNS 2002 / 2010

Global warming has arrived and is alive and well –
you must be blind or just do not care if you can't tell.
Divorce rates are at an all time high –
society has lost respect for marriage vows, it's all just pie in the sky.

Everyone driving emission emitting cars –
they may have stretched themselves too far?
Obesity is of no concern to the overweight –
they will not exercise or even learn to skate.

It's not a caring and sharing society –
people are only concerned with their own self-propriety.
There is far less discipline both at home and at school –
we have become a nation of over indulgent selfish fools.

Children today appear to be ever needy and greedy, they think the credit crunch –
Is something new to eat for lunch or brunch.
On our streets used condoms and rubbish are abound –
<left as a sign of ignorance, littering and fertility, in buses, parks and the playground>.

Increasing under aged pregnancy is ruining a life –
can't young parents see at their age it brings not joy but strife.
Unemployment has become a fact of life –
you just try telling that to your creditors, 3 kids and a wife.

Hundreds of illegal immigrants and terrorists in the UK
are alive and well –
but they will never see the inside of a prison cell.
Thousands of illegal claimants are getting the dole –
they don't care about others or seem to have a soul.
The war in Iraq was a needless attack, gone are church steeples –
along with thousands of dead innocent people.
Our Government keep letting more immigrants in –
can't they see the political system and country are financially
sinking.

With banks, building societies and businesses going bust –
the people and investment houses have lost their trust.
We have eleven year old children being shot in the park –
this is not accidental or a bit of a lark.

Innocent people are being blown up on buses and trains –
can't terrorists see that religiously there is nothing to be gained.
Religion fuelled wars and terrorism can never, never win –
Can't these fascists see that in the eyes of any God –
they are committing a sin.

Note to the reader – Just a list of thought provokers – are they worth thinking about?

WHAT IS THIS LIFE

What is this life if, full of concern and care –
There is no time to stand and stare?

No time to communicate and share and talk –
No time to fornicate in green fields and walk.

No time to see the pain of life etched on a face –
No time and no wish to try and keep pace.

No time to even see in broad daylight –
Or the streams of stars in skies at night.

No time to watch and take a glance –
At a beautiful woman with feet that dance.

What is life if one cannot take their chance –
No time in life to help make a difference.

No time to wait until a woman's mouth can –
Enhance that sexy smile her eyes began.

What is this life if, full of concern and care –
There is no time to stand and stare?

Note to the reader – This is my adaptation of a poem entitled 'Leisure' by W. H. Davies – 20/04/1871 – 26/09/1940.

DEPRESSED OR DEPRESSION

To wander lonely as a cloud –
O'er high mountains of sadness –
O'er a world bent on self-destruction –
O'er once green valleys now of blackness.

To wander lonely as a cloud –
O'er swollen seas of trepidation –
O'er bleak and baron unforgiving deserts –
O'er decimated and dying forests of depletion.

To wander lonely as a cloud –
O'er hills and slopes of self doubt –
O'er ghettos and fields of horror and badness –
O'er plains of pain and darkness that cannot shout.

To wander lonely as a cloud –
O'er constant thermals of unpleasantness –
O'er rapids and rivers of greed and selfishness –
O'er villages, towns and cities of fear and unhappiness.

To wander lonely as a cloud –
Who is tired with a diet of anti-depressants –
Who can't but really wants to scream and shout out very loud –
Who wants to see an end to this incessant – shroud.

Note to the reader – A lonely cloud who wants a depression to come so he can burst and wash away with fresh rain – the depressing anxiety and pain.

A DREAM

There is no shortcut to a dream –
You cannot just think one up.
Sometimes, it may make one scream –
As if you have trodden on your pup.

A dream is very special, and yours to keep –
You do not have to share it with anyone.
A dream will come to you when you sleep –
But you do not just have to have one.

It may be an ambition that you hold –
Or you may think about a person that is dear.
But a dream can never really be for told –
Or when it will happen or what year?

Your dream may not have an end in sight –
It may make you slightly sad.
And your feelings you must not fight –
As when a dream comes true, it will make you glad.

Dreams are a reflection of one's sub-conscious mind –
They cannot be planned or designed.
Good dreams may be hard to find –
But a dream is normally very nice and kind.

Martin Luther King, had a dream of equality for all –
Nelson Mandela, dreamed of peace in South Africa.
Neither of them were aggressive, strong or tall –
But both were massive in nature and stature.

Note to the reader – I enjoyed writing this poem as I am sure both gentlemen mentioned above would agree, you see a dream to me represents hope and calm and happiness with all that it brings, as opposed to a nightmare of which I do hope you have few, as I have had my fair share – but let's not go there – Phew!

Disaster

ELEVEN

An eleven year old Everton boy called 'Rhys' went out to play –
Nobody knew at the time but 'He Would Not'
come home 'That Day'.
He went out on his bike to see his mates, and 'Have Some Fun' –
He never saw the face of the boy that 'pulled the trigger' –
which Fired The Gun.

His back was turned he had no 'Time to Dash' –
He did not see or hear the gun it's not as if he had 'Loads of Cash'.
After the gun went off 'young Rhys' was laying
'Down on The Floor' –
In just a few minutes his young life would end,
he would be 'No More'.

The invisible trigger pulling thug, and now killer just 'Cycled Away' –
But only he will know what he did until 'His Dying Day'.
But 'young Rhys', the eleven year old boy that dying lay –
Will never say 'come on you blues',
when his favourite 'Footy Team' play.

Poor Rhys's Mum and Dad were devastated and Mortified,
Bitter, angry and sad –
To learn of the horrific death of, 'Their Young Lad'.
It's hard to believe but the murder took place in a 'Public Car Park' –
It wasn't late or even dark –
It wasn't a joke that backfired, or went wrong,
they weren't 'Having a Lark'.

Three shots were fired 'at Rhys' like a professional killing,
'The Witnesses Said'.
But nobody saw the invisible young killer that fled.
Where do these boys get guns from?
Where does the money come from?
Is it from their drug dealing or drug pushing gang leader
called 'scar faced' Tom!?

Note to the reader – I wrote this in memory of young Rhys (aged 11) who was shot dead playing in a Liverpool Pub car park, it was read out on City Talk FM Radio in Liverpool – So very sad for his family especially his devoted Mum and Dad.

GLOBAL WARMING

This poem is not meant to frighten, dismay or distress.
But it really is about time that the whole human race realised –
That Global Warming has been arriving o'er a long time –
and our planet is in a mess!

I do not wish to confuse the issue or to panic or over complicate.
You see harmful CO_2 emissions and other carbon gases –
Are being emitted and released into our atmosphere,
at an alarming rate.

This has o'er time, weakened the planet's defence –
Called the 'ozone layer'.
It is letting in very harmful UV rays,
from our all powerful heat giving Sun.
We cannot blame the Chancellor for this one –
The responsibility lies with Everyone.

Now our planet Earth is a very clever place –
and will try its level best to compensate.
Which it has been for years and is now, still doing.
I think by now you the reader will realise –
that we and the planet are in quite a state.

We live in little old England with no fear –
in the northern hemisphere.
Spring is nice, Summer is great, Autumn is grey –
and Winter brings snow each year.
In recent years our weather patterns have been changing,
it is now time to shed a tear.

But the ignorant among us will still go and buy –
a CO_2 spewing large 4x4 anyway.
They do not tow, they do not need one,
it just looks good parked in their driveway.
The cars give out massive harmful fumes,
it is 'not our fault', you will hear them say!

Polar ice caps at either end of our planet earth,
are melting more and more each day.
The thick ice sheets for millions of years,
are now thin like our ozone layer.
We blame scientists and meteorologists or the Prime Minister –
but it is the whole human race at fault –
the earth's message is very clear and sinister!

Note to the reader – Having sold these large 4x4 cars myself I know from literature that Car Manufacturers are under massive pressure to reduce all domestic vehicles CO_2 emissions down below 149gkm by the year 2013, when you think an average standard 4x4 emits nearly 300gkms this is a mammoth task!

THAT DAY ON 9/11

It was just another ordinary sunny morning –
That fateful day in New York on 9/11 –
There was no Warning!
As happy workers went on their way to work at seven.

The Twin Towers, which once stood so tall and proud –
In beautiful silvery tandem, on that day on 9/11.
Would soon be shrouded in an evil 'Death Cloud' –
Which would send thousands of innocent people up to Heaven.

Carol and I were visiting her sick mother who was in pain.
I happened to glance up at the TV screen –
I had to look again, and then, again.
I could not believe what I was seeing.

At first I thought it was a new shock action movie being released.
The 'planes of death' that were flown in to The Shimmering Towers –
Would make thousands deceased –
That fateful day on 9/11, literally within hours.

For all the people, who, that fateful day, died –
And for their friends and families, we were mortified.
We could not believe that day on 9/11, what we all saw, and just cried.
We sat down in complete shock, and said 'Oh Dear God' and sighed.

Those innocent workers all needlessly 'Crushed and Killed'.
Their children and families, mothers and fathers that are now left –
With much angriness and bitterness, at their sad loss, are filled.
And now very sadly are forever bereft.

Note to the reader – I think the whole World was left in shock and sadness, at the events on that fateful day on 9/11 in the USA, except the perpetrators of course.

LONDON 07 JULY 05

It was raining tears – in London on the 7th July in the morning.
The bombs that went off killed and maimed innocent people –
and left families and friends in deep shock and mourning.

A bus was blown up – with passengers still in their seats –
bits of humans lay on the ground –
terrorists blew up trains on the underground.
The sad thing is, that the cowards who did this –
will never be found.

They left blood spattered buildings and cars –
which had been trashed –
shards of glass were strewn and littered the streets –
people had been cut and mashed.
We must find the evil bastards that did this –
and their evil network must be smashed.

The leaders are all in shock and dismay –
as they waited for this fateful day.
As innocent men, women and children – in the gutters lay.
'Vengeance is mine' sayeth the Lord –
but we must make these evil murderers pay.

The 7th day of the 7th month of the year has left Londoners in –
dismay and fear –
Are we then to worry, about the 8th day of the 8th month –
the 9th day of the 9th month –
The 10th day of the 10th month etc – each and every bloody year?

Note to the reader – Why is it always the innocent people who have to suffer?

UNDERGROUND

Fed Up

FED UP

I am fed up with all the wars and battles and fighting and hitting –
I am fed up with showering and shaving –
and brushing bad teeth and shitting!

I am fed up with terrorists and terrorism –
and bombers who commit suicide.
I am fed up with bad news and reading and hearing about it –
until I am sick inside!

I am fed up with violence and stabbings and shootings –
and death in our inner cities.
I am fed up with women who want plastic surgery –
and ever big false titties.

I am fed up with the greedy, selfish and overpaid
and over indulgent fat cat bankers.
I am fed up with drug pushers –
and users and pimps and abusers they are all wankers!

I am fed up with the lazy who sit on loungers all day
and don't earn any pay.
I am fed up with beggars and thieves and benefit scroungers –
who get away with it each day!

I am fed up with those people who are lazy
and think the world owes them a living.
I am fed up with robbers and rapists and criminals –
their lack of concern and real giving!

I am fed up with businesses and the NHS –
and politicians who say they can and will.
I am fed up with underpaid doctors and nurses –
because it just makes us all ill!

I am fed up with the credit crunch and recession –
and mortgages that are too high.
I am fed up with millionaires and billionaires –
and snobs up their own arses who think it's all pie in the sky!

I am fed up with those thoughtless people –
who say just leave things to lady luck.
I am fed up with people who won't share and don't care –
and who don't help anyone or really give a fuck!

I am fed up with sending our young soldiers off to stupid wars –
in far flung places.
I am fed up with their needless deaths –
and seeing the strain and pain etched on their devastated families faces!

Note to the reader – If you have something to say – then say it! (Sorry for swearing)

THE SEX AND FAME AND PAIN GAME

There is no photo in the frame –
There is no winner of the game.
They will not pay the price of fame –
They just want the sex and more of the same.

Men just work hard for their money –
And those women they all call, 'love or honey'.
Life always seems so good, rewarding and funny –
When those cloudy days become, 'warm, sexy and sunny'.

But when there is only, 'wind and rain' –
We all seem to really feel more, that pain.
Your whole body, and muscles, seem to ache –
And everyone around you seems to be on the take.

Then in your stomach you start to feel really sick and ill.
But you know it's just that you cannot pay those mounting bills.
So you go to your bank, or get more ripped off –
with a Secured Loan.
Which after the bills are paid, you can't afford –
and start to 'panic and moan'.

And then things start to look, very bleak –
As there is no help, when you seek.
You have to be tough, and made of teak –
As you sit and feel, so tired and weak!

Note to the reader – If you have not got a lot – I bet that one cheered you up – Not!

WHY

Why wars and conflict and trouble and strife –
Why soldiers and their loss of life.
Why premature death and devastation –
Why children dying of lack of food –
Why so much bad in life and not good.
Why do third world countries rich in minerals –
Suffer?

Why do we have recessions –
Why are bankers paid massive bonuses –
Why do investment brokers, go broke –
Why do banks go bust.
Why are investors mistrustful –
Why have ordinary people lost their –
Trust?

Why so much stress and anxiety –
Why the lack of self respect.
Why no self propriety –
Why are we all so circumspect –
Why is there no care or concern –
Why don't governments learn –
Greed?

Note to the reader – A big part of life is having to suffer and to have to put your trust both in people and banks, but I am fed up with the needy and greedy they seem so seedy! (Please read poem 'Fed Up'.)

I CAN'T TAKE ANYMORE

I sit in my flat listening to the pouring rain – on the window pane.
The TV is on, what a pain –
Coronation Street is on again and again.
Ken Barlow has been in it for years – He must be eighty four –
Or more?
What about a good funny 'Carry On' film from 1974?

I can't take anymore!

I use my remote again and switch channels.
There is a Political Debate – about the credit crunch –
On Freeview Channel 8.
Oh God! A repeat of Man Alive from 1965 – on Channel 5.
With American baseball scores on Channel Four.

I can't take anymore!

I grab the remote yet again –
Flicking through the multitude of channels – as I often do.
There is a Japanese film on about the Samurai on BBC 2 –
There is a Life of Grime on – there is CSI crime on –
There are Holidays from Hell on channel 64 –
I will have to lay on the floor!
There is the death toll of British dead –
Afghanistan versus Iraq on Channel 24.

I can't take anymore!

I use the remote to flick forwards – and back.
I am fed up with death and wars –
And hearing about the attacks on Iraq.
Eastenders is on 5 times a week – I will press this button –
It's auto seek.
There is a film on later tonight – called 'Poor Cow' –
Starring Carol White.
Pity it's not on right now – wonder what else is on tonight?
Doesn't seem to be a great choice –
Do you know, I think I'm losing my voice?
Am now watching a repeat of the football scores – what a bore.

I can't take anymore!

Note to the reader – I wrote the above one wet and windy lonely night in my flat!

WHY SHAVEN HEADS AND TATTOOS AND DOGS?

Why do a lot of these shaven headed men –
own an ugly Staffordshire pit bull?
You never see these men with a poodle or a whippet or a big greyhound.
Is it because like the dog's owner they are perceived –
as a fighter who is not dull?
Does it make them feel like a UFC fighter –
punching and pounding on the ground?

Why do men with hair shave their heads –
Is it just the fashion, or is to make themselves look hard and tough?
Does it impress the women and help to get them in to their beds?
I think it makes them look ugly and older –
and catch the sun and look rough.

Don't they all realise that if they wait a few more years –
they will go bald anyway?
I think they do it to look like a hardened nightclub doorman.
You know the type that are supposed to frighten you away –
And say 'Oh hi babe, nice to see you' –
and to the drunks 'No way man, no way man!'

And what are all these costly and painful
unsightly tattoos on their necks n' arms?
Do they think it is attractive?
Does it help them charm?
I wonder if they have tattoos done upon their genitals,
or the inside of their palms?

Perhaps it's to make them look like they are very ill with Cancer?
And are undergoing chemotherapy.
Don't they see that really it just makes them look –
like a bully a crook or a chancer?
Or perhaps it's to make them feel big and strong, in the gents –
when they have a pee?

Note to the reader – Sorry folks it's just my opinion.

WHAT'S WRONG WITH THAT

The Earth's Ozone Layer is becoming thinner and thinner –
Polar ice caps visibly melting, watched by an uncaring population.
Hey Mum going out for a drink and a fast drive –
what time is dinner?
What's Wrong With That?

Broken beer bottles and diseased syringes –
dumped on a beautiful beach.
Corrupt and power crazed, needy and greedy, selfish politicians.
Nobody wants to listen and learn –
or help to read a book of life and teach.
What's Wrong With That?

Everyone on Facebook pretending to be friends on the internet
or having a Twitter.
Children out playing on their bikes getting shot dead in a park.
Young single parents sad and alone who can't afford a babysitter.
What's Wrong With That?

Overpaid investment brokers giving bad advice and going broke.
Ungovernable governments and an uncaring voting public –
It's true it's not cockney rhyming slang, it's not a bloody joke!
What's Wrong With That?

Terrorists living among us planning to create havoc –
and death on our streets.
Footballers and fat cat bankers being paid –
millions of pounds each year!
While the hard working public struggle to pay –
increasing bills with fear.
What's Wrong With That?

Needless futile expensive unwinnable religion fuelled –
Middle eastern wars –
Against an unseen invisible ruthless unrelenting
fascist driven enemy.
Send more body bags or tell you what it will save space – send jars!
What's Wrong With That?

Note to the Reader – Well I expect you have liked a good moan now and then?

TODAY

Today we all have to think, act, drive, work and –
live our lives at such a frantic pace –
It's like being in a losing race.

Today we have recession and redundancy –
the interest rate is 0 percent –
The housing benefit is heaven sent.

Today war or anti-terrorism has become a full time but dying job –
As terrorists appear to have an unlimited amount of bombs to lob?

Today divorce rates are very high –
marriage has become a forgotten institution.
Many couples end up broken and broke –
sad and lonely in destitution.

Today children get used and abused –
bullied at school and tortured –
Instead of being loved, helped, valued, respected and nurtured.

Today it seems politicians and people in power –
are always on the take –
They have become selfish, needy and greedy –
not happy with their slice of cake.

Today our police force do not earn respect –
and are largely treated as a joke.
  Is it any wonder then, why our youngsters roam the streets –
doing weed and coke?

Today due to a bad Government making us suffer –
the country is forced to borrow.
  Can't they see the grief it causes –
with the subsequent underlying sorrow?

Today our financial future and livelihood –
appears, uncertain and unclear.
  As ordinary working class people have to live –
in debt, poverty and fear.

Note to the reader – I wrote 'Today' because I could see, read and hear what was going on around me and cared about it – does anybody feel the same as me out there? Or is it just me?

TOXIC WASTE

Our toxic waste –
I will agree with you all –
It's not to everyone's taste.
Where does it go to?
It can't simply vanish in to space.

We have hundreds – if not thousands –
Of derelict fridges and freezers –
Being dumped every week on our lands –
By unscrupulous hard looking geezers –
With lads in battered white vans.

Come on now we have ICI – BP – Esso and Shell
What happens to their 'Toxic Waste' –
Please some responsible body – please do tell?
Or do we just wait until the smell – gets too bad
Or their staff – become sickened and sad.

But all I am asking is – where does all the toxic waste go?
Is there anybody who cares – out there?
Or better still – is in the know,
Or if they tell us – though –
Will they be too scared – to show us – where?

Note to the reader – Where do you think our 'toxic waste' goes – perhaps in to our rivers – which we then drink – so perhaps it is destroying our livers – who knows – what do you all think?

LOVES AND HATES

I Love people who both care and share for and with others.
I Hate people who manipulate, and are bullies and cowards.
I Love people who respect and love their families.
I Hate people who are greedy, needy and selfish –
and just sit for hours.

I Love people who are strong of body and soul and of their mind.
I Hate people who are cold, uncaring and unfeeling –
with bad intentions.
I Love people who get pleasure from pleasing –
and giving and who are kind.
I Hate people who can't see outside of the box –
or admire others' inventions.

I Love people who read and want to gain knowledge –
and want to learn.
I Hate people who mistake an openness for arrogance –
instead of confidence.
I Love people who have aims and goals in life –
and who want to provide and earn.
I Hate people who just sit and watch others work or suffer –
and who sit on the fence.

I love people who are intelligent and enjoy making others –
'Laugh and Smile'
I Hate people who are not punctual, don't keep in touch –
or are always late
I Love people who can tell jokes and try and create happiness –
all of the while.
To be honest – I don't know why I am writing this –
as I hate people who hate!

Note to the reader – If Love makes the World go around – what does Hate do?

Time and Seasons

DAYS

What are Days for?
Days are where we live –
They come and go every day –
And have so much to give.

Days come time and again – it really is a feat –
Daytime passes to her friend – Night Time.
Together they make our Days complete –
Then they allow us peace and quiet, while we sleep.

Days are happy to be in –
For where else can we live but days?
Days are always there to help us enjoy things –
In so many different ways.

Note to the reader – My own interpretation of 'Days' – a Philip Larkin poem.

MODERN TECHNOLOGY IT'S A RAP

We have had BETA Max – VHS with 6 track and 12 track
Now we have I – Phones and Blackberries with
MMS with E Mail and TV's –
With Walkmans and DVDs and IPODs plus MP3s –
And CD's with Megabytes and PC's with burners.
We have Mobile Phones with Cameras –
Taking Mega-Pixel Digital Pictures for learners –
To download on your Facebook and Fish 4 Friends – for show –
And give strangers a look – you haven't met yet –
and don't even know?

To view on your laptop or verify via Firefox – or just take a look
On your Intranet or Internet – you can place a bet.
You don't need a book to read or course to learn –
you can e-mail a vet – for your pet.
You can Scan or Google – print a spreadsheet –
do your accounts or just log-on.
One can even Nudge and Wink – Twitter or Blog-on.
What with CCTV and HDI plus SKY + and Freeview too –
I can't keep up anymore – can I please leave it all up to you ?
What happened to the record player with cassettes –
and how much is Freeview?

I just don't know what to do ?

I have just been offered a new CD-ROM with a
bundle and a dongle –

and a new Hard Drive with an upgraded Hub?

Are you confused as well?
Why not come and Join our Club?
We won't tell.

Note to the reader – Try and sort of rap when you read this one – it's good fun!

A CHILD'S VIEW OF CHRISTMAS

My poor dad slipped getting out of the car and fell over on the ice.
He dropped all my presents on our driveway –
Which for both of us was not very nice.

My Mum plugged the Christmas lights in.
She said the turkey would have tasted great –
Had she remembered to put it in the Tin.

My Grandad's car broke down in the snow.
It did not come to a complete standstill –
But had to move so very slow.

My Grandmother was worried in case this made them late.
She does not normally panic like that –
But worked herself up into quite a state.

My Sister just wanted to stay in bed and watch TV all day.
When she knew very well –
That I needed her to play.

My Brother wanted to play with his new I- Pod and his CDs and MP3.
When there was an almighty crash and a bang –
Oh dear me! All the lights had fused on our Christmas tree!

My Auntie had knitted me a very nice mohair woolly jumper.
It had a Big Rabbit on it in four different colours –
I just had to call him Thumper.

My Auntie had also made me a hat and a matching scarf.
But the hat was too big and the scarf was 8 feet long –
I just said thank you, but then I really had to laugh.

Note to the reader – I am sure that if not as a child, then we have all had one or more of the experiences mentioned in the above poem or we know somebody who has? Have you noticed that even my happy poems have a degree of Adversity? – It's just my style of writing!

AGE

We are all born out of a woman's womb, so wondrous of life's beginning –
Our love is unconditional and carried for our Mother,
until the end of our life.
We hopefully enjoy the wealth and richness of our life,
even with hair thinning –
Man may stay single but sometimes happy and
brave enough to take a wife.

The learning process and growing up –
may prove to be hard and confusing.
With the requirement for education –
and academic achievement now so great.
It can prove too difficult for some –
but for others enjoyable and amusing.
Whether one is at school or university –
are easier when shared with a mate.

As we gain more experience and knowledge in life –
we do get wiser and older.
Unfortunately, our skins get thinner and
blotchy dry patches appear on our faces.
Muscles which once gave us our strength –
have given way to pain in our shoulder.
Laughter lines which once graced our face –
now turned to wrinkles in other places.

Now with age comes wisdom and family concerns –
which demand answers so kind.
They may require much thought and help or money –
or even help from God above.
Acquiring age and experience –
helps in life, because we develop strength of mind.
Age gives us answers to many questions –
except that posed by what is True Love?

Note to the reader – If knowledge is power why doesn't age give us all the right answers, all of the time, and give us the wisdom, to convert problems into solutions?

WHEN I'M EIGHTY FIVE

I do hope that I am reasonably fit and well –
And alive –
When I'm 'eighty five'.
With all the reading and writing – I have done in my life –
I will have so much information to impart and tell –
I do hope I don't start to smell!
At least my ex-wife –
Will be older than me – at the ripe old age of 87 –
Unless she has gone to heaven?

Looking back I enjoyed and was glad – being a son –
To my mother – but not to my dad.
He was an abusive, alcoholic – angry man, so sad.
Anyway thank God – he is now gone.
I think I liked being a child –
All meek and mild.
I have been and as far as I know – I still am –
An ex-husband – an ex-businessman – a divorcee –
A Father to 3 daughters and now Grandfather to Callum –
Yes that's me!

But when – 'I'm eighty five'.
I want to do a tandem Parachute jump –
and abseil down tall buildings –
That's just for a start – and show people I am still alive.
I hope I can still enjoy sex – and will not be too old, or vexed –
Not be a dribbling old misery – unable to fart!
Wearing a purple shirt and mustard coloured baggy trousers –
For hours.
Giving everybody grief – creating inconvenience –
And giving others the hump.
And having curvature of the spine or a big lump!
No I want to shout out loudly at people –
And climb to the top of church steeples...

...Hello – Good Morning ! – Wakey – Wakey – rise and shine...
It's your favourite nurse with a nice hot cup of tea –
I have brought a straw with a bend at the end...back in ten minutes,
to help you get dressed –
So don't get all angry and stressed... and vexed...
See you in a mo... bye – bye... now don't burn yourself on the cup!

Note to the reader – Like most people I don't really want to become senile – it's vile!

COLD COMFORT

There is no comfort in being cold –
There is nothing to stop us growing old.
To become fragile and sick before dying –
There is no point in even trying.

To be old and cold is such a shame.
Is the government to blame –
Or one's friends, neighbours or family?
To just have someone who comes to see.

To have somebody to share or care –
And see you sit in your cold lair –
With old skin and bones and balding hair.
People just look and stand and stare.

You don't want much –
Just a friendly word or kindly touch.
Or a warm smile –
Or someone to sit with you for a while?

To be old and cold on the outside –
But to feel young and warm on the inside.
Makes one feel so lonely and sad –
Not happy and contented in senior years – not glad.

There is no comfort in being cold –
There is nothing to stop us growing old –
To lose one's dignity whilst trying to be bold –
There is no comfort in being old and cold.

Note to the reader – I wrote this whilst visiting the old and sick during the coldest winter for nearly 100 years – whilst working for The Energy Savings Trust (EST).

WINTER

Cold mornings and dark misty nights –
Woolly hats and scarves –
Thick socks and tights.

Frost and rain and sleet and snow –
Wet clothes and shoes and frozen noses –
Traffic with drivers either too fast or too slow.

No warming sun for hours and hours –
Dark shrouded and shapeless grey blanketed clouds –
Heavy soaking precipitation with showers –
but no colourful flowers.

Slippery dangerous, unsalted icy roads –
no leaves on trees – no frogs or toads.
With no flocks of singing birds on high –
and S.A.D. affected people passing by.
Poor young foxes searching for road kill – but killed on the same road.

With glowing fires – and presents giving, festive Christmas cheer.
With over indulgence – and fuel costs rising each and every year.
Heads and feelings numbed by mulled wine –
spirits and lots of beer.

Off licences and pubs and clubs and bars – that are far too busy.
Increased drinking and driving – accidents and crimes –
We rush around – over spend and over shop –
until our heads are far too dizzy.

Yes! – Winter brings us lots of merriment - joy and good cheer.
Along with colds and flu – family arguments and expense and fear –
Now let us thank God! – that it only comes once a year!

Note to the reader – How do we all survive Christmas each year?

THE SNOW IS COMING

Day 1.
The snow is coming –
The snow is coming.
Let's get the gritting lorries out on the streets –
Go and buy thigh high wellington boots,
to protect our legs and feet –
The snow is coming –
The snow is coming.

Day 2.
The snow is coming –
The snow is coming.
Let's all buy buckets of salted sand,
to put on our pathways and driveways –
Go and buy a new 4 x 4 car, you know –
One that doesn't slip and slide sideways –
The snow is coming –
The snow is coming.

Day 3.
The snow is coming –
The snow is coming.
Let's all go to Sainsbury's and buy 20 loaves of bread,
in case we get snowed in –
Go and buy candles, spades with long handles,
and foodstuffs contained in a tin –
The snow is coming –
The snow is coming.

Day 4.
The snow is coming –
The snow is coming.
Let's get down to B & Q and spend hundreds of pounds –
Re-insulating our roof –
Go and download the weather reports –
Send e-mails to everybody and Auntie Ruth –
The snow is coming –
The snow is coming.

Day 5.
The snow is coming –
The snow is coming.
Let's be as prepared as we can – down to the last man –
For fuel, get a spare can...huh
What's that? – the snow isn't coming to England –
And it's on it's way to Iceland –
Well who said that? Oh! It was on TV was it? –
The BBC Weatherman...
So the snow isn't coming now then?
Well, what are we going to do with all the stuff we've bought then?

Note to the reader – We seem to panic and get excited when we hear about snow.

SPRING AND AUTUMN

Years ago we used to have 4 defined seasons of the year.
Spring then summer, then autumn then a, winter that froze.
Now those seasons appear so close together, so near.
I have asked quite a few people but nobody seems to care or know.

I remember when young, picking wild daffodils for Mum.
I had a tortoise called 'Tommy' who slept a set pattern each year.
Nowadays, he would sleep too early –
and wake up too late with his nose numb.
Or get frostbite or damp rot in our changeable weather –
and lose a foot or an ear!

Or get hypothermia on his way to his box, and fall asleep forever?
Our winters seem longer and wetter and summers are hotter.
Global warming has definitely changed our seasons and weather –
It's probably OK if you live in the water, like a 'beaver or an otter'.

But us humans cannot –
And do not –
And I don't know about you lot –
But I can't stand it too Hot.
I suppose, we'll just have to put up with what we've Got?

I mean in,the summer when it's too hot you can have a swim –
or stay in the shade.
And in the winter if it gets too cold,
you can wrap up all warm, or light a fire.
What do you do in the autumn when it's warm –
wet and dark buy a lampshade?
Or in the spring, when our high tides are increasingly higher –
Buy or rent a boat –
In order to keep afloat.
Or wear a rubber tyre?

Note to the reader – I don't know about you but I think we have become all SAD with that Seasonal...Affected...Disorder... (perhaps it should be Spring and Autumn Disorder instead?)

HOT SUMMER DAYS

Summer comes but once every year.
It brings with it the sun and good cheer.
If we don't use SPF, it also gives us sunburn that can blister –
You should've seen the chest and shoulders on our sister!

Summer brings lovely flowers the birds and bees –
But when the sun gets hot it can burn your knees.
The sun doesn't care it will burn your eyes and thighs.
And many other places, but most of all it seems to burn
Our arms and faces.

Summer makes us all happier and tans and turns us brown –
It makes us smile and laugh a lot, never frown.
We go on holiday both at home and away,
some people even go to the USA.
But some people are poor and cannot even afford a holiday.

Summer heightens our awareness about global warming –
We don't seem to want to listen or heed their urgent warnings.
We just sit playing cards and drinking too much –
underneath a Carlsberg awning.
Drinking beer and yawning, waiting for a new day dawning.

Note to the reader – I am sure some people think global warming is a new type of electric blanket to keep your bed warm in the winter months and that SPF is an erectile dysfunction cream that aids sexual penetration – We are not listening!

THOSE YEARS AHEAD

I have no fears for those years ahead –
I am not worried by the greying hair growing out of my head.
Those grey nasal hairs that could hardly be seen just the other day –
Appear to have really come to stay.

My skin is thinning, going all blotchy and crinkly –
It won't be long before it's all pale and wrinkly.
The affects of ageing are all too clear –
But the years ahead will hold no fear.

I will exercise and ride my bike –
I will run and hill climb and take a hike.
My body has gone all saggy –
My clothes appear to be all baggy.

I seem to have become increasingly grumpy –
My belly is not flat anymore – it's gone all hairy and lumpy.
There's a big bald patch on top of my head –
But I am not frightened by those years ahead.

After all life is a stairway that we all have to climb –
And with a properly constructed diet – I will feel sublime.
I will eat lots of salads – have massages and rub creams in instead –
I will have no fears for those advancing years ahead.

Note to the reader – If you have any fears – it can help to write about them!

Young People Today

YOUNG PEOPLE TODAY

Young people get a much better –
More informed education today.
They are given invariably more support and more gadgets and play –
Than their parents ever had, and have considerably more to do and say.

My three daughters knew much more academically –
Than I did at the same age.
Although I do realise –
And I know it's not right to generalise –
But it does vary greatly and is very difficult to gauge.
They certainly get less discipline today, both at home and in school –
This is quite clear to see – by any fool.
But what really annoys me very greatly –
Is that they will not listen to their teachers, their mother, or even me.

Yes, the quality of education and subjects –
Has vastly improved, this is quite clear.
Can you kindly explain to me, and do please be concise, and sincere
Then why – when they leave school today they simply have no fear?
Of drugs or drink – no they can go to rehab they think –
Or a job – no I can simply live at home or, on benefits –
Or of money – no I have got mum and dad both in the pink –
Of a boyfriend – yes we sleep together because he says he likes my bits.

A girl today says 'I am 15 and now I know everything' –
I can even be a diva, as I can sing –
My boyfriend wants sex all the time without a condom –
He says it's because he wants to show me how much he loves me Mum –
And after all, he drives a new Corsa sport – and is very handsome.
I did not really want to, but he really enjoyed himself –
And it seems to make him so very happy.
He has left me now – I am pregnant, it's as if I am left upon a shelf –
Who will help me now to pay for food, and for cash to buy the nappies?

....I am on my own now you see –
........But I want to go to university –
............And travel and maybe –
................Get a car and visit different places –
....................I don't see the stress it causes to everyone, and the baby.

Or the pain from the strain – now etched on my parents faces!

Note to the reader – Just look around you at the rise in under aged pregnancy, and the peer pressure placed upon our children, and their unfortunate lack of common sense.

SCHOOL, SOCIETY THEN AND NOW

THEN – Right let's see your hands and nails,
hair brushed, cap straight have a nice walk to school
and don't be late home or else you will have your dad to answer to.
NOW – I am not wearing that it's just not cool at school –
get the car – chill mum laters!

THEN – A bully said I am a fat and ugly bastard –
and that my belly is raw because it drags on the floor
so I hit him and got caned 3 on each hand –
and made to stand under the school clock.
No tea for you and your dad will be in soon – go to your room!
NOW – My friends say I am overweight can I go for liposuction?
I want to be slimmer.
If not can you go and buy me a months supply –
of that new Ally slimming drink?
Why not mum?
Well I won't wash and I will bloody well stink OK?

THEN – Here is 2 shillings (10p) go down to Harry's
and get a short back and sides, then to the Launderette.
and pick up our washing, lunch will be ready in an hour OK?
There's a good boy and don't speak to any strangers on the way.
NOW – Can I have £20.00 cos I want me hair done –
like Gareth Gates, and I need new trainers but only Nike –
the same as all my mates –
Why not?
Well put it on the magic plastic you carry in your purse, huh!
Mum, my mates in year 6 have got their own.

THEN – Thanks mum and dad I got my TUF school shoes
re-healed and soled it cost 6 shillings and sixpence (32.5p) –
here is the change from that pound note,
was wondering if I could have a new pair –
of white or black plimsolls please – or a rain coat?
NOW – Hey mum! When we go to see dad –
can you mention that I need a new Ipod
and an MP3 player for my CD Rom?
If he says no tell him I need it for schoolwork –
or I won't get to University.
You know what to say, you can sweet talk him for me –
Pleeeeez! Pretty mum?

THEN – Mum I have cut the grass and cleaned the mower –
and took nan's washing to the Launderette for her –
and have done my paper and milk rounds –
but I want to take Christine Kimmings to the pictures tonight.
Could you loan me a 10 bob note until next week please?
I will pay you back out of my 5 shillings pocket money each week.
NOW – Hi mum erm... Mandy (aged 15) says –
I am going to be the father of her child but I did wear a condom –
it's her fault she should have been on the pill.
Will you go around dad's flat and tell him –
he is going to be a granddad,
Do you think he will be very wild?

Note to the Reader – Is it just me or have you noticed changing values and lack of discipline/concern over the years?

QUESTIONS AT BEDTIME

Dad – Why is the sky so high?
And what is the Ozone and Global Warming?
Don't know son go to sleep.
Mum – why is the sea so deep?
And where do all the fish keep coming from?
Save it for school please son it's very late –
You are up early in the morning now please go to sleep.

Dad – Why is the grass always green –
And what does amphibious mean?
Please dad I want to know?
Didn't you hear your mum son, now please go to sleep?
Mum – How far away is the moon?
And what is it made of I need to know soon.
Now look son it's very late, please go to sleep.

Dad – How do aeroplanes and jets take off and fly?
And stay up in the air for hours, please dad why?
Listen son, why do you need to know now, it's late?
We are all tired, it's the end of the day and we are all in bed –
why can't it wait?
Mum – Why do we always go to sleep at the same time every night?
And why do the bullies at school keep hitting me –
and always want a fight?
What bullies son? Who, When, Where and Why?
Did they hurt you son?

It's very late now dad let's all go to sleep!

Night... Mum... Night ...Dad.

Note to the reader – Just to show that whatever the time we should try and listen.

SPOILT OR SPOILED

I have just watched a TV programme.
They say that children today are undisciplined, spoilt and to blame –
I think they mean over nurtured or over indulged, it's not the same.
If you have taken a good look –
At the poems contained within this book –
You will clearly see that a lot of young people today,
have just lost their respect.
For Police, for Parents, for Teachers,
for themselves with under aged, unloving Sex!

I think it started in the seventies with pornography and nudes.
With less discipline at home and in school –
This led to a more over relaxed attitude –
And young people not in school but acting the fool.
Which has led to youngsters with reduced values.
Saying Hi Man or Hey Dude, I don't know that song,
Information and Technology then came along.
Young people did not have to listen and learn –
They simply got a PC off their busy parents n' played songs –
Or learned how to be a Game boy or design web sites,
so they can sit at home and earn!

Men and fathers became less important,
and less effective, at home and in life –
Women ruled the roost, went to work, not happy at just being a wife.
Girls became more liberated and life aware –
Boys wanted more than their fair share–
Parents earned more money, and had no time to care.
Their children were left at home, to their own desires –
Over the years boys and girls kept lighting each others fires.
They became over indulgent –
Not young ladies and young gents –
They became more clever, but had lost their common sense.
But they were all doing exactly the same –
And now we are looking for someone to blame!

My opinion on all this is that quick evolution is really at fault –
It was a culmination of things, a series of events, plus a need.
For a better more luxurious life and flexibility and money of a sort –
It bred selfishness and materialism which led to more greed.
Teachers and parents and children did not mean to lose respect or sight –
But if nothing is done by the next generation it may be too late, a fight.

Note to the reader – Have I earned my membership to The Grumpy Old Man club?

NO NURSERY RHYMES

Mary did not have a little lamb –
There was no fleece of snow.
It didn't follow her anywhere –
Because they had nowhere to go

Mary, Mary was not at all contrary –
She had no garden to grow.
There were no silver cockle shells –
So they did not grow all in a row.

Goldilocks never met three bears or fed –
On their unsweetened porridge, or slept in –
Or even tried out their three beds.
You are all clutching at childhood threads.

And whilst we are on the subject, Little Bo Peep –
Never kept any sheep.
She did not even exist, so how could she?
Now then, now then please don't weep?
There was no little Red Riding Hood –
Or a forest or a big bad wolf of any kind.
It was just a story developed by mankind –
To frighten and stay in a child's mind.

Very sorry folks! But Snow White did not exist either –
There were neither –
Seven vertically challenged alive –
Funnily dressed, differently named little people.
Honestly, I will bet you all a fiver!

And last but not least –
Sorry kids, there is no Father Christmas – only good cheer.
There is no Rudolph or any kind of flying Reindeer – each year.
There never was and never will be OK.
Now that's all I've got to say...

Note to the reader - Except try and remember that poor turkey you're eating was probably laying an egg just the other day!

Love, Marriage and Divorce

THE PULL

You go in to a pub or a club or a bar –
It doesn't really matter where you are.

You are looking good and smelling fine –
Perhaps you are drinking some beer or wine.

You look around for that encouraging smile –
Then you sit and wait for a while.

You suddenly catch that fleeting glance –
Yes! There's eye contact it's not just chance.

You see her face and then her eyes –
Look she is giving you a flash of her thighs.

You can see her breasts rising both up and down –
She is smiling at you there is no frown.

You walk over slowly and say Hi! or Hello! –
She thinks 'Oh bloody hell – here we go'.

You think she reminds you of your ex –
She wonders if you're like most men and just want sex?

You both feel the chemistry straight away –
And you know it is only a matter of time before you both share
that overnight stay!

Note to the reader – My above poem was read out on City Talk FM Radio in Liverpool and two lady listeners called in to ask for my telephone number – what a lovely compliment for me – thank you!

THE GARDEN OF LOVE

And I have visited the garden of love –
In the hope of trying to find –
My lasting and true turtle dove.
A woman fine in thought and kind of mind.

And I have visited the garden of love –
So many, many lovely times –
And prayed to Holy God above –
In words and verse that do rhyme.

And I have visited the garden of love –
And trodden on sharp needle pines –
And sat waiting with arms entwined.
Listening to those church bells chime.

And I have visited the garden of love –
She gave me her body and her sweetness.
But would not or could not give undying love –
We both enjoyed each others fruits, no less.

And I have visited the garden of love –
With hope of joy and glee –
And what she gave me I could feel and see.
Which I returned with verse and words of poetry.

And I have visited the garden of love –
I saw what I would never had seen –
For if I had not visited there before –
I am now very happy to have been.

Note to the reader – It is lovely, loving to be loved and to give love, isn't it?

WHAT A SHAME

It's so nice to be kind –
Sensitive, warm and sharing.
To be giving and caring –
Intelligent with a good mind.
There is nobody to blame –
What a shame.

It is great being the sort of man –
And to try and always be true.
A man who is pleased to please another and do –
What it says on the side of my can.
There is nobody to blame –
What a shame.

What a pleasure, not a bother –
To give pleasure to another.
To have a big kind heart –
Just like that of your Mother.
There is nobody to blame –
What a shame.

How good it is to be able to give love –
And to have that love returned.
Not to be taken advantage of –
Or hated, hurt or spurned.
There is nobody to blame –
What a shame.

There is no photograph in this frame –
There is no real winner of the game.
But now there is nobody left to blame –
What a shame.

Note to the reader – Love could be fantastic if it wasn't such a shame!

TO FIND A LOVE

What does a man or woman have to do?
'To find a love' that is honest and true.
To stop one feeling unloved and blue –
Is it up to me or is it up to you ?

It must be a real joy –
'To find a love' –
Whether you're a girl or a boy,
Somebody you can call your own turtle dove?

'To find a love' do you need real chemistry?
Or is it just down to sex and trust and what will be
Or confidence, control, power and security –
Or just laughing at adversity with false personality?

They say to give is better than to receive –
But 'to find a love' is very hard to believe.
Is it best to be clever and true or naïve –
Or does everyone try to be – but then deceive?

People say to each other – Oh! I do love you!
I really do want you in my life –
And become that husband or that wife.
Then they leave each other, to try 'to find a love' that's true.

Lots of folk over more recent years –
Have said it's hard 'to find a love' that lasts.
That does not bring with it, loads of baggage and fears –
With issues raised, and pain and stress and tears.
This kind of love just evaporates,
and in to the ethos it disappears so very, very fast!

Note to the reader – I do hope you have found your true love and are very happy.

OH WHY?

On that day you said I love you –
And I always will.
Through sickness and in health – for better or worse –
Even though I was never really ill.

Oh Why Do You Hate me So?

On that day we both said 'I do' –
Because you loved me –
And I loved you.
To marry and be happy – Our whole lives through.

Oh Why Do You Hate me So?

On that day at the altar, we both agreed to marry –
And my pet name for you was Carie.
I was so very proud – and wanted to shout out loud!
On the horizon there were no clouds.

Oh Why Do You Hate Me So?

On that day we both gave our vows –
For all those years there were no rows.
You called me your rock and your hubby –
And I called you sexy or honey.
We had lots of good times then –
When we did not worry about money.

Oh Why Do You Hate Me So?

Note to the reader – I think this poem is now definitely one of my favourites, which one is yours? Do please tell me on a postcard it would be great to hear from a reader.

I WANT

I want somebody to care –
I want somebody to share.
I want somebody to have and to hold –
I want somebody before I get too old.

I want somebody to cuddle –
I want somebody who gets in a muddle.
I want somebody to walk with –
I want somebody to talk with.

I want somebody who laughs a lot –
I want somebody who is moody not.
I want somebody who is not too deep –
I want somebody who likes their sleep.

I want somebody who is smart and slim –
I want somebody who is not too thin.
I want somebody to share the driving –
I want somebody who likes swimming or diving.

I want somebody without grey hair –
I want somebody who is not easily scared.
I want somebody who likes a hug –
I want somebody who is not scared of bugs.

I want somebody who can be a friend –
I want somebody whose garden they tend.
I want somebody who has got good vision –
I want somebody who likes to watch television.

I want somebody who tells the truth –
I want somebody –
As long as their name is not Ruth.
I want somebody who is a Libra or Taurus I think –
I want somebody whose feet don't stink.

I want somebody who is fun but not too loud –
I want somebody who stands tall and proud.
I want somebody who is not totally disabled –
I want somebody who likes making love –
Upon a bed or even a table

Note to the reader – I wrote this in an egotistical moment as the ladies from my lonely hearts advertisement kept asking me what I was looking for or wanted.

DIFFERENT LOVES

There is a lustful love.
There is a needful love.
There is a wanton love.
There is a caring love.
There is a sharing love.
There is a hard sexual love.
There is a cold callous love.
There is a selfish love.
There is a soft love.
There is a friendly love.
There is a warming love.
There is a vengeful love.
There is a hate filled love.
There is an explosive love.
There is a financial love.
There is a reliable love.
There is an emotional love.
There is an unconditional love.
There is an undying love.
There is an all consuming love.
There is the love of God above Love.

Note to the reader – I am sure you can think of many more different loves.

LOVE OR JUST LUST

Is it love – or is it just lust?
I hope it is – oh please, it must.
If not, it would seem so unjust.
We both so want that total trust –
That lovers share.
When they are aroused and bare.
Is it love – or is it just lust?

Is it love – or is it just lust?
In each others arms and minds we trust.
A cuddle in the car park –
A tender kiss after dark.
A warming hug – a snug –
Sex on the rug.
Is it love – or is it just lust?

Is it love – or is it just lust?
We don't need those mirrored ceilings –
We both have those heartfelt feelings.
Feelings so urging strong and sublime –
Is it a mountain we both have to climb?
Can a crevasse in a life, be traversed – within this verse.
Is it love – or is it just lust?

Note to the reader – Sometimes we get fooled by both love and lust don't we? But whatever it is it's jolly nice anyway – do have a good day and night!

A LOVER LIKE YOU

It feels so good having a lover like you.
You always know exactly what to do –
I think of little else but you.

It is just bliss to have a lover who –
With a kiss and a hand upon my thigh –
Turns my manly thoughts into a sigh.

You make me happy through and through –
It feels so good to be us two –
You always know exactly what to do.

Your smile and laughter are so true –
I think of little else but you –
Without you darling what would I do?

I feel so lucky to have a lover like you.
The movie in my mind, of you, is blue –
You always know exactly what to do.

But is it love? And is it true?
Who cares? – It feels so good having a lover like you –
I think of little else but you.

Note to the reader – As the song goes 'Love is a many splendour thing' – it feels great when you find true love – or is it just lust?

IF MUSIC BE THE FOOD OF LOVE

Somebody once said long ago, 'If Music be The Food of Love'.
I will bring me gramophone player around your house tonight –
Is that ok with you my little Turtle Dove?
I've got LP's by Roy Orbison, Eartha Kitt,
Desmond Decker and Box Car Willy
Can you please make sure you have that record of yours –
Dolly Parton's greatest hits?
What do you mean 'My Cup Cake' – why will you feel a silly billy?

I loved music so much when I stayed at The Approved Boys School –
So I joined their marching brass band –
I was the unlucky lad with the Piano.
I use to wonder why people would stop and stare outside the school –
I felt a fool.
Mind you as I got older I used to wonder –
If music was the food of love in life –
Why did I have to keep pushing my Piano to your house,
especially up that steep hill?
Then I thought – blinking 'eck what is an engagement?
And why do I need a wife?

Now I have changed my mind over the years –
and think 'words are the food of life'
I have finished writing that book called ' My Life in Verse' at long last –
May I now thank you for those wild nights of sex we had –
When you were my wife.
I don't suppose you fancy listening to my gramophone again?
It's tattered and torn.
However – it's still in perfect working order though,
and rises both up and down, fast.
But I have to warn you now that my stylus has been used a lot,
and is a little worn.

Oh! Thank you so much darling – that's good news 'My Little Cup Cake'.
I will see you at about half past eight –
Do you fancy some wine? – Shall I bring fillet steak?
We can have a good hug and a snug – With kisses for old times sake –
See you later on then my 'Honey Bun', I really cannot wait –
I promise you that you will enjoy yourself – and I won't stay very late!

Note to the reader – Whilst a poem does not have to rhyme all the time – it must have an opening, some story or content, and an end.

TRY AND REMEMBER

(Sent to my ex-wife after our marriage breakdown in 2002 –
well at least I tried for a reconciliation!)

Try and remember the good times we both had.
Try and remember all those days when we were glad.

Try and remember all the good and happy years.
Try and remember our lack of both tears and fears.

Try and remember the true love that we once shared.
Try and remember that it was fate that we were paired.

Try and remember the happiness we felt on our first date.
Try and remember how very hard it is to hate.

Try and remember that it was God who gave us both our health.
Try and remember the small blue box of love you placed upon my shelf.

Try and remember that I loved you and never did you any harm.
Try and remember that our home was always dry and warm.

Try and remember that life is a very steep hill that we all have to climb.
Try and remember that we are mortal and all only have so much time.

Try and remember that today is the first single day of the rest of your life.
Try and remember how once you were such a kind, caring, giving,
and loving wife.

Note to the reader – I sent many poems to my ex-wife and asked her to think about our senior years in life together – she said that she was as bothered about our companionship as she was about the weather – Oh Well – (what's 30 years between friends anyway).

NOBODY

Nobody calls or knocks or texts or phones –
Nobody now to hear my fears plans or moans.
Nobody to say hey I missed you today –
Nobody to say hey don't worry I will pay.
Nobody to say good morning dear –
Nobody to help make one full of cheer.
Nobody to hold you with warmth, love and care –
Nobody to talk with, or to make love with and to share.
Nobody to help, or be helped with that chore –
Nobody to walk with along the shore.
Nobody there now to have and to hold –
Nobody there now that one is growing old.
Nobody to help occupy an empty heart –
Nobody to even hear that embarrassing fart.
Nobody to sleep with on a cold winter night –
Nobody to be objective with but not to fight.
Nobody to cuddle or hug when you feel down –
Nobody to wear that spare dressing gown.
Nobody to care when you are sick or in pain –
Nobody to go on holiday with, even to Spain.
Nobody there now to say I do love you –
Nobody to say it's only a cold not man flu.
Nobody there to say I think you are doing it wrong –
Nobody to walk around sexily in that thong.
Nobody there to share those favourite songs –
Nobody there now – still it won't be very long.

Note to the reader – I suppose most divorcees must feel this way at first?

IT'S NOT NICE

It's not nice when one's marriage is unhappy and has run its course –
It's not nice for anyone concerned, when it invariably ends in divorce.

It's not nice when so long and hard you have fought –
It's not nice when you both have to go to that court.

It's not nice when one's romantic advances and favours, are not returned –
It's not nice when you're sad and alone in denial, hurting and spurned.

It's not nice when you lose a business, and your security in life –
It's not nice when you have lost that friend, you once called your wife.

It's not nice when one ends up losing lots and lots of money –
It's not nice if you can't laugh or don't find things very funny.

It's not nice when you find yourself all alone –
It's not nice when you have no home.

It's not nice when you have nobody who cares –
It's not nice when you have nothing to share.

It's not nice when you don't have a friend who talks –
It's not nice when you have nobody to share that walk.

It's not nice when you are made redundant for the fourth time,
it makes one mad!
It's not nice when you cannot find work or get that job, it makes one sad!

It's not nice when one feels compelled to
write this sort of verse and poetry –
It's not nice but worse things
happen in war and at sea.

Let's just sit down, cheer up,
tell a joke and have another cup of tea.

Note to the reader – You know when you are being nice, but people are not nice back to you? – It's just not nice is it?

NO PARTNER – NO LIFE

Following a divorce or separation –
It can become a somewhat lonely life.
It may not end up in depression or desperation.
No Partner – No Life.

When alone it is important to occupy your time.
Join a club or a gym –
Take up writing, drama or mime – Not drinking wine or gin.
No Partner – No Life.

Yes a holiday or two will do you good.
Or reading a crime thriller or that new book –
And do live well, exercise and eat good food.
No Partner – No Life.

Whilst you are being really lonely and sad –
Don't forget to chat and smile a lot, and have lot's of conversation.
And appear to be really happy and glad –
No Partner – No Life.

Try and meet new friends –
The old ones you had may not want to know.
Turn over a new leaf, be confident, positive and start afresh –
Think of new faces and places where you can go.
No Partner – No Life.

Get out and about, make friends with members of the opposite sex.
Don't phone expensive sex chat lines or become a sex text pest.
You may not need a husband or a wife –
But, remember, No Partner – No Life.

Note to the reader – Well I am writing mainly about what can happen to people in life! – What do you expect to read? All things bright and beautiful?

BEFORE AND AFTER

When you are young – they want you older.
When you are old – they want you younger and bolder.
When she has gone – you wish you had told her.
When she is back – you tenderly enfold her.

When you are cross – it's let's not fight dear.
When you are tired – it's come on, it's party time.
When you're penis is hard – and you want sex, it's no fear.
When you are worried or scared – she is full of vodka and lime.

When you are down and broke – she asks can you lend me a fiver?
When you are rich – it's go on get yourself down the gym.
When you are fat or overweight –
It's get off your bum and don't be a skiver.
When you are dying or dead –
It's 'Well he smoked all his life, Fuck him!'

Note to the reader – Well I am only saying what you would like to have said!

TOGETHERNESS

Glowing embers, fallen ashes –
 Fine wine sipped from crystal glasses.
Both warm and cosy on the settee –
 Cuddling up close, just you and me.

Candles flickering with music mellow –
 Of string quartet and a fine bass cello.
I softly kiss and hold you tight –
 Whispering sweet nothings into the night.

Another squeeze, a comforting hug –
 As we gently slide onto the rug.
Another glass of wine, with room now aglow –
 I think it's time for us to go.

Up the stairs and so to bed –
 Nothing else to be done or said.
Out with the light, are you ready –
 To fall asleep with me, your favourite teddy?

Note to the reader – I bet you thought the above poem was about a man and a woman.

HOT AND STICKY

It was Hot and Sticky that night in Billericay –
  As we both lay in each other's arms.

It was Hot and Sticky that night in Billericay –
  As I truly fell for your charms.

It was Hot and Sticky that night in Billericay –
  As you said please don't let me go.

It was Hot and Sticky that night in Billericay –
  As we both could not say no.

It was Hot and Sticky that night in Billericay –
  As on each other's skin we did blow.

It was Hot and Sticky that night in Billericay –
  As we kissed and hugged the night away.

It was Hot and Sticky that night in Billericay –
  As both in bed we stayed.

It was Hot and Sticky that night in Billericay –
  As your moistened head lay on my chest.

It was Hot and Sticky that night in Billericay –
  We were filled with lust and both said Yes.

It was Hot and Sticky that night in Billericay –
  As your damn earrings got caught in my string vest!

Note to all buyers of this book in Billericay or Essex – If I sell at least 500 copies of my book in the Billericay or Essex area – I will come and do a personal book signing with you all – I will tell you some of my old jokes as well (I love Essex).

Children's Poems

ALAN THE ANACONDA

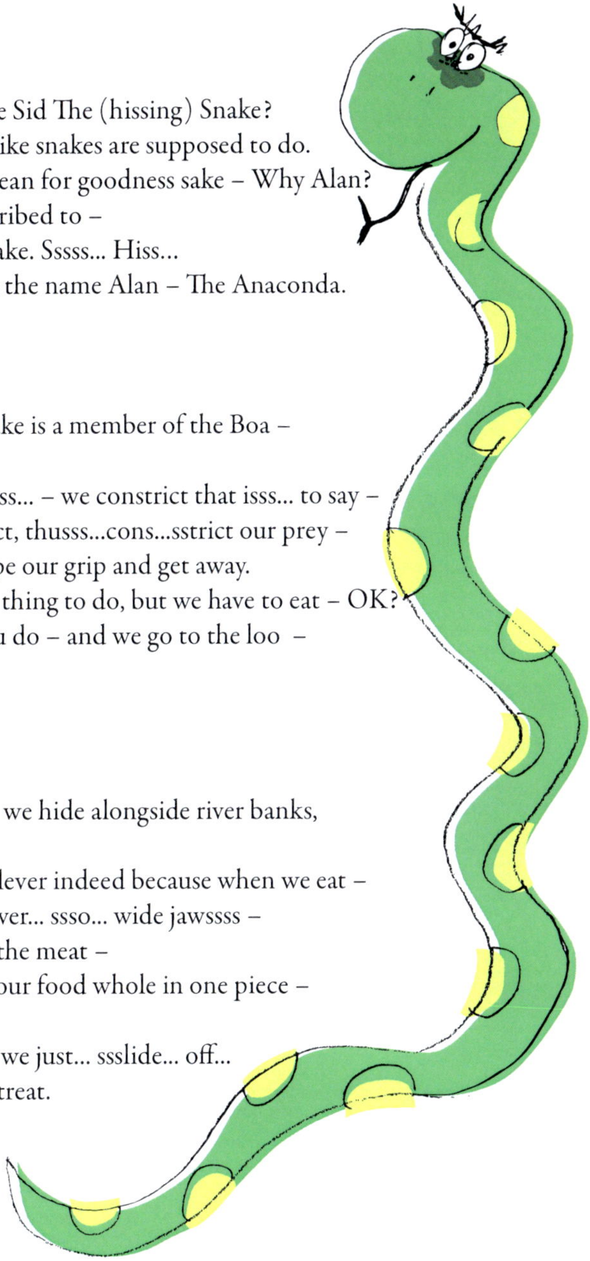

Why couldn't my name be Sid The (hissing) Snake?
I like to hiss ... n ... sisss.. like snakes are supposed to do.
Why call me Alan ? – I mean for goodness sake – Why Alan?
Perhaps the Author was bribed to –
He was probably on the take. Sssss... Hiss...
Ssss... Why Alan? – I hate the name Alan – The Anaconda.

Anyway an Anaconda snake is a member of the Boa –
Constrictors... Ssss..
Ssssee... what I mean... hisss... – we constrict that isss... to say –
We crush and re...ssss...trict, thusss...cons...sstrict our prey –
Sssso... they can't esss...cape our grip and get away.
Sssso... it's not a nicsss...se thing to do, but we have to eat – OK?
Just the – Ssssame... as you do – and we go to the loo –
Jussst... like you do OK?

We are very long snakes – we hide alongside river banks,
under bushes outdoors –
Anacondassss... are very clever indeed because when we eat –
We simply dislocate our ever... ssso... wide jawssss –
In order to eat the size of the meat –
And then we sss...wallow our food whole in one piece –
it really isss... quite a feat.
Then once we have eaten, we just... ssslide... off...
sssomewhere to a quiet retreat.

No! I heard what you... sssaid. I can hear you know –
I have got ears – you know!
We are not Rattle... Ssssnakes... or Vipers although we are –
Sssnipersss –
Ssso what you are... ssaying... is a load of old Cobras.
We Anacondas wrap ourselves around our prey
and put them to... sssleep.
Rattler...sss... and vipersss... and cobrasss...
have poissss...onous venom in their bites –
Please don't be frightened of us...sss though –
don't be ... sscared or weep –
We very, very rarely eat children – have a nice ... ssssleep –
nitey..nite...Ssss...Hisss...

Ssss... Alan! – fancy calling ME! Alan... Hisss...
It should have been hissing SID!

Note to the reader – A nice school or bedtime poem?

MAURICE THE MOLE

Hello there! I am Maurice the mole.
No! Not that kind of mole, found on your face or your neck –
What do you think I am? – blinking 'eck!
No not a stoat, a rat or even a vole –
Although I do believe we may be distant cousins.
And yes, you've guessed –
Moles do live in tunnels and holes.

Now just before you say anymore –
Let me assure you all that we do speak, and we are not at all dirty
We are not like you humans who need washing,
and get upset and all shirty –
At the least little thing – we know the real score.
Moles do not have violent tempers, or those mood swings –
Quite the opposite in fact –
Moles are decidedly very happy and clean.
We don't get all angry, like you humans, and go all mean!

We are quite solitary animals, there is only me and Mable –
Er that's my wife.
Although, at the last count we did have over 300 children –
But they have all moved on now –
To start their own mole holes in life.
Yes, just me and Mable now – she has been an absolute brick –
A brick! Not really one of my favourite words,
bricks make us moles very sick.
We meet a lot of them underground –
Always banging our heads on them in the dark.
Don't like motorways or footings either –
Oh no you will find me n' Mable in the park.

Well any well drained but moistened soil, or soft earth is very nice –
I don't like glass or ice or rubble or clay.
What's that you say? ... (dear) ...
I said any of the above two will suffice.
Sorry about that it was only Mable,
shouting at me from our food hole –
Lunch is ready mmm... crispy worm –
It's not such a bad life being a mole –
We don't have those utility bills, or taxes,
or large mortgages or rents to pay.

Whoops! I'm so sorry about that mate, I was going too fast –
I don't know how I bumped into him,
on such a straight bit of tunnel like that?
I don't normally speed, but I do have strong feet,
although I am sure this will not last –
You see the problem is that us moles don't see very well –
Although, when you meet us you will hardly be able to tell.
Strong sharp claws and brilliant noses –
You should watch us when we smell.
And great hearing too – we can hear a worm cough or sneeze,
from many yards away
Anyway – thank you for listening to me,
and please do have a very enjoyable day!

Note to the reader – It started as a poem and ended up a bit of a monologue – hope you liked it anyway?

BARRY THE BEAVER

Hi folks – It's Barry the Beaver here!
It's Christmas time again –
Only seems like 12 months ago that we had one last year.
I hope our river doesn't freeze over again – honestly, it's such a pain.
Beavers are expert swimmers,
and we can chew through the thickest of logs – no fear.
But I just don't like the Ice –
I don't know why, me and Bet (that's the missus) –
Could go ice skating.
It's not the cold, Beavers are used to that –
It's just that ice is not nice!

Bet hates Christmas shopping –
She never knows whether to have salmon,
oyster or a good goose or gosling –
For Christmas day dinner –
Mind you she is a great girl – It was a lucky day when we met –
Bet's a great Beaver, a real grafter – she's an absolute winner.
Nearly lost her last year – they were cleaning out the weir –
Me and the kids were all worried, and very full of fear –
Don't know what we would do if we lost her – she is such a dear.

We moved away from that weir after that – too much trouble –
Always full of shopping trolleys, or strands of dangerous wire –
Or used by fly-tippers, with lorry loads – full of bricks and rubble.
I remember a few years back –
Waking up and seeing about 200 rubber tyres –
Dumped at our end of the river – what blooming cheek!
It took me and Bet, her dad Bob, his friends Bill, Bert and Ben –
Working like beavers we were – to get it cleared up again! –
It took us well over 2 weeks.
Oh well! can't tread water all day chatting –
Got to go fishing – for river bass –
...Here's wishing you a very Happy bricks and rubble free Christmas...

(Singing)...gone fishing by a shady, shady tree – gone fishing.
Bye from Barry the Beaver...That's me!

Note to the reader – I have been trying my hand at writing a book of poems or monologues for schools – is this any good?

TERENCE THE TURKEY

It was fast approaching Christmas down at the farm.
Terence the Turkey was apprehensively, pensive in his pen –
Would he go to heaven?
He wondered if it was his year to be harmed – or just alarmed.
After all he was a big Turkey and now nearly seven.

Terence knew that the Farmer and his family had overheads –
But he was fed up each year seeing his friends scream and shout –
As they were all pushed and shoved – and fed – unloved.
Then unceremoniously taken to that dark smelly shed –
Never to come out!

You see Terence was quite aware what was going to happen –
Well he'd seen it all six times before –
He was a clever turkey and knew the score.
And that very soon the blood would be all over the floor.
It didn't stop Terence waiting, swollen –
Apprehensively and pensive in his pen.

The cheery, clucking, chickens quota had been done –
now the remainder were glum.
The indignity of it all,
and a special offer pack of FREE stuffing pinned on one's bum.
Terence knew his time was drawing near – would it be his year?
As the big proud Turkey waited apprehensively, in his pen –
With trepidation and fear.

As per usual the Turkey hens (or Turkettes),
seemed happy and relaxed –
They knew that cocks were bigger,
and if needed the hens would be last.
They were kind about it though,
and they hoped their untimely demise would be fast.
Terence the Turkey waited, apprehensively, pensive in his pen –
Was he for the axe?

His friends the Pigs – Polly, Holly, Molly, Bertie, Bill and Ben –
Had all said their goodbyes – sobbed and cried,
and would never be seen again.
These days it was very quick and clinical,
Terence didn't think they suffered any pain.

As Terence the Turkey waited apprehensively, pensive in his pen...
Again.
His beak was dry, and beads of sweat had built up –
All around his, feathered quill.
Terence saw the Farmer coming towards his pen,
he suddenly felt quite ill –
The farmer shouted to his staff that's enough for one day –
Goodnight Bill and Will...

...As Terence the proud Turkey waited apprehensively, pensive in his pen – Now still!

Note to the reader – It's both happy and sad – but I am glad not to be a Turkey!

STRANGELY NAMED ANIMALS AND INSECTS

The lesser spotted Ladybird.
No spots or feathers –
Can't fly –
In bad weathers –
Blows off on the wind –
And wonders why?
But it just gets on with life and doesn't cry.

There's the greater striped Tiger Moth –
Well it's mostly sort of black.
With two orange eyes at the back.
And two wings –
Both are black
Oh Yes! And it sings –
Well more of a hum and it stings.

The African front and rear White tailed Zebra –
Named, so that nobody can see it coming, and going in the snow.
With four black stripes on each side – so –
It can be seen crossing a busy road.
Hence the old expression, Zebra crossing.
It's quite slim and not very wide –
His best friend is the wide-mouthed toothless Toad.

The Ooomabelly bird of Papua, New Guinea
Who is quite fat with no legs at all –
And not very skinny.
Although hairy, and for a bird comparatively small –
Who, on landing very heavily and a little too fast –
Gives out the very strange call –
Ooomabelly! – Ooomabelly! – Only twice, it doesn't last.

Finally, and despite their size, they are good swimmers,
but by no means least.
We have The 8 Ton Hippopotamus!
Quite big for their size –
You see they do like to feast.
The Male only has one ear and two toes on each of his six foot feet
However the Female, at only 5 tons is a very solitary –
Long haired quite frail beast.
Whose face and mouth is nearly as big as her Bottom – is!

Note to the reader – Trying to create a lighter moment and use my imagination – Did I succeed?

Poetry Homework

LOSS

When I was born I didn't have any!
My brother did and mum and mad did –
Even granddad did and so did nanny, and our dog called Spot!
I often used to lay in my cot –
Pretending to be asleep, but secretly I was not.
I used to wonder why?
But it only made me cry.

As I grew up and got bigger and stronger –
These strange strands appeared from out of the top of my head.
I couldn't do much about them,
they just kept getting longer and longer –
Mum said 'I would be blonde like her' –
Dad said 'No you will be mousey instead'.
I really wondered what they meant,
as I lay in my bed, thinking about how long –
It was likely to get, used to bring me out in a cold,
uncertain, nervous sweat.

Much later on mum used to take me to the barbers shop and get it cut.
I used to say 'not too much off please and leave it low at the back' – But –
As mums often do, she countermanded my request and said I ought –
To have a crew cut, you know like soldiers and sailors do, nice and short!
It used to make me sad and sometimes very angry and somewhat mad –
But then thought better of it, because I would have to go home,
and face my dad.

Now I am in my senior years –
The long dark strands that once grew are no more.
They have changed their route,
and appear to be growing out of my nose and ears!
But unfortunately, at my age I know the score.
My follicles have been challenged and seem to have lost the fight.
Maybe it was the lack of Melanin or Keratin?
Either way it does not seem fair or right.
But I have concocted a cunning plan,
and am going to see a man called Stan.
You see he is a wig maker and specialises in hair loss –
and lives on The Isle of Man.

Note to the reader – I tried to make the above poem sound a bit like one of my heroes – the inimitable Pam Ayres – did I do it?

THE LIBRARY

My copy of The Oxford Concise Dictionary defines –
"'The Library' as a room or building in which is kept –
A collection of books, both public and private which –
May be used freely, by the public, without payment."
Said I am sure with good intent.

It does however, go on to say –
That one may reference from books freely on that day –
In which books may be consulted, but not necessarily taken away.
But that if books are 'loaned or taken out' –
and if not returned by the due date –
Which is stamped inside the front cover,
then it says that a fine will have to paid.

For instance, I have just loaned –
Or perhaps borrowed a book from 'The Library' –
Entitled 'Poem For The Day', it's edited by Nicholas Albery.
And sure enough and quite rightly inside it says –
Please return this book or item by the due date shown –
And a fine you will not have to pay.

I just love all types of words and books.
And enjoy reading or writing whilst drinking hot - preferably English Tea.
But being quite a broad shouldered chap I do get the strangest of looks –
When I tell people I meet, quite sincerely, –
That my first love is for Poetry.

Now then Dictionaries and Poetical Books all aside –
I would like to say that I use 'The Library' frequently,
and with much pride.
Where else in the world on a cold and wet winter's day –
Could you wait quietly inside –
And read or go on the Internet and Jobsearch or Twitter,
and Google or Blog –
Whilst you wait warm and freely for that appalling rainstorm to subside,
or turn to fog?

Note to the reader – I struggled a bit with this subject 'The Library' – hope you can't tell?

GLUE

Roll up! Roll up! Come and buy extra strength super glue –
It sticks anything to anything – you to me –
Even me to you –
Go on try it and see.

With extra strength super glue – there are lots of things you can do.
You can glue a fish's finger back on to the hand of a fish.
Try mixing it with red and green paint and make blue – super glue.
It will most certainly glue anything you wish.

You can use it on a model aeroplane –
And make it stronger and fly further and higher.
It will glue a car windscreen, or even a broken window pane.
Extra strength super glue has no bounds, go on be a tryer.

It will glue glass and iron – metal to plastic.
If you're brave you can glue an eyelash on or a false nail –
Back on to your finger.
Mind you it's very strong and quick acting –
That might seem a bit drastic.
Do please be careful it glues in seconds, you won't have long to linger.

Just one drop of this glue will do, two at the most should suffice.
You can even glue a brass handle back on to a wooden door.
I am reliably informed that, it's even glued a vice to a vice –
Believe it or not, you won't need screws or nails,
it will even glue down a floor!

Paper, Cardboard and Hardboard and Plywood,
are joined in one straight away.
Whatever you do when using it, please don't splash it in your eye.
Roll up! Roll up! Everybody, buy extra strength super glue today.
Don't delay!
It really does what it says, on the side of it's 20lb tin, honestly,
not a word of a lie.

Note to the reader – The poem had to have a message that stuck in one's mind!

GOLF OSCAR LIMA DELTA

One will not find it on the floor – or behind a door,
unless it is locked at night.
In its raw state it is not easy to even see – it can be foolish alright.
It sounds as if it is old – and if sold, would cost quite a few pounds.
A precious metal can be found – pounded into the ground –
But not lying around.

What I can say is that for a metal – it is quite soft –
But is found in hard places.
Back in the 1850s it was dugout of the ground –
By men with tough blackened faces.
No! – You are thinking about coal – which is black,
But can burn hot and bright.
Other rare metals to be found –
In the ground – are uranium and titanium, they are light.

The Incas, Egyptians and Romans –
All coveted this precious metal very highly.
For it, they would fight wars – kill, bribe, steal and have dealings,
almost nightly.
This metal I am describing – can be found in lots of different things –
Such as – old cups and bracelets –
Brooches and things with diamonds in.

What? – You still don't know what metal I am describing,
so fully and sincerely?
You're not paying attention are you – or thinking very clearly?
Some more clues then – contrary to misguided belief,
the streets are not paved with it.
One can find it in thread – but not in a bed –
It can even be found in a liquid.

Note to the reader – How are you doing with all the clues? – Are you anywhere near the answer? – Look it rhymes with sold and is millions of years old, come on now have an educated guess – be a chancer? The answer is – Atled – Amil – Racso – Flog ! (it's the title - back to front).

MY NEXT POEM

Hello and good evening…

This is not technically my next poem.
However, it would have been –
If you had seen me writing my last poem.

You see my next poem will be the one after this one.
But it won't be my next poem when I am composing it.
It will be my current poem,
of course this poem would become my last poem.

No not the last poem I ever write –
Just the last poem written by me.
I do hope you enjoy reading my next poem.

That is, this poem –
You see, that is what it is called.
'My Next Poem' that is the title of the poem.

Anyway, I do hope you have not become totally confused –
About what a next poem is, or indeed what it isn't?
Sorry I have got to go now, as I am going to start my next poem.

It might help you to understand what I am trying to explain.
If you can remember that –
Today was tomorrow just yesterday – OK?

Note to the reader – Confused or not confused that is indeed the question.

ASGARD II – TALL SHIP

The Tall Ships came once more to the port of Liverpool –
One was The Asgard II representing the Irish Sail Training Association.
Forming a small part of the proud flotilla of ships – it took its station,
among the other multi-masted ocean goers, from many varied nations.

With five full time experienced crew and twenty sailing trainees.
The proud little Irish ship since 1981, had sailed the seven seas –
Many times in the past twenty nine years.
Through storm force 9 and 10 gales without any fears.

The flotilla had paraded so serenely in Liverpool's protective harbour.
Many thousands of people came to view the wondrous fleet in awe –
Huge crowds stood lining both sides of the Mersey shores.
They brought flasks of hot tea and coffee –
Plus sandwiches, chocolate and toffee.

People were adorned with zoom cameras –
And tripods and deckchairs and binoculars.
School trips were organised which brought scholars.
Old mariners and ex-sailors came who seemed –
Eccentric and most Peculiar.

The parade was over, the flotilla set its sails on the last day –
The Asgard II sporting the Irish ensign was bound for the bay of Biscay.
The proud twin – master set sail for disaster,
that fair but fateful Thursday.
In calm seas the tall ship hit a submerged container –
And at 2am was in great dismay.

There was a catastrophic influx of water –
The ship and crew stood no chance.
Captain Newport shouted "Abandon Ship!" –
Twenty miles from the coast of France.
The ship was lost – the crew were saved, but were in total devastation –
The Irish sail training association – have since held an investigation.
But this will never hide the sadness felt,
by the whole of the Irish nation.

Note to the reader – This Illustration has been provided by a poetic friend and fine artist (James Gordon) as it was one of our poetic subjects. At least there was no loss of life involved when the ship when down. (Many thanks for the painting Jim – nice one.)

DO CLOTHES MAKETH THE MAN?

It has been said that clothes maketh the man.
It is also rumoured that this was said –
By an eminent Jewish tailor in London.
Yes clothes can enhance one's appearance –
But may give the wrong impression.
It largely depends on one's attitude to dress code,
means and profession.
We can discuss this in greater depth during another session.

Another much used term is appearances can be deceptive.
It normally pays to look more deeply in to the person,
as they may not want to deceive.
Your observational powers may be tested,
it depends if you are receptive and receive.
Can you make a judgement about their honesty on oath –
Or judge their politeness or intentions just from their clothes?

We all say that it is wrong to judge a book just by looking at its cover.
But is it not true that sometimes we glimpse the forward –
And do not really bother.
We are influenced by what others say about the author,
and their possible derision –
Instead of taking our time and reading the book,
and then making one's decision.
Some people read a book as if they were a surgeon,
with many incisions.

I suppose what I am trying to say within these various words –
that I treasure.
Is try and look before you leap and end up in a heap.
And do not act in haste as one may repent at leisure.
Always try and look for the good things in people, nobody is perfect –
and you may find a true friendship that will last and that you can treasure.

Note to the reader – We had to write a poem about 'Clothes'. I enjoy our homework.

NEW

New year!
New job – May even earn a few bob.
New hopes and fears.
New challenges...

New friends!
New work patterns and resolutions.
New opportunities.
New solutions...

New route to work!
New hours and a long but happy working week -
New duties to seek.
New knowledge to be gained too...

...to my new employer and the Jobcentre I say Thank You.

Note to the reader – On starting another new job after Christmas, I went and thanked my Jobcentre for their help. It's not nice being unemployed is it?

NEW 2

A new day dawns across a wide open meadow –
A new sun rises over a shimmering ocean –
A new fledgling takes it's first flight –
A new born baby must wonder at their sight.

An old man but with new ideas –
An old warrior with new weapons but no fears
An old poet but with new thoughts and words –
An old car but with a new engine which purrs.

Note to the reader – Just some poetry homework on the subject 'New'.

SONGWRITER OR POET

I think a Songwriter is a really a Poet.
Or can a Poet be a Songwriter?
Although unless you compose yourself –
You may not even know it?
I am only talking about the lyrics and words
to almost any song you care to mention.
I just love words and writing I am not having a go,
there is no bad intention.
Poets can't write music though, well The Beatles did,
now they were a great invention.

'Let it be' that I'm 'Glad All Over' and what I really mean to say –
As I said to our 'Mr Postman' – (Fred)
Just 'Yesterday' all my troubles seemed so far away,
now it seems they're here to stay.
Then I woke up got out of bed, got dressed,
and dragged a comb across my head.
Made my way downstairs and drank a cup,
looking up, I noticed I was late.
Grabbed my coat and grabbed my hat,
I made the bus in seconds flat...
It would be 'Dear Prudence' who said 'She Loves You'.
Words are music to my ears.
Just like The Beatles, what a group they were,
and they went on for years and years.

You would have to be an 'Animal' to say –
'Who' is 'Gary Glitter' or 'Leo Sayer'?
But it really does not matter what you call yourself –
it can even be The Slayer.
As long as the words to the music and your song are good,
and it becomes a payer.
The main thing is that you enjoy it and like to give enjoyment –
And don't try too hard to look for any remuneration or payment.
Mind you 'The Rolling Stones' have done very well for themselves,
haven't they?
Mick Jagger reads a lot of Poetry and he is a good poet,
but his passport does not say –
He is a 'Paperback Writer' by far,
instead it says he is a Rockstar, so there you are!

Tar-Tar!

Note to the Reader –Well one compliments the other?

SILLY, AS THE SAYING GOES

He who laughs last, at nights – wearing tights –
Laughs the strongest and – the longest.
They who are bad and wrong all the rights –
Are a bunch of losers – and are the wrongest.

Cast not a doubt –
Until May is out.
What about – global warming?
By May the African killer bees are swarming.

You cannot make a silk purse –
Out of a sow's ear – who would want one – that's worse.
Another stunning piece of useless information –
The words just flow – like a bad urination.

Many a true word has been spoken in jest –
Many men's skin has gone cold – clad only in a vest.
Lots of miles walked in one man's shoes – can give one blisters –
Especially if they are ill fitting – like the ones worn by my sister.

One swallow – does not make a summer –
What with global warming – who needs one anyway –
What a Bummer.
I have got a foot – and a 12 inch stool –
But I try not to use them both – as a rule.

Don't judge a book by its cover –
Read the bloody thing.
Then on Sunday morning have unbridled sex – with each other.
And afterwards – both go to church for some bible bashing –
And a good sing!

Note to the reader – Can you think of any really meaningless outdated sayings?

VULCAN (Volcanus)

The Volcano is millions of years old –
They live within a fissure, as a fistula within our Earths' Crust.
When or where they will next erupt cannot be foretold.
To live anywhere near one, you must in God place your trust.

A Volcano may lay dormant for thousands of years –
But just the mention of an active one –
Whether it be far away or near –
Will to its local population surely engender great worry and fear.

Seismologists and geologists – using supersonic Seismometers,
and other electronics –
Can and do monitor Volcanic activity,
with increasing efficiency and accuracy.
But only the Volcano (Vulcan) will know –
When it is about to blow itself in to the sea.

First a Volcano will start to shake, shudder and then smoulder.
Sending up a giant pall of harmful ash in a glass laden deadly cloud.
Blocking out our powerful Sun's rays,
then will spew out smoke and boulders.
The mountainous Volcano will vibrate and explode,
in a gaseous poisonous shroud.

In the final stages of an eruption its own power will destroy itself.
By fracturing, exploding and giving forth rivers of white hot molten lava.
But whilst this Roman God of Fire –'Vulcan' –
Disintegrates on the Earth's shelf.
The fiery lava when cooled creates a new land mass,
as it did just East of Java.

Note to the reader – Our planet earth is a truly wondrous beautiful but worrisome and violent place.

Politics and War

ATTACK ON IRAQ

The troops are moving in on Baghdad –
I do hope they don't kill our dad.
My mum says the troops are mad – to go in to Baghdad –
It's full of mines.
They will get blown to pieces – I think they are all swines.

They have killed their own people with poisonous gas –
That Sadam is a real ass.
He uses the money from his oil – to cause death, destruction
and turmoil.
Sadam's soldiers all fight in fear –
Because they are too frightened to hear.

The bombs have killed innocent people –
The blasts have blown down church steeples.
The shops are all gone – the job's nearly done.
But where is Sadam Hussain?
He's gone away again – he does not want to see his people's pain.

The Generals all pat themselves on the back –
As they leave the attack on Iraq.
They may have become the slayer –
But who will foot the bill for this needless war?
Why it's you and I the Taxpayers!

Note to the reader – As if the world needed another bloody war!

THE CREDIT CRUNCH

We have had bad news now for months, week in and week out
Is it any wonder why people are fed up and keep freaking out?
With overdrafts withdrawn, the credit crunch and mortgage trap –
Ordinary people are now depressed, fed up with just hearing crap.

It's constantly on the radio and in newspapers,
TV and always on the news.
With those poor investment bankers lying –
With their ever-warped views.
Businesses, Banks and Building Societies at an alarming rate –
Are going bust.
Can't they see that their customers don't earn any interest –
And have lost their trust?

Even The Bank of England has reduced interest rates –
To an all time low.
One can't get a bank loan though or mortgage,
unless you are in the know.
Landlords, Lenders and Loan sharks are making a killing,
and getting very tough.
Unemployment figures rising with redundancies,
can't they see we've had enough?

What is this Credit Crunch I hear you all say and shout and cry?
Is it a new high fibre breakfast cereal?
Where did it come from and why?
Changing one's job or even finding one –
Has become a near impossibility.
And have you seen the hourly rates of pay today?
They're verging on stupidity.

Why didn't the Government see –
That people have been living beyond their means?
And in the last few weeks have you seen the increase –
In the price of a tin of beans?
People have been living on invisible extended credit –
For years and years.
The bubble had to burst sooner or later –
And reveal those inevitable tears.

I suppose our wonderful Government are trying –
to do their level best.
But it is really putting the Country's purse strings –
To the ultimate test.
The current world financial problems did not just happen overnight.
I blame Selfish, fat cat Investment Bankers,
and highly paid clever Actuaries who should have monitored,
but lost sight,
of our current plight!

Note to the reader – Just another financial/political observation on life.

IT'S WAR AGAIN

President Bush is on the push –
For more war against Sadam Hussain.
It's War Again –

The troops are all geared up and prepared –
The enemy is frightened and scared.
It's War Again –

It's not really very fair –
As stealth bombers take to the air.
It's war Again –

The ships of war are on the sea –
Soldiers will be maimed and killed, just wait and see.
It's War Again –

The buildings are all crumbled –
'Was it really necessary?' someone mumbled.
It's war Again –

The bereaved all form an orderly queue –
Is it for me or is it for you?
It's War Again –

Note to the reader – Why do we go to war?

COUNCIL TAX

Council Tax – I think is really here to stay –
Whose idea was it anyway?
Senior citizens keep saying that 'they cannot afford' to pay.

We have a fuel tax, value added tax and income tax –
A capital gains tax, inheritance tax and a road fund tax.
Do we really need another annually increasing tax?

All these extra costs in our life cause us extra stress and tension –
Is it any wonder why then –
That people cannot afford to pay an increasing pension?

Older people worry at this extra cost and sometimes go all pale –
Pay all your taxes and your rates – or you will end up in jail!
That's what our Government say –
They don't care if the sick or old cannot pay.

Why won't the government hear their plea –
Or simply open their eyes and see?
That when one is older, incomes are lower –
And taxes seem far too high?
They think it's all just 'pie in the sky' – that's why.

The authorities think that people lie –
When really they just don't want to listen –
Or see old or sick eyes full of 'fear and worry' –
With tears that make eyes glisten.

Why does the 'Council Tax' go up every year –
Why is it so very high?
Why won't they listen or show concern when ordinary people cry?
I wonder Oh why? – Oh why?

Note to the reader – An elderly neighbour (a widow in her eighties) gets a single occupancy rebate, but still pays over £100 per month – she only gets her state pension – To survive has she got to sell her semi-detached house?

BANKS AND POVERTY

They say that poverty is caused by money –
Now you may think that very funny.
But I can assure you that it's not –
Because, it largely depends, on how much you have got?

Banks borrow money at a lower rate that they invest –
The difference is called profit or interest.
But when their returns are less than they can borrow –
It all leads to much confusion, loss and sorrow.

These fat cat bankers annoy people quite a lot –
As they pay themselves, large salaries and bonuses –
Out of what we've got.
But when the finance industry is under pressure, and in a mess –
They will not pay themselves any the less.

Instead of cutting back on their lifestyle,
expenses and making a stand –
They just pick the phone up and cry help! –
To The Bank of England.
Or phone another bank, who then gives them a bigger loan –
Until it becomes too late –
And they make their valuable customers moan.

These bankers are very big and clever, until they lose their clout –
Then they all scream to The Government,
'Please come and help bail us out!'
Then once the banks have merged and employees are left jobless,
with tension –
The big clever bankers just bugger off and live,
on their badly earned pensions.

You would think that The Banking Ombudsman,
would have something to say.
But he doesn't really care,
as he has probably done the same thing anyway.
Oh and by the way –
They all play golf together quite happily,
on a Friday, Saturday and Sunday!

Note to the reader – As the saying goes – there is no honour amongst thieves!

GORDON BROWN (Read out on City Talk FM 2009)

Can Gordon Brown bounce back?
The Country have put him on the rack.
Shall we put him in traitors gate –
Or simply use him as the bait?

Can Gordon Brown be strong?
Has he been so very wrong?
What is this Credit Crunch?
Is it for breakfast munch?

Can Gordon Brown come through?
Will he fight off those blues?
Perhaps the Lib Dems will get in –
Maybe even the greens will win?

Can Gordon Brown bounce back?
Do you think he is on the right track?
The Millionaires do not seem to care –
Will they continue to receive the lions share?

Can Gordon Brown save the people's money
Will we all end up eating bread and honey?
We have all been there before –
But do we really know the score?

Can Gordon Brown really win us all over?
Or will those bankers be jumping off the cliffs at Dover?
I bet some of them won't be able to suffer the tension –
Poor souls, but then they can always retire,
and live off their ill-gotten fat pensions!

Note to the reader – In a funny sort of weird way, I feel sorry for this Scotsman – the head of an English Parliament – do you think he's getting his own back *Braveheart* style?

HAVES N HAVE NOTS

The Haves keep getting more and more –
Whilst the Have Nots keep getting less and less.
The Capitalists are winning but the Country is in a mess.

Mortgage costs are causing a credit crunch –
Lenders are becoming very picky.
The situation is real.
For the Have Nots things are getting very tricky.

They say that a big recession is on the way from the USA –
But the Haves don't really give a shit!
Because it is the normal people that will have to take the hit.

Shop owners can take tax free cash from their tills –
But we all know that if a recession comes –
It will be the Have Nots that cannot pay their bills.

Rich Football Clubs will put up prices for all ages –
To help pay their rates –
And over priced players' wages!

The gas, electric and phone companies will also increase profits –
At the Have Nots expense.
They won't be happy until people are all living intensely in tents.

As the saying goes 'money goes to money' –
But it's the Haves that keep getting it.
Don't you think that strange or funny?

Note to the reader – The above poem was written by me in response to another City Talk Radio Show as callers kept asking why do prices keep going up but their wages seem to go down?

THE HAUNTED CLOUDS OF WAR

The hallowed sky is not the same anymore since –'The War in Iraq'.
Now the clouds rush by o'er our 'green and pleasant land,'
all 'Angry and Black.'
They used to be 'White and Fluffy' with 'Small Flecks of Grey'
Now they look dark, satanic and haunted 'Each and Every Day'.

Weather patterns have changed a lot since these sinister 'War Years'.
Now the world's weather brings 'Tsunamis and Floods and Fears' –
Accompanied by people's losses and worries,
with added 'Tears and Pain'.
They say 'Global Warming' is to blame,
and weather will not be the same again.

Environmentalists say it is caused by fumes –
Given off by cars, trains, planes and boats.
Scientists are even trying to blame methane filled farts –
Given off by 'Cows and Goats'.
What silly 'arses' they all are –
Can't they all see that it is largely down to the war?

You see when our troops threatened Sadam,
and his army of Black Guards in Kuwait –
He exploded 800 oil wells on his cowardly retreat –
He just simply 'Could Not Wait'.
The 'Haunted Clouds of War' have darkened our skies,
for at least a millennium.
This is why the troops we send are not to defend,
but to save the oil and uranium.

If you look up today into those haunted clouds of war,
you may see a trace –
Of a dead soldier's face –
Wondering why –
Up in a now ever darkened, haunted sky.

***Note to the reade*r** – Maybe it is Global Warming – But just call me an old cynic!

Adult Humour

DIGGORY THE DOG

Hickory horny Diggory the dog –
Lived in a very nice house –
With his owners Patrick and Roz.
There was no cat and only a computer mouse.

Hickory horny Diggory the dog –
One day went o'er the sea to France –
To make friends with chienne (frog dogs).
He was a randy dog and hoped he would seize his chance.

Hickory horny Diggory the dog –
Thought that getting laid –
Would be as easy as falling off a log.
He found a Dandy and a Honey who both wanted to be paid.

Hickory horny Diggory the dog –
Found his need was greater than theirs –
So undecided was Diggory he had his wicked way with both dogs.
He was attracted to both –
And he found it very difficult to split hairs.

Hickory horny Diggory the dog –
Travelled home to Ledbury with Patrick and Roz soon after –
But was to become the subject of much laughter –
As Diggory was sitting, sniffing and licking –
They found a tick on the end of his dick.

Note to the reader – A true story from a good friend Jane re Roz's dog!

A COCKNEY RHYME

There's this geezer walking down the 'frog n toad'.
Just passing the old 'rubber dub' The Crown,
He finds a 'lady godiva' as he looks down.
At his first glance –
He thinks somebody is having a 'tin bath'.
So he picks up the note and legs it around the 'jack horner'.
He had been football training and his 'birds n bees' were stiff.
Passing the 'greasy spoon' café he calls the blue moon he whiffs,
Home made 'kate n sidney' pie with 'jockeys whips' – he finks –
'Shall I eat or get down to 'Marks n Twisters' me feet 'pen n inks'?'
He finks – 'I could do with some new 'almond rocks' – nah,
I'll be there for hours'.
'Mind you' – he finks again – 'I do need a new pair of 'callard n bowsers'.'
He could also do with a few pairs of 'Alan Whickers'.
Should he give it a miss?
All of a sudden he has a pain, then feels thirsty, but needs a 'gypsies kiss',
and needs to 'siphon the python', but hopes it not a 'Brad Pitt' as well.
He pops in the 'rubber dub' orders a 'pigs ear',
and sprints up the 'apples n pears'.
Standing in the 'To-Let' he finks –
'I've made some 'folding green' and nobody to tell!'
There's a geezer grunting and groaning he sounds in pain, and really poor –
In trap number four!
He's either shagging or being shagged or has fallen on the bleeding floor.
He sounds in pain – 'Ere mate are you awight?' – He shouts.
He shouts back – 'Shut up mate I'm trying to bang one out,
Let me concentrate or, I'll give you a bleeding clout.'
A typical cockney, when in drink, likes to shout and yell.
All of a sudden there's a Ffwoommph... noise –
Like an arrow from William Tell.
'Cor blimey! – F*** me mate have you apple tarted? –
What's that bleedin' smell?'
Would you 'Adam n Eve' it?
I fink he's finished his 'Eartha Kitt', 'Brad Pitt', 'Tom Tit' –
Or call it what you will

It smelled 'pony n trap', like 4 day old pigswill.
He runs down the 'apples' and outside and down the 'frog' to get some fresh air.
He puts his hand in his 'sky rocket' to get his 'bangers n mash'.
He's puzzled and scratches his 'barnet fair'.
Oh large round fings, the 'lady godiva' is not there!
He can't find the note, must have left it on the pub counter.
He searches everywhere.
So back to the 'battle cruiser' and to an empty glass he did dash
Some 'Ron Hunt' had drunk his 'pigs ear'
and 'cattle trucked' off with his cash!

Note to the reader – In memory of many a night out as a young man in London you would always find some money on the streets especially at the weekends, it came in very handy – I found a ten pound note once, it lasted me nearly 2 weeks!

IT'S JUST NOT TENNIS

I am watching the Tennis from Wimbledon again.
They have spent £5 million on a roof over centre court,
so they don't mind if it rains!

To be perfectly honest I could not tell a cross court slice,
from a passing shot with spin –
Or an overhead top spin lob from a lobbed drop shot –
As long as the umpire calls it in!

Poor Great Britain have not had a male player in the final,
since 1948!
Despite millions of pounds of investment in our game,
it really is in a poor state!

We have had lots of players in between, with Taylor, Henman
and now Murray.
But nobody seems to want victory as much as the USA –
There is not much worry!

Our women have done marginally better –
With wins by Ann Jones and Virginia Wade.
But come on folks even the women have won nothing –
In more than two decades!

Realistically, our best chance of a Wimbledon win,
is from Murray – he is no dope.
But to be honest, there is more chance of me getting a date –
From a black female pope!

It does not seem to matter whether it is the singles,
doubles or mixed doubles.
Our players always work and train hard enough –
To burst their own bubbles!

Wimbledon is the most revered prize,
and world centre of the tennis game.
What a shame that over the years,
our British players' game has been so lame and so very tame!

It's just not tennis!

Note to the reader – Anyone called Dennis or Denise for Tennis?

COMMENTARY ON A SLOVENIAN FOOTBALL MATCH

Welcome to the Lujbankovic Stadium in Slovenia –
For the match between Slovenia and Bosnia.
The winner of the match will of course play Croatia –
In the final which will take place in Herzogovenia.

As the whistle is blown by referee Eric Reckcicz –
Passed forward to Pukic by Stanic –
Headed on to the tall centre forward Policz –
A good header but saved by the Bosnian keeper Lukic.

A long ball out from Lukic but intercepted by Revanovic –
The ball played square by the defender to Stanovic –
Who plays it through to Pukic but tackled by Vazsic –
And again collected by keeper Lukic.

Lukic this time rolling to right back Snatchovic –
Down the line to their winger Flavovicz –
In to the path of their attacker Clingonovic –
A terrific shot, but saved by Slovenian Keeper Slovicz.

Slovicz switches play to midfielder Michelovic –
Who plays a tremendous pass to Policz –
But is tackled by the tough looking defender Slivovic –
And passed safely back to the big hands of keeper Lukic.

Kicked right up field to Clingonovic on to Revanovic –
But saved again by Slovicz and passed to Stanovic –
On to Revanovic square to Pukic –
Who shoots and scores, the ball passing under keeper Lukic!.

Note to the reader – Well I think it's funny if you like football – how about you?

Me

A YOUNGER ME (A WALTER MITTY MOMENT)

I would like to have been a professional sportsman.
Not someone who is vertically challenged with a big belly.
Mind you, I know perfectly why I seem to have acquired one –
It's because, I have sat too much at a desk and ate meals,
whilst watching the telly.

I would like to have been a javelin thrower, a sprinter or a runner –
Or a very fit footballer, with loads of pace and speed.
But I have ended up being a bit of a grower and gardener –
Who is very good indeed – at sowing their seed.

I would like to have been a Formula One racing driver.
Because since Fangio – I have always been a big fan.
But I think it would have cost me more than a fiver –
And all I would have probably got, are several driving bans.

I would like to have been an Airline Pilot –
Flying high up above the clouds, in Blue Skies.
Unfortunately, I've ended up working at McDonalds –
Serving up those 'healthy burgers' and crispy French fries.

I would like to have been a Millionaire –
With loads and loads of Money.
But I have become a friendly cuddly bear –
Who has eaten too much bread and honey.

Note to the reader – Well that's ME folks – but I do like reading and writing and words – Don't you ?

A JOURNEY TO LONDON (MONOLOGUE)

For a weekend journey to London.
I would leave about 5am on a Saturday.
The main reason being is that as a Londoner myself –
we work hard n' play hard –
The bulk of the inhabitants, of our beautiful,
overcrowded capital city,
will still be fast asleep upon my morning arrival.
The outskirts in particular, the M25 and M40 motorways
will be relatively free from heavy traffic, as this normally builds up,
throughout the day. (Journey time 4 hours).
When I lived in London the motorways, mentioned previously,
were known as the free car parks!
It's 5am, I take the Birkenhead Road out of sunny Hoylake,
where the locals call our beach God's Golden Mile with a smile,
but said with style and great belief!
Via Meols, which under Roman rule was a small fishing harbour,
used to supply fresh fish on a daily basis to their troops –
In fact Roman Road is still there today.
Over the railway bridge past Carr Farm down the stretch,
to Moreton Cross, turning right at the roundabout,
on to the Upton Road and follow signs for the M53 (800 yds).

The M53 runs the length of the Wirral peninsular,
from Liverpool to Chester,
which by car takes normally 30 minutes,
at the maximum allowable speed of 70 mph –
It used to take Roman Soldiers approximately 10 to 12 hours,
to march the same distance.
On the M53 I have passed Upton, Prenton, Clatterbridge,
Ellesmere Port and Hooton –
In what felt like only a few minutes.
Shortly I will turn left before Chester on to the M56 signposted to
Warrington, Manchester, Birmingham and The Beautiful South.
I have half eaten my first sausage roll, and some plain salted crisps,
as I get ready to turn my windscreen wipers on
as I approach Manchester.

(All together now – it always rains in Manchester).
Apparently more umbrellas are sold per head in Manchester that
anywhere else in the Country – I was told.

Having turned on to the M6 motorway,
I can really put my foot down today as traffic is minimal,
as hoped and planned.
I finish my sausage roll and bottle of water –
I am soon in Staffordshire passing mile after mile of green fields
(interrupted only by the odd advertising board for Eddie Stobbart.)
With Cheshire now far behind,
and the first of many signposts for Birmingham passed –
15 minutes ago –
I have something else on my mind – Yes! – A comfort break...

I stop at Hilton Park Services which has everything – well almost – all
I need is a Pee a Hot Mug of Tea –
And 2 slices of lightly buttered toast.
It is still very early as, freshly watered and fuelled,
I rejoin the M6 motorway normally intolerably busy –
at this time of day but not on a Saturday – Hooray!
I gather much haste, less speed so to speak,
and head towards my London home.
Oh Dear how obscene, I have nearly consumed –
The whole contents of a family pack of jelly beans,
before I had even seen the sign for Luton Airport,
I am at Junction 14 –
Not long to go now you know, 3 hours on the go,
now that's not too slow!
The weather report last night said it would be quite clear, and now my
windscreen has started to smear,
with blobs of rain mixed with that shitty oily stuff, what a pain!
Never mind I have reached my destination, by South Harrow station,
home again.

Note to the reader – An imaginary journey home – I miss my Southern based family so much, sometimes.

TV – THINKING AND DRINKING

The TV is on –
My God this film is so boring –
Whoops! I've dozed off again – I hope you didn't hear me snoring!

I like the sport –
And quiz games and shows too –
And documentaries about nature and the zoo – I've just sneezed –
Perhaps it's flu?

Repeats, repeats – repeats –
The same old programmes on again –
Even the weather report says it's rain.
My headache 's getting worse and worse –
Do you think it could be a migraine?

Am now laying on the floor –
can you hear that noise from the kids next door –
God it's gone very cold – perhaps it's me just getting old –
Oh! For goodness sake Graham, get told –
Will you go out and join the fold?

Well the evening's gone again – what a pain – and night is here –
The TV has finished – let's all cheer!
Please, please no more repeats –
perhaps tomorrow I'll drink wine and not beer ?

I've started talking to myself, since the divorce –
I should get out more – get a life –
It's no good sitting in, thinking and drinking –
Because I don't have a wife –
There is no need for anymore – 'Trouble and Strife'.

Note to the reader – Attention all divorced men out there – What did you do? Did you go out on the pull or sit in watch TV, read and drink and think in self pity?

THE WRITER IN ME

I always wanted to become a writer or an actor –
Or someone who is good with speech or words.
Because as the old saying goes –
'The pen is mightier than the sword'.

Somebody who is really clever –
Not just a 'Tim nice but dim' type like me.
A person who has great vision with ever –
Solutions to life that only they can see.

I think a writer or an actor is someone who can be proud –
In verse that can make eyes with interest 'glisten'.
When that person is speaking out aloud –
You feel compelled and really want to 'listen'.

You see the written word will last much more than a day –
Much longer, than one can ever speak or say.
Because, once you have put 'pen to paper' and, have paid –
A publisher to produce a book, your words are there to stay.

With words you can write short stories, quite fully –
Also anecdotes, and 'plays and poems'.
If one just thinks about a subject long and carefully –
They can be written, sometimes, without even knowing.

I would like to become a writer or an actor –
For the reasons that I have already stated.
But if for some reason I end up driving a tractor –
I will not be totally and utterly devastated.

Note to the reader – Now redundant for the umpteenth time and in my fifties – my advice to everyone, is try and decide what you want to do and be as soon as you can and then work as hard as you can to achieve your chosen ambition – Good Luck!

MY SOLDIER BOY (In honour of Pam Ayres)

My soldier boy wears a blue cockade –
It's technical name is Durex.
He always wears one when we have sex –
The trouble is he never knows when to stop –
Because he also wears a Hearing Aid –
And can never hear me saying for God's sake get off!

My soldier boy would come with me to various gigs –
And drink too much beer –
And smoke those bloody horrible smelly cigs.
But I loved his bones and he brought me good cheer –
Not just for a week or a month, but year after year.
He used to get drunk and start to shed tears of joy –
My soldier boy.

My soldier boy and I travelled everywhere by 'Crappers Coaches'.
We went to many backstreet pubs and clubs and dives –
And stood among discarded dog ends, sandwiches and cockroaches.
It's a wonder we never caught a cold or herpes or hives.
My soldier boy wears a blue cockade –
But he doesn't smoke anymore, is overweight,
and drinks mainly lemonade.

Note to the reader – A little humorous 6 liner in honour of the inimitable Pam Ayres – I wonder if she is still married to Dudley Russell of Dolphin Concert productions – I bet she still lives in Oxford though.

A GEORDIE LAD (Written for Dave Stocks)

There was a Geordie Lad called Dave,
who did not know that he was brave.
With tattoos and a smile so wide,
his nostrils could have breathed in the tide!

Newcastle was his pride and joy,
he was certainly born to be a boy.
He split up from his long time ex,
because he wanted too much sex!

With friends he was such a hit,
and Oh my God he could shit.
On the dance floor he was such a mover.
In my youth we would have called him a groover!

His jokes were mostly sometimes very funny,
and his attitude and smile were always very sunny.
Alan Shearer was his true footballing hero,
If Dave had met him he wouldn't half bend his ear hole!

There was a Geordie Lad called Dave,
Who just loved to get out and drink and rave.
Some people thought that he was barking mad,
But to have known him made you glad!

Note to the reader – I worked with Dave Stocks at Toyota in Liverpool – a nice bloke.

A QUIET LIFE

The holiday is over now, it's back to work.
To face the stress and strife –
It's such a quiet life.

The job is hard with staff bitter – the boss is a real shitter.
But I am no quitter.
It's such a quiet life.

The pace of life and the traffic are bad.
To have a job I am so glad.
It's such a quiet life.

Pay day is here at last the bills are paid so quick –
I am not well, but have to work, I feel so bloody sick.
It's such a quiet life.

I can't afford a new raincoat just yet –
So, I will just have to get very wet.
It's such a quiet life.

Working over 60 hours per week –
Makes me feel so very weak.
It's such a quiet life.

The drunks at night keep ringing my doorbell –
But there is nobody there to tell.
It's such a quiet life.

My three girls are the light left in my life –
I am over the divorce and losing my wife.
No, I am not reaching for that knife!

It's now such a peaceful life.

Note to the reader – Marriage can be a very fulfilling rewarding institution – but treat marriage wrongly, and you could end up being resident in one!

A LONELY POEM

Nobody –
Writes –
Or calls or phones –
Nobody there now to even share a moan!

Alone and broke but not yet broken.
The peace and quiet with no words spoken –
Oh bugger! The iron's just broken!

To busy ones self with that little job.
Oh sod it! I've burnt my baked beans on an over hot hob!
Never mind I will just shove them in my gob!

The carpets are hoovered and the stairs are brushed.
I feel so tired I'll sit down for a rest –
Oh blow it! My crisps I've just crushed

I sit alone with thoughts running through my aching head.
Too much to plan for and hope for – oh well another day gone –
I guess I'll just have to go to bed and think instead!

Note to the reader – I wrote this about 3 months after moving in to my flat and as any divorcee or separated person knows after many years of living with a wife and 3 children – You are just not used to the prolonged bouts of total silence! My advice is put the radio and TV on – it sounds like you have got company even if you haven't.

A TERRORIST AT WORK – A true story.

I went to work at my travel agents one day in 1984,
my counter staff Tracey and Louise were out at lunch.
A Middle Eastern looking man came in through the door –
He had dark eyes, a dark shirt and dark hair, plus body odour.
The unsmiling man wore dark jeans, a dark jacket, and a dark stare –
He said nothing and just sat there.

I said how can I help you Sir?
He was quiet and looked all around.
He was about 26 and said his name was Mukhtar Mohamed Amir,
and worked at Kennings the cleaners by the cricket ground.
He wanted an open air ticket to Nicosia Airport, Cyprus,
with rooms quite near.
I understood exactly what he had asked for,
but then started to fill up with fear.

How could I book rooms or a hotel,
when I did not know when he was going?
I phoned Nicholas Brothers Cyprus,
and got a list of accommodation in Nicosia.
The air ticket was booked from Heathrow on a BA –
Tristar or a Boeing.
The man gave me a gold credit card for payment,
he would also need a visa.
He said his Mother was Egyptian and his father was from Pakistan –
Well I knew one thing, his name certainly would not be Stan!

I made £100.00 profit on the open dated ticket,
Heathrow to Nicosia and return.
But needed more information for the visa application,
which was valid for 90 days
I gave him a visa application form for completion,
and signature, and details to learn.
Having copied his Egyptian Passport, credit card and address,
my head was in a daze.
I got his telephone number at work –
He did not have a phone at home –
Which I thought funny.
But I had made another £50.00 on his visa for Cyprus,
and had taken all the money!

I met Sgt. Bob Stewart in the pub that night,
and told him what had happened that day.
We went back to my shop,
and I gave him copies of all the documents to keep.
Bob said 'Thanks a lot mate, you have done the right thing',
then went on his own way.
By this time my head was banging,
and when I got home I could not get to sleep.
Two plain clothes men came in the next day,
and told me it was OK and not to worry.
The men smiled saying 'You can keep the money,
Mr.Amir will not be back in a hurry.'

Note to the reader – I had never been so nervous that week, I remember hearing the news about 2 months later and that there had been an explosion at Nicosia Airport!

FUNDRAISING

Hoylake Cottage Day Care need to raise £1.5m,
to start the re-building phase.
This means there is lots and lots of money that we need to raise.
There are many options available in order to achieve this task –
But whatever we choose and whatever options are used,
it is still a very big ask.

We could do lots of car boot sales,
but would we sell enough car boots?
We could do cash in the attic sales,
but how would we get people up the stairs?
We could do a series of one legged sponsored races,
but do it in pairs?
But whatever we do and in whichever way we choose,
we still need lots of loot.

They say that Charity begins at home –
So what can we all do to help make us money?
We could go fruit picking on a summer day,
and make homemade jams, but no honey.
We could have a bakers' day twice a month say,
and sell sponge cakes with jam in.
I could write poems that are funny –
and ask visitors to put their money into our tin.

We can arrange bring and buy sales of unwanted items,
and other donated stuff.
We cannot do a gymnastics display or run around the park,
we would run out of puff.
All the nursing staff could enter themselves in a sponsored
parachute jump.
But I don't think there would be many volunteers,
as they all may get the hump!

How about arranging a sponsored car wash?
I have heard that can bring in lots and lots of dosh.
We could sell recycled cycles to poor cyclists, that would be a lark.
Or what about asking a local brass jazz band –
to come and play quietly in our car park?

We can ask local shops to give prizes for a raffle,
and of course we would say thanks.
I know a much quicker way to raise these much needed funds –
But it involves the robbing of Banks –
The Army with about 40 soldiers –
And a couple of getaway drivers of 100 ton tanks!

Note to the reader – I am a Voluntary Worker for our local Hoylake Cottage Hospital and wrote the above to heighten awareness of their monetary but charitable needs.

A POEM TO MUM

Dearest Mum I am so sad that I was not with you,
the day you passed away.
You'd had the operation, which you said 'went well',
and 'you felt sore but OK'.
I had told the girls that their Nanny was a fighter,
because you had been all your life –
You were the very best of Mum's that one could ever have,
and you were a good wife to our toughened, alcoholic,
and aggressive, child and wife beating Dad.
I don't know how you put up with him all those years?
To experience it and see it, made us all very sad.
Together we shared so many tears and fears –
But you were so brave dearest Mum, the best we could have had!

You know that day I was 200 miles away,
when you slipped over to the other side.
As long as you know that if I had thought for one minute
that you would die –
I would have driven through the night to have been with Cliff,
at your bedside.
We all cried rivers of tears for you Mum,
the girls said why daddy, oh why?
They want me to thank you for teaching them to play cards,
scrabble and such.
The girls will always remember your smile and laugh,
and kindness so very much.
They wanted to thank you, for your thoughtfulness,
and your caring loving touch.
I told the girls that their 'Nanny Pearl' will still be loving us all –
From up above.
And that if you could, you would fly down to see us –
On a shining white 'turtle dove'.

Always in my and our thoughts Mum,
gone from sight but never from our hearts.

Note to the reader – This poem is dedicated to my lovely Mum (Pearl).

MY BROTHER (in honour of my brother Clifford)

My brother is clever and witty and strong of body and mind.
My brother is generous, a good father and kind.

My brother and I are both Arsenal fans through and through.
My brother is a very good golfer too.

My brother is a socialite and a 'great drinker of beer'.
My brother always tries to be happy and full of cheer.

My brother is always first to send –
A Christmas or birthday card each year.
My brother was always there to lend, that helping hand –
And show no fear.

My brother would be there to defend to the end.
My brother is Clifford – my best friend!

Note to the reader – Somebody once said "If you Love a Person For God's Sake Tell Them when they are Alive so that they know it, because you are a Long Time Dead!"

HORTICULTURAL HELPERS OF HOYLAKE

We are a group of people who like to sow the seeds –
Which then grow in to flowers and plants which we water and feed.
We are The Horticultural Helpers of Hoylake!

Hoylake in bloom is one of our wishes –
It gets us out of the house and we can sometimes avoid –
Doing the dishes.
We are The Horticultural Helpers of Hoylake!

With our trowels and forks and quality company and soil –
You will often see us at the planters toil.
We are The Horticultural Helpers of Hoylake!

The work we put in the planters of flowers we treasure –
Because we like to see the peoples smiling faces and give pleasure.
We are The Horticultural Helpers of Hoylake!

Our members go out in all sorts of weathers –
We go with friends and very rarely reach the end of our tethers.
We are The Horticultural Helpers of Hoylake!

We all take a pride in our work and it never becomes a race –
The thing I like most is when the work is done –
We all have a drink and stuff our face.
We are The Horticultural Helpers of Hoylake!

Note to the reader – Following my divorce and another redundancy I decided to try and become more environmentally friendly so I joined 'Flowers in Bloom' my local horticultural society – I always liked gardening I think working with the soil and flowers and plants brings its own rewards.

JTG @ EST AND EPP

We all went to work for the EST –
And ended up together at the EPP.
That's Jack and Terry and me –
We post and chat and fill and file,
but not all of the while –
Most of our time is spent walking – mile after mile.

You see not only do we go door to door –
And deliver from house to house.
Sometimes we sit at a PC manipulating a mouse.
And provide facts and figures all written in techno babble and scouse.
The three of us all use our nouse –
And at the end of the day we wash and – just need to de-louse.

At the moment we are calling on homes near New Brighton station –
Advising on the benefits of cavity wall and loft insulation.
Plus smoke alarms and fire safety checks.
All in search of the holy grail, in the form of – a HECs.
Despite lots of customer procrastination –
We do have good fun with the extraction of required information.
Then we return to the office with our HECs intact,
like a retrieving dalmation.

We are all from different backgrounds –
Terry is an engineer who teaches people, dogs and hounds –
Jack our mentor is an ex-Teacher of people,
a PC expert and passable cook –
Then there is me, I just watch in amazement,
as I am writing a poetical book.
It's only taken me 56 years to live it – and write it,
so it should not be too long

Note to the reader – I went to work for Energy Savings Trust/ Energy Projects Plus with two of the nicest men I have ever met – I dedicate this poem to Terry and Jack (they know who they are...)

CITY TALK 105.9FM

I like listening to Dean Sullivan on
City Talk 105.9 FM in Liverpool do you?
It offers a new voice and choice, debates,
and a different point of view.

It does not have pop songs,
advertising and jingles blasting away all day.
But it opens doors on various subjects,
and lets ordinary people have a say!

Liverpool is the City of culture for England in 2008 –
City Talk FM is the station.
Because it represents the news and views,
not just of Liverpool but the Nation!

The subjects chosen by Dean Sullivan are current,
and interesting in every way.
It can be politics or poetry but always pertinent,
at least that's what he told me to say!

So come away from that radio station that only gives repetitive ads,
and music power –
And switch to Dean Sullivan at City Talk 105.9 FM,
you will find him up a tower!

Note to the reader – This was written by me for The Dean Sullivan radio show which I read out live on air! So in a way it was semi-published!

CELEBRITIES I HAVE MET

I met became friends with a nice man,
Russ Abbot from Madhouse on TV Fame.
He introduced me to Bonnie Tyler, Les Dennis –
and Bella Emberg from his show!
I have also met Jimmy Tarbuck and Bruce Forsythe –
of the TV Generation Game.
I hope you don't think I am a name dropper but there are others,
I have met and know.

There is Bob Carolglees of TV fame –
With his dog 'Spit' he now runs a Candle Shop!
I once met Benny Hill and Kenny Everett long ago,
with The Pams People Dancers.
Would you believe I met Severiano Ballesteros in Liverpool,
at Anfield in The Kop!
Oh what a laugh when I met Mel Smyth and Gryff –
what a couple of funny chancers!

I met Ossie Ardillles n' Ricky Villa when I was at Spurs –
They played for Argentina!
And of course Steve Perryman and Glen Hoddle,
and others from the Spurs Team!
But I am quite sure that I have never met or been out with –
a lady called Bettina?
At the Sheraton I met Barry Sheene and another Kenny –
with their Mean Machines!

A couple of comedians I met were Norman Collier and Jim Bowen –
Having a piddle!
I have met both Roy Walker and Tommy Cooper once –
On a flight from Heathrow!
But I don't think I have ever met anybody who did or could –
Play Violin or a Fiddle!
By now you will be thinking I am a right bighead but am not,
there are others I know!

I met Alan Sugar, now a 'Sir', when I was at Spurs,
God he was a miserable bugger!
To Me the greatest men I ever met at Sheraton were –
Our Henry and Mohamed Ali!
Another Boxing Great there that night,
although he is now Australian, was Joe Bugner.
He must have had a tummy upset –
Because he was at the back of the hotel in an alley!
I met Rodney Marsh and Georgie Best at a lunch once –
they were both drunk!
Bill Beaumont and Will Carling were both great,
the women thought they were hunks.

Note to the reader – Bet you think I am a right name dropper don't you? But don't be jealous with envy or blue because you see all of the above is simply quite true!

THE EARLY YEARS

The early years for me and my brother were sad and stark.
With a violent drunken dad who, when he came home –
We would try and humour, but he beat us in the dark!

The early years for our family were hard –
At night we would always to be on our guard.
We would worry for both ourselves, and our dear mother.

The early years for us as children were really rotten –
With worn out school shoes and clothes of cotton.
Not of Adidas, Nike, mohair, wool or silk –
Because mum had to pay the rent and food and milk!

The early years when dad was drunken –
We would have to live in fear and tears –
With our young spirits sad and sunken!
Is it any wonder then we lost those years?

The early years spent in a council dwelling –
I remember lots of stray cats and dogs all smelling –
And neighbours with kids all fighting and yelling!
The early years at a tough school were spent with fright –
We tried our best to learn to read and write –
The playground at lunchtime, was always full of fear and fights!

The early years spent on a council estate in London –
Was like living in a darkened dungeon.
We learned to think quick and be street wise and keep on the run –
But went around worrying, alone, scared and undone!
The early years were endured with pain and sorrow –
All we could hope and pray for was a far better tomorrow!

Note To The Reader – I Hope That Children Have It Better Today!
(I should have called this poem 2x3s, 2x4s and 2x6s, anyway, do you get the picture?)

THE PAIN OF A CHILD

It was a Friday night – dad's pay day –
When my brother and I heard an almighty thump in the hallway.
The front door slammed and shut tight –
It gave us such a fright!
And in the hallway, our dear mum lay.
We heard our mum stumbling and crying –
For a minute or two we thought she was dying.
As in the hallway she lay.

Mum tried to tell us she had fallen over –
But we both knew it was not true.
You see her coat was ripped, some buttons were missing –
And her face was black and blue.
On that Friday night mum had gone down the pub –
To get some money off dad –
Before he had drunk it all away.
Mum was bloodied and had a broken nose!
This had swollen her face the next day –
She looked terrible that night –
As in the hallway she lay.

You see mum had shown dad up that night in front of his mates –
So dad being a drunk had dragged her around the back –
Beaten her up, and thrown her over some metal beer crates.
Mum had staggered home that night because she was not a driver,
and for the beating she took all she got was a fiver.
Poor mum only wanted the money to buy food for us all,
the next day.
We bathed her face with warm salt water that sad night –
As in the hallway she lay.

Note to the reader – Not a nice thing to see at any age, let alone aged 9. What a sick man my dad was to have done this to my mum – makes my blood boil.

MY FLAT

In 2002 after marriage or heart failure – well that's what I call it –
Some folks call it a separation or a divorce.
Anyway, whatever you call it –
It had run the course.

I had nowhere to live so I rented a flat above a fine cheese shop.
It was next to a post office,
and opposite a large church with a steeple.
With red brick walls all around, with red carpets –
And a red roof it was like the Kop.
It was a bit like the church because I did not see many people.

On Wednesdays my three daughters (abc),
would visit me after school.
I would burn a pizza, buy them Dr Pepper drinks,
or go down the chippie.
We used to laugh a lot, pig out and talk –
The girls would argue or play the fool.
I loved Wednesday nights I was happy living like a hippie.

At about nine or ten or when they were tired –
I would take them home to their Mum's.
Occasionally they would help and tidy up first –
And put their rubbish in the bin.
I loved Wednesday nights and seeing my girls –
We were more like mates or chums.
Sometimes I would have to work late in Liverpool –
And would not be on time or in.

My flat was unfurnished so I bought a sofa,
bed and large pine table and 6 chairs.
Our old neighbours Dave and Jimmy and Sandy,
were very handy and had a van.
They were the only people to help me move –
And get the furniture up the steep stairs.
I will always be grateful to them –
As it was hard to try and find a strong helping hand.

As time rolled by I could see my girls doing final exams –
And growing into women.
They were not interested anymore in playing with games –
And those Mcdonald's toys.
Looking back now I so wish they had taken up acting,
or gymnastics or swimming.
But as young women do, their attentions were hormonally tuned in –
To those nice boys.

I am now a granddad to Callum whom I love,
more than words can say.
And seven years older than I was when I moved in to my flat,
I guess things have worked out relatively okay.
Although Abigail's password on my PC is lads r twats –
But that's enough of that.

Note to the reader – My Flat was built in 1878 it's clean inside, not in a state!

54 AND FEELIN' FINE

Well I drink whisky and I drink wine –
I drink some beer and I like to go out to restaurants and dine.
I'm 54 Feelin Fine.

I like to think and I like to write –
Yes I like women in short skirts and black tights.
I'm 54 Feelin Fine.

I like to walk and cycle and go swimming,
and yes I do like the women.
I'm 54 Feelin Fine.

I do not try to find fault with the human race,
and yes I just love a woman with a pretty face.
I'm 54 Feelin Fine.

There's people who laugh and people who cry,
there's people who work hard –
And people who don't even try.
I'm 54 Feelin Fine.

Out of all the ladies that I have met –
I have not met the right one yet.
I'm 54 Feelin Fine.

There is Jackie and Jill and Gayle and Lynn,
there was a Sue an Anne and a Chris –
I don't really know which one I miss.
I'm 54 Feelin Fine.

I know I carry a bit of weight around my belly – too much telly –
But I shower and wash each day and my feet are not too smelly.
I'm 54 Feelin Fine.

I realise that I will not be much of a catch at 54 with a bald patch –
But I won't give up searching until I have found my perfect match.
I'm 54 Feelin Fine.

To all you lonely men out there,
don't sit on your arse in a pub somewhere.
Don't drink too much and sit and stare because if you do,
nobody will care.
I'm 54 Feelin Fine.

Note to the reader – Guess what? I wrote this on my 54th Birthday!

DAUGHTERS

ABIGAIL –
Abigail is hebrew and means father's great joy!
I don't know what we would have called her had she been a boy –
Probably Roy.
She does not cycle do sports or read books.
She won't believe me when I say she is slim,
but she has very good looks!
Abigail is strong and knows her own mind,
and is considerate, good and kind.
She has eyes which are lovely and are a greenish, greyish, blue.
I think she will end up slim and about 5'2".
She can't really decide what she wants from life –
I can't see her being just a loving wife.
Abigail needs to save, not rave and have a good drink.
I wish she would just stop sometimes and think.

BEVERLEY –
Beverley is a beautiful place in Yorkshire,
and is built on very hard rock.
She has drive and ambition, but her thoughts,
you will have to unlock.
Beverley earned her corporal's badge in the army cadets –
Which made me proud!
She used to be quite quiet, but says she's going deaf –
And now speaks very loud.
She has long dark brown hair until recently –
When she dyed it flame red.
Her skin is like porcelain, and is very creamy and dreamy and fair.
She is strong like me, and just you try hitting her, if you very dare.
Also like me, she really enjoys her work and food and sleep –
And her bed.
Although I love her very much,
she knows I wish she had gone in the army, instead!

CARA AMI –
Cara is Gaelic and Italian and French it means a beautiful friend.
And for herself she has drive and ambition, is tough and can defend .
I don't think a garden she will tend?
She is strong and slender with fresh skin,
it's all that clarins, and she is slim.
She just lives for fitness, and should move in down at the gym.
She drives her car for miles and miles.
Her friends really love her beautiful smile!
Cara is a beautiful girl and works in beauty therapy.
She is always on the go.
The lads all fall in love with her –
Because she is so very kind and nice to know.

Note to the reader – I love my girls as you can see, more than words can say, and I am so very proud to be their father, it is plain to see, that I am a million times better, than mine ever was to me!

PEOPLE I DO AND HAVE ADMIRED

Norman Wisdom was such a funny man,
he used to make me laugh when I was a boy.
Oh such Joy!

Harry Secombe a comedian, an actor.
A complete twit with an operatic voice.
A natural choice!

Spike Milligan a clever, funny, happy, witty man,
a depressive manic and a Goon.
We won't see the likes of him again very soon!

Dick Emery, Benny Hill, Kenneth Williams and Sid James,
all not right in the head.
Great funny men but unfortunately now dead!

Stephen Fry for his intelligence, knowledge, openness,
and such an aristocratic voice.
Another must and obvious choice!

Dawn French, Jennifer Saunders, Pam Ayres and Hattie Jaques
were all so very dear.
I thought I'd better mention some women,
in case you thought I'd gone all queer!

Doris Day, Marilyn Monroe and Ursula Andress,
to me were so very sexy and grand.
I would have liked to have thanked them,
for the strength I now have in my right hand!

Russ Abbot, Bruce Forsythe, Mike and Bernie Winters,
plus Morcambe and Wise.
Are and were so very clever – Well I never!

Kirk Douglas for Spartacus and The Vikings,
with Mel Gibson for his Braveheart.
Well they will do for a start!

Russell Crowe in Gladiator – he always got a great looking woman,
I bet he was Glad-He-Ate-Her!
(Well the Publisher does not like swearwords)

Richard Burton in Cleopatra and Anthony Hopkins,
for Silence of The Lambs.
What very fine actors, for me the best in the land!

David Jason in Only Fools and Horses, the best comedy on the telly,
made me so glad.
And have you seen him as Inspector Frost?
So great but somehow so very sad!

Oh well what fun!
There are so many more to mention I could go on for ages.
I have run out of space just now,
perhaps I will do some more in those later pages!

Note to the reader – Haven't we admired them all for years?

TO MY 3 DAUGHTERS

My girls, whom I cherish, your mum and I have parted.
But we will still try and be mates.
We won't sleep together as man and wife anymore –
Or go out on any dates.

Remember that we both do love you still –
And that we always will.
Because mums and dads are special people –
Whose Christmas stockings for you, we fill.

We both cared for you when you were little –
And used to love tucking you up, all snuggled in bed.
Your mum and I used to worry about you all, so very much –
When one of you fell or bumped your pretty heads.

We took you to the doctors or the hospital –
When any of you were ill or sick.
We took you Christmas shopping –
To show you presents for you to pick.

We will always try to help you and to guide you,
with problems that you have come across.
We try to stay calm and happy –
And never did get very cross.

We wanted to give you far better than we both ever had –
But most of all my dearest daughters.
We will always be so very proud and glad –
To be your mum and dad.

Note to the reader – I penned this one after marriage breakdown – so sad a time for us all!

OUR PET DOG HONEY

Let's all say good night, god bless and a loving goodbye –
To our wonderful pet dog Honey.
She was a very good dog, now girls, please don't cry.
I know but she just got old and unwell and needed to die.
She was always well behaved and could be very funny –
All she ever wanted was our love, she didn't need money.

She so enjoyed a walk in the woods or a run in the park.
Honey liked her food but did not like going out in the dark.
If anybody came near the house –
The paper lad or milkman with his cart –
Even the noise of a noisy field mouse –
My goodness, you should've have heard her bark!

When Honey was younger she could run very, very fast!
But poor honey, as she got older –
She became a lot slower and, much less bolder.
I think we all knew that she was not well and would not last!
We will never know the exact age of our pet dog Honey –
She could have been nine, ten or even eleven.
But although she has gone and left us now –
I think honey will be looking down from heaven.

Let's all say 'we loved you' and goodbye to our pet dog honey!

Note to the reader – I am sure that you either have or had a family pet and feel the same way we did about our pet dog Honey – She was a lovely crossed Labrador.

THE CAR SALES JOB

After losing my business, my home, and nearly, my mind and marriage,
I thought my life, which I had been in control of for years, was all over!
We rented a place, not a home,
but it had a large dolls house and double garage.
Then a scouse mate told me,
they were looking for salesmen in Liverpool at Rover.

It was in Kensington, one of the toughest areas by far –
But at least I had wheels, and sold their new, badly prepared cars.
After 2 years, redundancy beckoned, the garage closed down –
Just like my spirits had, and I'd started to frown.

I thought Oh well! I will get a job selling Fords instead –
So I phoned around every Ford garage and at last,
'Come on over' they said.
A job selling Fords back on the Wirral –
Under the tunnel in lovely Birkenhead.
Working in a 'salt mine' would have been easier –
I should have stayed at home in bed!

The business centre at Toyota was next where I sold fleet.
Let me say, that a Toyota is one of the best cars on the road.
Up and down streets and those spiral stairs, I had blisters on my feet.
But the Japanese care as much about pain,
as they would about eating a toad.

I got offered a job at Jaguar cars, they paid your fuel,
and it was only 5 days a week.
The first day I got my company car,
the smell of the leather and wood, better by far.
Selling jags was hard, and I did not meet targets –
So another job I would have to seek.
At least I taught the girls about quality –
And I just loved driving home in a jaguar!

Unemployed again! Should have been the title,
of this wonderful poem, by me.
After a few months on the old 'rock and roll',
I soon found another car job –
Selling a fantastically fast, range of very great cars.
They were called the Mitsubishi.
I liked the job which had seen a succession of tough managers –
But they hated my gob.

Note to the reader – I would spend Over ten years in the most unrewarding, uncared for and totally unappreciated job I ever had, some of the many managers I worked for were the most ignorant, clever, selfish, greedy and needy and ruthless bastards I had ever seen. As I said to my ex-wife once, 'you only get 2 years for GBH!'

THFC PLC

From 1980 to 1983 I worked for THFC PLC.
It stands for Tottenham Hotspur Football Club in London City.
That means Spurs to a football fan or someone like me.
Although I am not a fan, the club is steeped in football history!

The Club itself was and is massive with over 250 Staff –
I travelled abroad a lot with the team and supporters –
We really had a good laugh.
I made all the travel arrangements which included –
a ticket, lunch and a scarf –
But supporters would lose their money and membership,
if they acted daft!

I remember sitting in the Spurs travel shop,
one dull and rainy Monday.
When the phone rang, it was Peter Day the secretary –
To ask if I wanted to play.
I panicked for a minute, then he said –
No! You fool, can you play golf on Wednesday?
Glen Hoddle and Alan Brazil had dropped out of the team –
I did not know what to say.

I said why yes of course! He said good,
be at Barnet Golf Club at nine.
He said have you got some decent golf clubs?
If not you can borrow mine.
I said no thanks I have got a set of Ben Sayers clubs,
he said don't worry they are fine.
He added that the prize for the lowest score on the day –
Would be a case of wine!

It was great, I played with Steve Perryman –
You have probably never heard his name.
We both had a really good game.
The weather was dry and fine –
But we didn't win the wine!

Note to the reader – If you were or are a Spurs fan you would have been green with envy but I just told myself that as a senior member of staff it was a perk of the job! They weren't very impressed though, when they found out I was an Arsenal Fan I never got invited to play again!

UNFORTUNATE

Following our move from London to Liverpool in 1988,
my wife was not very well after the birth of our twins.
They said post natal depression was the cause.
UNFORTUNATE everybody said,
it happens to a lot of people.

One of the twins had a bowel infection and was jaundiced,
and not well at all for quite a long time.
UNFORTUNATE everybody said,
but children are stronger than you think –
She will bounce back and be right as rain.

My wife's brother who was very fit, did not drink or smoke,
although he was a nervous bloke,
came home from work one day, had a light lunch,
and went off for a swim.
30 minutes later he was dead, cholesterol they said.
UNFORTUNATE.

As a Londoner living on Merseyside in 1989, I could not get a job,
despite sending off over 50 job applications.
I had no luck finding work for months.
UNFORTUNATE our friends and relatives said –
it's not as easy as living in London is it?

In the end I was forced to start my own business,
and become self employed as I could not get a job.
Living in Merseyside was very insular,
but the children were now at school and doing well,
but my business failed and I lost thousands.
UNFORTUNATE.

An ex- business colleague, let's just call him David,
owed me about ten thousand pounds,
but unknown to me he was in severe financial difficulties himself,
and he took the coward's way out and committed suicide.
How UNFORTUNATE they all said.

Despite working all the hours I could,
and being the best father and husband I could be,
I had lost too much money over the previous 5 years,
and could not keep up repayments on the mortgage,
we lost the house.
How UNFORTUNATE they all said.

I was working in the Car Sales Industry for over 10 years,
the job was hard but I had no fears,
as long as I could put food on the table.
It was UNFORTUNATE however, to be made redundant,
4 times in 6 years which led to much anxiety and depression.

During this time both my father and mother-in-law,
had passed away, it was such a sad time.
And then my Mother was diagnosed with stage 5 terminal cancer,
at the age of 73, she died on my birthday.
How UNFORTUNATE everybody said, but I was devastated.

After all the hardships and problems my wife and I had endured,
we had stayed strong she called me her rock.
But following her mother's death in 2002,
my wife was left her mother's house,
she asked for a divorce on my birthday.
UNFORTUNATE and it caused lots of tears,
well it would after 29 years.

Note to the reader – Yes life can be unfortunate sometimes can't it? But unfortunately there is always somebody a lot worse off than you.

STRONGER

It seemed to me to be strange, to be single again,
after nearly 30 years of married bliss,
for all those happy together years,
to end in much sadness, bitterness and fear.
The decree nisi had arrived in the post today, so i wrote this in tears –

Now I am divorced and feeling bitter,
but I am not a quitter.
The girls are all grown up now so I don't need a babysitter,
I sit alone and play my records –
I bet you won't remember Gary Glitter.

With a balding head and greying hair,
I don't mean to sit at the window and stare,
just like a lion in its lair – I feel caged, but it seems so sad and unfair!
I reach for another large glass of quality merlot –
And begin to try not to care.

The loneliness goes on and on and on –
My home, my wife, my business, my girls are from my daily sight,
gone!
My hopes and ambitions are all done –
Perhaps I should get fit and go for a run?
My daughters whom i love so dear – said
'Hey dad you're still young, have fun'.

The days are long the nights are longer
I need to work hard at a job I hate –
Although i have lost a mate I must be strong,
I don't feel like dancing the conga –
I hope this mental pain does not last too long.
But as grandmother used to say –
'What does not kill you will make you stronger'.

Note to the reader – What doesn't kill you will make you stronger.

Graham Robinson at work

Graham Robinson